Beneath Heavy Pines in World War II Louisiana

Beneath Heavy Pines in World War II Louisiana

The Japanese American Internment Experience at Camp Livingston

Hayley Johnson and Sarah Simms

LEXINGTON BOOKS
Lanham • Boulder • New York • London

Rowman & Littlefield
Bloomsbury Publishing Inc, 1359 Broadway, New York, NY 10018, USA
Bloomsbury Publishing Plc, 50 Bedford Square, London, WC1B 3DP, UK
Bloomsbury Publishing Ireland, 29 Earlsfort Terrace, Dublin 2, D02 AY28, Ireland
www.bloomsbury.com

Published by Lexington Books
An imprint of The Rowman & Littlefield Publishing Group, Inc.
4501 Forbes Boulevard, Suite 200, Lanham, Maryland 20706
www.rowman.com

86-90 Paul Street, London EC2A 4NE, United Kingdom

Copyright © 2023 by The Rowman & Littlefield Publishing Group, Inc.

All rights reserved. No part of this publication may be: i) reproduced or transmitted in any form, electronic or mechanical, including photocopying, recording or by means of any information storage or retrieval system without prior permission in writing from the publishers; or ii) used or reproduced in any way for the training, development or operation of artificial intelligence (AI) technologies, including generative AI technologies. The rights holders expressly reserve this publication from the text and data mining exception as per Article 4(3) of the Digital Single Market Directive (EU) 2019/790.

British Library Cataloguing in Publication Information available

Library of Congress Cataloging-in-Publication Data

Names: Johnson, Hayley, 1982– author. | Simms, Sarah, 1981– author.
Title: Beneath heavy pines in World War II Louisiana : the Japanese American internment experience at Camp Livingston / Hayley Johnson, Sarah Simms.
Other titles: Beneath heavy pines in World War 2 Louisiana
Description: Lanham : Lexington Books, [2023] | Includes bibliographical references and index. | Summary: "This study examines the Camp Livingston site of Japanese alien internment in Louisiana during World War II. The authors analyze the experiences of one extended family and the trauma, uncertainty, and injustice they experienced"— Provided by publisher.
Identifiers: LCCN 2023007953 (print) | LCCN 2023007954 (ebook) | ISBN 9781666923360 (cloth) | ISBN 9781666923377 (epub)
Subjects: LCSH: Japanese Americans—Forced removal and internment, 1942–1945. | Kohara family. | Miyamoto family. | Camp Livingston (La.) | Miyamoto, Buntetsu, 1888–1982—Family. | Kohara, Saki, 1893–1969—Family. | Crystal City Internment Camp (Crystal City, Tex.) | World War, 1939–1945—Concentration camps—Louisiana. | World War, 1939–1945—Concentration camps—Texas. | World War, 1939–1945—Japanese Americans—Louisiana—Biography. | World War, 1939–1945—Japanese Americans—Hawaii—Biography.
Classification: LCC D769.8.A6 .J64 2023 (print) | LCC D769.8.A6 (ebook) | DDC 940.54/72730976369—dc23/eng/20230307
LC record available at https://lccn.loc.gov/2023007953
LC ebook record available at https://lccn.loc.gov/2023007954

To all the men confined beneath the pines of Camp Livingston.

There is nothing more mysterious than destiny, after all.

—Reverend Buntetsu Miyamoto

Figure 0.1 View of Haleʻiwa Jodo Temple from the Ocean. Courtesy of Haleʻiwa Jodo Mission.

Contents

Words Matter: A Glossary of Terms ... xi

I Hear You Call, Pine Tree ... xiii

A Stillness in the Archive ... 1

Acknowledgments ... 15

PART I: FOUNDATIONS IN A NEW LAND ... 17
1. A Consequence of Birth ... 19
2. *Tengoku* or Heaven ... 31
3. A Community Emerges ... 39
4. Haleʻiwa, Hawaiʻi ... 51
5. A Temple's Foundation ... 57

PART II: PRELUDE TO WAR ... 71
6. The Watchers on the Eve of War ... 73
7. New Residents among the Pines ... 87
8. When the Tigers Pounced ... 101
9. Looking Westward ... 107
10. Becoming an Enemy Alien ... 111

PART III: WARTIME EXPERIENCES   117

  11 ISN-HJ-131-CI   119

  12 Let Photographs Tell the Story   133

  13 "Koton, Koton"   139

PART IV: CAMP LIVINGSTON   141

  14 Life in Camp Livingston   143

  15 Prisoners under the Pines   159

  16 Art, Community, and Resistance   175

  17 Connections to the Outside World   183

PART V: A FAMILY REUNITED   201

  18 The Road to Repatriation   203

  19 Reunited Behind Barbed Wire   211

PART VI: AFTER WAR   231

  20 Life beyond War   233

  21 Mysterious Memories: A Remembrance of Those Who Did Not Return   241

  22 What Remains   247

  23 Talk Story   253

Epilogue   261

Appendix I   271

Appendix II   281

Index   287

About the Authors   297

Words Matter: A Glossary of Terms

Incarceration: describes the illegal detention of over 120,000 persons of Japanese ancestry in American concentration camps overseen by the War Relocation Authority. Those held in these camps included *Issei* and *Nisei*. The forced removal of these Japanese communities, mostly from the western United States, was authorized by Executive Order 9066. The focus of this book is the story of internment; however, it is important to know the difference in terms and steer away from euphemistic language.

Internment: describes the "legally permissible, though morally questionable"[1] confinement of "enemy" aliens during times of war. During World War II, over 31,000 people were affected by the internment program and held in camps run by the Army or Department of Justice.[2] These camps and the treatment of those held within were governed by the provisions of the Geneva Convention relative to the Treatment of Prisoners of War (1929).

Issei: the term used for Japanese immigrants who were born in Japan, or "first generation." The majority of *Issei* migrated to the United States before 1924 and were legally barred from becoming naturalized American citizens by anti-Asian naturalization laws that would not be repealed until 1952.

Kibei Nisei: the term used for members of the *Nisei* generation who were born in the United States but sent to Japan for their education.

Nikkei: the term used for persons of Japanese ancestry living outside of Japan or the persons who constitute the Japanese diaspora. This can include emigrants as well as their descendants.

Nisei: the children of *Issei* parents, or "second generation." In the United States, the *Nisei* were born on American soil and are U.S. citizens.

Toritsuginin: the Japanese term for consular agent, a misunderstood voluntary position held by *Issei* leaders within the Japanese community. The job of a consular agent was akin to a notary public in that they assisted community members in filing reports and legal documentation to Japan. Consular agents also assisted with expatriation requests.

For more information on terminology, please see the Japanese American Citizens League's "Power of Words Handbook: A Guide to Language about Japanese Americans in World War II, Understanding Euphemisms and Preferred Terminology"[3] and Roger Daniels' five-part series, "Words Do Matter: A Note on Inappropriate Terminology and the Incarceration of the Japanese Americans."[4]

NOTES

1. "It's Time to Retire WWII-Era Euphemisms for Japanese American Incarceration," *Densho* (blog), April 26, 2019, https://densho.org/time-to-retire-euphemisms-for-japanese-american-incarceration/.

2. Tetsuden Kashima, *Judgment Without Trial: Japanese American Imprisonment During World War II* (Seattle: University of Washington Press, 2003), 124.

3. This can be found here: https://jacl.org/power-of-words.

4. Daniels' series can be found at the Discover Nikkei website: http://www.discovernikkei.org/en/journal/2008/2/1/words-do-matter/.

I Hear You Call, Pine Tree

By Yone Noguchi[1]

I hear you call, Pine-tree, I hear you upon the hill; by the silent pond where the lotus flowers bloom, I hear you call, Pine-tree!
What is it you call, Pine-tree, when the rain falls, when the winds blow, and when the stars appear, what is it you call, Pine-tree?
I hear you call, Pine-tree, but I am blind, and do not know how to reach you, Pine-tree. Who will take me to you, Pine-tree?

NOTE

1. Yone Noguchi, *Selected Poems of Yone Noguchi* (Boston: The Four Seas Company, 1921), 77–78. This work is in the public domain in the United States.

A Stillness in the Archive

In war truth is the first casualty.

—*Aeschylus*

The attack on Pearl Harbor is a tragedy ingrained in the American consciousness, the echoes of which still reverberate in our cultural memory—through the veneration of the lives lost that day at a national historic landmark, the countless textbooks and historic tomes dedicated to unraveling how this could have happened, and through its depiction in popular culture. The attack on Pearl Harbor effectively pulled the United States into World War II and caused a ripple effect, more akin to a tidal wave, that touched communities far and wide: those who lost their lives at Pearl Harbor, those who would lose their lives on the battlefront, and their families who would feel this grave loss. For the Japanese community of the United States and even, in some cases, those in Central and South America, their lives would forever be changed on that day. Within months of the attack, over 110,000 Japanese Americans in the United States, two-thirds of whom were American citizens, would be forced to leave their homes and spend the remainder of war held behind barbed wire in War Relocation Authority (WRA) incarceration camps. An additional 10,000 people would enter the camps in some capacity after the initial forced removal, whether as adults entering the camps or babies born behind barbed wire. This culmination of individuals entering into or being born into the camps brings the commonly referenced total number to 120,000 people incarcerated.

Another 17,477 Japanese from the United States and Latin America would be interned at Army and Department of Justice camps.[1] Issei residing in the United States were perpetual aliens, immigrants to the United States who were barred from American citizenship because of racist anti-Asian legislation. At the entry of the United States into war with Japan, these Issei were designated as enemy aliens, and a select group were arrested and placed into internment camps. A majority of this group were men, arrested within hours of Pearl Harbor, separated from their families, and shuttled around to various internment camps overseen by the watchful eyes of the Army and Department of Justice. The impetus behind this egregious injustice was fueled by racist and xenophobic fears that had been growing in the country since the late nineteenth century. And while the WRA camps that held families and U.S. citizens are not as widely known as they could or should be, the program of enemy alien internment during World War II remains an all but unknown facet of the American war machine.

In the pine forests of central Louisiana, an enormous Army installation known as Camp Livingston was built in 1940 as the country began to prepare for the possibility of war on foreign shores. Remembered with great nostalgia as the site of the Louisiana Maneuvers and an important Army training facility, Camp Livingston today is just a memory, having been decommissioned with the conclusion of the war. The pine forest has reclaimed the space that once played host to over 400,000 men. If you ask anyone in the area about the camp, they'll likely share stories handed down from their families about the building of the camp or even of the Prisoners of War (POWs) who were held there at one time.

But there is a darker history to Camp Livingston; a history that had been misremembered, forgotten, or unknown. From 1942 to 1943, over 1,000 civilian men of Japanese ancestry considered enemy aliens by the U.S. government were held behind barbed wire fences in an internment camp that had been built within months of the attack on Pearl Harbor. How could internment camps and enemy alien designations occur in the United States, let alone in Louisiana? And how had it been forgotten? The authors, both librarians, began their quest with these two seemingly simple questions. Now, seven years later, we have traversed the country from Washington, DC, to California to New York and even to Hawai'i in an attempt to piece together this very complicated part of our American history.

UNCOVERING CAMP LIVINGSTON AND ENEMY ALIEN INTERNMENT

Oftentimes, idle curiosity is just that—curiosity that exists without purpose or effect and passes fleetingly. Occasionally, curiosity can evolve into a project that spans years and takes one outside of their professional discipline. Through a chance reading of a *Los Angeles Times* article published in 2016—a time when political rhetoric was, and continues to be, mired in fear of the "other"— this article cut through the clamor and showcased children of the Muslim faith reading letters written by Japanese American children incarcerated during World War II to living survivors of those American incarceration camps. The connection between the two, seventy-five years apart, was chilling and foreboding. After reading the article, the startling similarities of racial discrimination and isolation that existed between both groups prompted us to begin to think about Louisiana's history during World War II and the many stories of Prisoner of War (POW) labor utilized throughout the state for sugarcane farming and logging. We asked ourselves, "Did Louisiana have internment camps as well?"

Hayley, a Louisiana native, had a distant memory about a camp near Alexandria, Louisiana, that held Japanese during World War II. But whether that was true and why the Japanese were held there was unknown. We could find nothing related to Japanese internment in Louisiana utilizing our usual channels of exploratory research. Through an inquiry made to the Louisiana History Museum in Alexandria, Louisiana, about Camp Livingston and internment, we quickly realized that this history was unknown to the many historical and academic organizations that would have been places of memory regarding this historic site. We contacted the Louisiana Maneuvers and Military Museum, Louisiana State University at Alexandria, the National World War II Museum, and other cultural institutions and were consistently met with resounding holes and lack of knowledge of this history. Time and again, we were told that only POW camps for the Japanese had existed in the state. No one knew anything of internment. We only had one lead to follow: the name "Kohara." This family name had been given to us by the curator at the Louisiana History Museum who explained that the Koharas were a Japanese family who lived in Alexandria for many years, and if we could find them, they may have some information regarding Camp Livingston.

Through some initial research and email correspondence, we were able to find the remaining Koharas of Alexandria, and our journey into the history of internment at Camp Livingston officially began. We had the pleasure of being able to interview Mrs. Marion Kohara Couvillion. Marion was a teenager during World War II, and she was eager to share memories of her life in Alexandria with us. Marion recounted her family's history and arrival in Louisiana, her life growing up in Alexandria, and how the Kohara family were the only Japanese family in the area. She vividly remembered when Pearl Harbor was attacked, the struggles her family underwent including the week-long FBI investigation of her family, as well as visiting surrounding WRA camps in Arkansas. Strikingly, Marion discussed how she learned about Camp Livingston and the men held there. The husband of her father's first cousin, a Buddhist priest from Hawaiʻi, was held at Camp Livingston as an enemy alien internee. We were shocked that a civilian family man with a religious vocation would be taken from his home and placed into internment camps. Discussing Camp Livingston with her began to unlock connections that were too unbelievable for us to logically comprehend. Hungry to know more, we started our research journey in earnest in the hopes of discovering more about the story we had just been told.

With the discovery of the Kohara family cousin, Reverend Buntetsu Miyamoto, we now had a name and lead to begin trying to find information on Camp Livingston and the internment that occurred. We were able to speak with Reverend Miyamoto's youngest son, Clifford, in Hawai'i about his memories of life during World War II. We were shocked to learn that Reverend Miyamoto was arrested the same day as Pearl Harbor and spent almost four years in internment. We also learned that Reverend Miyamoto's wife and children were not spared from the camps and were eventually interned in Crystal City, Texas.

To learn about this camp's history through the voice and memory of individuals affected by it has guided our entire research. If written about, the internment camp at Camp Livingston exists as a footnote or a temporary stopover. There aren't many details, and the names of the men imprisoned there aren't included. And while we have not encountered an archival silence per se, we have instead encountered a stillness. The records do exist, scattered across the country, but in many cases have not been included in the historical dialogue. Through archival research, we have been able to uncover government documents regarding the building of the camp as well as rosters of names of the men held there which are published in this book for the first time. We have found letters written by fathers and husbands while in Camp Livingston that were sent home to their children and wives. We have found artwork created by these men as well as never before published photographs of the men and camp. We have used primary sources, such as government documents, oral histories from both the Miyamoto and Kohara families as well as others held in the camps, in addition to numerous secondary sources.[2] These finds were instrumental in recreating the environment of Camp Livingston. It wasn't until we went to Hawai'i, however, and were able to meet the sons and grandchildren of Reverend Miyamoto, spend time where he once lived and preached, and were able to dive into the oral histories of those who were in camp with him in Hawaiian archives, that this book started to fully crystalize into a complete and cohesive story reflecting the human heart at the center of this saga. This story had been waiting patiently to be told and revealed itself to us in its own way and in its own time.

STRUCTURING MEMORY

We feel it appropriate to remind the reader that the authors of this book are not historians, but are, in fact, two librarians. To become a librarian, one gets a master's degree in the theory of information organization, and to put it simply—practical facets of how to find and organize information. We're experts at finding information and might even be considered trained document detectives in a sense. Hayley is a government documents librarian, and her specialty encompasses all the information created and curated by the U.S. government. As a teaching librarian, Sarah focuses on connecting with people to make them better researchers and global citizens. All this to say, we are not historians by trade and thus have stumbled through this project in the way only a librarian can—finding seemingly hidden information and working backward to then put that information into a historical context. And so, we have decided to share our research findings the way we uncovered and have come to understand them—through the experiences of the Miyamoto and Kohara families. By approaching this particular history in this way, we have effectively laid out a counter-narrative that is part biography and part critical exploration of a forgotten chapter in American history.

The goals of this book are twofold. First, and foremost, we want to share the story of Camp Livingston as a site of enemy alien internment. When we began this project, we naively thought the story of Camp Livingston was solely a Louisiana story. But through years of research, we have learned the story of Camp Livingston is a many-layered and complex one which extends thousands of miles beyond the Louisiana state line. In that vein, our second goal with this book is an exploration of the immigrant experiences of the Miyamoto and Kohara families and how enemy alien internment affected them as just one example of how the Japanese community was affected during World War II. We use the experiences of these families with much care and consideration, and we are mindful that a community is not a monolith and with the understanding that many of their experiences were mirrored with others in the Issei Hawaiian community.

This book is divided into six parts that comprise a chronological retelling of the histories of the Miyamoto and Kohara families set during the years approaching, during, and after World War II. Before we introduce the families, we thought it prudent to explore the differences between the incarceration camps run by the WRA that held 120,000 Japanese and Japanese Americans and the internment camps run by the Army and Department of Justice that held Japanese civilians considered enemy aliens by the U.S. government with our entry in the war. We have made this distinction in "A Consequence of Birth," a chapter outlining these differences so the reader has a baseline understanding of what Reverend Miyamoto and his family are subjected to as victims of enemy alien internment starting with his arrest on December 7, 1941. Central to our story is Reverend Miyamoto, so the remainder of the chapters contained in this first part, *Foundations in a New Land*, explore the history of Hawai'i as a place of Japanese immigration, the strengthening of that community, and the threat this posed for the white elite on the Islands, as well as Reverend Miyamoto's place within this community upon his arrival in 1915. Though located in an idyllic landscape, life for the Issei community and Reverend Miyamoto could be harsh and unforgiving. This adversity helped to strengthen the resolve and resilience of the Islands' new settler population through community, language, and religion.

In the second part of this book, *Prelude to War*, we examine how these same attributes that helped the Japanese Issei community thrive in Hawai'i would make them targets for suspicion by the surveillance arms of the Army, Navy, and eventually FBI. From this surveillance, lists of names were created of Issei men who were leaders within their communities on the Islands; lists which would be used in the hours after Pearl Harbor to arrest and intern over 300 men on the Hawaiian Islands. Reverend Miyamoto was one of these men. Four thousand miles away, in Alexandria, Louisiana, we meet the Miyamoto cousins, the Koharas, Issei parents who immigrated from Japan to start a new life. As they build their lives and photography business in this central Louisiana town, twelve miles away Camp Livingston is being built as a training garrison for U.S. Army troops as the threat of war looms ever closer. The remaining chapters in this part serve as the turning point for this story. First, with the attack on Pearl Harbor, then with Reverend Miyamoto's arrest, and finally how a community of alien residents became "enemy" in the eyes of the U.S. government with Presidential Proclamations 2525, 2526, and 2527.

The next three parts of the book each deal with aspects of life during World War II. In *Wartime Experiences*, we follow Reverend Miyamoto's arrest, trial, and internment journey as he makes his way to Camp Livingston. We also revisit the Kohara family and learn of their experiences during the war, so different than that of their Hawaiian cousins. We have dedicated an entire part to the internment camp itself, *Camp Livingston*, wherein we explore the physical layout of the camp, the prisoners being held there, their coping mechanisms, and visitors to camp. It must be noted here that up until this part, we have been able to construct an image of Reverend Miyamoto's life from family memories, newspaper articles, photographs, and government documents. But upon his arrival at Camp Livingston, Reverend Miyamoto seemingly goes silent. The only contemporary records we have pertaining to Reverend Miyamoto in Camp Livingston are the camp rosters, records regarding repatriation and lost luggage, and a note found while at the Japanese Cultural Center of Hawai'i that listed the barrack he was assigned. We have used journal entries, oral histories, and other various documents written by others held in Camp Livingston to explore daily life within camp during this time. But as you read, it is easy to visualize Reverend Miyamoto living alongside these men, a shadow of sorts, existing amid their whispered memories from almost eighty years ago. We can imagine how he felt, the fear of his arrest and internment, the sense of loss and indignation as he was moved from camp to camp, and the monotony of each day filled with longing for his family. But this loss of voice should not come as a surprise. Not all letters between families were kept. Not everyone kept journals during their time in camp. Many affected by the internment did not speak of their experiences after the war, not even to their families. The fifth part, *A Family Reunited*, sees the trials that Fumi Miyamoto and her children faced as they choose voluntary internment in the hopes of being reunited with Reverend Miyamoto. We follow along on their journey from Hawai'i to a type of internment hotel in North Carolina and finally to Crystal City, Texas, where after over a year apart, the Miyamoto family was finally together again albeit behind barbed wire under the hot Texas sun. It is here in Crystal City through a chance conversation with one of her friends in camp that Fumi learns her cousins, the Koharas, have been living in Alexandria and playing host to family members visiting their fathers and husbands in Camp Livingston. Fumi and her oldest daughter are allowed to visit the Koharas, and it is this meeting that nearly eighty years later Mrs. Marion Kohara Couvillion relayed to us one afternoon in her apartment. This story of two families, four thousand miles apart, connected by blood, and reunited by a chance meeting in the summer of 1945 is made all the more remarkable by yet another chance meeting almost eighty years later. This meeting between two curious librarians and one of those original family members feels as though time and place converged once more to ensure this story is told.

In the final part, *After War*, the Miyamoto family are released from their internment to return to their home in Hawai'i and the post-war fates of both the Miyamoto and Kohara families are shared. In stark contrast, chapter 21, "Mysterious Memories," reveals that not everyone held in U.S. internment camps made it home. Based on a sermon that Reverend Miyamoto gave at the age of ninety-two, we discovered that some of the men who had been held alongside him at Camp Livingston and then Crystal City had chosen to be repatriated with their families back to Japan. We share the tragic fates of Reverend Jikyo Masaki and Shoichi Asami lost at sea on their way to Japan in the tragic sinking of the *Awa Maru* at the hands of the USS *Queenfish*. This is a significant find as we have been unable to find any written connection between the enemy alien internment program at Camp Livingston and the sinking of the *Awa Maru* to date. The book concludes with reflections on present-day rhetoric and xenophobic actions being taken by our government, an exploration of the symbolism of the pine, and a short chapter on our research process. You will find a list of names of the men held in Camp Livingston as transcribed from the rosters we were able to find at the National Archives. This is the first time that these names have been compiled together and shared outside of a government file folder created decades ago, and it is our hope that by sharing these names we pay homage to the memory of these men who were torn from their families and unjustly interned by the U.S. government.

WHY THIS MATTERS

In a bid to raise money for the base of the Statue of Liberty, Emma Lazarus penned her now-famous sonnet *The New Colossus*. Taught in schools, quoted in books, recited by political pundits on both sides, and enshrined in bronze on this most famous of American landmarks, it reads:

Not like the brazen giant of Greek fame,
With conquering limbs astride from land to land;
Here at our sea-washed, sunset gates shall stand
A mighty woman with a torch, whose flame
Is the imprisoned lightning, and her name
Mother of Exiles. From her beacon-hand
Glows world-wide welcome; her mild eyes command
The air-bridged harbor that twin cities frame.

"Keep, ancient lands, your storied pomp!" cries she
With silent lips. "Give me your tired, your poor,
Your huddled masses yearning to breathe free,
The wretched refuse of your teeming shore.
Send these, the homeless, tempest-tost to me,
I lift my lamp beside the golden door!"

Often cited as an American ideal and a welcoming beacon for those coming to America, this poem and its location on the Statue of Liberty help to perpetuate the idea of America as a land of opportunity with open doors for all regardless of race, religion, sex, creed, or even lot in life. In that vein, America *has* admitted millions of immigrants in its relatively short history, but if one was to pull back the curtain and inspect any decade of American history they would find that, in actuality, America's xenophobia, racism, and "othering" did its best to barricade these doors to any person or group not in favor. We can look to the writing of Lazarus' poem as just one example of this complex dichotomy of lofty goals compared to base action. *The Great Colossus*, penned by an advocate for Jewish refugees fleeing Russia, redefined the bronze woman in New York Harbor as the "Mother of Exiles." But just one year before Lazarus put her famous words to paper, the United States passed the Chinese Exclusion Act of 1882, barring the immigration and naturalization of Chinese immigrants to America. This race-based legislation would pave the way for more anti-Asian measures culminating in the Immigration Act of 1924 that effectively banned all immigration from Asia and denied naturalization to those who had already immigrated, such as the Issei community in Hawaiʻi. So we must wonder who this poem, a national anthem in and of itself, was written for, both then and now.

Not confined to the nascent stages of our nation and the missteps that were taken, nor relegated to a century ago, the Janus-faced nature of American history is something that we are grappling with as a country today. In 2020, a once-in-a-century global pandemic has rocked the entire world while systemic, institutional and individual racism, monuments, and the dominant historical narrative we have been taught, our own history, has been challenged at all levels of society, especially here in the United States. This deep questioning of the very ways in which we understand ourselves, our place in society, and our history has shaken many to their core as well as their beliefs of what America is, and what it isn't. As Ibram X. Kendi noted in his September 2020 *Atlantic* article, "we are living in the midst of an anti-racist revolution."[3] He goes on to describe this country that we call home:

> The United States has often been called a land of contradictions, and to be sure, its failings sit alongside notable achievements—a New Deal for many Americans in the 1930s, the defeat of fascism abroad in the 1940s. But on racial matters, the U.S. could just as accurately be described as a land in denial. It has been a massacring nation that said it cherished life, a slaveholding nation that claimed it valued liberty, a hierarchal nation that declared it valued equality, a disenfranchising nation that branded itself a democracy, a segregated nation that styled itself separate but equal, an excluding nation that boasted of opportunity for all. A nation is what it does, not what it originally claimed it would be. Often, a nation is precisely what it denies itself to be.[4]

It is time for an honest and critical look at our history and how we share that history. Just as there are two sides to every story, the history that we are taught does not often capture the full experiences of the given period. To fully appreciate American history, the good and the bad must be confronted. When we imagine history like a nesting doll, we begin to understand the ways in which we must deconstruct this larger historical narrative into smaller, and more personal experiences for an understanding of how these details, often hidden, are integral to the makeup of a true and accurate accounting of our history. Confronting and reinstating those challenging histories that are left out of the dominant historical narrative require individuals to also challenge their very conception of what the United States stands for and reveal America for what she really is. She is a land of contradictions emanating from her stated ideals and unconscionable actions. She is at once gleaming and tarnished, open to the tired, poor, huddled masses and closed to those deemed "other," a land of opportunity and a land of oppression. Her history is complex and oftentimes ugly, but it is a history that must be confronted to break the cycle. But how can we do this? As Anthony W. Dunbar argues, we can:

> move beyond the famous and well-documented cultural moments to include the daily-lived experiences and existence of underrepresented populations . . . Historical representation is a strong tool of control by dominant cultures and a consistent point of critique for counterstories.[5]

To push back against the dominant historical narrative, we must discover the truth that counter-narratives provide, and it is here especially that archives and other cultural memory institutions are one important piece in moving forward.

Emiko Hastings shares one powerful and compelling example of the effects of the restoration of memory through the use of archives in the story of Aiko Herzig-Yoshinaga. According to Hastings, it was through Herzig-Yoshinaga's determined and steadfast work in the National Archives that she was able to piece together thousands of documents pertaining to the incarceration and internment of Japanese and Japanese Americans during World War II. This seminal research and documentation helped spur the Redress Movement forward effectively serving as the foundation for the report by the Commission on Wartime Relocation and Internment of Civilians as well as the reopening of the Hirabayashi, Yasui, and Korematsu cases before the Supreme Court.

> This episode in Japanese American history illustrates the power of archival records to document injustice and promote social change. The very documents that were originally used to control the Japanese American population became the documents that enabled recognition of injustice and led to the conclusion of the redress movement.[6]

Despite this inspiring example, recently it has felt as though there are more instances surfacing that reflect the implications of forgotten or misplaced memory. One reason this happens is the "othering" of the experiences and stories that don't align with the dominant historical narrative, and these stories consequently being relegated to the outskirts of history. But history is not simply what is written in a book. Like so much of life, history is about what happens in the spaces in between. Entrenched in this is the notion of power as well. As Terry Cook writes:

> . . . archives are constructed memories about the past, about history, heritage, and culture, about personal roots and familial connections, and about how we

are as human beings; as such, they offer glimpses into our common humanity. Yet memory is notoriously selective—in individuals, in societies, and yes, in archives. With memory comes forgetting. With memory comes the inevitable privileging of certain records and record creators, certain functions, activities, and groups in society, and the marginalizing or silencing of others. Memory, and forgetting, can serve a whole range of practical, cultural, political, symbolic, emotional and ethical imperatives and is central to power, identity, and privilege.[7]

This was the case with Fort Sill, an Army base in Lawton, Oklahoma, that made national headlines in 2019 as a proposed detention site for migrant children, the same role it had filled in 2014 as well. But Fort Sill's difficult history reaches back farther to its founding in the mid-nineteenth century as an outpost in the Indian Wars that served as both the site of a Native American boarding school that separated Indigenous children from their families and a POW camp for members of the Chiricahua Apache tribe in the late nineteenth century, notably being the site of imprisonment and eventual burial of Geronimo.[8] Having done extensive research into Camp Livingston and Reverend Miyamoto's internment journey at this point, we were well aware that another facet of Fort Sill's history included the internment of over 700 Japanese civilian men, many of whom would eventually be interned at Camp Livingston. Similar to Camp Livingston, Fort Sill's internment camp was located on an active Army installation. But in the news coverage we were reading, the type of internment that occurred and the people that were interned were misidentified, and more distressing still was the silence around the tragic death of Kanesaburo Oshima at the hands of a Fort Sill guard. When interviewed about the history of Fort Sill as a site of internment, Darrell Ames, spokesman for Fort Sill, explained that while there was information indicating the building of an internment camp for Japanese Americans at the behest of the U.S. government, there was no record that any had been held there and that it had only been used to hold POWs from Germany, Italy, and Japan.[9] When officials at the Fort Sill National Historic Landmark and Museum were asked the same question, they responded that "they have no information about the base's use as an internment or POW camp because that part of its history is not part of its mission statement."[10] A forgotten chapter, a forgotten tragedy, and a site shrouded in repeated trauma. We were struck by the parallels between the internment history of Fort Sill and Camp Livingston and are left to question who is responsible for keeping this historical memory alive. We believe that this duty and calling falls to librarians, archivists, and other memory curators to ensure that these memories, stories, and histories are sought out, dusted off, and brought to the forefront of the historic chronicle. The implications of the loss of memory are stinging; however, "Fort Sill is not an anomaly, but it is a reminder of the ongoing violences of settler colonialism, racism, and xenophobia that have defined far too much of our nation's history."[11]

There is power in our archives.

> Archives contain the evidence of what went before. This is particularly germane in the modern world . . . the archives remains as one foundation of historical understanding. Archives validate our experiences, our perceptions, our narratives, our stories. Archives are our memories.[12]

In another eighty years, how will our actions as individuals, institutions, and a nation be recorded and remembered? Not unlike the present, the story that we are presenting is one of a nation wracked with fear of an "other," a group that people believe is challenging and eroding the ideals of America. From 1942 to 1943, Camp Livingston operated in the geographic center of the state of Louisiana as a site of internment. This Army installation was an integral component in the United States' success in World War II as the site of the Maneuvers which transformed the fighting forces of the United States. This legacy of military triumph still looms large in the state's history today. But the history of Camp Livingston as a site of an internment camp for Japanese civilian men has fallen into obscurity; a darker history that challenges the popular ideal of what constitutes America. The history of the internment of Japanese civilian aliens and the larger history of Japanese enemy alien internment within the confines of DOJ and Army camps is a history that has drifted away from the mainstream historical memory. To share this chapter of our history, we must do the work of finding the experiences of those affected—their names and their voices which were muffled for decades. The importance of this work cannot be overstated. As Verne Harris writes:

> the work of memory is fundamentally spectral . . . The ghosts demand that we take responsibility before them. Not responsibility *for* them—responsibility *before* them, in front of them, seeing them, seeing them again, and re-specting them. They demand that we work to make our lives meaningful by working to make their lives meaningful. The work of memory, and the work of archives, in these framings, is about just such a taking of responsibility.[13]

There is power in our stories. With the expanding digitization of numerous collections in archives and other memory institutions the world over, hope springs eternal for the democratization of information and knowledge by tearing down barriers to access and the scholarship that will be born of these efforts. The following story of two families is one such example of the powerful but often overlooked histories held in our archives and other cultural memory institutions. Throughout this journey, we have used an archival approach wherein we allow the documentation unearthed to "talk story"[14] with one another to further the exploration of the history of Camp Livingston and those that experienced it. We use this as a call to archivists, memory curators, the academy, and to layman alike to uncover, acknowledge, and share these historically excluded stories and ensure they remain embedded within our rich historical tapestry.

NOTES

1. Kashima, *Judgment Without Trial*, 124.
2. We have used English language resources as our primary sources of information. Any Japanese language sources utilized have been translated for us, but because of monetary constraints the majority of items translated are related specifically to Reverend Miyamoto.
3. Ibram X. Kendi, "The End of Denial," *Atlantic* 326, no. 2 (2020): 50.
4. Kendi, "The End of Denial," 54.
5. Anthony W. Dunbar, "Introducing Critical Race Theory to Archival Discourse: Getting the Conversation Started," *Archival Science* 6, no. 1 (March 1, 2006): 115, https://doi.org/10.1007/s10502-006-9022-6.
6. Emiko Hastings, "'No Longer a Silent Victim of History': Repurposing the Documents of Japanese American Internment," *Archival Science* 11, no. 1–2 (2011): 26, https://doi.org/10.1007/s10502-010-9113-2.
7. Terry Cook, "Evidence, Memory, Identity, and Community: Four Shifting Archival Paradigms," *Archival Science* 13, no. 2–3 (2013): 101, https://doi.org/10.1007/s10502-012-9180-7.
8. W.J. Hennigan, "Trump Administration to Hold Migrant Children at Base that Served as WWII Japanese Internment Camp," *Time*, June 11, 2019, https://time.com/5605120/trump-migrant-children-fort-sill/; David Rogers, "Kid Shelters at Military Posts to Close," *Politico*, August 4, 2014, https://www.politico.com/story/2014/08/border-children-no-military-facility-housing-109692; Nina Wallace and Natasha Varner, "Fort Sill is a Site of Ongoing Trauma," *Densho* (blog), June 12, 2019, https://densho.org/fort-sill-is-a-site-of-ongoing-trauma/#:~:text=The%20Trump%20Administration's%20plan%20to,were%20incarcerated%20there%20during%20WWII.
9. Adam Kealoha Causey, "Oklahoma Base Set for Migrant Site was WWII Internment Camp," *Associated Press News*, June 13, 2019, https://apnews.com/article/b7ce3584b3fe412783028445e2258621.
10. Causey, "Oklahoma Base Set for Migrant Site was WWII Internment Camp."
11. Wallace and Varner, "Fort Sill is a Site of Ongoing Trauma."
12. Joan M. Schwartz and Terry Cook, "Archives, Records, and Power: The Making of Modern Memory," *Archival Science* 2, no. 1 (March 1, 2002): 18, https://doi.org/10.1007/BF02435628.
13. Verne Harris, "Antonyms of our Remembering," *Archival Science* 14, no. 3–4 (2014): 217–218, https://doi.org/10.1007/s10502-014-9221-5.
14. "Talk Story" is a common Hawaiian phrase denoting storytelling or the sharing of histories in familiar conversation.

Acknowledgments

This manuscript is a culmination of seven years of research, and the support that has accompanied our efforts has been remarkable on every level. This achievement doesn't happen without a community, of which we are abundantly blessed.

First, we owe a huge debt of gratitude to the Miyamoto and Kohara families. Without their assistance and support, there would be no beating heart at the center of this book. We want to first thank Marion Kohara Couvillion for sharing her memories with us and setting us down the path of discovery. To Clifford Miyamoto, we thank you for your kindness, hospitality, and openness.

We want to thank members of the Kohara family: Connie Haydel, Sydnie Kohara, Becky Broussard, and Karen Schlichting, Mike Murashige, Lynn Edwards, and Walter Edwards. We also want to thank JoAnne Kohara Thompson for her support, friendship, and lending us her talents to create artwork for the book cover. From the Miyamoto family, we want to thank David Kanji and Ethel Miyamoto and their daughters Karen and Susan for welcoming us into their home and sharing their stories, food, and spectacular Hawaiian hospitality as well as Garret Miyamoto for his constant and continued assistance.

We also want to thank the other families who helped us to uncover the history of Camp Livingston through their assistance and willingness to share their stories, histories, and artifacts: Jennifer and Addie Kano, Robert Cardinaux, Renko Ishida Dempster, and Ella Miyeko Tomita, née Ohta.

This book also would not have been possible without our friends and scholars who have supported us so greatly. From Hawai'i: Barbara Ritchie (the best tour guide this side of anywhere); Mary Campany and Jane Kurahara at the Japanese Cultural Center of Hawai'i; Jodie Mattos at the University of

Hawaiʻi Mānoa; Danee McFarr at the Honolulu Museum of Art for letting us play out a hunch; and especially George and Willa Tanabe for taking the time to share their knowledge, insight, and kindness with us. From California: Jamie Henricks at the Japanese American National Museum. From Louisiana: Richard Moran at the Louisiana Maneuvers and Military Museum as well as Yoshinori Kamo for his translations. From Canada (by way of New York): Greg Robinson for his continued support and encouragement.

We would like to thank LSU Libraries for allowing us to pursue a project of such magnitude and importance even though it falls outside of what some deem the traditional bounds of librarianship. Special thanks to Allen LeBlanc for assistance with translations, and Kevin P. Duffy, Randa Lopez Morgan, and Gabe Harrell for their assistance with images. And we would be remiss if we didn't thank our Citation Krewe: Allen, Audrey, Danielle, Jazz, Narcissa, Randa, and Sam.

Funding for research provided by: American Library Association Carnegie Whitney Grant (2017 and 2018); American Library Association Government Documents Roundtable (GODORT) Newsbank Award (2017 and 2018); Louisiana Board of Regents Awards to Louisiana Artists and Scholars (ATLAS) Grant (2019).

We would also like to especially thank Duncan Ryūken Williams who from the very beginning was an advocate and proponent of this work. Words fail to express our deep gratitude for your continued support, sage advice, patience, and the kindness that you have shown us.

And finally, to our families: Without your love, support, understanding, and encouragement, our work wouldn't have been possible.

Part I

FOUNDATIONS IN A NEW LAND

Chapter 1

A Consequence of Birth

December 7, 1941, is a date that resonates with every American. On this day, America's isolationist stance ended abruptly when the Empire of Japan attacked the U.S. Naval fleet docked at Pearl Harbor in Hawai'i. This preemptive military strike by the Japanese hurtled the United States into war and is known as one of the worst military and naval disasters in American history. A secondary catastrophe that resulted from the attack on Pearl Harbor was the effect it would have on the Nikkei communities throughout the United States and the territory of Hawai'i. This manifested in the forced mass removal and incarceration of approximately 120,000 Nikkei into incarceration camps in the western interior of the United States. Of those 120,000 incarcerated, some two-thirds were American citizens.

THE WAR RELOCATION AUTHORITY

Approximately two months after Pearl Harbor, President Franklin Delano Roosevelt signed Executive Order 9066 on February 19, 1942, authorizing the military to exclude any persons from designated "military areas" without trial or hearings.[1] A month later, Executive Order 9012 was issued on March 18, 1942. This order established the War Relocation Authority (WRA), a civilian agency within the Department of the Interior that was tasked with confining and housing the evacuated population for the duration of the war and sometimes beyond. Within days of the order establishing the WRA, the first Civilian Exclusion order was issued by the Army on March 24, 1942. This exclusion order was followed by others—108 in total—over a five-month period until August 1942. When these orders were posted, families were notified they had a week to make arrangements for or dispose of their property. In addition, they had to register at a designated civil control station where the family was assigned a number. When the family reported on the day of removal, they were only allowed to bring what they could carry. Their bags were tagged with their family number and shipped off to the "assembly centers" to await their arrival, thus starting their journey of imprisonment. Today, it is difficult to imagine what these families must have felt as they faced a deadline to abandon the lives they built for themselves by order of a government that was supposed to protect them.

By June 6, 1942, all Japanese Americans had been removed from Military Area 1 and individuals would be removed from Military Area 2 by August 18th.[2] The Wartime Civil Control Administration was responsible for the "assembly centers" to which Nikkei were first forcibly removed. These "assembly centers" were located at fairgrounds, livestock yards, horse racetracks, and other locations. Families were forced to live in animal stalls or other shoddily built dwellings spending up to six months in these conditions before being moved to incarceration camps. As the families waited, the WRA was setting up its relocation centers in barren and desolate locations in the interior of the United States. These sites were located on sparsely populated federal lands that had nearby railroad access and agricultural potential. Additionally, the sites were away from any strategic installations such as power lines and reservoirs.

In total, ten WRA camps[3] located in Arizona, Arkansas, California, Colorado, Idaho, Utah, and Wyoming were built to house the forcibly removed Japanese Americans for the duration of the war.

The housing conditions for the families and individuals being forced into these camps could be described as spartan, at best.

> The new physical mould into which people had to fit was a rigid one. The relocation centers were built by Army engineers according to standard plans for housing a young, unmarried, male population. They were Army camps of a type called theatre of operations, that is, temporary constructions designed for only a few years' use.[4]

These barracks were not built for families nor, in many cases, the elements as they were wooden barracks covered in tar paper. The expectation was that family life would center around these barracks. Since the purpose and location of these camps were to effectively segregate Nikkei from the rest of the U.S. population during the war, the camps were designed to be communities unto themselves.

> [They were] complete with hospitals, post offices, schools, warehouses, offices, factories, and residential areas, all surrounded by barbed wire and guard towers. Since the centers were supposed to be as self-sufficient as possible, the

residential core was surrounded by a large buffer zone that also served as farmland.[5]

The extremity of the measures taken by the U.S. government against those of Japanese ethnicity went so far as to include even those Japanese American children under the care of orphanages. Karl R. Bendetsen,[6] a key figure in drafting the "exclusion" of Japanese Americans from the West Coast, "[was] determined that if they have one drop of Japanese blood in them, they must go to camp,"[7] and gave the order to begin removing children from orphanages on April 28, 1942.[8]

While testing the allegiance and patriotism of the incarcerated Japanese Americans through Loyalty Questionnaires began in 1943, that same year, the WRA recognized the hypocrisy the relocation centers made of the democratic principles which they were trying to measure in the Nikkei population. Dillon S. Myer, the director of the WRA, said the following in a nationally broadcast speech:

> In spite of the fact that the War Relocation Authority is responsible for managing ten relocation centers—we don't feel that they are desirable institutions, or anything in which the people of the United States can take pride. It isn't the American way to have children grow up behind barbed wire. It may be possible to make good Americans out of them—but the very surroundings make a mockery out of principles we have always cherished and respected. It's difficult to reconcile democracy with barbed wire—freedom with armed sentries—liberty with searchlights.[9]

But even with this realization, the Nikkei being held in the WRA camps would not be released until Executive Order 9066 was "unofficially rescinded" in December of 1944.

The long-held racism against Japanese and Japanese Americans held by the U.S. government and the public at large would affect thousands.[10]

> Each [the Issei and Nisei] carried a personal burden of rage or resignation or despair to the assembly centers and camps which the government had hastily built to protect 130 million Americans against 60,000 of their fellow citizens and their resident alien parents.[11]

After being released from the camps, the vast majority returned home to nothing having lost everything in the blink of an eye. A long and arduous road lay ahead as they tried to rebuild their lives from scratch. Ultimately, no charges of disloyalty or sabotage were ever brought against any of these citizens. Their civil rights had been violated, and it would not be until the Redress Movement of the 1960s and 1970s that the call for justice would stop falling on deaf ears. Executive Order 9066 was officially rescinded on February 19,

1976—over thirty years after its initial signing. In 1982, the Commission on Wartime Relocation and Internment of Civilians published *Personal Justice Denied*, which found that the incarceration of the Nikkei communities was a "grave injustice" rooted in "race prejudice, war hysteria and a failure of political leadership."[12] The work done by the Commission on Wartime Relocation and Internment of Civilians opened the door for the passage of the Civil Liberties Act of 1988 acknowledging the "fundamental injustice of the evacuation, relocation, and internment of United States citizens and permanent resident aliens of Japanese ancestry during World War II."[13] An official presidential apology was given as was the sum of $20,000 for those eligible. It must be noted that by the time this legislation passed, many of the older generation who had experienced wartime incarceration and internment had already passed away; redress had come too late.

The ten WRA camps and the incarceration of 120,000 Nikkei are visually documented in the haunting and bleak photographs of Dorothea Lange, Clem Albers, and Ansel Adams and are the subject of numerous literary efforts, both popular and scholarly. For most Americans, this is where the history of Japanese American incarceration ends. Despite the magnitude and questionable legality of this incarceration, history books usually devote only a few pages to this travesty of justice when covering the history of World War II.

THE ENEMY ALIEN INTERNMENT PROGRAM

What few Americans know, however, is that these WRA camps are not the complete story of the experiences of Nikkei during World War II.[14] Thousands of other individuals of Japanese ancestry were placed into a parallel but separate set of detention centers run by the Department of Justice and the United States Army, effectively severing familial units in the process. The exploration of this particular history has largely remained dormant.

As Pearl Harbor was still under siege, the FBI began its dragnet roundup of Japanese men who had been surveilled and deemed to be "dangerous" based on nothing more than their place of birth (Japan) or their position within their community. The Enemy Alien Internment Program had been officially activated. All aliens of Axis nations residing in the United States and its territories were now officially classified as "enemy" aliens and could be arrested and interned. These men, who were now considered enemy aliens, were Japanese immigrants or Issei, long-term residents of the United States who had been denied citizenship due to discriminatory anti-Asian laws. Overnight, the status of these men changed from resident alien to enemy alien. Unlike the WRA program that gave the Nikkei community notice that they were being removed, the men arrested as enemy aliens were given no notice with many being taken from their homes in the middle of the night, pulled from their places of worship, their workplaces, or wherever they happened to be, and sent to temporary detention stations and held with no information given to their families regarding their arrests or whereabouts. The fear in the community was palpable. Stories of these initial arrests began to circulate around the communities, and many would wait in fear for the moment they too would be arrested, not knowing why or where they would be taken. At these temporary stations, the men were isolated from what was occurring in the outside world, unable to see their families, and left in a state of darkness as to what was in store for them. Eventually, the men were transferred to Justice Department Camps.[15] There were nine Justice Department Camps which were run by the Immigration and Naturalization Service, an arm of the Justice Department. At these camps, the men could receive hearings. Upon the outcome of the Alien Enemy Hearing Board decision, the men would then be transferred to a new camp run by the U.S. Army.

There were approximately eighteen U.S. Army camps[16] in which the Issei were held. This book focuses on one of those eighteen Army camps, Camp Livingston, as a representative example of all the Army camps that have been left out of the historical narrative. Even though our primary focus is on one specific Army camp, all eighteen of the camps were remarkably similar in their operation. Internees received treatment at each camp that was dictated by the Geneva Convention (1929), the tenets of which both those imprisoned and those overseeing the imprisonment were well-versed. Each camp was surrounded by barbed wire and guarded by soldiers with guns. Oftentimes, even the names and faces of internees remained the same as the men often traveled together when being moved from camp to camp. But despite this imprisonment, the solidarity of the men imprisoned as well as the protocols set forth by the Geneva Convention led to "an almost uninhibited expression of Japanese culture and even non-militant patriotism with the acknowledgment if not approval of the camp administrators" in these particular camps.[17] The biggest differences between the eighteen U.S. Army camps can be found in their geographic locations. Located from the very north of the United States in Bismark, North Dakota, all the way to the southern part of the country in central Louisiana, the natural environs of the Army camps would vary greatly in climate, vegetation, and wildlife. At Camp Livingston, located in central Louisiana, the men were especially moved by the vast amount of pine trees in the camp—pines that reminded them of Japan. These men would remain under the control of the Army until May 1943. At that time, they were transferred back into the custody and control of the Department of Justice for the duration of the war because the Army was tasked with detaining military prisoners of war. For much of their detainment, these men were separated from their families, some of whom had been forced into WRA camps, while others voluntarily, or in some cases inadvertently, chose to be interned in Department of Justice camps with the hopes of reuniting with their loved ones.

While there are differences in the incarceration of those forcibly removed to WRA camps and those interned as enemy aliens in Army and Department of Justice camps, namely demographics (Issei versus Nisei), treatment, and resources made available to those imprisoned, there are shared connections between the two—the most obvious being a shared ethnicity, the shared imprisonment behind barbed wire, and innocence of the Nikkei community of any wrongdoing. But there is one constant that appears in camp life itself—the practice of *gaman*. A form of cultural identity, *gaman* is commonly known to mean bearing the seemingly unbearable with dignity and patience. *Gaman* is also a display of tenacity, self-restraint, and resistance oftentimes manifested in the creation of various types of artistic works created in camp. In *Artifacts of Loss*, the art created by the Nikkei is described as:

> Displaying a wide range of interests, form, materials, and style, these works of art provoked ideas, resistive practices, and strategies for improving both physical and mental conditions. Here, internees connected and formed attachments with the purpose of improving their lot in life. Embedded in these artifacts were subversions, with internees speaking about the control exerted on their lives. For people confined in barren and monochromatic environments, art shows also offered counter-landscapes, adding vibrancy and color to camp palates dominated by shades of tan.[18]

This is something that we first discovered through photographs taken at Camp Livingston. Initially, we were perplexed by the photographs taken of what appeared to be an art exhibit with the men proudly displaying hand-carved wooden crafts. Through research and further investigation, we have found instances in numerous other camps as well and have been moved by the collective coping mechanism that was utilized by many in the camps—both WRA and Army/Department of Justice—to both heal the psychological wounds caused by incarceration and internment and to face the indignity and injustice of their forced removal in their own chosen way.

A RECKONING THROUGH RECOGNITION

This program of detaining enemy aliens during times of war is legally permissible under the Alien Enemies Act of 1798. Although legally permissible, it is morally questionable. Over 7,000 Japanese nationals (Issei) from the United States and Latin America were held in internment camps overseen by the Department of Justice and the U.S. Army.[19] Throughout our own journey with this history, we have constantly asked ourselves why the enemy alien program, specifically the camps located within Army installations, seems to have been pushed by the wayside, inevitably resulting in a feeling that this particular facet of internment history is not as widely known. The esteemed scholar Duncan Ryūken Williams has also pondered this question. He noted, "What research exists naturally focuses on the confinement sites that held larger populations and operated for longer durations."[20] The difference in numbers of those imprisoned in WRA camps compared to those held in Army and Department of Justice camps is staggering and could indeed explain why the enemy alien program is not more widely known. Another possible reason is that the experiences of many of those held in the Army camps was a topic not often discussed after their release—with anyone. The traumatic experiences paired with the shame and stigma of their internment often led to many in an entire generation remaining silent. There has been ongoing research into the transgenerational trauma experienced by those held in WRA camps during World War II; however, this research mainly focuses on the effects and coping mechanisms of the Nisei and even Sansei.[21] And while the focus has been on later generations who suffered incarceration in the WRA camps, we can use this information to describe and understand the silence of many Issei about their internment experiences. Donna Nagata, in her 1990 article *The Japanese American Internment: Exploring the Transgenerational Consequences of Traumatic Stress*, wrote about the effects of being unjustly imprisoned being:

> similar to that of rape victims[—having] done nothing to provoke the imprisonment, they felt ashamed of what had happened and responsible for their situation... [and] many Nisei adopted both immediate and long-term defense mechanisms of repression, denial, rationalization, and identification with the aggressor [here Nagata is building upon the work of Hansen and Mitson (1974) and Zimbardo (1981)].[22]

This silence in the community was pervasive. Nagata went on to say:

> Most obvious, however, has been the general lack of communication about the internment by those who experienced it, a phenomenon which has been so pervasive that one scholar (Daniels, 1986) referred to it as a "collective social amnesia."[23]

In 1981, hearings were held in conjunction with the Commission on Wartime Relocation and Internment of Civilians regarding the events that had happened some forty years prior marking the first time the event and the experiences of those incarcerated were publicly discussed.[24]

But perhaps the major reason the history of enemy alien internment has been relegated to the margins and footnotes of historical analysis of World War II is tied to human nature and the need to simplify and streamline history. With the desire to compartmentalize and condense history into neat chapters, the complexities of what happened to the Nikkei after Pearl Harbor become diluted and consequently conflated into one shared experience—that of the WRA incarceration camps and related Japanese American experiences.

Gerald Ford's 1976 Presidential Proclamation 4417 officially terminated 9066 and ended with an "American Promise." This promise constituted a recognition of learning as well as a vow to not repeat the same tragic history. The subsequent passage of the Civil Liberties Act of 1988 under President Reagan issued a formal presidential apology to every surviving U.S. citizen or legal resident immigrant of Japanese ancestry who was incarcerated thus extending upon Ford's 1976 proclamation.[25] While a presidential apology was issued, however, it is important to note that the law that allowed for the internment of those deemed enemy aliens, The Alien Enemies Act of 1798, is still very much an active law that can be wielded against similar groups today. The distinction between incarceration and internment highlights the dichotomy present in the experiences of Japanese American citizens versus those classified as non-citizen or resident aliens. The result of this conflation has meant that the differences between internment and incarceration have remained largely unknown to the general public culminating in a misplaced memory.

Throughout the following chapters, we hope to reinstate the memory of internment into the larger historical narrative through the focus on the experience of the Miyamoto family of Hawai'i. While their internment journey was unique to them, their story and experiences serve as a representation of what individuals in the Department of Justice/Army system had to suffer because of the place of their birth. The Miyamoto family's story is intrinsically tied to their life in Hawai'i, so that will be our first sojourn on this historic journey.

NOTES

1. On March 2, 1942, Arizona, California, Oregon, and Washington states were declared military areas under the direction of the Western Defense Command led by General John L. DeWitt with Public Proclamation No. 1. Military Area No. 1 was comprised of western portions of Washington, Oregon, and California, and some parts of Arizona, while Military Area No. 2 encompassed the remaining portions of these states. DeWitt's Proclamation No. 1 stated that "persons or classes of persons as the situation may require" would be excluded from Military Area No. 1 with the general understanding that this would include those from the Nikkei community. Initially, those of Japanese descent living in Military Area 1 were encouraged to "voluntarily evacuate" either to Military Area 2 or further east. Although some were able to move to Military Area No. 2 or areas beyond, the vast majority of the Nikkei population could not leave their lives behind so quickly. However, all of this became a moot point on March 27th with Public Proclamation No. 4 which banned "all alien Japanese and persons of Japanese ancestry who are within the limits of Military Area No. 1 . . . from leaving that area for any purpose." These proclamations are the precursors to the mass forced evacuation of the Nikkei population, including those that

had already "voluntarily evacuated" to Military Area No. 2. (Headquarters Western Defense Command and Fourth Army, *Public Proclamation No. 1,* March 2, 1942, https://cdm16855.contentdm.oclc.org/digital/collection/p16855coll4/id/12134; Headquarters Western Defense Command and Fourth Army, *Public Proclamation No. 4,* March 27, 1942, https://cdm16855.contentdm.oclc.org/digital/collection/p16855coll4/id/12194; Brian Niiya, "Military Areas 1 and 2," *Densho Encyclopedia,* last modified June 10, 2020, https://encyclopedia.densho.org/Military_Areas_1_and_2/; Brian Niiya, "Voluntary Evacuation," *Densho Encyclopedia,* last modified July 29, 2020, https://encyclopedia.densho.org/Voluntary_evacuation/).

2. Brian Niiya, "Civilian Exclusion Orders," *Densho Encyclopedia,* https://encyclopedia.densho.org/Civilian%20exclusion%20orders/ (accessed May 15, 2020).

3. Manzanar and Tule Lake, California; Minidoka, Idaho; Gila River and Poston, Arizona; Topaz, Utah; Heart Mountain, Wyoming; Amache, Colorado; and Jerome and Rohwer, Arkansas.

4. Edward Holland Spicer et al., *Impounded People: Japanese-Americans in the Relocation Centers* (Washington, DC: U.S. Govt. Printing Office, 1946), 39–40.

5. Jeffrey F. Burton et al., *Confinement and Ethnicity: An Overview of World War II Japanese American Relocation Sites,* (Washington, DC: U.S. Department of the Interior, revised 2000), https://www.nps.gov/parkhistory/online_books/anthropology74/ce3h.htm.

6. Bendetsen, an attorney, assisted in the drafting of EO 9066. After the order was signed, Bendetsen was promoted to oversee the "exclusion" program which he helped to conceive. He served as the director of the Wartime Civil Control Administration (WCCA). Bendetsen claimed that he "'conceived the executive order' and that he 'conceived the method, formulated the detailed plans for, and directed the evacuation of 120,000 persons of Japanese ancestry from military areas of the West Coast'" in his 1942 military record. (Klancy de Nevers, "Karl Bendetsen," *Densho Encyclopedia,* https://encyclopedia.densho.org/Karl%20Bendetsen/ (accessed May 16, 2020)). Note: This number of persons evacuated includes 110,000 forcibly removed and an additional 10,000 who later entered the camps. Later in life, Bendetsen vehemently denied his role in the forced removal and exclusion of Japanese Americans.

7. Michi Nishiura Weglyn, *Years of Infamy: The Untold Story of America's Concentration Camps* (New York: William Morrow and Company, Inc., 1976), 77.

8. Anyone with 1/16th or more Japanese blood was included. According to *Due Process,* "Some 2,000 children under 5 years of age, 15,500 children under 10 years of age, 2,000 persons over 65 years of age, and 1,000 seriously handicapped or bedridden persons were all shipped off to detention camps." (National Japanese American Historical Society, *Due Process: Americans of Japanese Ancestry and the United States Constitution, 1787–1994* (San Francisco: National Japanese American Historical Society, 1995), 32). To house these orphans, Manzanar Children's Village was constructed. Manzanar Children's Village was the only orphanage in the ten camps and held 101 children. Children's Village functioned as its own camp within the larger confines of Manzanar with three barracks to house the orphans and staff who relocated with the children.

9. Typescript of address by Dillon S. Myer over the National Broadcasting Company Network, July 15, 1943, Papers of Dillon S. Myer, The War Relocation Authority and the Incarceration of Japanese-Americans during World War II, Harry S. Truman Library, https://www.trumanlibrary.gov/library/research-files/speech-dillon-s-myer-over-national-broadcasting-company-network-july-15-1943.

10. This racism was the result of hysteria around the "Yellow Peril." The Nikkei community was seen as a threat to the economic and cultural mainstays of the United States: white economic supremacy and Christian values. Anti-Asian legislation began in the 1880s with the Chinese Exclusion Act, culminating in the Immigration Act of 1924. Newspapers and other media also fueled the flames as did societies like the Native Sons of the Golden West and Native Daughters of the Golden West.

11. Commission on Wartime Relocation and Internment of Civilians, *Personal Justice Denied: Report of the Commission on Wartime Relocation and Internment of Civilians* (Washington, DC: Government Printing Office, 1982), 94–95. (Hereafter cited as *Personal Justice Denied.*)

12. *Personal Justice Denied*, 18.

13. "Public Law 100-383, 100th Congress, Session 2, An Act: To implement recommendations of the Commission on Wartime Relocation and Internment of Civilians," U.S. Statutes at Large 102, no. Main Section (1988): 903, https://www.govinfo.gov/content/pkg/STATUTE-102/pdf/STATUTE-102-Pg903.pdf.

14. Some seminal scholarly works include Michi Weglyn's *Years of Infamy*; Roger Daniels' *Prisoners without Trial: Japanese Americans in World War II* (Hill and Wang, 1993); Commission on Wartime Relocation and Internment of Civilians, *Personal Justice Denied*; *Japanese Americans From Relocation to Redress*, edited by Roger Daniels, Sandra Taylor, and Harry Kitano (University of Washington, Revised Edition, 1991); Greg Robinson's *By Order of the President: FDR and the Internment of Japanese Americans* (Harvard University Press, 2001) and *A Tragedy of Democracy: Japanese Confinement in North America* (Columbia University Press, 2009). In addition to treatment by scholars, there are scores of personal narratives and novels that emerged from the WRA camps including Jeanne Wakatsuki Houston and James D. Houston's *Farewell to Manzanar* and John Okada's *No-No Boy*, to name just a few.

15. Kooskia, Idaho; Fort Missoula, Montana; Fort Stanton, New Mexico; Old Raton Ranch, New Mexico; Santa Fe, New Mexico; Fort Lincoln, North Dakota; Crystal City, Texas; Kenedy, Texas; and Seagoville, Texas. Crystal City and Seagoville are unique among the Department of Justice camps in that Crystal City was a family internment camp while Seagoville held single women and some families.

16. Fort Richardson, Alaska; Florence, Arizona; Fort McDowell, California; Griffith Park, California; Camp Blanding, Florida; Honouliuli, Hawai'i; Sand Island, Hawai'i; Camp Livingston, Louisiana; Fort Howard, Maryland; Fort Meade, Maryland; Camp Lordsburg, New Mexico; Fort Sill, Oklahoma; Stringtown, Oklahoma; Camp McCoy, Wisconsin; Camp Forrest, Tennessee; Fort Bliss, Texas; Fort Sam Houston, Texas; Fort Lewis, Washington.

17. Paul Frederick Clark, "Those Other Camps: An Oral History Analysis of Japanese Alien Enemy Internment during World War II" (Master's Thesis, California State University, Fullerton, 1980), 26.

18. Jane E. Dusselier, *Artifacts of Loss: Crafting Survival in Japanese American Concentration Camps* (New Brunswick: Rutgers University Press, 2008), 103. Artwork ran the gamut from wooden carvings to calligraphy to paintings or even delicate needlework, and this list is by no means exhaustive. The ephemeral nature of some of these pieces has meant that its very survival is a feat unto itself. It must be remembered that these items were made with materials found on hand which speaks to the ingenuity of its creators. Delphine Hirasuna compiled a beautiful collection of exemplary pieces of artwork that survived the camps titled *The Art of Gaman: Arts and Crafts from the Japanese American Internment Camps 1942–1946* (Ten Speed Press, 2005).

19. Burton et al., *Confinement and Ethnicity*.

20. Duncan Ryūken Williams, "Fort Sill and the Incarceration of Japanese 'Enemy Aliens' during World War II," [2019], 1, https://static1.squarespace.com/static/5ba3e3df1516ba05fbbe1801/t/5da5363a9e0ada5e379c5b78/1571108410776/Revised+Fort+Sill+History+10132019.pdf.

21. Translated to third generation. Their parents were Nisei, and their grandparents were Issei.

22. Donna K. Nagata, "The Japanese American Internment: Exploring the Transgenerational Consequences of Traumatic Stress," *Journal of Traumatic Stress* 3, no. 1 (January 1990): 51.

23. Nagata, "The Japanese American Internment," 51.

24. Nagata, "The Japanese American Internment," 51.

25. Sharon Yamato, "Civil Liberties Act of 1988," *Densho Encyclopedia*, https://encyclopedia.densho.org/Civil%20Liberties%20Act%20of%201988 (accessed August 6, 2022).

Chapter 2

Tengoku or Heaven

"History came to Hawaii by way of the sea."[1] Surrounded by the vibrant blue waters of the Pacific Ocean, Hawai'i, which comprises eight islands spread out over 1,523 miles of ocean, is the longest archipelago in the world. Hawai'i is also one of the world's most isolated population centers located 2,390 miles from California and 3,850 miles from Japan. Hawai'i's geographic location and history have made it a meeting place between East and West which has long been noted by scholars and observers alike.[2] In 1924, Reverend Albert W. Palmer, a minister at the prominent Central Union Church in Honolulu, wrote a study on the race problems in Hawai'i in which he cited Hawai'i and Constantinople as the two places in the world where East and West were intensely intermingled. Palmer's study articulated the struggle many Americans faced when pondering the future of the Hawaiian Islands.

> Will Hawaii at last be American or Japanese? Will it be Christian or Buddhist? East and West are meeting here—which will prevail? . . . Or will they meet to fight and snarl at one another or to appreciate and understand each other to the helping of the world?[3]

Palmer's questions were in response to the influx of Asian workers to the Hawaiian Islands that had begun in the 1880s to supply the labor needed for the growing sugar plantations peppering the Islands. As the whaling industry declined, the sugar plantations were on the rise. Sugarcane grew naturally on the Islands, and those who could control the production of this cash crop would experience economic windfalls allowing them to pull the strings of local politics in their favor.[4] Growing sugarcane was all well and good, but if you lacked a labor force to harvest the tough stalks, it was all for naught.

Making phrases about it was easy, especially for missionaries who were just beginning to take a serious interest in the agricultural prospects of the kingdom: the harvest was ready, they said, but the laborers were few. Finding a remedy was harder.[5]

The planters first sought a remedy at home. The native Hawaiian population, estimated to be around 300,000 to 400,000 in 1778 at the time of Captain Cook's arrival, had fallen to about 40,000 by 1884.[6] The small number of Hawaiians, coupled with their strong sense of independence, necessitated the bringing in of contract laborers to handle Hawai'i's now-booming sugar industry.[7] Between 1852 and 1884, 25,256 Chinese contract laborers were brought to Hawai'i and accounted for approximately 49 percent of the sugar plantation workforce by 1882.[8] With large numbers of Chinese laborers leaving the plantations upon the conclusion of their contracts and moving into the urban areas, the white elite of Hawai'i began looking to balance the large numbers of Chinese brought to the Islands. The plantations continued to look to the East and Asian labor as being the most economical source, and they began to import Japanese laborers.

The Japanese immigrants who arrived on Hawai'i's shores beginning in 1868 represent the timeless immigrant story of sojourning to an unknown place for the chance at a better life. This first band of 149 laborers, also known as *gannenmono*, or "first years" denoting the year 1868 as the first in the Meiji period, faced harsh working conditions and unfair treatment by plantation owners. Forty of the original 149 returned to Japan before their contracts had expired.[9] All formal immigration from Japan to Hawai'i ceased for seventeen years. By the 1880s, both King Kalakaua's Hawaiian government and Emperor Meiji's Japanese government were willing to try again, and the first 943 Japanese immigrants arrived as contract laborers to the Kingdom of Hawai'i in 1885.[10] The number of Japanese immigrants continued to increase as recruiters were sent to advertise the work available in Hawai'i to the Yamaguchi, Hiroshima, Fukushima, and Kumamoto prefectures.[11] The Hawaiian Majesty's government provided "free steerage passage and proper food from Yokohama to Honolulu, in first-class passenger steamers," as well as guaranteed monthly wages.[12] In the *Report of the President of the Bureau of Immigration to the Legislative Assembly of 1886*, Dr. William Hillebrand, the Bureau's Commissioner, stated "First and nearest to us lies Japan, inhabited by a people generally considered akin to the Hawaiians and who, we all agree, would be desirable immigrants."[13] Many of the immigrants wanted to leave Japan because of natural disasters that affected agriculture, economic turmoil due to modernization, as well as the fear of being conscripted into the military by the Meiji regime which was getting ever closer to going to war with China.[14] The Japanese who signed on as contract laborers were eager to leave for the land they called *tengoku* or heaven.[15] They believed that *tengoku* was a land of opportunity where through hard work, they could earn money and return home as rich men.

When the Japanese immigrants arrived in Hawai'i, they quickly found out that their heaven on earth was, in truth, a hell ruled by the plantation overseers or *lunas*. Life for the immigrants was harsh and unforgiving. Coming to the Islands as contract laborers meant working ten-hour days for a contracted three-year period. Monthly salaries for men amounted to $9.00, and for women only $6.00. The ratio between men and women was five to one. The labor on the plantations was a far cry from the agricultural work the Japanese had done in their homeland. Grueling days spent toiling in the sun at a swift pace set by pacesetters, men who were paid about ten cents extra per day to push the pace and output of the group to a higher level, were followed by nights in dire housing conditions. Oftentimes, the housing for laborers was substandard and overcrowded with inadequate sanitation facilities. "Under the minimum requirements established by Hawai'i's housing law, preannexation plantations had to provide only 300 cubic feet per laborer—the equivalent of a closet-like enclosure six feet high and seven feet square."[16]

Suffering poor treatment alongside deplorable living conditions, many of the immigrants became increasingly rebellious. The men turned to various vices to cope with the lives in which they were confined. Often described as "*sake, onna, bakuchi* (alcohol, women, and gambling)," these activities were often sanctioned by the plantations as an attempt to keep the men docile.[17] To escape their lives on the plantation, many laborers deserted the plantations in an attempt to break free from their contracts. Deserters would be captured, brought back to the plantation, and have additional time added to their contract to make up for their disobedience. Sometimes, they would be beaten as punishment for their *ha'alele hana* or desertion.[18] Deserters occasionally escaped to plantations where the managers were more benevolent or to communities of fellow deserters and other free laborers where they would take on a new name to distance themselves from their contractual duties. "The coffee fields of Kona on the Big Island and the farms of Waimanalo on Oahu were favorite destinations for Japanese deserters."[19]

The laborers often sang what are known as *holehole bushi*[20] while working in the fields. The *holehole bushi* are Japanese folk songs composed and sung by the immigrant plantation workers providing reflections of the experiences of the Issei who left Japan to work the plantations of Hawai'i.[21] The following is an excerpt from one *holehole bushi* which details how the Issei arrived with dreams of fortune and found only horrors and disappointment in their new lives in Hawai'i.

Kane no naru ki mo	Money trees were
Aru yō ni omotte	In my thoughts when I came but
Kite mir'ya Hawai wa	Hawai'i turned out to be a
Ikijigoku	Living hell
Kuni wo deru tok'ya	I left home
Egao de deta ga	With a smile on my face
Kyō no kachiken	Cutting cane today
Jigoku dani	A valley of hell[22]

In addition to the contract laborers, other ambitious men immigrated to Hawai'i without labor contracts. These free immigrants were classified as "Hi-Imin" or nonlabor immigrants and included priests and ministers, doctors, businessmen, educators and students, as well as newspaper editors.[23] By 1894, approximately 30,000 Japanese immigrants had settled in Hawai'i.

In 1898, the Spanish-American war broke out, and the United States realized the military significance of Hawai'i and her naval bases, prominently Pearl Harbor, as a way station to the Spanish Philippines. This recognition in light of war finally tipped Congress to approve the annexation of Hawai'i. Fearing that Hawai'i's annexation would cause the territory to follow suit with mainland laws outlawing contract labor, Hawaiian planters rushed to import some 26,103 Japanese contract laborers in 1899. This was the largest number of Japanese laborers brought into the Islands in a single year.[24]

The following year, the Organic Act of 1900 prohibited any further importation of contract labor into Hawai'i and effectively rendered all prior labor contracts null and void. With contract labor legally ended, many Japanese who were dissatisfied with their plantation existence migrated into the cities in large numbers and could now immigrate to the mainland for work. As Japanese immigration away from the plantations increased considerably so did "public apprehension and resentment" toward the Japanese who were moving into metropolitan areas and taking jobs requiring more skill.[25] Another effect of the passage of the Organic Act of 1900 was that workers could now engage in legal strikes in order to protest substandard wages, living conditions, and poor treatment. "There were more work stoppages in 1900 than ever before."[26]

In 1907, labor immigration from Hawai'i to the United States was prohibited as part of the Gentlemen's Agreement.[27] Because of this, Japanese immigrants had few alternatives available to them on the Islands. "Low, demeaning plantation wages could no longer be escaped by immigrating to the states. Return to Japan with no money or savings was impossible without losing face."[28] With the realization that returning to Japan without wealth or fortune would result in shame, Japanese immigrants began to focus on building their lives permanently on the Islands. Japanese laborers embraced a new idea of *eiju dochaku* meaning "settle down to the soil."[29] This desire to settle on the Islands precipitated the bringing over of families and of picture brides, which began in 1908 and culminated in 1924 wherein tens of thousands of Japanese women arrived to the Islands to create a new Japanese community identity built on a familial unit rather than temporary laborers without ties to the Islands.[30]

The first Consulate General of Japan was established in Honolulu in 1886 with the primary charge of looking after the well-being of its constituents, the Japanese immigrant community, and acting as a representative of the Japanese government in a foreign land. This included recording vital statistics and life events (birth, death, marriage, divorce, etc.), overseeing military and travel documents, and fostering communication and trade. The consul was an important facet of life in the Japanese-born immigrant community, or Issei. The role of the consul became even more important in 1900 when Hawai'i become a U.S. territory. The Issei would be consistently denied American citizenship through legislation that reflected the anti-Asian sentiments of the American public at the time culminating in 1922 with *Ozawa v. United States* which maintained the ban on Japanese naturalization.[31] This ban would remain in effect until 1952.[32] This meant that despite their hopes of becoming citizens of their adopted home, they were barred by law and made to retain their Japanese nationality, "subject to Japanese laws and military draft," while also subject to laws of the United States.[33]

The citizenship of American women who married Issei men was also affected. In 1907, Congress passed the Expatriation Act which declared that U.S. women who married non-citizen men lost their status as American citizens. When women gained the right to vote, they challenged the Expatriation Act of 1907, and in 1922, the same year as the Ozawa case, the Cable Act or Married Women's Independent Nationality Act was passed. The Cable Act ensured that women who married men who were *eligible* to become naturalized citizens did not automatically lose their American citizenship simply by marrying a non-citizen. Except, that is, if the woman married an Asian man. With the decision handed down by the U.S. Supreme Court in the Ozawa case that same year, it was determined that Japanese were not white and therefore could not become naturalized U.S. citizens. This served to further alienate and "other" the Issei as a non-assimilable group.

Although the Issei were forced by legislation to exist as perpetual resident aliens in their adopted country, their children were considered American citizens by their birth on U.S. land or *jus soli*. Complicating this matter was the principle of *jus sanguinis* whereby the children born of Japanese fathers, no matter their location, were automatically considered citizens of Japan through blood. This meant that the children of the Issei born in Hawai'i, the Nisei, were both citizens of the United States and subjects of Japan, "technically subject to Japanese law and military draft... [but] also *bona fide* American citizens with the accompanying constitutional rights and privileges."[34] In 1924, Japan instituted a law wherein those born before December 1, 1924, could renounce their Japanese nationality through documentation, effectively expatriating themselves from Japan. For children born after this date, their parents would have two weeks to register their birth and claim their Japanese nationality at the local Japanese consulate.[35] In the 1930s, only 8 percent of Nisei had expatriated from Japan, while 40 percent of Japanese parents had registered their children for dual citizenship.[36]

The Issei were caught in a no-man's land fraught with contradictions. They were establishing lives and building futures in a country that would not allow them to become naturalized citizens while automatically granting their children the very rights they were denied. Continuing to register their children for dual citizenship after 1924 was one way that Issei parents could ensure their child's future if they were forced to return to Japan. For many white Americans, the issue of dual citizenship among Japanese was especially troubling as they equated dual citizenship with dual allegiance. This was simply not the case. Germans and Italians were also granted citizenship based on *jus sanguinis* or right of blood; yet, individuals of European descent were not often looked upon differently due to their dual citizenship nor was their loyalty to the United States constantly in question.

The Issei faced difficulties in fully integrating. While immigrants often retain a natural affinity to the country of their birth, another reason an immigrant can hold onto vestiges of his mother country is the difficulty he faces when attempting to assimilate.

> An immigrant clings to his mother country also in proportion to the difficulty he experiences in becoming a member of the new country. An immigrant always finds difficulty in adjusting to a new community, especially so, when his physical and mental characteristics are quite different from those of the people who constitute the community.[37]

Initially welcomed with open arms, "by the end of the century they were being talked about as a yellow peril more insidious even than the Chinese, threatening the very existence of Western civilization at the islands."[38] For the Issei in Hawai'i, the discrimination they faced was a primary hurdle in completely adjusting to the new country in which they chose to live. The inability to be accepted into the larger fabric of the community caused the Issei to establish institutions in an effort to ease their lives in Hawai'i, and by doing this, the Issei, unknowingly, widened the gulf between themselves and the white ruling class of the Islands.

NOTES

1. Gavan Daws, *Shoal of Time: A History of the Hawaiian Islands* (New York: MacMillan Company, 1968), 395.
2. As librarians, we would be remiss not to suggest Gavan Daws' 1968 tome *Shoal of Time: A History of the Hawaiian Islands* to our readers. Covering the history of Hawai'i from the arrival of Captain Cook in 1778 to its official statehood in 1959, Daws' writing is at once informative and poetic.
3. Albert W. Palmer, *The Human Side of Hawaii: Race Problems in the Mid-Pacific* (Boston: The Pilgrim Press, 1924), xiii.
4. Daws, *Shoal of Time*, 173–178.
5. Daws, *Shoal of Time*, 177–178.
6. Roland Kotani, *The Japanese in Hawaii: A Century of Struggle* (Honolulu, HI: The Hawaii Hochi, Ltd., 1985), 2.
7. The signing of the Reciprocity Agreement with the United States in 1875 ushered in a new age of sugar economics on the Islands. The Agreement stipulated free trade between the Kingdom of Hawai'i and the United States meaning that sugar was now a duty-free product. Between 1875 and 1900 "the acreage under cane in the islands increased 1,000 percent, reaching a total of one hundred and twenty-five thousand acres in 1898" (Daws, *Shoal of Time*, 208). As the acreage grew, so did the profits. "In 1879 the total value of the kingdom's sugar estates was less than ten million dollars; by the end of the century the plantations were capitalized at something like forty million dollars" (Daws, *Shoal of Time*, 208). Although it must be noted that like any agricultural product dependent upon a foreign market, in this case the United States, there were boom years and lean years.
8. Kotani, *Japanese in Hawaii*, 2. The Chinese Exclusion Act or Immigration Act of 1882 was a U.S. federal law which prohibited Chinese laborers from entering the United States as well as excluded Chinese nationals from being eligible for U.S. citizenship. This was the first immigration law that excluded an entire ethnic group.
9. Gary Okihiro, *Cane Fires: The Anti-Japanese Movement in Hawaii, 1865–1945* (Philadelphia: Temple University Press, 1991), 22.
10. The 943 passengers consisted of 676 men, 159 women, and 108 children (Okihiro, *Cane Fires*, 25).
11. Okihiro, *Cane Fires*, 24.
12. "Proclamation," *Pacific Commercial Advertiser*, March 10, 1886.
13. Quoted in Eleanor C. Nordyke and Y. Scott Matsumoto, "The Japanese in Hawaii: A Historical and Demographic Perspective," *Hawaiian Journal of History* 11 (1977): 163.
14. Franklin Odo, *Voices from the Cane Fields: Folk Songs from Japanese Immigrant Workers in Hawai'i* (Oxford University Press, 2013), 3.
15. *Tengoku* is what the Japanese laborers called Hawai'i in the 1880s. *Tengoku* translates to Heaven. (Tara K. Koda, "Aloha with Gassho: Buddhism in the Hawaiian Plantations," *Pacific World: Journal of the Institute of Buddhist Studies*, Third Series, no. 5 (Fall 2003): 241).
16. Kotani, *Japanese in Hawaii*, 15.
17. Odo, *Voices from Cane Fields*, 43.

18. Kotani, *Japanese in Hawaii*, 19.

19. Kotani, *Japanese in Hawaii*, 19. "In 1890, there were 7,612 Japanese contract laborers on the plantations, and 5,706 arrests and 5,387 convictions for desertions" (Kotani, *Japanese in Hawaii,* 19.)

20. *Holehole* is the Native Hawaiian word for the dead and dying leaves on cane stalks. *Holehole* also refers to the job on the sugar plantations which consisted of stripping those dead or dying leaves from cane stalks. This work was extremely demanding and was often assigned to women. *Bushi* is a Japanese word for tune or melody.

21. Odo, *Voices from Cane Fields*, 3.

22. Odo, *Voices from Cane Fields*, 117.

23. Yukiko Kimura, *Issei: Japanese Immigrants in Hawaii* (Honolulu, HI: University of Hawai'i Press, 1988), 11.

24. Kotani, *Japanese in Hawaii*, 24.

25. Andrew Lind, *Hawaii's Japanese: An Experiment in Democracy* (Princeton: Princeton University, 1946), 11.

26. Kimura, *Issei*, 89.

27. This agreement between the United States and Japan stopped the migration of Japanese laborers to the United States. Japanese women could still immigrate if they were wives of U.S. residents. This agreement stopped the movement of Hawaiian Japanese laborers from seeking out better working and living conditions on the mainland.

28. Dennis M. Ogawa and Glen Grant, *To a Land Called Tengoku: One Hundred Years of the Japanese in Hawaii* (Honolulu, HI: Mutual Publishing of Honolulu, 1985), 15.

29. Ogawa and Grant, *Land Called Tengoku*, 11.

30. Ogawa and Grant, *Land Called Tengoku*, 13.

31. In addition to the ban on naturalization, the United States enacted numerous laws aimed at decreasing Asian immigration beginning with the Chinese Exclusion Act of 1882, then more pointedly toward Japanese immigrants with the Gentlemen's Agreement of 1907 and finally the Immigration Act of 1924 which effectively ended Japanese immigration to the United States.

32. This race-based legal discrimination would eventually be overturned post World War II with the Immigration and Nationality Act of 1952, also known as the McCarran-Walter Act.

33. Dennis Ogawa, *Kodomo no tame ni, For the Sake of the Children: The Japanese American Experience in Hawaii* (Honolulu, HI: University Press of Hawai'i, 1978), 228.

34. Ogawa, *Kodomo no tame ni, For the Sake of the Children*, 229–230.

35. John Stephan, *Hawaii Under the Rising Sun: Japan's Plan for Conquest After Pearl Harbor* (Honolulu, HI: University of Hawai'i Press, 1984), 24; Ogawa, *Kodomo no tame ni, For the Sake of the Children*, 228–230.

36. Stephan, *Hawaii Under the Rising Sun*, 24.

37. Paul Junichiro Tajima, *Japanese Buddhism in Hawaii: Its Background, Origin, and Adaptation to Local Conditions* (Honolulu, HI: University of Hawai'i Press, 1938), 65–66.

38. Daws, *Shoal of Time*, 212.

Chapter 3

A Community Emerges

As Issei decided to permanently settle in the Hawaiian Islands and raise families, several essential components arose to assist in the social, religious, and educational needs of the developing Nikkei community. In a 1920 census, the Japanese population of Hawai'i numbered approximately 110,000 out of the total population of 250,000. Only half of the 110,000 individuals of the Japanese population were Japan-born, the other half were native-born U.S. citizens.[1] In order to support the needs of almost half of Hawai'i's population, consular agents or *toritsuginin*, Buddhist priests, and Japanese language schools, as well as other services and institutions, began to proliferate across the Islands including four Japanese daily newspapers in Honolulu and over eighty Buddhist temples or Shinto shrines.[2] These growing services were a necessity to the Nikkei community allowing them to function in a society in which they were not fully accepted. Ultimately, these services aimed to foster community for the Nikkei; however, these same services made the Nikkei community the targets of xenophobic *haole*[3] planters and government officials who did not understand the cultural significance and support these services provided. They were not seen as "American" or "white," and were therefore considered a threat to the current sociopolitical structures in place around the Islands. It was a "paradox" that had arisen before. Hawai'i's economy was inextricably linked with the United States and that economy had to be supported by immigrant laborers from Asia, but too many Asian immigrants "would endanger Americanism at the islands."[4] The outcry against these supposedly "un-American" civic, religious, and educational institutions arose in an attempt by the white minority to maintain political control of the Islands.

With the growth of the Nikkei population across the Islands, the Japanese Consulate needed help in liaising with their constituents—both Issei and

Nisei. To effectively serve the Japanese communities, the Japanese Consulate asked for volunteers or appointed leaders within the community to act as *toritsuginin* or part-time consular agents to serve for a period of two years. These volunteers would assist those in their community in filing the necessary reports and legal documentation required by Japan—birth, marriage, death, and deferment of service with the Japanese military.[5] Consular agents would also assist with expatriation requests.[6] The position was considered a very "worthwhile public service job" and like the letter-writers[7] of old, "a real convenience to the illiterate people who were quite numerous among the laborers."[8] As war between Japan and China progressed in the 1930s, a conflict in which the United States would remain neutral, many of the *toritsuginin* would oversee the collection of funds and *imonbukuro* or comfort kits that were sent to Japanese soldiers on the front. These comfort kits held "non-prescriptive medicine, literature, and an assortment of dry goods all designed to provide comfort on the front."[9] Even though the role of a *toritsuginin* was voluntary and received no funding from the Japanese Consulate, *toritsuginin* could receive small payments from those they served. This position could also raise an individual's status, for if they were not already a community leader, they soon became "highly visible . . . and an individual's main connection with Japan."[10] The role of the consular agent in Hawai'i was filled by those who could perform the necessary tasks—read and write—and as such, these roles were filled by those in the community endowed with these traits, namely priests and teachers. These community leaders undertook an additional role as a public service to their communities without knowing the backlash that would follow.

It is impossible to fully understand the Japanese communities in Hawai'i without also discussing the religion that many of the Japanese immigrants brought with them to the Hawaiian Islands—Buddhism. Arriving with the first Japanese immigrants in 1868, Japanese Buddhism continued to grow as the numbers of Japanese arriving on the Islands continued to flourish. Buddhism can be described as "an elastic, hospitable compromising religion; one that transforms and adapts itself to a new environment whenever necessary."[11] The Japanese immigrants mostly came from the Hiroshima, Yamaguchi, Kumamoto, and Fukuoka prefectures where the Pure Land and Hongwanji Sects of Buddhism were especially strong.

The first Buddhist priest to arrive in Hawai'i was Reverend Kagahi of the Nishi Hongwanji in 1889. He, and others like him, came to support the spiritual needs of the Japanese immigrant laborers around the Islands. The Jōdoshū mission was opened in 1894, followed by the Nichirenshū (1899), Sōtōshū (1903), and the Shingonshū (1914).[12] As the Japanese immigrant population spread beyond the confines of the sugarcane and pineapple fields, so did the Buddhist priests and their congregations. The spread of Buddhism throughout the Islands was not without its challenges. When Buddhist priests initially came to the Islands, their ministry to plantation workers was difficult as many of the plantation men had developed lives of debauchery in order to cope with their harsh living conditions. Additionally, ministers had to devise ways to encourage Buddhists to attend services. Oftentimes, the immigrants felt humiliated to attend Buddhist services as they were very aware that they came to a Christian country to live and that Christians received priority.[13] Many affluent Japanese had converted once they were in Hawai'i, including the Consul General and his consulate staff. Bishop Imamura of the Hongwanji Sect became intrepid in his efforts to encourage participation in Buddhist services by looking beyond the Japanese community for support. Knowing that Hawaiian Queen Lili'uokalani had interest in both Japan and Buddhism, Bishop Imamura invited her to a service commemorating the birthday of the founder of the Hongwanji Sect. On May 19, 1902, Queen Lili'uokalani attended the ceremony, and according to Bishop Imamura:

> This was the first time for the Hawaiian queen to attend a gathering of a Japanese institution and the news was published in the *Jiji Shinpo Daily* of Tokyo and in the *Osaka Mainichi Daily* with big headlines. This helped to increase self-respect in our Buddhist believers.[14]

Two short years after Queen Lili'uokalani's attendance boosted the esteem of Buddhism, another win came through the pivotal role that the same Buddhist minister played during the 1904 Waipahu strike. This strike began like all others. Laborers were dissatisfied with living conditions, wanted higher wages, and were tired of the harsh treatment of the *lunas* or plantation overseers. The Japanese Consul from Honolulu tried to calm the strikers but was unsuccessful. Bishop Imamura was asked to speak with the strikers because of his history of ministering to the plantation workers. He was able to calm the strikers, and they returned to work after eleven days of striking.[15] Bishop Imamura noted:

> After this incident, the planters and the Caucasians in general recognized the fact that Buddhism had important meaning to the Japanese and was necessary to stabilize the labor population on the plantations. Since that time the plantations provided land for a preaching center [temple] and when the temple was newly built or rebuilt, they made monetary donations and also they helped us in various ways, thus enhancing our spirit as Buddhist missionaries.[16]

This support of Buddhist temples by the plantation owners was something that would be seen time and again across the Islands. Plantations donated land, money, and even helped in the building of other facilities for the plantation workers, such as recreational facilities. This was all done to entice laborers to settle permanently in their plantation communities thus ensuring the plantation's workforce long-term. While many of the plantation owners supported the Buddhist communities working their plantations, there were others on the Islands that did not welcome the arrival of this Eastern religion. For white Christian missionaries who had taken up residence on the Islands since 1820, "the mere arrival in their midst of immigrants who happened to be Buddhist felt like a threat . . . [and they] therefore advocated stemming the tide of migration."[17] The view that America and her territories were first and foremost a Christian nation was pervasive and the antagonistic belief that Buddhism was "a heathen religion to be eradicated by the civilizing force of Christianity" was widely held beyond the fields of the plantation.[18] The Christians were unsuccessful in their efforts to eliminate Buddhism on the Islands, and Buddhism persisted as a font of faith, strength, and support for the many adherents. As the Buddhist community grew, the apprehension surrounding this seemingly "un-American" religion continued on.

With the civic and religious lives of the community taken care of, the Nikkei also sought to provide both care and education for their children. The first Japanese language school opened in 1893 on the island of Hawai'i as "compulsory education for all children from six to fifteen was not mandated in Hawaii until 1896, thus many Japanese children did not receive any formal education unless they went to a local Japanese language school."[19] Others around the Islands soon opened, including the Taisho Gakko[20] in Hale'iwa in 1914, and by 1920, there were 163 Japanese language schools spread throughout the Islands serving 20,000 students.[21] As public schooling became the norm by the turn of the twentieth century, the Japanese language schools provided after-school instruction, usually one to two hours, in the Japanese language, history, physical education, and morals—"a cultural education, emphasizing moral conduct and traditional Japanese values."[22] The instruction of the Japanese language also assisted with helping Nisei children communicate with their Issei parents, many of whom did not speak English, or at least not well. "Japanese immigrants perceived the Japanese language schools as their communal center, cultural property, symbol of their success, and source of ethnic pride in an alien land."[23]

The proliferation of Japanese language schools coincided with the ending of World War I and an intense rise of nationalism and push for Americanization throughout the mainland and Hawai'i. As xenophobia swept the country, "diversity signified disloyalty"[24] and the Japanese language schools and their association with Buddhism challenged the Anglo-Saxon Christian idea of what constituted being American. This idea was also perpetuated in the battle between the Japanese communities' Buddhist and Christian groups. Competition among language schools was strong, and the Buddhist schools prospered igniting an internal religious rivalry within the Japanese community. One prominent Japanese Christian, Reverend Takie Okumura of the Makiki

Christian Church, led the charge in perpetuating the idea that the Buddhist schools were un-American. In a speech given in 1920, Reverend Okumura listed reasons as to why there was anti-Japanese sentiment in Hawai'i. One reason given by Reverend Okumura was the paganization of the country by Japanese. Reverend Okumura said:

> America is a country of religious freedom. But can the American people sit quietly by and gaze at the rapidity with which their country is being repagnized [sic]? Hawaii, a Christian country, is being thoroughly re-pagnized [sic]. Idols are being imported. Temples are being erected in every nook and corner of the Territory, and pagan rites are being held. Traditional Sunday observances are giving way to noisy festivals and wrestling tournaments at the temples and shrines.[25]

Reverend Okumura was a staunch proponent of Nisei being completely "American." To do that, they must disregard all culture, language, and traditions of Japan and adopt fully American speech, religion, and most importantly, accept and continue their parent's roles within the plantation culture and system.

This accusation flung toward the language schools as being un-American did not go unnoticed by the Japanese community. To counter these claims, the Hawai'i Japanese Educational Association was founded in February 1915. This association encompassed almost all the language schools throughout the Islands, and its first order of business was to tackle the revision of school textbooks that were previously provided by the Imperial Department of Education to train Japanese subjects.[26] By the fall of 1917, new textbooks were in schools alongside new policies and practices that put the Japanese language schools in line with American and Hawaiian ideals.[27] The efforts of the Japanese to alleviate the suspicions tied to their schools through their organized and concerted efforts to transform the curriculum went unnoticed. There was still a tug of war to be played out over which group would control the future of the Nisei in the Islands.

The fight for the Americanization of these 20,000 Nisei in order to guarantee their loyalty to the United States was paramount to the white ruling class of Hawai'i. After all, these schools were educating the future voters of Hawai'i—a group made up of 44.5 percent of Hawai'i's Nikkei population.[28] The idea that these future voters were being educated by the Issei in Japanese language schools worried the white ruling class who feared this group would take control of the Islands once they came of voting age. The crackdown on language schools was not unique to Hawai'i as the mainland had seen similar reactions with states passing laws outlawing foreign language instruction in an attempt to force all immigrants after World War I to fall into the idea of America as "one language under one flag."[29] The struggle to control the Japanese language schools in Hawai'i was a product of that same desire to Americanize the immigrant community. In 1919, a bill was introduced to Hawai'i's Territorial Legislature that would abolish all foreign language schools. The Nikkei community of Hawai'i responded loudly to the governmental intrusion on their right to educate their children, and the legislation was defeated.

Just as the Nikkei were willing to fight for their rights to keep their language schools, they were also more motivated than ever to demand fair treatment and wages from the plantation elite that had long held them down.

What the planters wanted was for "immigrants to be servile laborers. A man should work out his contract and then if he would not sign up again he should go home, preferably at his own expense, to be replaced by a laborer just like him."[30] Bringing families was frowned upon because of the extra expenses incurred until the children were of working age.[31] The expectation of a solitary existence for the workers was compounded by the model of a *luna* overseer. Oftentimes, the *luna* was of a different race than the laborers, usually white, and this model was conducive to "prevent 'collusion'" among the workers.[32] But collusion did occur, manifesting in strikes for better wages and living conditions. And though strikes had become a common occurrence after 1900, the lives of Japanese laborers were still little improved. In 1909, five thousand Japanese laborers struck for higher wages. "The planters' policy had always been to adjust wages to racial background," and at this time, the "Japanese were getting eighteen dollars a month for twenty-one days' work; Portuguese and Puerto Ricans were getting twenty-two or twenty-three dollars for the same work."[33] But the planters were not deterred and brought in strikebreakers who were paid a daily rate of $1.50 to harvest the sugarcane—double what the Japanese laborers had been making for the same work before the strike. The striking laborers could not hold out indefinitely and eventually conceded to returning to work. To add insult to injury, they went back to work for the same wages they had been paid before the strike.[34] After World War I, the cost of living increased while the pay to Japanese laborers remained stagnant at seventy-seven cents per day for a ten-hour workday or $20 for twenty-six workdays per month. This low standard of living was not seen as favorable to the Americanization of the plantation labor force as detailed in an annual report to the U.S. Department of Labor and Commerce.

> This difference between what is required to content the American as distinguished from the other laborers mentioned [Oriental, Puerto Rican, or Filipino] has of itself a strong tendency to set so low a standard of wages and living as to discourage the Americanization of the islands.[35]

This strike highlighted the "awakening consciousness among the workers, a transformation from sojourners to settlers, from Japanese to Japanese

Americans."[36] This desire to participate in American ideals can be seen through the words of the strikers written to a plantation manager in 1909. In a pamphlet titled, "The Higher Wages Question," the Japanese authors wrote:

> It is a fact that the laborers have made up their minds to stay here and to join their destiny with that of Hawaii. The formation of family, the establishment of schools and churches are the strongest evidences of this fact.[37]

In the end, the pamphlet continued that "Hawaii will have, not in a very distant future, a thriving and contented middle class—the realization of the high ideal of Americanism."[38]

In his study of racial issues in Hawai'i, Albert Palmer noted that "it must always be remembered that here in Hawaii we have no white laboring class for the Japanese to antagonize by competition and that the Japanese, moreover, never pushed themselves into Hawaii. They came by invitation."[39] Palmer is accurate that the Japanese were brought into Hawai'i to fill a labor shortage need that the white planters and European laborers were unwilling to fill. While there was no competition between the Japanese and white laborers, the Oahu Sugar Strike of 1920 saw the Japanese workers greatly affect the monetary gains and challenge the absolute control of the white planters and ruling class of Hawai'i. This was something that could not be tolerated.

The Oahu Sugar Strike of 1920 was the first time that strikers received widespread support throughout the Japanese community. Evicted strikers were housed in temples, churches, hotels, and even an old sake brewery and were supported by Japanese merchants and community leaders.[40] The 1920 strike was also the first interracial strike in the Islands with Filipino and Japanese immigrants joining to push for higher wages and better living and working conditions shattering the planters' goals to prevent "collusion" among laborers of different races.

Unlike previous strikes which had been led by the intelligentsia bemoaning the unfair treatment of the Japanese, the 1920 strike movement was spearheaded by the laborers themselves. Another difference from previous efforts was the involvement of the Young Men's Buddhist Associations (YMBAs) which could be found throughout the Islands.[41] YMBAs were organizations formed as arms of the Buddhist church and "served as a training ground for *nisei* youth in developing leadership skills and as a forum for studying and debating wages and working conditions on plantations."[42] The support and assistance of the YMBAs formed a powerful pathway for the laborers to communicate with fellow strikers throughout the Islands.

When the strike began, 97 percent of Japanese workers struck in conjunction with an additional 92 percent of workers of other nationalities from the six affected Oahu plantations.[43] Around 77 percent of the plantation workforce on Oahu had walked out and practically brought plantation operations to a halt.[44] The planters quickly retaliated by evicting all strikers from their plantation-provided housing during a major influenza outbreak that was ravaging the Islands. In total, 12,020 people were evicted, including 4,137 children.[45] To counter the efforts of the strikers, the planters hired over 2,000 strikebreakers at two to three times the wages asked for by the strikers.[46] Wasting no time, the planters also tied the reason behind the strike to the desire of the "oriental" peoples to control the sugar industry and thus the Islands as a whole. The planters reframed the strike into a racial standoff between America and Asia and bemoaned the strike as "a deliberate attempt on the part of the conspirators to 'Japanize' the islands."[47] A clear capital-labor dispute had been reframed as a racial aggression against the white ruling class. The *Honolulu Star Bulletin* ran this editorial during the strike:

> What the alien Japanese priests, editors and educators are aiming at, in our opinion, is general recognition of their claim that they can absolutely control the 25,000 Japanese plantation laborers of this territory.
> If they could gain that point they would be as completely the masters of Hawaii's destiny as if they held title to the land and the growing cane. [. . .]
> If the alien agitators could establish their pretensions to control of labor, Hawaii would be as thoroughly Japanized, so far as its industrial life is concerned, as if the mikado had the power to name our governor and direct our political destiny.
> It was the same alien Japanese agitators who are now solely responsible for and the executive directors of the strike on Oahu who a year ago led the fight against enactment by the legislature of the measure to suppress the foreign language schools. [. . .]
> As might have been expected, the agitators—the priests, the editors and the educators—regarded the defeat of the foreign language school measure as a clean-cut victory for them, a recognition of their pretended power to control the labor of the territory, and they were encouraged to take the next step in the conspiracy to Japanize Hawaii, the present effort to force recognition of them as the dictators of labor by the sugar planters. [. . .]
> Never lose sight of the real issue: Is Hawaii to remain American or become Japanese? A compromise of any nature or any degree with the alien agitators would be a victory for them and an indirect but nonetheless deadly invasion of American sovereignty in Hawaii. The American citizen who advocates anything less than resistance to the bitter end against the arrogant ambition of the Japanese agitators is a traitor to his own people.[48]

Reverend Palmer proposed a path to rapprochement wherein the Japanese would end the strike and look toward the creation of an "interracial sugar worker's organization" to settle disputes, as opposed to a Japanese Labor Federation, then the planters would restore the striking workers to their previous positions and allow for representatives within the community to be elected to negotiate issues with the planters in the future.[49] The striking workers accepted Palmer's proposal; the planters rejected it outright. "They had insured their crops, and their plantations were being worked by strikebreakers . . . They were in a position to outstay the Japanese, just as they had done in 1909."[50] Eventually the Japanese were forced to abandon the strike, and as before, "went back to work on the same old terms, hoping that the planters would make improvements in wages and conditions."[51] Many Japanese decided to leave the plantations after the strike. In 1920, there were 19,474 Japanese male plantation workers in Hawai'i. By 1930, that number had fallen to 8,955.[52] The Filipinos eventually became the largest labor force on Hawai'i's plantations. "Thousands of laborers [Japanese] moved into the urban areas of Hawaii and began to enter the skilled trades, small businesses and other non-agricultural labor opportunities that gave them economic freedom and opportunity."[53] Their Chinese predecessors who had left the plantations for a chance at success in the cities of the Islands "were criticized as relentless invaders, unfair competitors, subverters of the established order," and the Japanese who followed suit to "compete with the white men and natives in the same way" were painted in the same light.[54]

The inflammatory language being published in Hawaiian newspapers labeling the strike supporters "alien agitators" with a nefarious desire to wrest control of Hawai'i away from the white elite was effective in gaining the attention of the territory and casting even more doubt onto the Japanese community. With a firm line drawn dictating either full support of an "American" side or risk being deemed a traitor, the people of Hawai'i viewed the strike and the efforts of the Japanese not through the lens of strikers attempting to better their lives to support families, but through the lens of a greedy, ambitious, and nefarious yellow peril that was flexing its muscles with the intent of taking over the sugar-producing jewel of the Pacific. Ultimately, the viewpoints, as expressed in editorials, colored not only the strikers and their actions and intentions but also those institutions that supported strikers in their time of need. Buddhist priests become agitators and "un-American" in their care and support of their Japanese congregants who were striking for better wages. They were also "condemned for their protracted training periods in Japan, the 'curious' mysticism of their indigenous beliefs, and for 'developing Japanese spirit and for holding before their adherents Japanese ideas.'"[55] Inherent in this thought was the idea that they were "part of a larger fraternity of secret Japanese sects fanatically loyal" to the Emperor.[56] By extension, Japanese language schools, run by these so-called agitators, were accused of being cloisters of Japanese nationalistic centers planting seeds against America and indoctrinating the Nisei as puppets for imperial Japan. The fight that began in the Territorial Legislature in 1919 would flare again during the strike. In a 1920 Special Session of the Legislature, Act 30 was passed which required the "licensing of schools, examination of teachers and revision of text-books."[57] The battle to control the language schools was far from over and would continue for several years.[58]

The strikes only showed the "surface of a contested terrain."[59] Boiling beneath the building tensions around labor and wealth benefits was the inherent battle over which culture would prevail in the Hawaiian Islands.

Would the culture be dominated by the Anglo-American planter class, or would it be enriched with the traditions and customs of the Japanese as well as of the other nationalities in Hawaii? Culture was critical, for it had the power to deny or provide a way for people to affirm their individual and self-esteem and positive group identity.[60]

In the end, every single facet of the Nikkei community—*toritsuginin*, Buddhist priests, and Japanese language schools—had been tainted in the eyes of the whites simply for coming together as a community to practice their rights as Americans and fight for their American dream—a dream of racial and economic equality.

NOTES

1. Palmer, *Human Side of Hawai'i*, 104.
2. Palmer, *Human Side of Hawai'i*, 104.
3. *Haole* is a Hawaiian term used to refer to a non-Polynesian person, especially a white person. It can also be used to denote a foreigner.
4. Daws, *Shoal of Time*, 285.
5. Tom Coffman, *How Hawai'i Changed America, Book One: The Movement for Racial Equality 1939–1942* (Honolulu, HI: Epicenter, 2015), 224–225.
6. As war between the United States and Japan became more plausible, expatriation campaigns, hosted by Japanese civic clubs and associations, were held throughout Oahu, including in Waialua and Hale'iwa. At these events, leaders from the Japanese community would explain to Issei parents the importance of expatriation as well as the process in an effort to help those born in Hawai'i "sever their dual citizenship status" ("Waialua Club Plans Expatriation Drive," *Honolulu Star-Bulletin*, April 21, 1933). By 1940, an expatriation petition had been created with the hope of easing the process with a goal of 20,000 Nisei signatures—Waialua's signatures numbered 551 ("Goal of 20,000 Nisei Signatures Neared on Expatriation Petition," *Honolulu Advertiser*, December 2, 1940). Expatriation from Japan had come to serve as an example of American patriotism on the eve of war, and this was aided by Japanese consular agents or *toritsuginin*.
7. "This arrangement clearly placed the volunteers within an immigrant tradition associated with the plantations, in which a learned person helped the many less educated people with letters, translations, and an understanding of the regulations and laws. The shorthand title for this supportive role was 'Letter Writer'" (Coffman, *How Hawai'i Changed America, Book One*, 222).
8. Kazuo Miyamoto, *Hawaii: End of the Rainbow* (Rutland, VT: Charles E. Tuttle Company, Inc., 1968), 335.

9. Bob Kumamoto, "The Search for Spies: American Counterintelligence in the Japanese American Community 1931–1942," *Amerasia Journal* 6, no. 2 (October 1979): 63, https://doi.org/10.17953/amer.6.2.rw2212q8724mw376.

10. Michael John Gordon, "Suspects in Paradise: Looking for Japanese 'Subversives' in the Territory of Hawaii, 1939–1945" (Master's Thesis, University of Iowa, 1983), 20, https://doi.org/10.17077/etd.s62y8u3x.

11. Tajima, *Japanese Buddhism in Hawaii*, 3.

12. Duncan Ryūken Williams and Tomoe Moriya, "Introduction, Dislocations and Relocations of Issei Buddhists in the Americas," in *Issei Buddhism in America*, ed. Duncan Ryūken Williams and Tomoe Moriya (Champaign, IL: University of Illinois Press, 2010), xi.

13. Kimura, *Issei*, 154.

14. Kimura, *Issei*, 155.

15. Kimura, *Issei*, 155.

16. Quoted in Kimura, *Issei*, 155.

17. Duncan Ryūken Williams, *American Sutra: A Story of Faith and Freedom in the Second World War* (Boston: Harvard University Press, 2019), 24.

18. Williams, *American Sutra*, 23.

19. Noriko Asato, "The Japanese Language School Controversy in Hawaii," in *Issei Buddhism in America*, ed. Duncan Ryūken Williams and Tomoe Moriya (Champaign, IL: University of Illinois Press, 2010), 47. The first Japanese language schools founded in the Islands were Christian. The first school was started on the island of Hawai'i by Reverend Shigehide Kanda in 1895. The second was on Maui by Seiji Fukuda in 1895, and the third was started by Reverend Takie Okumura in Honolulu in 1896 (Kimura, *Issei*, 186). As noted earlier, the first Buddhist priest didn't arrive in Hawai'i until 1889.

20. *Gakko* is the Japanese word for school.

21. Kotani, *Japanese in Hawaii*, 49.

22. Asato, "The Japanese Language School Controversy in Hawaii," 49.

23. Noriko Asato, "Religious Conflict among Hawaii Nikkei and How Japanese Entered the Public School Curriculum, 1896–1924," *Japanese Language and Literature* 42, no. 1 (April 2008): 66.

24. Noriko Asato, *Teaching Mikadoism: The Attack on Japanese Language Schools in Hawaii, California, and Washington, 1919–1927* (Honolulu, HI: University of Hawai'i Press, 2006), 21.

25. Takie Okumura and Umetaro Okumura, *Hawaii's American-Japanese Problem: A Campaign to Remove Causes of Friction between the American People and Japanese. Report of first year's campaign, January to December, 1921* (Honolulu, HI, 1922), 6.

26. Ernest K. Wakukawa, *A History of the Japanese People in Hawaii* (Honolulu: Toyo Shoin, 1938), 269.

27. Wakukawa, *A History of the Japanese People in Hawaii*, 270.

28. Asato, "Religious Conflict among Hawaii Nikkei," 66. The Nisei of Hawai'i gradually increased their voter strength as they matured. In 1920, they made up 2.5 percent of Hawai'i's registered voters. By 1930, the percentage had risen to 13, and by 1940, Nisei made up 31 percent of Hawai'i's registered voters (Eleanor C. Nordyke and Y. Scott Matsumoto, "Japanese in Hawaii: a Historical and Demographic Perspective," *Hawaiian Journal of History* 11 (1977): 166.)

29. German was the second most commonly spoken language in the United States when the U.S. went to war with Germany in 1917. The use of English as the primary language with immigrants was a way to prove loyalty to the United States. Legislation to ban foreign languages in schools quickly went into effect in several states. The U.S. Supreme Court ruled that the Nebraska ban on foreign language education was unconstitutional in *Meyer v. Nebraska* [262 US 390] 1923)

30. Daws, *Shoal of Time*, 211.
31. Daws, *Shoal of Time*, 211.
32. Daws, *Shoal of Time*, 211.
33. Daws, *Shoal of Time*, 304.
34. Daws, *Shoal of Time*, 304.
35. United States Department of Commerce and Labor, *Reports of the Department of Commerce and Labor 1904–1912: Report of the Secretary of Commerce and Labor and Reports of Bureaus* (Washington, DC: G.P.O., 1905–1913), 276.
36. Ronald Takaki, *A Different Mirror: A History of Multicultural America* (New York: Back Bay Books/Little, Brown and Co., 2008), 243.
37. United States Department of Commerce and Labor, *Bulletin of the Bureau of Labor, No. 94, May 1911* (Washington, DC: G.P.O., 1911), 741.
38. United States Department of Commerce and Labor, *Bulletin of the Bureau of Labor, No. 94, May 1911*, 742.
39. Palmer, *Human Side of Hawai'i*, 104–105.
40. Kotani, *Japanese in Hawaii*, 48.
41. Edward D. Beechert, *Working in Hawai'i: A Labor History* (Honolulu, HI: University of Hawai'i Press, 1985), 197.
42. Okihiro, *Cane Fires*, 68.
43. Beechert, *Working in Hawai'i*, 204.
44. Okihiro, *Cane Fires*, 71.
45. Beechert, *Working in Hawai'i*, 204.
46. Okihiro, *Cane Fires*, 72.
47. Daws, *Shoal of Time*, 305.
48. R.A. McNally, "What the Japanese Agitators Want," *Honolulu Star-Bulletin*, February 13, 1920.
49. Daws, *Shoal of Time*, 306.
50. Daws, *Shoal of Time*, 306.
51. Daws, *Shoal of Time*, 306.
52. Kimura, *Issei*, 100.
53. Ogawa and Grant, *To a Land Called Tengoku*, 17.
54. Daws, *Shoal of Time*, 303–304.
55. Quoted in Kumamoto, "The Search for Spies," 65.
56. Kumamoto, "The Search for Spies," 65.
57. Wakukawa, *A History of the Japanese People in Hawaii*, 270.
58. The Supreme Court sided with the Japanese language schools in 1927 in *Farrington v. Tokushige*, unanimously striking down previous legislation passed in Hawai'i.
59. Takaki, *A Different Mirror*, 246.
60. Takaki, *A Different Mirror*, 246.

Chapter 4

Hale'iwa, Hawai'i

Hanohano no Hale'iwa   Distinguished is Hale'iwa
Ku'u home aloha   My beloved home.

From *Hale'iwa Hula*

While the history of the Japanese in Hawai'i presented in previous chapters represents the general political and cultural climate of the time, we now turn our attention to the beachside town of Hale'iwa—a place that is as central to this story as the family who settled there and called it home. Nestled on Oahu's North Shore, the Waialua *moku*, or district, was settled by Hawaiians in the early fifteenth century. The district had plentiful rainfall and rich, fertile soil perfect for growing crops, mainly taro and sweet potatoes, as well as an abundance of native Hawaiian fishing ponds. The first missionaries, Reverend John and Ursula Emerson, arrived in 1832 and founded the first Christian church originally housed in a grass hut. The church grew and eventually became the church where Hawaiian Queen Lili'uokalani would worship when staying at her summer home. The arrival of the missionaries also brought the *haole* or white man who began to settle the area. Once the *haole* settled, plantations began to spring up, and the rise of the sugar plantations, along with pineapple and rice plantations, precipitated the growth and settlement of the area. By the 1800s, Waialua, the largest population center of the district, grew to have "three churches, four schools, and a female seminary."[1]

Sugar had always been a part of the native Hawaiians' crops. In the 1880s, the Halstead family pioneered sugar cultivation on the North Shore and had the first mill on the island. The mill burned in the 1890s, but Castle & Cooke purchased the Halstead family's holdings in 1898, consisting of approximately 600 acres. They established the Waialua Agricultural Company, Ltd., which would later become known as Waialua Sugar Company.

With the steady growth of Waialua Sugar, the founding of the Dole Plantation in nearby Wahiawa, along with other plantations in the Waialua *moku*, a demand for plantation workers also grew. This growth brought in an ethnic diversity of agricultural laborers needed to work the fields. Native Hawaiian workers were initially recruited to work the fields, but their cultural traditions didn't fit into the long-term commitment required of plantation work nor the long hours of fieldwork required. The first sizable group of laborers brought in to work the plantations were Chinese. Chinese laborers were readily available and already had knowledge of how to cultivate and manufacture commercial sugar, but the independent nature of the Chinese workers caused many to leave the plantations after their work contracts expired in order to start their own private businesses within towns.[2] The next large-scale group brought in as plantation workers were the Japanese. In the end, "The plantations hired Koreans, Portuguese, Japanese. . . even Swedes and Norwegians. . . finally Filipinos. In doing so, they crafted the diverse ethnic mix that makes up Haleʻiwa today."[3]

Agricultural production could only grow so much as the larger and larger crop yields could not be efficiently transferred to the port in Honolulu. Benjamin Franklin Dillingham was a first mate on merchant ships when he boarded the *Whistler* for a voyage to Hawaiʻi. While in Honolulu in 1865, Dillingham was thrown from a horse, broke his leg, and was left behind on the island to recuperate. Dillingham decided to make Hawaiʻi his home and began investing in local businesses. During his time on the island, Dillingham saw the large amounts of land that could be cultivated in the countryside. He dreamed of a railroad that would connect Honolulu to those undeveloped rural areas and envisioned the agricultural expansion that would be possible if a means of transportation was developed. Many scoffed at Dillingham's railroad dreams citing them as "Dillingham's Folly." It was thought an impossible task to acquire the financing and build the railroad; however, Dillingham persisted through the taunts of his "folly." In 1886, Dillingham received a charter from King Kalakaua to build a railroad from Honolulu to Ewa to move the increased sugar production from the fields to docks in Honolulu.[4] On August 31, 1888, the Hawaiian Legislature passed a bill giving Dillingham an exclusive franchise to build the railroad on Oahu. The following year on September 4, 1889, the first train left the Honolulu station for an excursion trip to the end of the line, then only about two miles away.[5] By 1898, the Oahu Railway & Land Company completed a 71-mile rail line around the coast of Oahu.[6]

Ever the resourceful businessman, Dillingham wanted to capitalize further on his investment and wondered what other cargo could be transported via his railroad. His solution: passenger travel. Dillingham leased land in the vicinity of the town of Waialua on the scenic North Shore and constructed the finest hotel of the time. Built on land located between the Anahulu River and the Pacific Ocean, Dillingham's fourteen-room Victorian hotel opened in 1899 realizing his resort vision more than a year before Waikiki's first hotel opened in 1901. Dubbed by Dillingham as the Haleʻiwa Hotel, the word haleʻiwa[7] translated means the "house of the ʻiwa, or frigate bird." Dillingham wanted a name that would capture the majesty of his hotel, and the ʻiwa bird represented beauty in Hawaiian culture.

As the first destination resort on Oahu, the Haleʻiwa Hotel quickly became a popular country weekend getaway for the affluent residents of Honolulu. A round-trip, two-day excursion on Dillingham's railroad from Honolulu to Haleʻiwa cost $10 and included an overnight stay at the Haleʻiwa Hotel, a tour through the Waialua Sugar Mill, and a carriage ride to tour the pineapple plantations in Wahiawa.[8] Haleʻiwa quickly grew to be an epicenter of tourism due to its idyllic scenery and its location far removed from the hustle and bustle of Honolulu. One visitor stated:

> I cannot leave this beautiful land without expressing my enthusiasm, not only with Hawaii in general, but particularly of the trip over the Oahu Railway, through rice and cane fields to Haleiwa, Waialua, which is a veritable paradise—a haven of rest.[9]

Due to the growth of the area surrounding the hotel caused by tourism and plantation work, the town that sprang up formally took on the name Haleʻiwa.

With a diverse group of plantation workers and business owners settled into the area, services for these groups needed to be established. Waialua Sugar "operated in benign isolation"[10] and owned and operated its own stores where plantation workers could purchase food and other goods on credit and at a fair price. The plantation also had its own hospital and doctors to serve the community. A movie theater, gymnasium, and community center were also built. Waialua Sugar provided housing for its workers at a fair price and paid more wages than neighboring plantations. With that, services catering to the religious and educational needs of the children of plantation workers were also necessary. With the large Japanese population of plantation workers, Buddhism was a predominant religion in the community. Plantations welcomed the Buddhist priests into the communities. They recognized that "the priests emphasized patience and endurance of adversity, non-violence, resignation, and peaceful cooperation."[11]

Reverend Jitsujo Muroyama of the Jōdoshū sect arrived in Hawaiʻi in 1909 and initially began his missionary work on the island of Kauaʻi. Upon learning that the North Shore of Oahu did not have a Jodo mission, Reverend Muroyama left Kauaʻi and headed for Waialua. Jōdoshū, the sect of the Pure Land, was the second-largest Buddhist sect in the Hawaiian Islands.[12] Founded in Japan by Honen Shonin in 1175 AD, Jōdoshū teaches that an individual's salvation is attainable, not through their own merits or deeds, but only through their faith in Amida Buddha's power of salvation. Honen's teaching dictated that "the grace of Amidha [sic] Buddha had accomplished countless good works for the benefit of mankind during many ages past."[13] To display one's faith in Amida Buddha, the recitation of the Nembutsu was all that was necessary. The Nembutsu or prayer of "Namu Amida Butsu" means "I take refuge in Amida Buddha."[14]

Honen's focus on faith and prayer to Amida Buddha was revolutionary for the common people. With one simple prayer, Jōdoshū could be practiced anywhere and at any time. Honen made Buddhist principles accessible to the masses by removing any obstacles to practicing the faith such as philosophy, meditation, or elaborate rituals. "The faith of this [Honen's] simple doctrine and its easy discipline spread like fire in a summer field; and the Amidha [sic] Buddhism, the doctrine of the Pure Land, the Jodo shu, was firmly established in Japan."[15]

With an abundance of plantation workers in Haleʻiwa being Jōdoshū sect adherents, Reverend Muroyama arrived in 1912 and rented a house in Haleʻiwa. In May 1912, he held a dedication ceremony to place a statue of Amida Buddha on the altar of the rented house thus signifying the start of the mission.

Reverend Muroyama needed a permanent site for the temple, however, and he began looking in earnest. To raise funds to build a temple and school, Reverend Muroyama traveled from house to house on horseback. His fundraising efforts were successful. In 1913, with assistance from Jōdoshū members, Reverend Muroyama purchased the Seaside Hotel along with adjoining land for $2,500. The second floor of the hotel was used as the *hondo* (main temple hall) which was opened in December 1913, and the downstairs was opened in January 1914 as the language school or Taisho Gakko as well as the minister's residence. The location of the Mission was described in a 1903 newspaper article. "The location is unsurpassed. The finest of sea bathing is close at hand. A wonderful view of ocean, mountain and field refreshes the eye, in every direction. Winter or summer, the climate is all that could be desired."[16]

In 1915, after establishing the new temple site and opening the Japanese language school for the Jōdoshū members, Reverend Murayama returned to Yamaguchi-ken, Japan. The community awaited the arrival of the new priest of the Haleʻiwa Jodo Mission.

NOTES

1. Wayne Muromoto, "Sugar, Midkiff and the Japanese Worker in Waialua," *Hawaii Herald* (Honolulu, HI), May 2, 1986.

2. Tom Jacobs, *Haleʻiwa: A Pictorial History* (Haleʻiwa, HI: Pau Pono Pub., 2006), 9–11.

3. Jacobs, *Haleʻiwa*, 11.

4. Joseph P. Schwieterman, *When the Railroad Leaves Town: American Communities in the Age of Rail Line Abandonment* (Kirksville: MO, Truman State University Press, 2004), 113–114.

5. "Dillingham's Folly Now One of Hawaiʻi's Greatest Enterprises," *Honolulu Star Bulletin* (Honolulu, HI), October 20, 1924.

6. Schwieterman, *When the Railroad Leaves Town*, 114.

7. Haleʻiwa was the name of the dormitory building of the Waialua Female Seminary, a Protestant school built on the banks of the Anahulu River.

8. "History & Tours," North Shore Chamber of Commerce, https://www.gonorthshore.org/history-and-tours/ (accessed April 15, 2016).

9. "Through Rice Fields and Cane Fields," *Austin's Hawaiian Weekly* (Honolulu, HI), November 11, 1899.

10. Jacobs, *Haleʻiwa*, 11.

11. Dorothy Ochiai Hazama and Jane Okamoto Kemeiji, *The Japanese in Hawaiʻi: Okage Sama De* (Honolulu, HI: Bess Press, 1986), 80.

12. Tajima, *Japanese Buddhism in Hawaii*, 22.

13. Tajima, *Japanese Buddhism in Hawaii*, 24.

14. "Namu Amida Butsu," The Soka Gakkai Nichiren Buddhism Library, https://www.nichirenlibrary.org/en/dic/Content/N/13 (accessed August 6, 2022).

15. Tajima, *Japanese Buddhism in Hawaii*, 25.

16. "Mortgagee's Notice of Intention to Foreclose and of Foreclosure Sale," *Hawaiian Gazette* (Honolulu, HI), February 20, 1903.

Chapter 5

A Temple's Foundation

Miyamoto
宮 (miya) *meaning* "temple, shrine, palace"
本 (moto) *meaning* "base, root, origin"

On July 19, 1915, a twenty-seven-year-old Buddhist priest arrived in Hawai'i on the *Tenyo Maru* to serve as the priest and principal of the Hale'iwa Jodo Mission and attached Japanese language school. His name was Buntetsu Miyamoto, but he was not born with that name. He was born Buntetsu Kano. Upon dedicating himself to becoming a Buddhist priest, he was adopted by the Miyamoto family patriarch, also a priest, and took on the last name of Miyamoto. Miyamoto translated means the foundation of a temple, and Buntetsu would earn his name tenfold over the course of his service in Hawai'i.[1]

Born in Oita Prefecture on September 3, 1888, Buntetsu apprenticed as a Jodo priest from the age of eleven and followed no other occupation. Upon graduating from the Shukyo Daigaku in Tokyo, he was appointed a Buddhist priest on March 29, 1915. A few short months later, Reverend Miyamoto left for Hawai'i to serve as a priest to the large Japanese population on Oahu's North Shore. He arrived at the Hale'iwa Jodo Mission and Taisho Gakko on July 19, 1915, and took over from Reverend Muroyama, the founder of the temple and school.[2] Ambitious, civic-minded, and a gifted orator, Reverend Miyamoto was always properly dressed and emanated a dignified bearing that affirmed his role as a leader within the community.

Five months after arriving in Hale'iwa, the S.S. *Persia* arrived in December 1915 carrying Nui Miyamoto, Reverend Miyamoto's wife. Reverend Miyamoto and Nui began the work of establishing their lives within the community and continuing to foster the growth and development of the temple and language school. The success of their efforts could not be denied when the growth of the school was analyzed. On January 22, 1916, it was reported that the Taisho Gakko had about sixty-four students.[3] In October of 1919, the Taisho Gakko had 113 pupils.[4]

While the temple and school were thriving, life for the Japanese and other immigrants living and working on the plantations was grueling. The plantation workers felt their only course of action was to strike, so they did. During the Oahu Sugar Strike of 1920, the plantation *lunas* forced strikers out of their plantation housing. With nowhere to go, many strikers sought refuge in their local temples. Fortunately for the Japanese Waialua strikers, the Hale'iwa Jodo temple housed and fed almost 100 individuals beginning on February 2, 1920. But circumstances soon took a turn for the worse. An influenza epidemic battered the Islands with the death toll reaching 2,338 persons in Hawai'i[5] and an estimated 52 people in the local area.[6] Coupled with the influenza outbreak, subpar sanitation conditions resulted from the strike.[7] This combination claimed many lives including Nui Miyamoto who died suddenly on March 19, 1920, after caring for strikers.[8] Reverend Miyamoto and the community mourned Nui's sacrifice and sudden passing, and the temple underwent a brief hiatus. While Reverend Miyamoto and Nui did not toil in the fields as the plantation laborers did, they still sacrificed dearly to serve their community.

Three months later, Reverend Miyamoto returned to Oita-ken, Japan, for a period of about six months and married his second wife, Fumi. The couple returned to Hale'iwa in 1921 and quickly began to expand both their family and the temple. Soft-spoken, patient, generous, and kind-hearted, Fumi was an excellent teacher and much-loved figure in the community. Raised in a samurai family, Fumi displayed an uncommon dignity and grace. In 1922, Reverend Miyamoto and Fumi welcomed their first son, Osamu, who was followed by another boy, Kanji (b. 1924). They welcomed their first daughter, Taeko (b. 1925), a year later (see figure 1). While growing their family, Fumi also grew her involvement within the Taisho. She became a licensed teacher after taking an examination that determined the eligibility of individuals to teach in foreign language schools.[9] With Fumi serving as an instructor, the Taisho now had three instructors to serve its growing enrollment.

By 1926, there were two Japanese schools in the Hale'iwa district. One was the Taisho Gakko tied to the Jodo Mission and led by Reverend Miyamoto and the other was the Waialua Japanese Language School. The Taisho Gakko had an enrollment of 330 students while the Waialua Japanese Language School only had an enrollment of 140 students. Given its smaller enrollment, parents of children attending the Waialua Japanese Language School had to shoulder more of a financial burden than parents of the Taisho students. To stabilize the inequity, the two schools merged with the Waialua School being absorbed into the Taisho Gakko.[10] With this amalgamation, the Taisho now had approximately 470 students over which Reverend Miyamoto presided.

As the school grew, Reverend Miyamoto understood the importance of being involved in the Japanese Educational Association of Hawai'i. When the association held a meeting in 1927 to discuss revising textbooks for all Japanese language schools in Hawai'i, Reverend Miyamoto attended. Leading educators from across the Islands convened to discuss revising textbooks with the "motive of training Hawaiian-born Japanese in Americanism."[11] Beyond simply being an attendee at meetings, Reverend Miyamoto also took on great responsibilities and served as chairman of the association's annual meeting on several occasions.[12] Reverend Miyamoto understood the criticisms leveled at the language schools and was proactive in responding to those criticisms by the white planters and elite of the Islands. He was active in helping to transform the practices and image of the language school and have it align with American ideals.

Reverend Miyamoto also founded the *fujinkai*[13] and the Meisho Young Buddhist Association (Y.B.A.) in Hale'iwa.[14] Not only concerned with the education of the community, Reverend Miyamoto formed these clubs to provide for the social lives of members of the community as well. As the wife of the minister of the temple, Fumi was also involved in social clubs, such as leading the *fujinkai* and serving as the president of the Girls Friendly Society. Reverend Miyamoto was also an active member of the Waialua Japanese Red Cross Society serving as vice president.[15] Another role which Reverend Miyamoto undertook was that of consular agent or *toritsuginin*. As an educated member of the community, Reverend Miyamoto could assist community members with letter reading and writing and the completion of necessary forms. Undertaking these duties was a way for Reverend Miyamoto to further serve his community, and he did this believing that he was assisting in the betterment of the lives of those he helped.

The Hale'iwa Jodo and Taisho continued to grow and swell with students. In the 1930s, the temple buildings were renovated which allowed for the Taisho to expand, and by the middle of the decade, the Taisho had five teachers, three ministers, and their three wives all teaching. Reverend Miyamoto continued to grow in his leadership abilities and also served as the chairman of the territorial conference of the Jodo Mission of Hawai'i showcasing his abilities as a leader and an up-and-coming figure in the Jodo community.[16]

Thoughtful and gracious, Reverend Miyamoto looked after members of his community and left an impression on those he met. This was exemplified in the meeting between Reverend Miyamoto and Mrs. Saito, the wife of the Japanese ambassador to the United States. In 1938, Reverend Miyamoto, along with Bishop Kubokawa, the head of the Jodo Mission of Hawai'i and North America, sailed to the mainland for a two-month visit to the Pacific Coast. During this visit, Reverend Miyamoto called on Japanese Ambassador Hiroshi Saito and Mrs. Saito to personally thank them for the kindness and courtesy shown toward his former student, Tomiko. Far away from home, Tomiko was serving as a maid for the family of an Army surgeon that was formerly stationed at Schofield Barracks near Hale'iwa. Extremely homesick, Tomiko had called upon Mrs. Saito during her distress and was warmly received at the ambassador's residence in D.C. The following year, Mrs. Saito's husband, Ambassador Saito, passed away and the Hawaiian Senate honored him by passing a resolution mourning his death and adjourning to show their respects. While on their way back to Japan, Mrs. Saito and her daughters came to Hawai'i for a ceremony, and a contingent of Hawaiian elite greeted them. Among the group were two men from Hale'iwa, Tomiko's father and Reverend Miyamoto. Mrs. Saito immediately recognized Reverend Miyamoto and recalled his visit the year prior.[17]

Amid expanding the temple, school, and social structures within the community, Reverend Miyamoto and Fumi welcomed three more children. Terufumi (b. 1928), Kayoko (b. 1933), and Keiko (b. 1934) came in quick succession. Having six children (Osamu, Kanji, Taeko, Terufumi, Kayoko, and Keiko) in the span of twelve years, coupled with the growth of the temple and school, kept the Miyamoto family extremely busy. This new life in Hawai'i was not without its trials though. Still considered "others" by those in power, discriminatory practices would puncture this idyllic bubble. For example, at birth, the Miyamoto children were given Japanese names. When they started their American schooling, however, each child was assigned a more "proper" or more "American" name by their teachers, essentially giving them a new identity as true "Americans." This tension is reflected still as each child has a preference as to whether their Japanese, American, or a combination of the two names is used. We have honored their requests from this point forward in the story as follows (in birth order): Osamu, David Kanji, Carol, Clifford, Kayoko, and Keiko.

The temple's location directly on the ocean meant the children spent lots of time swimming, snorkeling, and even surfing. The children also participated in kendo, boy scouts, girls' camps, school choral performances and plays and participated in school contests such as hobby contests where the children always placed in the stamp collecting category. Reverend Miyamoto also assisted in some of the children's activities. He directed a kendo demonstration during the Inland Oahu District of the Honolulu Council of the Boy Scouts of America Scoutfest Program.[18] The railroad that passed in front of the temple meant train rides into Honolulu and the joyful shouting of children calling for pineapples to be thrown from the train as it passed the temple carrying its cargo.

While life on the edge of the North Shore was picturesque and led to many halcyon memories of childhoods spent frolicking in the sea, it could also be fraught with danger.[19] Kayoko, the Miyamoto's fifth child, was only fifteen months old when she was swept into the ocean and succumbed a day later from exposure. The family was bereft and completely heartbroken. In answer to this sorrow, Reverend Miyamoto erected a statute of Jizo at the top of the beach overlooking the ocean.[20] Jizo, a bodhisattva, was believed to protect the spirits of children who had departed this life. Haleʻiwa was like a beautiful dream, but like many dreams, the beauty obscured the dangers lurking just under the surface.

As children of the religious leader of the temple and the principal of the Japanese language school, the Miyamoto children were representations of their father. The idea of filial piety known as *oyakoko* was a concept Reverend Miyamoto enforced with both his own children and his students.[21] A daughter of a Japanese school principal on the Big Island recalled knowing the importance of proper behavior. She said:

> Because of our father's leadership position in the community, we were expected to serve as model children and were not to bring shame to him or to our family. Our lives and our behavior centered around my father's role.[22]

Because of his role as a community leader, her father also saw to it that "we were exposed to many people, places, and events. Whenever anyone came to our house, we had to drop whatever we were doing to greet our guests."[23] Expectations were similar for the Miyamoto children, and they were aware of the example they set for others.

The high standards expected by Reverend Miyamoto for his children's behavior extended to their education as well. Reverend Miyamoto recognized the value in education outside of the small town of Haleʻiwa. The Mid-Pacific Institute located in Honolulu was known as a top private, Catholic school that many Japanese Nisei attended. While it was a Christian school, students were allowed to practice whatever religion they wanted; however, everyone was required to attend a Christian church service on Sundays.[24] Because the school was located in Honolulu, students attending lived in dormitories on the school's campus. Mineo Katagiri, a former student of Reverend Miyamoto and student of Mid-Pacific, would often spend time sitting and talking with Reverend Miyamoto at the Jodo. He recalled that Reverend Miyamoto and Fumi always had kind words for him and that Reverend Miyamoto was a much-esteemed man in the community. During one of his vacation visits home from school, Mineo visited Reverend Miyamoto and recalled that Reverend Miyamoto said to him, "Mineo, you good boy *ni natta yo.*"[25] Reverend Miyamoto asked if Mineo could assist in getting his oldest son, Osamu, into MidPac, as the school was commonly known. Mineo approached the school president and learned there were scholarships available for the children of ministers, and scholarship guidelines didn't specify the ministers had to be Christian. And so, Osamu was able to attend

MidPac.[26] Reverend Miyamoto was very open-minded about allowing his children to be educated in a different religion as he saw the value in the quality of education they would receive. Osamu, the first Miyamoto child to enroll, graduated from Mid-Pacific Institute in 1939.[27] Osamu then went to Tokyo to attend the Buddhist University as he planned to take over Reverend Miyamoto's role as priest of the Haleʻiwa Jodo Mission when the time came.

A strong and unwavering dedication to his family, church, community, and the education of the Japanese community whom he served meant that Reverend Miyamoto was an extremely busy man who embedded himself within the organizations that were necessary to promote and institute changes that would affect his pupils and community. In his role as religious and educational leader of the Haleʻiwa Jodo and Taisho, Reverend Miyamoto was in contact with many other community leaders. But his position, influence, and connections were not viewed in a positive light by everyone on the Islands. As the roots of the Japanese communities around the Islands grew deeper, much like Reverend Miyamoto's, so too did suspicions around their loyalties, ways of life, community ties, and seemingly everything in between. The inability by many in positions of power to separate the lives and aspirations of the Japanese now comfortably settled in Hawaiʻi from the government and military of their homeland would have tragic consequences. Concern that there were subversive elements within the Japanese community had plagued the Islands for most of the early twentieth century. The practice of creating lists of individuals became a favorite surveillance tactic by military and governmental agencies stationed on the Islands. With the Japanese victory over Russia in 1905, the expansionist policies of the Japanese government and its military prowess growing, Japan became a matter of concern for the United States. President Theodore Roosevelt believed that "if irritated [Japan] could at once take the Philippines and Hawaii from us if she obtained the upper hand on the seas."[28] In response to Japanese encroachment in the Far East, in 1906 the Office of Naval Intelligence, in partnership with other departments in the Navy, began to outline strategies and plans in the event of war with Japan. "The suggested plans included securing lists of possible espionage agents, setting up confidential cable codes and security and counterespionage measures for the Hawaiian Islands."[29] Tensions began to escalate in the 1930s as Japan's nationalist government and military-backed expansionist policies in the region led to recurring clashes and eventually war with China, which threatened American interests in Asia. As relations between the United States and Japan worsened, a policy of selective internment had been decided for Hawaiʻi because an evacuation of the entire Japanese population would have been "economic suicide" as the Japanese population constituted 40 percent of the Islands' workforce and one-third of its population.[30]

Suspicion was placed on these individuals, many of them resident aliens, because of their position in the community and their occupation. These lists were the effort of years of surveillance and the combined efforts of the Office of Naval Intelligence, the Army's Military Intelligence Division, and eventually the Federal Bureau of Investigation. Driven by the fear of sabotage in the event of a Japanese invasion or attack and other activities associated with Fifth Column agitators,[31] these lists were built on hearsay, opinion, and a general misunderstanding of the Japanese community and culture. Targeting the leaders of the Hawaiian Japanese communities, "Considered the front line of Fifth Column forces, those deemed sinister enough to warrant top billing included fishermen, produce distributors, Shinto and Buddhist priests, farmers, influential businessmen, and members of the Japanese Consulate."[32] The names on these lists reflect the "erroneous and racist view held by many in the intelligence community . . . that Japanese Americans, being communal people, would not pose any risk without their leaders" and that the arrest, incarceration, or internment of these leaders would "inspire fear, and with it obedience, among the masses of Japanese Americans."[33]

As relations between the United States and Japan began to deteriorate in the 1930s, this plan of domestic intelligence gathering centered on the Japanese communities in Hawai'i was reinforced with the newly updated 1936 Army-Navy Joint Defense Plan.[34] That same year, the Army-Navy Joint Planning Committee submitted a report to FDR outlining issues regarding the defense of the Hawaiian Islands. Of particular interest and concern was the perceived threat of Japanese vessels being visited by the local Japanese community on Oahu while docked in harbor. On shore leave, these Japanese sailors might be delivering mail from Japan to the local community, visiting with family, or frequenting many of the local Japanese businesses. The Joint Planning Committee conveyed that this was a prime opportunity for these sailors to share "the 'greatness' of Japan, her virility, and her absolute superiority over all other countries. In fact, every effort of Japanese naval personnel ashore here appears to be deliberately calculated to advance Japanese nationalism and to cement bonds of loyalty."[35] Accepting the report's synopsis of a pervasive and persuasive Japanese element interacting with a local community of dubious allegiance, FDR responded:

> One obvious thought occurs to me—that every Japanese citizen or non-citizen on the island of Oahu who meets these Japanese ships or has any connection with their officers or men should be secretly but definitely identified and his or her name placed on a special list of those who would be the first to be placed in a concentration camp in the event of trouble.[36]

These meetings between the local communities and ships were not restricted to Honolulu. As Reverend Miyamoto recalled:

with the exception of Honolulu, there were no groups other than the Waialua Japanese who gave constant receptions to the naval training squadron, naval oil tanker personnel and merchant marine cadets of the Japanese Imperial government. This trend of receptions by the Waialua Japanese probably occurred due to the peculiar location of the Waialua district on the highway around the island rather than because of any desire of the whole Japanese community to give such receptions.[37]

These community receptions were not mired in surreptitious activities, as was feared by the military authorities, but rather can be considered an expression of the pairing of Japanese hospitality (*omotenashi*) with Hawaiian hospitality (*Ho'opika*).

The Office of Naval Intelligence was not alone in gathering surveillance on the local Japanese communities in Hawai'i. Since at least the 1920s, the Military Intelligence Division of the Army (G-2) had been conducting their own domestic intelligence despite a lack of funds, personnel, and negative public opinion of these activities during peacetime. In 1924, the Assistant Chief of Staff G-2 of the Hawaiian Department bemoaned the recent restrictions on domestic surveillance activities ordered by the War Department. In a letter to the War Department General and Special Staffs, the Assistant Chief of Staff G-2 of the Hawaiian Department:

> protested that owing to the peculiar racial conditions existing throughout his area and the absence of any other governmental agency capable of keeping him properly informed about the domestic situation, it was necessary for him to carry out investigations similar to those described in the recently rescinded War Department countersubversive pamphlet. He requested permission, therefore, to continue maintaining "the close watch and supervision that is now being kept on our alien and other racial groups" in Hawaii.[38]

Before making the rank of General, George Patton was stationed in Hawai'i from 1934 to 1937 as the Assistant Chief of Staff for the Army's Hawaiian Department. Sometime during his tenure, most likely between 1935 and 1937, he drafted *A General Staff Study, Plan: Initial Seizure of Orange Nationals*.[39] In addition to step-by-step guidelines on practical Army movements in the event of war with Japan,[40] Patton's plan called for the arrest and internment of 128 individuals from Oahu and surrounding islands.[41] The plan stipulated for military personnel "To arrest and intern certain persons of the Orange race who are considered most inimical to American interests, or those whom, *due to their position and influence in the Orange community, it is desirable to retain as hostages*."[42] In addition to names and addresses, Patton's list provided the occupations of the individuals in question, including, but not limited to, employees of the Japanese consulate, various types of merchants, hotel managers, writers, publishers, medical professionals, ministers, priests, and bishops of the Shinto, Buddhist, and Christian faiths, as well as Japanese language school teachers.[43] Despite the Supreme Court ruling in favor of Japanese language schools a decade earlier, the schools and those teaching in them were still viewed with suspicion as can be seen in Patton's listing of possible hostages. Listed in the North Sector, as part of Group 18, Reverend Miyamoto's name appears as one of the identified hostages. His occupation is listed as Language School Principal.[44] This would not be the last time that Reverend Miyamoto's name would appear on a list.

For almost thirty-five years, the ONI and MID led the charge on intelligence gathering and surveillance of the Japanese communities in Hawai'i. But as the prospect of war with Japan transitioned from possibility to almost certainty, these two offices would soon be eclipsed in 1939 when the Federal Bureau of Investigation would open its Honolulu offices. Using the lists and information gathered by the ONI and MID as a basic model for island surveillance, the FBI would narrow their focus to a handful of community leaders—especially those who served as consular agents, Buddhist priests, and Japanese language school teachers. "Largely oblivious to the vigilant and invisible eye of the government, few in the community could have realized that they were being secretly watched. They had, after all, no reasons for harboring guilty consciences."[45] Despite concern by military intelligence and even the *haole* elite, there were those on the Islands who were white and allies of the Japanese communities. One individual who was especially prominent within the sugar community would take a stand for Reverend Miyamoto and others like him; his name was John Midkiff.

In Hale'iwa and Waialua, John Midkiff was an important and powerful fixture. Midkiff began working at Waialua Sugar Company in 1924 as an overseer or *luna* and quickly moved up the ranks, becoming manager in 1932. "It was a time when the community was to all extents and purposes, the sugar company. And the sugar company did the bidding of the plantation manager, an almost all-powerful entity in the town."[46] As manager of Waialua, Midkiff "directed his efforts not only to sugar production but also to the development of a model community of contented, industrious employees."[47] He worked to improve plantation life and living standards through the development of social and recreational activities and an emphasis on civic mindedness.

Midkiff understood the importance of Japanese community leaders like Reverend Miyamoto. When messages needed to be conveyed to the Japanese population, Midkiff entrusted Reverend Miyamoto and the three other local church leaders with communicating those to the community outside of the plantation. The importance of working with community leaders and supporting their community organizations was also important to Midkiff. To show his support, Midkiff was a frequent principal speaker at various community events including the local Y.B.A. that Reverend Miyamoto founded at the

Jodo temple. Midkiff would attend the assemblies and banquets of these meetings and often allowed the use of the Waialua Plantation social hall or gymnasium for such functions.[48] In November 1937, Midkiff was the principal speaker at the first general assembly of the United Oahu Y.B.A. which was held in Waialua and was attended by more than 200 delegates from across the island.[49] Midkiff recounted his speeches to the Y.B.A.

> I had made speeches to the Young Buddhist Association, and was advocating it [Americanization]. Of course, many of them had dual citizenship. I suggested to a great many of them they give up that dual citizenship and quite a good many did. Lot of other people thought, well, why should we? We're not doing anything, and if we travel to Japan, as a great many of them did to see their relatives, there's quite an advantage to be a Japanese—to have Japanese citizenship, too. But that didn't mean that they weren't loyal to America.[50]

Midkiff interacted with the Japanese community of Waialua and Hale'iwa on a constant basis, and he knew that war would be coming. In March 1941, Midkiff wrote a newspaper article in which he directed Hawaiians that it was time they accepted the loyalty of the Japanese without question and let the Japanese community know they wholeheartedly supported them. He wrote about the multiple generations of Japanese living in Hawai'i and said:

> For the past twenty-three years, I have lived among these people and worked with thousands of them. I am going on the assumption that they can be wholeheartedly trusted, and I am sure that if history is going to be made history will prove that my feeling is justified.[51]

That very same month, Midkiff attended an event to see the second contingent of draftees from Waialua off to their military training. At this event, Reverend Miyamoto as well as Reverend Ryuten Kashiwa of the Waialua Hongwanji were chosen to speak to the draftees and community members gathered. The very next day, Midkiff circulated transcriptions of these two speeches along with his comments about Reverend Miyamoto and Reverend Kashiwa. He wrote:

> In the days to come everyone may have to take some definite stand. I feel that these men representing the older generation of Hawaii have taken the proper stand and have fully appreciated their responsibilities to their adopted country. The fact that they cannot legally become citizens of this country makes their allegiance to it all the more important. I hope that in the days to come all Americans will recognize this fine stand and that all the older Japanese will take a similar position. Their children in the generations to come are going to be immeasurably benefited by this fine attitude.[52]

With Midkiff's words of admonition hanging heavy in the air, tensions and uncertainty floated within and around the Japanese community as everyone waited for what would happen next. For Reverend Miyamoto, his family, and the community at large, there was no choice but to continue life normally.

NOTES

1. Clifford Miyamoto, in discussion with authors, February 2017.
2. Buntetsu Miyamoto Alien File, RG 566, Series: Alien Case Files, 1944–2009, National Archives, San Francisco, CA.
3. "Japanese Schools of Territory are Largely Attended," *Pacific Commercial Advertiser* (Honolulu, HI), January 22, 1916.
4. "20,000 pupils in Japanese Schools Many Directed by Buddhist Priests MacCaughey Checks up on Teachers," *Honolulu Star Bulletin* (Honolulu, HI), October 7, 1919.
5. Robert C. Schmitt and Eleanor C. Nordyke, "Influenza Deaths in Hawai'i, 1918–1920," *The Hawaiian Journal of History* 33 (1999): 115.
6. Muromoto, "Sugar, Midkiff and the Japanese Worker in Waialua."
7. Seiichi Miyasaki, Transcript of an oral history conducted in 1976 by Norma Carr, in *Waialua & Haleiwa: The People Tell Their Story, Volume V: Japanese*, Ethnic Studies Oral History Project, University of Hawai'i at Mānoa, 208.
8. "Vital Statistics," *Pacific Commercial Advertiser* (Honolulu, HI), March 21, 1920.
9. "62 Alien School Teachers Pass in Test; Eleven Fail," *Nippu Jiji* (Honolulu, HI), July 25, 1924.
10. "Two Schools in Waialua Merge for Efficiency," *Nippu Jiji* (Honolulu, HI), April 18, 1926.
11. "Hold Meeting on Textbooks," *Honolulu Star Bulletin* (Honolulu, HI), December 22, 1927.
12. "Japanese Educators in Conference Here," *Honolulu Star Bulletin* (Honolulu, HI), June 23, 1931; "Election of JEA Officers Slated for Tomorrow," *Nippu Jiji* (Honolulu, HI), July 17, 1940.
13. Women's club that would facilitate activities at the temple. Kelli Nakamura, "Fujinkai," *Densho Encyclopedia*, https://encyclopedia.densho.org/Fujinkai/ (accessed December 4, 2019).
14. "Jodo Mission Bulletin – December 2012," LinkedIn SlideShare, November 21, 2012, https://www.slideshare.net/hawaii/jodo-mission-bulletin-december-2012.
15. "Waialua Society Reelects Kashiwa," *Honolulu Star Bulletin* (Honolulu, HI), December 11, 1937.
16. "Conference Underway Here," *Nippu Jiji* (Honolulu, HI), July 26, 1938.
17. "Widow Grateful for U.S. Honors," *Nippu Jiji* (Honolulu, HI), April 4, 1939.
18. "Court of Honor Held by Scouts at Atherton Gym," *Nippu Jiji* (Honolulu, HI), November 1, 1940.

19. Haleʻiwa is located on the western end of Hawaiʻi's Seven-Mile Miracle, a seven-mile long stretch of beaches that contain arguably the most celebrated and concentrated surf breaks in the world, including the infamous Banzai Pipeline. In the winter months, swells can reach heights over twenty-five feet.

20. John R.K. Clark, *Guardian of the Sea: Jizo in Hawaiʻi* (Honolulu, HI: University of Hawaiʻi Press, 2007), 82. This beautiful memorial to Kayoko's memory and for the protection of other children still stands at the Haleʻiwa Jodo Mission to this day.

21. Joe Fujimoto, interview by Ted Tsukiyama, April 20, 2000, Japanese Cultural Center of Hawaiʻi, Honolulu, HI, 4, https://jcch.soutronglobal.net/Portal/Default/en-GB/RecordView/Index/678.

22. Hazama and Kemeiji, *The Japanese in Hawaiʻi*, 56–57.

23. Hazama and Kemeiji, *The Japanese in Hawaiʻi*, 57.

24. Eileen Tamura, *Americanization, Acculturation, and Ethnic Identity: The Nisei Generation in Hawaiʻi* (Champaign: University of Illinois Press, 1994), 117.

25. Reverend Mineo Katagiri, interview by Yuri Tsunehiro, October 10, 1993, Japanese Cultural Center of Hawaiʻi, Honolulu, HI, 10, https://jcch.soutronglobal.net/Portal/Default/en-GB/RecordView/Index/4313.

26. Reverend Mineo Katagiri, oral history, 10.

27. "61 to Graduate from MPI June 5," *Nippu Jiji* (Honolulu, HI), May 6, 1939.

28. G.J.A. O'Toole, *Honorable Treachery: A History of U.S. Intelligence, Espionage, and Covert Action from the American Revolution to the CIA* (New York: Grover Press, 2014), 207.

29. Jeffrey Dorwat, *Conflict of Duty: The U.S. Navy's Intelligence Dilemma, 1919–1945* (Annapolis: Naval Institute Press, 1983), 39.

30. Gordon, "Suspects in Paradise," iv.

31. Fifth Column agents, as defined by Military Intelligence in 1940, were those whose "activities, based on previous, secret and intelligent planning, are coordinated in time and space with those of the uniformed forces of the enemy. [They] are dependent for success on local conditions and personnel." (Quoted in Kumamoto, "The Search for Spies," 53.).

32. Kumamoto, "The Search for Spies," 58.

33. Autumn Womack, "ABC List," in *Encyclopedia of Japanese American Internment,* ed. Gary Y. Okihiro (Santa Barbara: Greenwood, 2013), 4.

34. Robinson, *By Order of the President*, 55.

35. Quoted in Robinson, *By Order of the President*, 56.

36. Quoted in Robinson, *By Order of the President*, 56.

37. Reverend Buntetsu Miyamoto, "Memories of Sand Island," *The Hawaiʻi Herald* (Honolulu, HI), New Year Edition, January 1, 1949. (Briefly translated by George K. Matsumoto; translation in author's possession).

38. Bruce Bidwell, *History of the Military Intelligence Division, Department of the Army General Staff: 1775–1941* (Frederick, MD: University Publications of America, Inc., 1986), 280.

39. "Orange" being the military's code word for Japan before the onset of World War II (Michael Slackman, "The Orange Race: George S. Patton, Jr.'s

Japanese-American Hostage Plan," *Biography* 7, no. 1 (Winter 1984): 5, https://www.jstor.org/stable/23539134). This undated plan was marked as "obsolete" in 1940 and kept only for reference, but it foreshadows events and actions soon to occur. (Slackman, "The Orange Race," 6).

40. These measures included declaring martial law, censorship protocols, closing harbors to Japanese vessels, removing those of Japanese descent from military posts and similar areas, seizing all Japanese-owned amateur sending and receiving radio sets (names, addresses, and telephone numbers of those in question are provided), seizing Japanese-owned or operated cars and taxicabs, and closing all Japanese banks and language schools. Within the report, Patton also outlines a timeline and step-by-step account of when these events should occur.

41. Of the 128 individuals listed, 95 had resident alien status. The remaining thirty-three individuals on the list are designated as American citizens. Interestingly, two "Haoles," meaning white or Caucasian in Hawaiian parlance, also made the list—one is listed as a Shinto Priestess, the other as a Buddhist priest. (Slackman, "The Orange Race," 10).

42. Emphasis authors' own. (Slackman, "The Orange Race," 25).

43. Patton's was not the first list of this kind. In a 1922 report of the Bureau of Investigation (the precursor to the FBI), A.A. Hopkins compiled a list of 157 Japanese he considered possible subversives. This list was gathered from a confidential source in Hawai'i and included "40 merchants and storekeepers, 31 Buddhist priests, 24 Japanese-language school principals and teachers, 19 laborers, 10 Christian ministers, and 4 professionals." (Okihiro, *Cane Fires,* 118).

44. Slackman, "The Orange Race," 40.

45. Kumamoto, "The Search for Spies," 47.

46. Muromoto, "Sugar, Midkiff and the Japanese Worker in Waialua."

47. "Waialua Managers," *Waco News* (Waialua, HI), October 12, 1948. In authors' possession.

48. "Meisho YBA Meet Will Officially Close Tomorrow," *Nippu Jiji* (Honolulu, HI), June 26, 1937.

49. "John H. Midkiff Address YBA," *Honolulu Star Bulletin* (Honolulu, HI), November 11, 1937.

50. John H. Midkiff, Transcript of an oral history conducted in May 1977 by Vivien Lee, in *Waialua & Haleiwa; The People Tell Their Story, Volume I: Caucasians, Chinese, Hawaiians,* Ethnic Studies Oral History Project, University of Hawai'i at Mānoa, 27, http://hdl.handle.net/10125/21420.

51. John H. Midkiff, "Should Accept Loyalty of Japanese in Hawaii Without Question, Declares Midkiff," *Nippu Jiji* (Honolulu, HI), March 27, 1941.

52. John H. Midkiff, Manager of Waialua Agricultural Co. Ltd., Bulletin dated March 24, 1941. In authors' possession.

Part II

PRELUDE TO WAR

Chapter 6

The Watchers on the Eve of War

In the summer of 1939, an article appeared in *Foreign Affairs* titled "Preparing Civilian America for War," outlining the various ways in which the U.S. government was "laying plans, now in peacetime, to bring the full weight of its resources in men, materials and morale to the support of its armed forces in case it becomes involved in another great war."[1] War was coming. This was not breaking news to anyone who read the newspapers or listened to radio broadcasts. Japan and Germany grew more powerful and bellicose as they expanded their reach through invasion—Japan into China, Germany initially into Czechoslovakia. But when and where the United States would do battle was still a question that seemed to have no immediate answer. As the American war machine for battle abroad was being groomed, a secretive program of how America would deal with war at home was moving forward with haste.

That same summer, in August of 1939, Robert Shivers arrived in Honolulu, having been recently promoted to the rank of Special Agent in Charge of the newly re-opened Honolulu Division of the Federal Bureau of Investigation.[2] Considered an all-around efficient agent—"a well-informed investigator, diplomatic, and engaging"—this new assignment would prove to be a steep learning curve for Shivers.[3]

> For a Tennessean, who had never met an Asian, he was overwhelmed by his sudden immersion into a complex racial brew of Caucasians, Filipinos, Japanese, Koreans, Chinese, native Hawaiians, each with their own culture, history, tradition, and language, coupled with a rigid social and class stratification that dominated the islands.[4]

Having just opened, lacking Japanese language translators, and with no reservoir of their own intelligence to pull from, the Honolulu field office was in no position to take over the responsibilities of surveillance on the Islands.[5] Still a civilian in the summer of 1939, George Bicknell[6] helped Shivers and the Honolulu FBI office become situated. With previous knowledge about G-2 operations in World War I, Bicknell suggested ways in which Shivers could grow his surveillance on the Islands with the understanding that the FBI would share information with the Military Intelligence Division and the Office of Naval Intelligence, and vice-versa. In June 1940, in an effort to streamline efforts and communication and avoid duplication of effort, the Washington offices of the FBI, ONI, and MID agreed to the Delimitation Agreement which attempted to identify the area each intelligence division was to oversee. The MID would oversee counterintelligence cases related to the Army. ONI would oversee counterintelligence cases related to the Navy, and the FBI would handle counterintelligence cases related to civilians.[7] In the end, however, it was the FBI's pursuit of information and surveillance of the local population in Hawai'i that would have the greatest consequence for Reverend Miyamoto and hundreds of other men like him.

The local team of Shivers (FBI), Bicknell (G-2), and Mayfield (ONI) had already been working in tandem with each other for some time, even going so far as to have weekly informational meetings between them; the frequency of these meetings made all the easier when the G-2's Contact Office moved into offices neighboring the FBI's in the Dillingham building in downtown Honolulu.[8] Shivers found that the ONI and G-2 had:

> accumulated a store of information, or rather, the names of various and sundry individuals in Hawaii, Japanese agencies and people of Japanese blood who were considered to be suspicious, people who in their judgment should be interned in the event of hostilities involving the United States and Japan.[9]

Shivers requested that the Army and Navy share their lists of A and B suspects—meaning that in the event of war with Japan, those designated as "A" suspects would be interned and those designated as "B" would be kept under surveillance. The Army's "A" list numbered 700; their B list topped off near one thousand.[10] Shivers' opinion was "they had very little factual information to support such a list,"[11] and so began the FBI's thorough investigations of those on the list and a concerted effort to learn more about the Japanese on the Islands, what Shivers called "a Japanese survey."[12]

In order to help with the investigation and appraisals of the suspected individuals on these lists, Shivers requested help from the Honolulu Police Department. With six months under his belt as captain of the Honolulu Vice Squad, in December 1940, the Police Department appointed John Burns[13] as the head of its newly created Espionage Bureau. Burns was told to create a team of four men of his choice to make up this new unit. He chose men who represented the local communities—Japanese, Korean, Japanese-*haole*

(Japanese and Caucasian), and Hawaiian; of these four, three could speak Japanese. Burns and his team each had ties to the local communities, including the Japanese, which would help with their investigations. Burns taught his men the elements of investigative work or "how to get stuff out of people."[14] The FBI would send letters with names to the Bureau who in turn would "investigate his background, general reputation and activities to ascertain whether in the event of hostilities between this country and Japan his interests would be inimical to the United States."[15] The list was so extensive that the men did little else but investigate these individuals for an entire year.[16] The investigations were not without problems, however. As Kanemi Kanazawa, one of the four men that made up the Espionage Bureau, recalled:

> The investigations [. . .] were done discreetly and indirectly. You couldn't just walk up to a man and ask whether his interests were inimical to those of the United States. Our investigations were based upon second or third-hand hearsay evidence. It would never have stood up in a court of law.[17]

Ultimately, the separate agency lists furnished by the ONI, MID, and now the FBI with the help of the Honolulu PD Espionage Bureau were compiled together and submitted to the Department of Justice's Special Defense Unit. From this multi-agency compilation, the Custodial Detention List or "A-B-C" list was created. The Custodial Detention List was a compilation of names of individuals, mostly Issei, suspected of subversive activity or the *possibility* of subversive activity in the event of war with Japan. All names listed were those of alien residents, but it went beyond just those of Japanese ancestry or those living in Hawai'i or the West Coast. The surveillance being done on alien residents spanned the United States and included Germans and Italians as their countries of birth edged closer to war with the rest of Europe.[18] The purpose of this list, much like the previous lists produced by the three agencies over the years, was to document individuals who were to be arrested and interned in the event of hostilities with the Axis nations. The designation of each group and their "dangerousness" was signified by a letter, hence A-B-C list. "A" signified those that were "most dangerous" and "in all probability should be interned in the event of War;" "B" were those that were considered "somewhat less dangerous" and their "activities should be restricted;" and lastly "C" were those believed to be "least dangerous" and should also be restricted on their movements and "subjected to general surveillance."[19]

In addition to lists, the Contact Office had a large map of Honolulu and Oahu. Every address of a suspect on their list was indicated with a pin pushed into the map so that when it came time to "put out [their] dragnet" and pick up suspected individuals, it was a "comparatively simple matter."[20] In October 1941, Bicknell and Shivers "made and practiced . . . elaborate plans for rounding up dangerous aliens, especially Japanese, in the event of war with Japan."[21]

The FBI's list identified 347 suspects of Japanese descent across the islands of Hawai'i—338 Issei and 9 Nisei.[22] These lists would grow over time. Shivers' "self-stated goal" was to "'break the backbone of any Japanese alien resistance or organized attempt of interference'"—his answer to this was to focus on the leaders of the community, the Issei.[23]

He discovered that one way to weaken the community was through the Japanese Consulate. During his survey, Shivers came to believe that the Consulate was exerting control over the numerous Japanese societies that peppered the Islands as well as over the Issei population.[24] He became suspicious of the consular agents, or *toritsuginin*, believing they had the capacity to spy for the Japanese Consulate.[25] According to Shivers, "We saw and the Army saw and the Navy saw that if used as an espionage ring they would be in a position to furnish the Japanese consulate with espionage information from every corner of the Hawaiian Islands."[26]

Despite his lack of evidence that the *toritsuginin* were engaged in subversive activities, Shivers was quick to act on his assumption and compiled a list of 234 consular agents located on the Islands which he furnished to the FBI office in Washington in April of 1940.[27] This list was easy to compile as the names of the consular agents were regularly published in the Hawaiian Japanese Directory and local Japanese newspapers. Shivers wanted to investigate these consular agents immediately to determine if they had acted in any way that would allow for their prosecution, specifically for not having registered with the State Department as a foreign agent—a stipulation of the "Act governing the registration of agents of foreign principals and of foreign governments."[28] In this letter, Shivers admitted that his:

> office is not aware of the full extent of the duties of the consular agents, it is believed that they are required to look after the interests of the Japanese populace in their respective communities, to keep alive the Japanese spirit, and to do the bidding of the Japanese consulate. They are undoubtedly looked upon by the Japanese populace as representatives of the Japanese consulate and the Japanese Government and the Emperor of Japan, and for that reason wield considerable influence in determining the actions and molding the thought of the Japanese populace in Hawaii, especially among the alien element.[29]

While it is clear from this letter that Shivers did understand the basic services the agents provided to the community, his assumption of the nefarious intent of these agents stemmed from the composition of the group which was predominately Issei, their locations throughout the Islands, their leadership role within the local communities, his mistrust of the Consul and Vice Consul in the Honolulu Consulate, and finally the efforts of the *toritsuginin* to collect comfort kits and other forms of aid for the Japanese military.[30] At this time, the United States was not at war with Japan, but "counterintelligence had come to equate Japanese patriotic activities as anti-American—which was not the case."[31]

Even though Shivers had the support of the Criminal Division of the Department of Justice, the matter was put to rest with the vehement objections made by Lieutenant General Walter Short, the Department Commander of the Army in Hawai'i. Since there had been no attempt at enforcing the Registration Act on the Islands since 1939, Short recommended that a warning be sent to the consular agents alerting them of their need to register by a certain deadline as he believed from reviewing the information provided by the FBI that "not over ten per cent of the unregistered consular agents in Hawaii are aware they have violated our laws."[32] Short believed this was only "fair play."[33] At the time of Short's reply (July 21, 1941), he and the Army were in the middle of a successful campaign to strengthen both "loyalty" and "unity" among the Japanese communities on the Islands.[34] Short believed that arresting the consular agents would "unduly alarm" the Japanese on the Islands and effectively undermine the success of their campaign.[35] Short's opinion put the matter of criminal prosecution into a "deferred" status,[36] but the surveillance of the consular agents continued under orders from the Criminal Investigation Division of the Department of Justice.[37]

As these discussions were meted out through letters, memos, and radiograms between the heads of the investigative units of the military and those in D.C., Robert Shivers moved forward with the recommendation that Reverend Miyamoto's name be "considered for temporary custodial detention in the event of war" in a letter to J. Edgar Hoover dated January 19, 1941. In his letter, Shivers noted Reverend Miyamoto's role as a consular agent put him under suspicion, a suspicion that was couched in belief and not evidence. Almost three months later on April 7, 1941, Shivers sent Special Agent F.G. Tillman to the Miyamoto residence in Hale'iwa to interview Reverend Miyamoto in person. Carol Miyamoto, the Reverend's fifteen-year-old daughter, acted as language broker.[38] While Reverend Miyamoto was questioned about his life in Hawai'i— his arrival, his occupation as priest and principal, and his one and only trip back to Japan in 1920—the bulk of the interview centered on his role as a consular agent. Reverend Miyamoto told the special agent that he had served as a consular agent for a number of years with his last appointment being January 1, 1940. He laid out for the agent the duties expected of a consular agent—preparing reports related to birth, marriage, death, expatriation proceedings, and petitions for deferring service in the Japanese military. He likened it to the public letter-writer of the past, "in that they mainly aided the illiterate." For this, he received no payment from the Japanese Consulate and only received a small fee from those he helped, approximately a quarter for each report. Reverend Miyamoto informed Special Agent Tillman that these forms were purchased from the *Nippu Jiji* and *Hawaii Hochi* newspapers and were self-explanatory and that information on the filing procedures could be found in the Hawai'i Japanese Annual Directory which was "official and correct" as consular agents "could not ask the consul each time they wanted information." Reverend Miyamoto then informed Agent Tillman that he had returned his certificate of appointment to the Vice Consul at the Japanese Consulate effectively resigning from his position as a consular agent. He and other teachers and principals of Japanese language schools had decided to do this after a meeting of the Oahu Branch of the Hawai'i Education Association where Isao Ichiba, principal of the Ewa Japanese Language School, informed them that he received a letter from the Hawai'i (Japanese) Education Association raising concerns that many of them also acted as consular agents. The general misunderstanding of the role of the consular agent made it appear as though they were "for the Japanese Government" and it would reflect badly on the Japanese language schools. To avoid "embarrassing the Japanese Language Schools," all those in attendance vowed to return their certificates to the Japanese Consulate.[39]

Reverend Miyamoto's resignation as a consular agent did not matter to the FBI, even though the return of his certificate of appointment was noted twice in his FBI file—the first instance during his interview by Special Agent Tillman and then again with an addition to a memo that only said, "Subject has returned his certificate of appointment as consular agent to Okuda, the Vice Consul at Honolulu."[40] On May 23, 1941, J. Edgar Hoover requested Reverend Miyamoto's name be added to the official Custodial Detention List being compiled by the Special Defense Unit.[41] On September 30, 1941, under the directive of the Criminal Division of the Department of Justice, Hoover informed Shivers to continue investigating Reverend Miyamoto to ascertain whether he was "engaged in espionage, propaganda, or other activities inimical to the interests of the United States."[42]

This matter of designating persons in particular categories on the Custodial Detention List is a complicated one—based on assumption, hearsay, and cultural misunderstandings. And the list wasn't just limited to the *toritsuginin* either. Suspicion fell on other groups that promoted Japanese culture, heritage, religion, and language including Buddhist and Shinto priests and Japanese language schools.[43] "Military reports emphasized that Buddhism was an alien religion whose entire leadership collectively posed a threat to national security."[44] In a report compiled by the ONI and shared with interested parties (FBI, Army Intelligence, and State Department) in the days before Pearl Harbor, concerns as to the subversive nature of the Buddhist priests and community were laid bare.[45] In addition to noting how large the Buddhist community was, the report went on to say:

> Affiliated with the Buddhist and Shinto temples are Japanese Language Schools, welfare societies, young people's Buddhist societies, and Buddhist women's

associations. They provide excellent resources for intelligence operations, have proved to be very receptive to Japanese propaganda, and in many cases have contributed considerable sums to the Japanese war effort.[46]

The concerns surrounding the Japanese religious leaders echoed those that had been parroted regarding the consular agents. By December 4, 1941, the Custodial Detention List had a category just for priests. The names on this list were "mainly Konkokyo or Buddhist priests" from around the Islands.[47] Shivers also believed that Japanese language schools were preventing the "assimilation of the American way of life on the part of the Japanese," and he considered them one of the "worst subversive elements in Hawaii."[48] Much like the consular agents and the Buddhist priests, many of the Japanese language school teachers were alien Japanese. As has been previously stated, the individuals who became consular agents were those in the community who could read and write; thus, a majority serving in this capacity were priests and language school teachers with many often serving simultaneously in these roles. The list of 212 consular agents on the Custodial Detention List is not a complete picture of the men listed as such—they were so much more than that, to their families and their communities. First and foremost, Reverend Miyamoto identified himself as a Buddhist priest and second as the head of the Taisho Japanese language school. He had resigned from his position as a consular agent to avoid suspicion and embarrassment being brought down on the Japanese language school, but the stain of the *toritsuginin* could not be washed off so easily in the eyes of the authorities.

As relations between the United States and Japan further disintegrated, the nation braced for war. By monitoring and plotting Japanese naval transmissions in the Pacific, the United States was keenly aware of Japanese naval movements.[49] Additionally, in September 1940, the Japanese diplomatic codes were broken allowing for U.S. intelligence to read messages between Tokyo and her embassies, including those on U.S. soil.[50] This information was shared with a select few in the government and military. Hoover radioed Shivers around November 28, 1941, to alert him to the worsening situation between the two countries; Mayfield and Bicknell received similar messages.[51] Bicknell's Contact Office had been on "full alert" and on "24-hour watch" since November 1st, so this new alert "made no difference to [them]."[52]

"In the first week of December the best estimate was that Japan would launch a massive attack, probably within the next few days, almost certainly somewhere in Southeast Asia."[53] One week before the Japanese attack on Pearl Harbor, Shivers called Burns into his office to tell him, with "tears in his eyes," that the United States would be attacked "before the week is out."[54] Ever the agent, Shivers asked Burns to take his team from the Espionage

Bureau, "without letting anybody know it," into the local communities to see if there were any signs of "a catastrophe coming, or something gonna happen or anything like that or are they expecting anything." However, "Not a single one could find anybody doing any monkeyshines."[55]

It was in the first week of December that a flotilla of Japanese naval ships, including aircraft carriers, seemingly disappeared. The fleet had been tracked by American radio traffic analysts, but now the ships had gone silent. No alarm was raised because this had happened before. Once they entered their home waters off Japan's coast, the Japanese Navy used a radio frequency "that could not be picked up by American listening posts."[56]

Hoover informed his agents on December 5th to prepare themselves for the "immediate apprehension of Japanese aliens who have been recommended for custodial detention."[57] That same day, Hoover requested to be "advised as to the exact status" of the case pertaining to Buntetsu Miyamoto.[58]

His name had not, and would not, be removed from the Custodial Detention List.

NOTES

1. Harold J. Tobin, "Preparing Civilian America for War," *Foreign Affairs* 17, no. 4 (1939): 686.

2. Raymond Bativins, "The Hours Seemed Like Days: The FBI in Honolulu in 1941," *The Intelligencer: Journal of U.S. Intelligence Studies* 19, no. 3 (Winter/Spring 2013): 25. The Honolulu office was first opened in 1931 to manage immigration and criminal issues, but also in response to Japanese military growth in the Pacific. It was closed in 1934, to be reopened in 1937, only to close again the following year. ("FBI Honolulu History," found at: https://www.fbi.gov/history/field-office-histories/honolulu).

3. Bativins, "The Hours Seemed Like Days," 25.

4. Bativins, "The Hours Seemed Like Days," 27.

5. U.S. Congress, 79th Congress, First Session, Joint Committee on the Investigation of the Pearl Harbor Attack, *Hearings before the Joint Committee on the Investigation of the Pearl Harbor Attack* (Washington, DC: GPO, 1946), Part 23, 856. (Please note: The Pearl Harbor Hearings will hereafter be referred to in citations as PHH Part #, Page #.)

6. In October 1940, Colonel George Bicknell came on to active duty as the assistant G-2 of the Hawaiian Department in Honolulu. Bicknell was in charge of the counter-intelligence unit, comprised of twelve officers and thirty agents (PHH 9, 4355). The Contact Office under Bicknell was "responsible for the internal security of the islands, and for observations of all measures necessary, counter-intelligence measures necessary, to protect any information from getting into enemy hands, or prevent any espionage that might be conducted in the Hawaiian Islands" (PHH 10, 5090). This included keeping tabs on the "activities within the civil population on the

Island of Oahu," gathering information from those who had recently returned from both business and official trips to Asia in a bid to assess the situation there and acting as the conduit for information from various sources to be used in publications (PHH 10, 5089-5090).

7. Bidwell, *History of the Military Intelligence Division, Department of the Army General Staff*, 397.
8. PHH 27, 748.
9. PHH 23, 857.
10. PHH 23, 858.
11. PHH 23, 858.
12. PHH 23, 858.
13. Later to become governor of Hawai'i serving from 1962 to 1974.
14. John A. Burns, Transcript of an oral history conducted in 1975 by Paul Hooper (Tape 2), in *John A. Burns Oral History Project, 1975–1976*, Hawn Collection, University of Hawai'i at Mānoa Library.
15. John A. Burns, Transcript of an oral history conducted in 1975 by Paul Hooper (Tape 2), in *John A. Burns Oral History Project, 1975–1976*, Hawn Collection, University of Hawai'i at Mānoa Library.
16. John A. Burns, Transcript of an oral history conducted in 1975 by Paul Hooper (Tape 2), in *John A. Burns Oral History Project, 1975–1976*, Hawn Collection, University of Hawai'i at Mānoa Library.
17. Quoted in Dan Boylan, *John A. Burns: The Man and His Times* (Honolulu, HI: University of Hawai'i Press, 2000), 31.
18. In the end, however, the majority of those detained in the aftermath of Pearl Harbor would be Japanese.
19. Buntetsu Miyamoto FBI File No. 97-42, 1941, RG 389, Box 2626, National Archives, College Park, Maryland.
20. PHH 28, 1539.
21. PHH 9, 4348.
22. Kashima, *Judgment Without Trial*, 72.
23. Quoted in Kashima, *Judgment Without Trial*, 68. Robert Shivers' approach to the Japanese communities on the Hawaiian Islands is a dichotomy. Although his surveillance of leaders within the community as well as his testimonies at the Pearl Harbor Hearings gives him the appearance of being anti-Japanese, he also relied heavily on Charles Hemenway, a regent at the University of Hawai'i who "explicitly denounced racism as a fallacious, self-serving and generally preposterous notion" (Tom Coffman, "Robert Shivers," Densho Encyclopedia, http://encyclopedia.densho.org/Robert_Shivers/#cite_note-ftnt_ref3-3). In that same vein, Shivers was instrumental in creating the Council for Interracial Unity that met with the leaders of the various communities in the Islands, including the Japanese. The message promoted by the Council "returned constantly to the themes of inclusion and unity" among the many people in Hawai'i (Coffman, *How Hawai'i Changed America, Book One*, 212). Often, Shivers would have to quiet fears of mass internment or incarceration of the Japanese community, and to this end, he did remain true to his word.

24. PHH 23, 858.

25. Assumptions as to the purpose and motives of the Japanese Consul General and the *toritsuginin* had been previously noted. Naval Intelligence was alerted to the issue in 1918 in a letter from Robert Shingle, who purported that the Japanese Consul General oversaw over 100 agents who held honorary unpaid positions and reported on general conditions around the Islands. Concern for the political nature of the position was heightened with Shingle's assertion that the consular agents were under the Consular General's influence (Okihiro, *Cane Fires,* 105). Additionally in 1922, A.A. Hopkins as part of the Bureau of Investigation, precursor to the FBI, filed a report regarding the "Commercial Agents" located at "'strategic places and positions' by the Japanese consul for carrying out political, commercial, and military espionage" (Okihiro, *Cane Fires,* 118).

26. PHH 23, 858. Captain Irving Mayfield had arrived as the District Intelligence Officer for the Navy in March 1941 (PHH 26, 336). Under Mayfield's command, the practice of keeping watch on Japanese fishing boats, Japanese language radio broadcasts from the Islands, and Japanese consular agents was continued (PHH 26, 337-338). It was Mayfield's belief, which was shared by other intelligence branches, that the Japanese Consul General as the representative of Japan on the Islands utilized the consular agents, the numerous Japanese societies and organizations, and Japanese Language Schools "for the purpose of keeping them tied to Japan as closely as possible," especially as relations between the two countries continued to sour (PHH 26, 336). This is where the willful misunderstanding of the purpose of the consular agent is damning. Mayfield believed, but could "not substantiate by actual facts," that the consular agents spread around the Islands were committing some form of espionage against the United States (PHH 26, 336). This was not the case, but time and again, the supposition without proof, the *feeling* that the Japanese population, especially the Issei, were doing something nefarious made them targets for intelligence services on the Islands.

27. PHH 23, 858.

28. PHH 23, 859. Throughout the Pearl Harbor Hearings this law appears to be referred mostly as "the Act" or "Registration Act." Interestingly, some scholars associate it with the Federal Agent Registration Act of 1938 while others cite the Espionage Act of 1917—even within testimonies given to the Joint Committee on the investigation of the Pearl Harbor attack there are discrepancies as to what "Act" was being enforced! In testimony given by a Naval Intelligence Officer William Stephenson, he refers to concerns surrounding the Act of 1938 (PHH 26, 350) while a paraphrased telegram sent by General Short to the War Department clearly states "Espionage Act of June 15, 1917 referred to in your radio of July 19, 1941, has been in effect here since August of 1939 with no attempt at local enforcement" (PHH 23, 861). While the two acts are tangentially related, the Espionage Act of 1917 does not require the registration of federal agents.

29. PHH 23, 859.

30. According to Coffman, Shivers "said his views were influenced by his conclusion that both the consul and vice consul in Honolulu had engaged in intelligence work in their previous assignments and as such were more concerned with spying than with humanitarian support of immigrants" (Coffman, *How Hawai'i Changed America,*

Book One, 225). While the Consul and Vice Consul might have conducted espionage from the Consulate, there has been no evidence that any of the consular agents throughout the Islands participated. These 212 men serving in their role as *toritsuginin* were subjected to years of internment on the mainland because of this assumption.

31. Kumamoto, "The Search for Spies," 59. In Miyamoto's *Hawaii,* an internee states that lists of contributors for Red Cross supplies, trucks, and tanks for the Japanese forces in China were considered especially pro-Japanese by the FBI. "Sure it is pro-Japan! But when we are denied naturalization and forever barred from becoming Americans we must remain Japanese. What is wrong in being pro-Japan! That should not be anti-American no matter how you try to interpret it. You can only be anti-China!" (Miyamoto, *Hawaii,* 336). This book was written by Kazuo Miyamoto, a Nisei doctor from Hawai'i, who was interned in various camps during World War II. While this is a work of fiction, Miyamoto began writing this book while interned and it draws heavily from the events of his own life. Miyamoto claimed that his writing "did not materially deviate from the truth" and that "had [he] not written this story there is perhaps no one else who could have presented it to the world as it actually happened in the concentration camps and relocation centers." (Kelli Nakamura, "Hawaii, End of the Rainbow (book)," *Densho Encyclopedia,* https://encyclopedia.densho.org/Hawaii,%20End%20of%20the%20Rainbow%20(book)/.) We have also used his work to elucidate experiences at Camp Livingston.

32. PHH 31, 3184.

33. PHH 31, 3184.

34. PHH 31, 3184.

35. PHH 31, 3184.

36. Buntetsu Miyamoto FBI File No. 97-42, 1941, RG 389, Box 2626, National Archives, College Park, Maryland.

37. Buntetsu Miyamoto FBI File No. 97-42, 1941, RG 389, Box 2626, National Archives, College Park, Maryland.

38. Carol would often act as her parents' language broker, or interpreter, especially for her mother during their arduous internment journey from 1943 to 1945.

39. Buntetsu Miyamoto FBI File No. 97-42, 1941, RG 389, Box 2626, National Archives, College Park, Maryland.

40. This memo has a handwritten notation that makes it appear as though it was received on August 30, 1941, but it was not officially recorded until November 25, 1941. Whether this is bureaucratic oversight remains unknown. (Buntetsu Miyamoto FBI File No. 97-42, 1941, RG 389, Box 2626, National Archives, College Park, Maryland.)

41. Buntetsu Miyamoto FBI File No. 97-42, 1941, RG 389, Box 2626, National Archives, College Park, Maryland.

42. Buntetsu Miyamoto FBI File No. 97-42, 1941, RG 389, Box 2626, National Archives, College Park, Maryland.

43. This is not excluding the various other professions and memberships that grabbed the attention of military authorities on the Islands, including the Japanese language press, businessmen, fishermen, and the various Japanese clubs and organizations, to name but a few.

44. Williams, *American Sutra*, 31. Although the majority of those arrested in Hawai'i in the aftermath of Pearl Harbor were designated as consular agents on the custodial detention list, there was a separate category for "priests"—both Shinto and Buddhist. Williams' *American Sutra* dives into how Buddhism was vilified by authorities and led to the internment and incarceration of thousands of Nikkei throughout the United States and her territories—both in Army and Department of Justice camps as well as the War Relocation Authority camps. *American Sutra* also reveals how Buddhism was a source of strength and resilience for those who faced the traumatic experiences of internment and incarceration. An interesting facet of *American Sutra* is the treatment of the Issei experience in Hawai'i. Many of the men and experiences found in *Beneath Heavy Pines* . . . are shared in *American Sutra* as well, but through the lens of the leaders within the Buddhist religion as well as the practitioners.

45. Williams, *American Sutra*, 31.
46. Williams, *American Sutra*, 31.
47. Kashima, *Judgment Without Trial*, 72.
48. PHH 23, 868.
49. Daws, *Shoal of Time*, 340.
50. Daws, *Shoal of Time*, 340. As the FBI immersed themselves with compiling lists of enemy aliens for arrest in time of war, the War Department in Washington, DC, was busy "perfecting its plans for the custody of enemy aliens turned over to it by the Department of Justice and other Federal agencies in the event of a declaration for war." (Letter from the Secretary of War to the Attorney General, March 7, 1941, Plans for Enemy Aliens RG 407, Japanese Internment and Relocation Files: The Hawai'i Experience, University of Hawai'i at Mānoa Libraries). This included planning for the internment of enemy aliens—both of foreign vessels and civilians. In a flurry of secret memoranda and letters in the early months of 1941 into the summer, general provisions were discussed including verbiage for any possible Presidential proclamations as well as scouting and identifying locations to serve as internment sites in case of war. (Memorandum for the Chief of Staff, January 13, 1941, Disposition of Enemy Vessels and Crew RG 407; Letter from Secretary of War to the Attorney General, March 7, 1941, Plans for Enemy Aliens RG 407; both found in the Japanese Internment and Relocation Files: The Hawai'i Experience, University of Hawai'i at Mānoa Libraries). By March 26, 1941, a step-by-step list of recommended procedures regarding the internment of enemy aliens had been agreed upon between the Department of Justice and the War Department ("Recommendations of Representatives of the War Department and of the Department of Justice for Cooperation Respecting Internment of Alien Enemies," March 26, 1941; Recommendation of Internment of Enemy Aliens RG 407; Japanese Internment and Relocation Files: The Hawai'i Experience, University of Hawai'i at Mānoa Libraries). Many of these recommendations would be put into effect within hours of the attack on Pearl Harbor. One of the most striking aspects of these letters is when they were written, and the realization that these documents were planning for action months before the United States was attacked, further reiterating how heavy the air must have been with the threat of war.

51. PHH 9, 4360.

52. PHH 10, 5101.
53. Daws, *Shoal of Time*, 340.
54. John A. Burns, Transcript of an oral history conducted in 1975 by Paul Hooper (Tape 2), in *John A. Burns Oral History Project, 1975–1976*, Hawn Collection, University of Hawai'i at Mānoa Library.
55. John A. Burns, Transcript of an oral history conducted in 1975 by Paul Hooper (Tape 2), in *John A. Burns Oral History Project, 1975–1976*, Hawn Collection, University of Hawai'i at Mānoa Library.
56. Daws, *Shoal of Time*, 340.
57. Quoted in Kumamoto, "The Search for Spies," 69.
58. Buntetsu Miyamoto FBI File No. 97-42, 1941, RG 389, Box 2626, National Archives, College Park, Maryland.

Chapter 7

New Residents among the Pines

Reverend Miyamoto was not the only person in his family to voyage across the Pacific Ocean for the chance at a new beginning in the West. Fumi's first cousin, Manabu Kohara, also a religious man, but in this case a Christian, boarded a boat in Japan that would convey him to his future in the United States where he would eventually settle with his family in the central Louisiana town of Alexandria. Sitting proudly on the southern bank of the Red River, Alexandria has been described as:

> an old mercantile town situated smack in the middle of the state, with a picture-window southern exposure that looks out on some of the fastest developing farm lands in America. Her legacy consists of cotton, livestock, oil, fish and game, and a history of rich romance punctuated by sharp tragedy.[1]

Converging cultures shaped both the city of Alexandria and the state of Louisiana as a whole, much like the tributaries, bayous, and lakes that feed and are fed by the mighty Red River. For much of early history, the Avoyel tribe made this area their home.[2] Small bands of immigrant tribes fleeing threats from other tribes as well as the British arrived to the area beginning in 1763 with a contingent of the Apalachee tribe from Florida. Members of the Mobilians, Pascagoula, Chacato, Alabama, and Biloxi followed soon after.[3] The history of the area from the European perspective begins in the late seventeenth century with the establishment of New France, the expansive French colony that extended from the base of the Mississippi River into Canada. It is possible that as early as 1690, a mission was established by Spanish Franciscan missionaries across the river from present-day Alexandria, at the place of the "Grand Rapids."[4] These rapids, or *rapide*[5] in French, were a defining feature of the area and during certain times of the year were impassable unless by portage. Traders and trappers soon arrived, and a French military outpost, known as Post du Rapide, was established in 1723. When the French holdings west of the Mississippi were ceded to Spain in 1763, the post eventually became known as El Rapido, Spanish for the rapids.[6] By 1800, the area was again in French hands only to be sold to the United States in 1803 as part of the Louisiana Purchase.

Between 1790 and 1793, Alexander Fulton and William Miller, two business partners from Pennsylvania, were given an exclusive grant from the Spanish government in New Orleans that allowed them sole rights to trade with the local American Indian tribes in the area.[7] "This grant was conditioned that they were to sell goods to these Indians at a fair price and upon long terms of credit."[8] Between 1801 and 1803, the debts from these credit lines were called in by creditors, and the lands of the Choctaw, Pascagoula, Biloxi, Apalachee, and Taensa tribes were used to settle their account with Fulton.[9] Some of these lands would form the basis for Fulton's new town—Alexandria.[10] Fulton had the area platted around 1805, and by 1819, it had been incorporated as a town. Fulton's Alexandria continued to grow, and by 1832, it was officially recognized with a city charter bestowed by the state of Louisiana.[11] The combination of cotton and river transport ensured the growth and prosperity of the town. The rapids near Alexandria proved difficult to navigate when the water dipped to low levels, and ships would have to unload their cargo and reload where the water was higher.

> Steam boats at times required two or three days to cross the falls and the hauling of freight around this point was a lucrative business for residents, and a tramway around the falls and a warehouse to store the freight was built.[12]

Throughout the early nineteenth century, more settlers ventured to the area, and cotton reigned supreme. Alexandria transformed from a frontier outpost into a paradigm of the Old South—genteel society relaxing on plantation verandas draped with crepe myrtles and magnolias, masking the dark truth of the thousands of men, women, and children in the enslaved community upon whose wearied backs the success of these planters was carried. The Civil War brought an end to this dichotomous way of life. By 1864, much of Louisiana had fallen to Union troops, but there was a Confederate holdout at Shreveport in northern Louisiana. Union forces moved to attack by land and river with thirty thousand ground troops under Major General Banks and a large fleet of thirty U.S. Naval warships under Rear Admiral Porter in what is known as the Red River Campaign. Unfamiliar with the terrain and waterways, Banks and Porter both faced disaster. Banks lost to Confederate troops at the Battle of Mansfield, and Porter faced the destruction of the fleet from the Red River being diverted by Confederate forces. Both Banks and Porter retreated to Alexandria where they were pursued by the Confederate Army.[13] Unable to pass the rapids at Alexandria, the Union fleet appeared to be in dire straits. Plans were put in place to destroy the ships to deny seizure by the enemy until Lieutenant Colonel Joseph Bailey suggested damming the river with trees, brick, and other materials found in Alexandria and her sister city across the river, Pineville.[14] On the Alexandria side, bricks from demolished buildings were "handed, brick by brick, to long lines of Union soldiers."[15] The plan worked, and the water rose enough for the fleet to escape.[16] Banks retreated from Alexandria soon after, and as his Union troops fled the city, fires were set to ensure there would be nothing for Confederate troops.[17] On May 13, 1864, almost every building in a twenty-three-block radius was burnt to the ground.[18]

After the conclusion of the Civil War, Alexandria slowly rose from the ashes left by the Red River Campaign. By the late nineteenth century, prosperity returned to the region with the arrival of railroads and local lumber barons. By the early twentieth century, "the golden age of the 'sawmill capital of the world' was dawning with 75 mills operating within 40 miles" of town.[19] Grand buildings like the Hotel Bentley (1908), Commercial Building (1915), and the Guaranty Bank (1919) began to fill downtown Alexandria again and reflected her economic growth. Merchants continued to prosper, and agriculture remained an important facet of the local economy. When the United States entered World War I, Alexandria experienced another economic boom when Camp Beauregard, a National Guard training facility six miles north of the city, was greatly expanded to serve as a cantonment for thousands of men preparing to be shipped overseas to Europe. Between 1880 and 1920, Alexandria's population grew from 1,800 to 17,510. By 1930, it would increase by another 30 percent to reach 23,025 individuals. Throughout its varied history, Alexandria has been home to many peoples and many cultures. American Indian, French, Spanish, Anglo-American, African American, Jewish, Italian, Greek, Mexican, and Syrian individuals looking for a home on the banks of the Red River have claimed Alexandria as their own.[20] In 1928, a single Japanese family joined the community of Alexandria in a bid for a better future.[21]

Manabu Kohara, a native of Ōita Prefecture, Japan, came to the United States in 1903 to start a new life as a theology student at the University of California Berkeley.[22] Upon graduation, he became an ordained minister speaking perfect unaccented English. In 1912, he met Saki Shima, also a native of Japan. She was quiet, affectionate, and loved to laugh. The two soon fell in love. Saki, aged nineteen, was sent to the United States by her grandfather to study religion. She arrived with a trunk full of western clothes, a Japanese *koto*,[23] and two maids. Manabu and Saki eloped in March 1914, and when word reached her grandfather, he called the maids back to Japan leaving Saki and Manabu on their own to navigate married life in San Francisco. Their first adventure as a young married couple took them to Denver,

Colorado, where Manabu was assigned a position as a youth coordinator at a local church. While in Denver, the couple's first child, a son, Susumu "Sammy," was born in 1915.

During this assignment, Manabu realized that a life in the ministry was not his true calling. Instead, he decided to pursue his hobby and passion for photography. The Koharas opened their first photography studio, but not long after, the family moved to Omaha, Nebraska, where Tomatsu "Tommy" (b. 1916) and Kay (b. 1920) were born. Eventually, the family settled in Council Bluffs, Iowa, where they welcomed their third son, Jack Minoru (b. 1922), and second daughter, Marion Sakaye (b. 1928). In total, Manabu and Saki had five children: Sammy, Tommy, Kay, Jackie, and Marion (see figure 2).

While living in Council Bluffs, Manabu traveled to the small farming town of Glenmora, thirty miles south of Alexandria, Louisiana, for a photography job. His assignment was to photograph farmland in and around Glenmora to be used in advertisements to entice farmers in the North and Midwest to purchase land and move south. But Manabu himself, however, became enchanted with the area and the fact that his family would be the sole Japanese family in the vicinity greatly aiding in their Americanization which Manabu found of great importance. In August 1928, Manabu moved his family from Council Bluffs, Iowa, to Louisiana where he abandoned photography in favor of a new vocation—truck crop farming. By the 1920s, truck farming in central Louisiana had become increasingly popular as mid-westerners flooded into the areas of Glenmora and Forest Hill. Aided by education from agricultural agents, crops like strawberries, potatoes (both sweet and the Irish variety), string beans, tomatoes, onions, and even peaches and Satsuma oranges thrived.[24] But after two years of struggling in the dirt and unrelenting heat, Manabu realized that he was not suited to farming life. He returned to his true calling, photography, and opened a new photo studio in 1930. The Kohara Photo Studio stood proudly on Murray Street in the bustling downtown of Alexandria, Louisiana.

Life for the Kohara family was not much different from any other family living in Alexandria during that time. In fact, the Kohara family probably had a bit more than the average white family living in the city then. Their large two-story home in the middle of downtown Alexandria had four bedrooms, one-and-a-half baths, screened-in porches on all levels of the house, and even had a room located off the living room where the maid would do the ironing. Louisiana life suited the Koharas.

Marion, the youngest of the Kohara children, recalled growing up in Alexandria.

> I think it was pretty much a typical small town. We didn't have air conditioning. The theaters were air-cooled and we had a town swimming pool—municipal

swimming pool—so we all went there during the summer. We rode bicycles. You know, pretty much what anybody did.[25]

Still deeply in love, Manabu and Saki would hold hands as they drove around the area during the family's weekly Sunday drives. Both Manabu and Saki wanted their children to be as American as possible. Although the children could count to ten in Japanese and use chopsticks, Manabu and Saki made a point not to speak Japanese with them. The only time Manabu and Saki spoke Japanese was to each other, and then only when they didn't want the children to know what they were talking about. Manabu and Saki's Christian faith remained strong. As practicing Christians in a very southern society, this most likely helped to ease their transition into the Alexandria community. Louisiana was a segregated society mired in prejudice—this was the Jim Crow South after all. In the early twentieth century, pockets of rabid anti-Japanese immigration sentiment sprung up all around Louisiana, fearful of a Japanese deluge—both culturally and economically. This culminated in 1921 when Louisiana successfully passed legislation blocking those of Asian ancestry from owning farmland, a continuation of racially based discriminatory legal practices that had been ignited with California's Alien Land Act of 1913.[26] Much like the situations in Hawai'i and California:

> the discrimination Chinese Americans and Japanese Americans faced in the South with landownership was a statement of their perpetual racial otherness and inability to assimilate and naturalize. The fear of what Asian immigrants *could* do as racial menaces more than what they actually *did* in the South shaped southern law.[27]

But the South can be a strange place. As Greg Robinson explains:

> Throughout the prewar era, Japanese Americans in Louisiana occupied a liminal space (as did the more numerous Chinese population) between the white and black populations, and associated with both. [T]here was ambient anti-Asian racism . . . yet individual residents were not treated as people of color, in contradistinction to black people.[28]

Robinson goes on to relay the story of Clifford Uyeda who took a seat in the back of a New Orleans streetcar reserved for those of color. The streetcar driver remedied this social faux pas by changing the sign in front of Uyeda from "colored" to "white," thereby ensuring that Uyeda was sitting in the "white" section.[29] The Koharas had settled in a Deep South that had long held to a social caste system that was underpinned with legalized racism and discrimination—at times puzzling or even downright deadly. While the family settled into the community of Alexandria fairly seamlessly, they did face isolated instances of racism. On one particular afternoon, Manabu was walking down the street with a white friend when someone yelled a racial slur to Manabu. Manabu's friend was quick to come to his defense, but Manabu appealed to his friend to ignore the offending man explaining that he was ignorant and not worth the trouble.

Despite some instances of discrimination, the Kohara Studio soon became known as a fine photography studio frequented by all the local residents who wanted to have pictures taken for special occasions (see figure 3). To have a Kohara photograph meant that you had achieved a certain level of success and was a mark of pride throughout the central Louisiana region. The studio carried the latest in photography equipment, even offering Technicolor moving pictures and free services such as checking cameras and advising on film.[30]

Manabu's gregarious and humorous nature, coupled with his technical photography skills, made him a skilled and successful photographer. A great portrait photographer, Manabu had a tried-and-true method of putting his subject at ease. When someone would come in to have their portrait taken, Manabu would take his time setting up the camera while making small talk with them. Since Alexandria was a small town, Manabu would slip in a personal detail he recalled about the person, which usually elicited a smile or brought a twinkle to their eye. At that moment, Manabu would trip the shutter he had casually been holding in his hand during the conversation. This trick allowed Manabu to capture a genuine moment of interaction with the person and helped to create a better portrait. Manabu also had a camera designed specifically to capture large group photos on which the lens housing sat on a track at the end of bellows. The track ran parallel to the film plane. The photographer could pull the lens to one side of the track, and once the shutter was tripped, a clockwork mechanism drove the lens housing down the track, making a broad sweep of a group of people posed on a long bench or low bleacher. Sometimes, Manabu would use this camera to take a photo of a group in which he was included. He would stand at one end of the line when the shutter was tripped and then playfully race behind the group as the lens housing made its way down the track managing to position himself at the other end of the line just in time for the lens to arrive and take his image for a second time. The resulting photograph would feature Manabu twice—once at each end of the same line of people![31]

Manabu was very involved in the local community and business groups. He was accepted as a member of both the Chamber of Commerce and the Alexandria Rotary Club. The Rotary Club even held business sessions at the Kohara home and were "served with delicious refreshments, cake, ice cream and coffee by Mrs. Kohara and her charming little daughter, Miss Marion Kohara."[32] He was also an active member in the Alexandria Arts and Crafts Study Club where he would sometimes exhibit his work.[33] Manabu felt enormous pride around his success and acceptance into these organizations. As the Koharas settled into their Technicolor life in Alexandria, war would come knocking at their door.

With Germany's invasion of Poland on September 1, 1939, the United States under President Franklin D. Roosevelt sat up and took notice. Within two days, France and Great Britain, Poland's allies, declared war on Germany. The United States watched anxiously as Europe plunged headfirst into war. Since the conclusion of World War I, still at this time known only as "the Great War," the United States had maintained a policy of isolationism and neutrality regarding international disputes.[34] The U.S. Military had been considerably downsized since the culmination of World War I. This postwar tradition of demobilization dated back to the American Revolution and was based on the "fear of a large standing army"[35] because of the costs this incurred. As of July 1, 1939, there were only 174,000 enlisted men on active duty in the U.S. Army, and funds for their training "were less than 5 percent of the annual War Department appropriations."[36] In the days following Germany's aggression, FDR reiterated the nation's attitude with his September 5th proclamation outlining the nation's neutral stance regarding the current conflict in Europe. But understanding that this position of neutrality would not hold out for long, FDR declared a limited national emergency three days later that allowed for the "strengthening of our national defense within the limits of peacetime authorizations."[37] This proclamation allowed for the increase of men in both the standing Regular Army and National Guard. FDR appointed George C. Marshall to oversee the training of these men as the Army's new Chief of Staff.

At the time of this proclamation, the U.S. Army ranked "seventeenth in effectiveness among the armies of the world, just behind that of Rumania."[38] It was time to prepare for the possibility of war.

The initial test of the current state of the Army came in May 1940 with the first "Louisiana Maneuvers." These war games pitted two Corps against one another in a mock battle to test not only the men in the field, but their commanders as well. General Marshall decided on central Louisiana as the site of the main "battle" due to the region's sparse population, favorable weather conditions, and diverse terrain.

> In addition, the terrain, the Louisiana coastal area, and the distances involved were comparable to Belgium, Holland, and the French coastal area east of the Seine River, where fighting would soon erupt. The river systems in Louisiana were similar to those in northern Europe, and the Sabine Pine Forest resembled the Ardennes and Argonne Forests. The South seemed the perfect place to practice if participation in the European conflict was a possibility.[39]

The first maneuvers succeeded in proving the need for these types of large-scale trainings, and "the maneuver area pleased army officials so well that they returned in the autumn of 1940, and in 1941, 1942, and 1943."[40] The second maneuvers was held in mid-August of 1940, wherein the Louisiana elements and their potential inconvenience were described as "Generals Weather and Mud" because of the month-long rainstorms which preceded the troops' arrival.[41]

The training of troops was also now seen as a necessity as France had been "eliminated as a world power and the British Army lost most of its heavy equipment" by June of 1940 as Germany progressed through Europe.[42] In the midst of the August second maneuvers, Great Britain was under air attack by the Luftwaffe and the United States listened raptly to Edward Murrow's reports from the Battle of Britain and the London Blitz. National opinion on the country's neutral stance began to change as the enormity of the danger posed by Nazi forces became clear. On September 16th, FDR signed the Selective Service and Training Act, also known as the Burke-Wadsworth Bill, enacting the first instance of a peacetime draft in American history. Within days, preliminary construction began on a camp located approximately twelve miles north of Alexandria amid the pine forests of the Kisatchie National Forest, just twelve miles away from the Kohara family.[43] Originally called Camp Tioga, within six weeks of initial construction, the name was changed to Camp Livingston by the War Department in honor of Robert Livingston, negotiator of the Louisiana Purchase.[44] Central Louisiana had become a favorite training ground for Army General Headquarters, and in order to house and train the influx of men now being drafted into the military, new sites would need to be built (Camps Livingston, Claiborne, and Polk), and old sites would need to be refurbished and expanded (Camp Beauregard). This new flurry of activity around Alexandria did not go unnoticed and would be a boon to the local economy. By September 24th, there were over 1,000 men working on the construction of camps in the local vicinity, by the end of October that number grew to 9,100, by the end of November there were 26,975, and in a final push to finish construction in January of 1941 there were 35,344 laborers—15,613 at Camp Livingston alone.[45]

In order to complete the camps by the spring of the new year, "Construction was carried on on a 24-hour-day-seven-day-week basis, the workmen laboring in shifts to get the camp ready for the soldiers."[46] The cost for the completion of Camp Livingston was originally estimated at $7.9 million, but by February 1941, it had doubled to $16.2 million; the final cost for the camp came to $32.5 million due to the ever-growing nature of the camp, as well as unforeseen weather conditions at the initial construction phase and increase in the cost of materials and labor.[47] It is said that:

> Enough lumber was used in building the original camp to construct a two-foot boardwalk from New York to San Francisco. And if all the nails used in this original construction were fused into one big nail it would be 5,000 miles long.[48]

Although construction wouldn't be completed until March 31st, the official activation date was February 10, 1941, with the arrival of the 32nd

Division, comprised of the Wisconsin and Michigan National Guard followed shortly thereafter by the 46th Field Artillery Brigade, the first African American Brigade in U.S. history. The first unit to actually train at Livingston was the 106th Cavalry from Illinois, the famous Black Horse Troop, as they arrived on December 29, 1940.[49] Camp Livingston would be home and training facility for "247 units totaling over 300,000 men" including the infantry divisions of the 32nd, 28th, 38th, and 86th as well as headquarters for the Third and Fourth Army. An average of between 25,000 and 30,000 were stationed at Camp Livingston during World War II with "the all-time high being reached in 1942 when 42,500 men were making use of the camp facilities."[50]

As was the case with the maneuvers in central Louisiana, Livingston was also considered "an ideal training ground" because it "[provided] terrain and semi-tropical conditions found in many of the world's battlefronts."[51] Now housing and training nearly 30,000 men at Camp Livingston alone, central Louisiana was primed for the General Headquarters (GHQ) Louisiana Maneuvers, referred to as "The Big One."

The Maneuvers of 1941 were, and still are, the largest peacetime maneuvers conducted by the Army in American history with over 350,000 men participating—many of whom were trained and garrisoned at Camp Livingston. Beginning in mid-September, the challengers were the Second "Red" Army under Lt. Gen. Ben Lear against the Third "Blue" Army under Maneuvers-veteran Lt. Gen. Walter Krueger with Dwight D. Eisenhower acting as Krueger's Chief of Staff. Apart from the size of these maneuvers and the number of participants, these maneuvers differed from previous iterations in that these were "free maneuvers"—where "there would be no elaborate, prewritten scenarios dictating the action in the GHQ maneuvers, and only a minimum of artificial constraints" to allow for experimentation and creativity in battle.[52] Since these maneuvers, like the ones that came before it, were simulated—using blanks in guns and tanks as well as flour sacks as bombs—artificial battle noises were produced by five sound trucks in some battles to ensure the men fighting would become "inured to the noise of modern battle."[53] The Blue Army even used propaganda pamphlets dropped from planes onto a retreating Red Army that said:

> Your commanders are withholding from you the terrible fact of your defeat. Your gasoline stores have been captured. From now on, if you move, you do it on the soles of your shoes. Your food stores have been captured. Your dinner today is going to be what was left over from yesterday ... Rout, disaster, hunger, sleepless nights in the forests and swamps are ahead of you—unless you surrender.[54]

Civilians in Alexandria, including the Koharas, got to experience the maneuvers firsthand as the armies clashed in the city. On the morning of September 15th, the Red Army blew up the main bridge in town with "a simulated bomb that supposedly shook every building in town and littered the streets with broken glass from shattered windows."[55] Mayor Bowdon was thrown from his office chair and cut his head when his windows were blown in, but he continued to work despite the injury and inconvenience. Drawn by the sounds of "rifle and machine gun fire, accompanied by the roar of bombers in the sky," Alexandrians watched from the riverfront as the battle played out before them.[56]

The GHQ Louisiana Maneuvers ended on September 28, 1941, just seventy days before the attack on Pearl Harbor. On that same day, Manabu Kohara suffered a paralytic stroke and passed away almost a month to the day on October 27th.[57] In an instant, the family had been ripped from their American dream. Saki lost her husband and partner and was left to run the photo studio with the help of her eldest son, Sammy. Saki and Manabu's youngest son, Jackie, left college and returned home to help his mother and brother. Tommy, the second oldest son, had been drafted into the Army in May 1941 where he served as a photographer both on the frontlines and behind enemy lines in Germany and France. While Camp Livingston was crackling with the electricity of battle preparations, the Koharas were reeling from Manabu's death and trying to put their affairs in order as the shadow of war between the United States and Japan loomed ever closer. Unknown to the Koharas, their connection to Camp Livingston would become personal in the following months.

NOTES

1. Harry G. Eskew and Elizabeth Eskew, *Alexandria 'Way Down in Dixie: An Informal Biography of an Old Louisiana City, The Cities of Louisiana Book Series* (New Orleans: Southern Printing Company, 1950), 2. Note: This particular book can only be described as a "product of its time"—the language used in certain parts can be quite problematic.

2. "Alexandria-Pineville," Works Progress Administration, 1930–1939, Louisiana Works Progress Administration Digital Collection, State Library of Louisiana, 4, https://louisianadigitallibrary.org/islandora/object/state-lwp%3A3799.

3. Donald G. Hunter, "Their Final Years: The Apalachee and Other Immigrant Tribes on the Red River, 1763–1834," *The Florida Anthropologist* 47, no. 1 (March 1994): 3–6.

4. G.P. Whittington, "Rapides Parish, Louisiana—A History (Second Installment)," *The Louisiana Historical Quarterly* 16, no. 1 (January 1933): 28.

5. *Rapide*, from which the parish (a county in Louisiana) around Alexandria claims its name: Rapides Parish.

6. Whittington, "Rapides Parish, Louisiana—A History (Second Installment)," 30–32.

7. G.P. Whittington, "Rapides Parish, Louisiana—A History," *The Louisiana Historical Quarterly* 15, no. 4 (October 1932): 579.

8. Whittington, "Rapides Parish, Louisiana—A History," 579.

9. Hunter, "Their Final Years," 17–18.

10. The origin of the name is debated—many claim the town was named after Fulton himself, while some say it was named for an infant daughter that passed away. (G.P. Whittington, "Rapides Parish, Louisiana—A History (Fourth Installment)," *The Louisiana Historical Quarterly* 16, no. 3 (July 1933): 437).

11. "The History of Alexandria Louisiana," https://www.alexandria-louisiana.com/alexandria-louisiana-history.htm (accessed August 11, 2022).

12. "Alexandria-Pineville," 6.

13. Justin A. Nystrom, "Red River Campaign," *64 Parishes*, https://64parishes.org/entry/red-river-campaign.

14. Terry L. Jones, "The Red River Rapids," *Country Roads*, January 22, 2019, https://countryroadsmagazine.com/outdoors/knowing-nature/the-red-river-rapids-pastimes/.

15. "Alexandria-Pineville," 8.

16. The rapids at Alexandria no longer exist. They were eradicated by a channel project overseen by the Corps of Engineers in the late nineteenth century. (Jones, "The Red River Rapids.")

17. James G. Hollandsworth, "The Burning of Alexandria," *64 Parishes*, https://64parishes.org/burning-alexandria.

18. "Alexandria-Pineville," 7.

19. "The History of Alexandria Louisiana."

20. Baham, "Alexandria, Louisiana Lee Street Negro District," Works Progress Administration, no date (circa 1930s), Louisiana Works Progression Administration Digital Collection, State Library of Louisiana, 1, https://louisianadigitallibrary.org/islandora/object/state-lwp%3A3850.

21. According to the 1930 Census, there were only 52 Japanese individuals residing across the entire state of Louisiana.

22. While at Berkeley, he watched as the 1906 earthquake destroyed San Francisco just across the Bay. (Sydnie Kohara, "Growing Up Asian in Louisiana," *Discover Nikkei*, September 29, 2005, http://www.discovernikkei.org/en/journal/2005/9/29/nikkei-heritage-louisiana/).

23. The *koto*, a 13-stringed instrument constructed from *kiri* wood, is the national instrument of Japan. It measures approximately 71 inches long and is in the zither family of instruments.

24. Works Progress Administration, "Description of Small Towns and Agricultural Communities Surrounding Alexandria, Louisiana," Louisiana Works Progress Administration Digital Collection, State Library of Louisiana, n.d., 1–2, https://louisianadigitallibrary.org/islandora/object/state-lwp%3A6959.

25. Marion Kohara Couvillion, interview with authors, July 12, 2016.

26. Greg Robinson, "The Astonishing History of Japanese Americans in Louisiana," in *Far East, Down South*, ed. Raymond Mohl, et al. (University of Alabama Press, 2016), 13–14.

27. Stephanie Hinnershitz, *A Different Shade of Justice: Asian American Civil Rights in the South* (University of North Carolina Press, 2017), 29.

28. Robinson, "The Astonishing History of Japanese Americans in Louisiana," 15.

29. Robinson, "The Astonishing History of Japanese Americans in Louisiana," 15–16.

30. "Technicolor Moving Pictures Now Made by Kohara Studio," *Alexandria Daily Town Talk* (Alexandria, LA), March 26, 1940.

31. Personal correspondence with Kohara family, April 2020.

32. "Church and Club Activities," *Alexandria Daily Town Talk* (Alexandria, LA), March 26, 1940.

33. "Art Club's Exhibit Here Outstanding," *Alexandria Daily Town Talk* (Alexandria, LA), November 4, 1938.

34. This was the "official" stance of the United States; however, the U.S. government and intelligence services had been watching with growing trepidation as Japan's nationalistic government and military invaded China—once in 1931, and again in 1937. Isolationism and neutrality did not mean that preparations for an eventual war with enemy nations in the East and West were not being made.

35. Mary Kathryn Barbier, "The 1940 Louisiana Maneuvers," *Southern Studies* V, no. III & IV (Fall & Winter 1994): 69.

36. George C. Marshall, *Biennial Reports of the Chief of Staff of the United States Army to the Secretary of War, 1 July 1939–30 June 1945* (Washington, DC: Center of Military History, United States Army, 1996), 3.

37. Franklin D. Roosevelt, "Proclamation 2352—Proclaiming a National Emergency in Connection with the Observance, Safeguarding, and Enforcement of Neutrality and the Strengthening of the National Defense Within the Limits of Peace-Time Authorizations," September 8, 1939, https://www.presidency.ucsb.edu/documents/proclamation-2352-proclaiming-national-emergency-connection-with-the-observance.

38. Christopher R. Gabel, *The U.S. Army GHQ Maneuvers of 1941* (Washington, DC: Center of Military History, United States Army, 1992), 8.

39. Barbier, "The 1940 Louisiana Maneuvers," 71–72.

40. Jerry Sanson, *Louisiana During World War II: Politics and Society 1939–1945* (Baton Rouge: Louisiana State University Press, 1999), 222.

41. "Troops Battle Mud in Louisiana Games," *New York Times*, August 6, 1940.

42. Marshall, *Biennial Reports of the Chief of Staff of the United States Army to the Secretary of War, 1 July 1939–30 June 1945*, 6.

43. As early as September 1940, the area around Alexandria had been identified by the Army for three training facilities in addition to Camp Beauregard. ("Options Obtained for Army Camp Sites in Rapides," *The Weekly Town Talk* (Alexandria, LA) September 14, 1940). By 1941, there would be a total of four large Army installations within a forty-mile radius of Alexandria, Louisiana: Camps Beauregard, Livingston, Claiborne, and Polk, as well as two airfields in the vicinity. ("Construction of Two Camps Opens Monday," *The Shreveport Times* (Shreveport, LA), September 22, 1940; "Here's the Inside on Livingston," *The Communique* (Camp Livingston,

LA), August 13, 1942; "1000 Working at Army Camps," *Alexandria Daily Town Talk* (Alexandria, LA), September 24, 1940.)

44. "History of the Surgeon's Office 1941–1942," Posts, Camps, and Stations; 1905–1954; RG 338 US Army Operational, Tactical, and Support Org. (WWII and Thereafter); National Archives at College Park, Maryland. Note: There was some debate as to who exactly the camp was named after—Robert Livingston, negotiator of the Louisiana Purchase, or his brother Edward, who became a prominent New Orleans lawyer; both were natives of New York but each had their own unique influence on Louisiana. ("Camp Tioga's Name Changed to Livingston, Evangeline to Claiborne," *Alexandria Daily Town Talk* (Alexandria, LA), October 30, 1940.)

45. "1000 Working at Army Camps"; "Builders Busy on Four New Sites at Camps," *The Shreveport Times* (Shreveport, LA), October 30, 1940; "26,975 Work on Army Camps Near City," *Weekly Town Talk* (Alexandria, LA), November 23, 1940; "35,344 Work in Camps," *Alexandria Daily Town Talk* (Alexandria, LA), January 18, 1941.

46. "Camp Livingston," *Chicago Sunday Tribune*, August 17, 1941.

47. "Army Adding Millions to LA. Spending," *The Shreveport Times* (Shreveport, LA), February 27, 1941; "Camp Livingston Looks Back on 4-1/2 Years of Training Troops for Global Conflict," *The Communique* (Camp Livingston, LA), September 14, 1945.

48. "Livingston Marks Second Birthday," *The Communique* (Camp Livingston, LA), February 5, 1943. By 1945, Camp Livingston had grown to encompass 48,087 acres. (War Department Office of the Chief of Engineers Post War Utilization Studies, "Camp Livingston, Louisiana," September 1945, Legal Branch Subject File 1942–1946; RG 389 (Provost Marshal General) Prisoner of War Operations Division; National Archives at College Park, Maryland).

49. On one particular night ride, all twenty-nine competing officers became lost at some point in the Kisatchie National Forest on the edge of Camp Livingston. ("Capt. Place Winner in 106th Cavalry Night Ride," *Weekly Town Talk* (Alexandria, LA), April 5, 1941).

50. "Camp Livingston Looks Back on 4-1/2 Years of Training Troops for Global Conflict."

51. "Camp Livingston Nearing Third Anniversary, Is Still Growing," *The Communique* (Camp Livingston, LA), August 27, 1943.

52. Gabel, *The U.S. Army GHQ Maneuvers of 1941*, 45–46.

53. Kent Roberts Greenfield, Robert R. Palmer, and Bell I. Wiley, *United States Army in World War II. The Army Ground Forces: The Organization of Ground Combat Troops* (Washington, DC: Historical Division Department of the Army, 1947), 44.

54. Arthur Carmody Jr., "The Louisiana Maneuvers of 1941: The Last Days of Innocence," *North Louisiana History* 39, no. 1 (Winter 2008): 12–13.

55. "Blues Take Alexandria," *Alexandria Daily Town Talk* (Alexandria, LA), September 15, 1941.

56. "Blues Take Alexandria."

57. "Kohara," *The Weekly Town Talk* (Alexandria, LA), November 1, 1941.

Chapter 8

When the Tigers Pounced

Oahu, also known as The Gathering Place, had been the headquarters of the U.S. Pacific Fleet for only a little over a year since taking up residence at Pearl Harbor in May 1940.[1] As the sun rose on the fateful Sunday of December 7th, residents around the island began to stir, anticipating another beautiful day in paradise. This peaceful start to the morning belied the tragedy that would unfold in mere hours.

3:42 a.m. HST: Close to the waters of Pearl Harbor, the mine sweeper *Condor* sights what they believe to be the "periscope of a submerged submarine."[2]

3:58 a.m. HST: The *Condor* signals to the nearby destroyer USS *Ward*, "Sighted submerged submarine on westerly course, speed nine knots."[3]

6:00 a.m. HST: Six Japanese aircraft carriers, *Akagi, Kaga, Soryu, Zuikaku, Hiryu* and *Shokaku* turn into formation 200 miles north of the Oahu coast.[4] These aircraft carriers and the supporting flotilla comprised of battleships, cruisers, destroyers, tankers, and submarines, are all part of the *Kidō Butai* or the Carrier Striking Force poised to wreak havoc on the unsuspecting island to the south and effectively bring the United States into World War II.[5]

6:15 a.m. HST: The initial strike force of 183 aircraft, led by Commander Mitsuo Fuchida, are in the air headed south to the island of Oahu.[6] A second wave of 171 aircraft, led by Lieutenant Commander Shimizaki takes off soon after.

6:45 a.m. HST: USS *Ward* fires on an unidentified submarine that is trailing the cargo ship *Antares* near the entrance of Pearl Harbor.[7]

7:00 a.m. HST: Flying above thick cloud cover, Fuchida turns on his radio direction finder searching for a radio signal from the island that he can use for navigation. He tunes into Hawaiian radio station KGMB using the signal to correct his course. A weather report interrupted the music: "Averaging partly cloudy, with clouds mostly over the mountains. Cloud base at 3,500 feet. Visibility good. Wind north, 10 knots." This means that there will be cloud breaks over Pearl Harbor. Fuchida realizes the visibility of their projected targets is a "windfall" for the attacking forces.[8]

7:02 – 7:39 a.m. HST: At Opana Mobile Radar Station, on the North Shore near Kahuku Point, Privates Lockard and Elliott observe a large contingent of planes, possibly 50, on their radar approximately 130 miles offshore. They report this to the Information Center at Fort Shafter. It is assumed that this is a flight of B-17s expected to arrive from California that morning. In reality, the two privates were seeing Fuchida's force approaching the island. Lockard and Elliott continue to track the incoming planes for practice, ending at 7:39 a.m. when the signal was lost. The planes were approximately 22 miles out.[9]

In the sleepy beach town of Hale'iwa, Reverend Miyamoto greeted the new day. The clear waters of Waialua Bay called to him. As the minister of the Hale'iwa Jodo Mission, he would be leading services later that morning, but for now, he made his way down the sloped sandy beach behind his home and the Jodo mission for his daily morning swim.[10]

7:30 a.m. HST: The clouds below finally break, and Fuchida sees the "long white line of coast" of the North Shore ahead.[11] Behind him, his squadron of 182 fighter pilots are awaiting orders.

7:40 a.m. HST: Fuchida fires a flare, or "black dragon," from his signal pistol indicating they had not been detected and were deploying a surprise attack.[12]

Walking back to the house after his swim, Reverend Miyamoto looked up in the sky and saw a group of planes flying overhead. He did not know, nor could he know, that he was witnessing Fuchida's initial attack squadron moments before deploying to their marks around the island.[13]

7:49 a.m. HST: Fuchida orders the attack with the radio signal, "To . . . to . . . to . . ." short for *totsugekiseyo* or "charge." With this order, each unit breaks off into their attack squadron for targets set around the island.[14]

7:55 a.m. HST: Hickam Field, Ford Island, and Wheeler Army Airfield are attacked by Japanese dive-bombers.[15]

7:57 a.m. HST: Japanese torpedo planes attack Pearl Harbor battleships.[16] U.S. Navy Commander Ted Hechler described the scene from his station on the *Phoenix* "as akin to trying to swat an angry swarm of bees in the confines of a telephone booth."[17]

8:00 a.m. HST: Japanese fighter pilots begin strafing air bases.[18]

8:05 a.m. HST: Japanese level bombers attack Pearl Harbor battleships. Fuchida then radios the fleet, *"Tora! Tora! Tora!"* (Tiger! Tiger! Tiger!) The code used to signify a successful surprise attack.[19]

8:55 a.m. HST: Shimizaki's second wave begin their attack.[20]

9:45 a.m. HST: The second wave have finished their attack on Oahu and are departing the island for their rendezvous with the carriers.[21] Wheeler Field, Schofield Barracks, and Kaneohe Naval Air Station have all sustained massive damage. Pearl Harbor and her battleships are on fire.

Beginning at 8:04 a.m. HST, local radio stations began putting out calls for military personnel to report to duty. Soon after, these same stations began summoning medical and defense workers to report for emergency duty. At 8:40 a.m. HST, an announcement was made that "A sporadic air attack has been made on Oahu . . . enemy airplanes have been shot down . . . the rising sun has been sighted on the wingtips."[22] Many listeners assumed this was just a simulated attack. Those in the vicinity of Pearl Harbor or any of the other bases had become used to the noises of military maneuvers.[23] It wasn't until 9:00 a.m. HST when Webley Edwards at KGMB began announcing the attack was the "real McCoy!" that people around the island began to understand what was happening.[24] On the North Shore, the Miyamoto family was settling into their Sunday morning. They had no idea that anything was happening at Pearl Harbor twenty-five miles away, nor did they know about the raids on the airfields scattered around the island (Wheeler was only thirteen miles away). "Realization of the attack came slowly to Islanders distant from the scenes of terror and destruction. Remote explosions were muffled. The drone of planes was not unusual. The dark smoke from Pearl Harbor mingled with the low-lying clouds."[25] They would not know about the events unfolding to the south of Haleʻiwa until they heard the news on the radio.[26]

It was 1:47 p.m. EST in Washington when Secretary of the Navy Frank Knox notified FDR about the attack on Pearl Harbor.[27] The official announcement from Washington came at 2:22 p.m. EST, or 9:22 a.m. in Hawaiʻi.[28] The grave news began to be broadcast nationally as radio networks picked up the story. At 2:26 p.m. EST, the Dodger-Giant football game in New York was interrupted by the announcement that the Japanese had attacked Pearl Harbor. Half an hour later, CBS repeated the bulletin during their broadcast of the New York Philharmonic concert at Carnegie Hall.[29] Four thousand miles away in bustling Alexandria, Louisiana, Marion Kohara, aged thirteen, was at her home on Bolton Avenue doing homework and listening to the radio. Her father, Manabu, had passed away just a little over a month prior in October, so her mother and brothers were at the family photo studio working on their Christmas orders to get them out in time. Marion noticed "Pearl Harbor" and "bombing" on the broadcast, but she didn't really understand what was going on. She didn't even know where Pearl Harbor was or why it was being bombed! When her mother, Saki, came home, she explained to Marion that Pearl Harbor was in Hawai'i and that it was the Japanese who bombed it. The dark realization of her mother's words washed over Marion that afternoon as her mother explained this meant the United States was going to war.[30] The news came across the radio at Camp Livingston, just down the road from the Koharas, and, for the rest of the day, everyone at Livingston "remain[ed] within hearing distance" of a radio so as not to miss any incoming reports.[31]

In just a matter of hours, the Pacific Fleet and surrounding bases had sustained devastating losses, both in terms of lives lost and the damage inflicted. Across the island of Oahu, fear and rumors spread like wildfire. By 3:30 HST that afternoon, Hawai'i would be under martial law.[32] That same day, Japanese forces would hit seven other targets in the Pacific: Malaya, Thailand, Singapore, Guam, Wake Island, Hong Kong, and the Philippines. War was upon us.

That evening, with smoke still rising from the embers of the attack, two FBI agents and a local policeman arrived at the Hale'iwa Jodo Mission. Reverend Miyamoto was handcuffed and taken away. This moment would mark the beginning of an internment odyssey, one in which he would be separated from his family for almost a year and a half.[33] He was not alone in this aberration of justice. Other men from the Japanese community would be arrested under the cover of nightfall—across the Islands as well as on the mainland.

In the dawn hours of Monday, December 8th, Corporal David Akui and Lieutenant Paul Plybon were canvassing the beach near Kaneohe Naval Station when they came across Ensign Kazuo Sakamaki, a Japanese midget submarine pilot, who had washed up on shore after abandoning his disabled midget submarine on a coral reef off the northern coast of Oahu. Upon his arrest, Sakamaki became Prisoner of War Number One.[34] Just a few hours later, FDR formally addressed a joint session of Congress. "Yesterday, December 7, 1941—a date which will live in infamy—the United States of America was suddenly and deliberately attacked by naval and air forces of the Empire of Japan."[35] From the twisted wreckage of Pearl Harbor, the slumbering giant that was the United States had awoken.

NOTES

1. Frederick D. Parker, *Pearl Harbor Revisited: U.S. Navy Communications Intelligence 1924–1941. United States Cryptologic History, Series IV: World War II, Volume 6, Third Edition* (Ft. George G. Meade, MD: Center for Cryptologic History, National Security Agency, 2013), 36.
2. Walter Lord, *Day of Infamy* (New York: Henry Holt and Company, 1957), 30.
3. Lord, *Day of Infamy*, 30.
4. Homer N. Wallin, *Pearl Harbor: Why, How, Fleet Salvage and Final Appraisal* (Washington, DC: Naval History Division, Government Printing Office, 1968), 88.
5. Michael J. Wenger, Robert J. Cressman, and John F. Di Virgilio, *"This Is No Drill," The History of NAS Pearl Harbor and the Japanese Attacks of 7 December 1941* (Annapolis, MD: Naval Institute Press, 2018), 65.
6. Mitsuo Fuchida, "I Led the Attack on Pearl Harbor," in *Air Raid: Pearl Harbor! Recollections of a Day of Infamy,* ed. Paul Stillwell (Annapolis, MD: Naval Institute Press, 1981), 8.
7. Lord, *Day of Infamy*, 40.
8. Fuchida, "I Led the Attack on Pearl Harbor," 8–9.
9. Recounted in both Gordon W. Prange, *At Dawn We Slept: The Untold Story of Pearl Harbor* (New York: McGraw-Hill, 1981), 499–501; Lord, *Day of Infamy*, 46–49.
10. Clifford Miyamoto, interview with authors, October 10, 2016.
11. Fuchida, "I Led the Attack on Pearl Harbor," 9.
12. Fuchida, "I Led the Attack on Pearl Harbor," 10.
13. Clifford Miyamoto, interview with authors, October 10, 2016.
14. Prange, *At Dawn We Slept*, 503.
15. Fuchida, "I Led the Attack on Pearl Harbor," 11.
16. Fuchida, "I Led the Attack on Pearl Harbor," 11.
17. Ted Hechler, "Like Swatting Bees in a Telephone Booth," in *Air Raid: Pearl Harbor! Recollections of a Day of Infamy,* ed. Paul Stillwell (Annapolis, MD: Naval Institute Press, 1981), 187.
18. Fuchida, "I Led the Attack on Pearl Harbor," 11.
19. The use of *tora* is related to the Japanese saying, "A tiger *(tora)* goes out 1,000 *ri* (2,000 miles) and returns without fail." A stated wish, perhaps, of a successful mission and safe return home. (Fuchida, "I Led the Attack on Pearl Harbor," 11).
20. Carl Smith, *Pearl Harbor 1941: The Day of Infamy* (Westport, CT: Praeger, 2004), 40.
21. Paul Joseph Travers, *Eyewitness to Infamy: An Oral History of Pearl Harbor* (Lanham, MD: Madison Books, 1991), 15.
22. Lord, *Day of Infamy*, 159.
23. Ronald Harry Lodge, Transcript of an oral history interview by Mike Gordon, March 2, 1981, Japanese Cultural Center of Hawai'i, https://jcch.soutronglobal.net/Portal/Default/en-US/RecordView/Index/5586.

24. Lord, *Day of Infamy*, 160.
25. Gwenfread Allen, *Hawaii's War Years 1941–1945* (Honolulu, HI: University of Hawai'i Press, 1950), 9.
26. Clifford Miyamoto, interview with authors, October 10, 2016.
27. "Pearl Harbor Documents," Franklin Delano Roosevelt Presidential Library, https://www.fdrlibrary.org/documents/356632/390886/Pearl+Harbor+Documents.pdf/405ef5ca-fb07-4a76-b651-2c756814eda4.
28. "Pearl Harbor Documents," Franklin Delano Roosevelt Presidential Library, https://www.fdrlibrary.org/documents/356632/390886/Pearl+Harbor+Documents.pdf/405ef5ca-fb07-4a76-b651-2c756814eda4.
29. Lord, *Day of Infamy*, ix.
30. Marion Kohara Couvillon, interview with authors, July 12, 2016.
31. "History of the Surgeon's Office 1941–1942," Posts, Camps, And Stations; 1905–1954; RG 338 US Army Operational, Tactical, and Support Org. (WW II and Thereafter); National Archives at College Park, Maryland.
32. Jane L. Schieber and Harry N. Scheiber, "Martial Law in Hawaii," *Densho Encyclopedia*, https://encyclopedia.densho.org/Martial_law_in_Hawaii/.
33. Clifford Miyamoto, interview with authors, October 10, 2016.
34. Sakamaki wrote a memoir detailing his experiences: Kazuo Sakamaki, *I Attacked Pearl Harbor* (Honolulu: Rollston Press, 2017).
35. Franklin D. Roosevelt, "'December 7, 1941 – A Date Which Will Live in Infamy' – Address to the Congress Asking That a State of War Be Declared Between the United States and Japan, December 8, 1941. (Transcript)," https://www.loc.gov/resource/afc1986022.afc1986022_ms2201/.

Chapter 9

Looking Westward

A ship set afloat
Laden with sweet offerings
Joyful spirits dance
Lanterns light the sky and sea
Guiding the ancestors home.[1]

The attack on Pearl Harbor signaled the end of life as the Miyamoto family knew it. Plucked from his family and temple in the blink of an eye, no one can know what Reverend Miyamoto's thoughts and feelings were in those moments as he was forcibly ripped from his family and the life he built. His internal struggle, his fears, and his confusion can only be imagined. As the car left the temple to ferry Reverend Miyamoto to an unknown future, did he look out over the temple and onto the unwavering sea and wonder what his destiny and that of his family would be? Did his mind flash through the nearly three decades spent dedicating himself to the care and nourishment of his temple community as he was being taken away?

As the minister of the Jōdo-shū, Reverend Miyamoto spent twenty-six years serving as a very important guide and beacon to his congregation helping them to navigate all of life's events including the joyous, sad, and momentous occasions. One important yearly celebration over which Reverend Miyamoto presided was O-Bon.[2]

Brought to Hawai'i by the Japanese immigrant workers of the nineteenth century, the practice of O-Bon from the early medieval period, commonly known as Bon,[3] is the time of year when the spirits of ancestors return to visit family and friends while the living celebrate both their ancestors and the gift of life itself. Summer in Hawai'i is synonymous with Bon season.

Each summer, Buddhist temples across the Islands host festivities to express gratitude and joy, and the Hale‘iwa Jodo was no exception.

During Bon season, families clean gravesites and *butsudans* (family shrines), make offerings to the ancestors, and light *chochin* (Japanese lanterns) to prepare to send the spirits back to their realm. The central part of the Bon celebrations takes place on the last night of the three-day celebration, which culminates in the Bon Odori or folk dances. On the temple grounds, a *yagura* (tower) is erected in the center of an open area and serves as the focal point of the Bon Odori. The *yagura* can be between fifteen and twenty feet high and is draped in red and white cloth, the traditional colors of Japanese festivals. Serving as the celebratory hub of the Bon Odori, the *yagura* is adorned with hanging lanterns and electric lights radiating from its center across the grounds illuminating the nighttime festivities while also serving as a beacon for the spirits. It is here, at the *yagura*, that the drummers, singers, and musicians take their places and entertain the crowds and spirits. To an observer, a bird's eye view of the festivities could be likened to a dharma wheel. The circle of dancers, or the round shape of the dharma wheel, represents the perfection of the Buddha's teachings. The cyclical motion of the wheel, the dancers circling the *yagura*, represents the cyclical nature of life in the world. The *yagura* itself is the hub of the wheel symbolizing the three treasures of Buddhism.

As the night goes on, more and more people join in dancing around the *yagura*. By night's end, there can be as many as six or more circles of dancers circumventing the *yagura*. To fully participate in the dancing, egos of the dancers must be thrown aside. Young and old, novice and seasoned, Buddhist and non-Buddhist, Japanese and non-Japanese all dance together in unison. Everyone is participating with the universal desire to honor their departed loved ones and celebrate life. The dancing serves to entertain the spirits of the ancestors and cheer them onwards on their journey back to the land of the dead.[4]

Reverend Miyamoto's temple in Hale‘iwa holds possibly the most special of all Bon celebrations on Oahu. In Hale‘iwa, the temple is located directly on the water—the sole temple on all of Oahu to be so uniquely situated. The temple grounds are raised above the beach offering a perfect view of the sun setting over the ocean as the day fades and night gathers slowly enticing more and more revelers around the *yagura*. Sea air mingles with incense from the temple ceremony and the smells of delicious foods like saimin, teriyaki, musubi, and sushi waft over the celebrations. Young and old savor the sweet shaved ice to cool down from the hot summer night and frenzied dancing. A visceral banging of taiko drums and the trill of flutes create a universal heartbeat to which the revelers move in unison around the *yagura* with jumps, claps, and song bursting forth as expressions of their joy.

Tsuki mo mam maru Da Yo
Moon is full moon,

Odo ri Mo Ma Ru-I Yo
Dancing in the circle,

Nushi To Wa Ta Shi Mo
You and me . . .[5]

Beyond the physical beauty which is obvious as one looks out over the temple and onto the ocean, the Haleʻiwa Jodo temple's location has a deeper significance. The temple faces the west cardinal direction looking out over the beach and ocean. The significance of the temple facing the west is tied to Pure Land Buddhism. In this school of Buddhism, facing westward is equated with facing the direction of heaven. Toward the end of the Bon Odori, the priests return to the temple and prepare the *saiho-maru* (the boat that heads to the west) for its procession to the sea filling it with offerings to the spirits so that it is ready to symbolically lead the spirits of the ancestors back to the Pure Land or heaven. From the temple stairs, the priests begin their chants of "Namu Amida Butsu" while ringing bells and reverently carry the laden motherboat down from the temple and toward the beach leading the procession of revelers to participate in the final send-off of ancestors. Once at the beach, the priests continue to chant and ring bells while the *saiho-maru* is lit with a lantern, placed into the water, and slowly pulled into the ocean beckoning the spirits to return westward with each ebb and flow of the boat with the ocean tide.

By December 1941, Reverend Miyamoto spent twenty-six years leading the Bon celebrations at Haleʻiwa. Twenty-six years were spent honoring ancestors, celebrating life, and placing the *saiho-maru* into the ocean while chanting blessings as it slowly floated out to the horizon. For twenty-six years, Reverend Miyamoto was the *saiho-maru* for the people of Haleʻiwa. He was the beacon that guided his congregation to follow the right path through his leadership, humanity, and dedication to creating a better life for the people of Haleʻiwa.

As the car into which Reverend Miyamoto was forcibly placed on December 7, 1941, sped away toward an unknown destination, Reverend Miyamoto must have been thinking of many things. December 7th began a four-year journey of suffering, uncertainty, and perseverance during which time he would look to the west every day. Reverend Miyamoto looked to the west in search of his family, his home and temple, and a land of purer intent that existed right beyond the horizon where the *saiho-maru* docked. A pure land. A just land. A free land.

NOTES

1. Original tanka poem written by author, Hayley Johnson, for the chapter after attending the Haleʻiwa Jodo Bon Dance and Toro Nagashi in July 2019.

2. The origins of O-Bon can be traced to the Ullambana Sutra which tells the story of Mokuren and the freeing of his mother from the realm of Hungry Ghosts. Bon stems from the Sanskrit term ullambana meaning "to salvage souls from the agony of being hanged head down" (Katsumi Onishi, "'Bon' and 'Bon-Odori' in Hawaii," *Social Process in Hawaii* 4 (May 1938): 49). Mokuren or Mahamaudgalyayana, one of Shakyamuni Buddha's closest and chief disciples, was the most gifted of all in his psychic powers and his extraordinary sense perceptions. Because of his powers, he was able to search the six realms of existence for his mother after her death to check on her well-being. Mokuren was both surprised and distraught to find his mother in the realm of Hungry Ghosts, hanging upside down and starved, suffering in a perpetual state of unsatisfied desire. With his powers, Mokuren immediately sent his mother food to satisfy her hunger, but each time Mokuren's mother attempted to consume the offerings, the food burst into flames as it neared her mouth. Realizing that his powers alone would not release his mother from her suffering, Mokuren went to Shakyamuni Buddha for help. The Buddha advised Mokuren to make a selfless offering to a group of monks upon the end of the rainy season retreat on the fifteenth day of the seventh month. Mokuren made the offerings on the prescribed day, and his mother was freed from her suffering in the realm of Hungry Ghosts. Upon seeing his mother freed and dancing in celebration, the normally reserved and dignified Mokuren became so consumed with tremendous joy that he too began dancing and clapping without restraint.

3. "'O–' is a Japanese honorific prefix usually used in conjunction with 'bon' when referring to the religious occasion, but not when referring to the dance performed on this occasion." (Judy Van Zile, *The Japanese Bon Dance in Hawaii* (Press Pacifica, 1982), 86.)

4. Onishi, "Bon and Bon-Odori in Hawaii," 50.

5. Lyrics from the Fukushima Ondo sung at the Haleʻiwa Jodo Obon. Translation by Howard Sugai. In author's possession.

Chapter 10

Becoming an Enemy Alien

Within hours of being notified of the attack on Pearl Harbor, President Roosevelt signed Presidential Proclamation 2525 authorizing the arrest and detention of Japanese aliens residing in the United States who were considered "dangerous to the public peace or safety of the United States by the Attorney General or the Secretary of War."[1] The names of those suspects had already found their way onto the Custodial Detention Lists that had been prepared in the months before the attack. By December 8th, FDR had signed Proclamations 2526 and 2527 authorizing the arrest and detention of Germans and Italians, respectively. With these proclamations, President Roosevelt had invoked the Alien Enemies Act of 1798 (50 USC 21-24), and it was at this moment that all aliens of Japanese, German, or Italian birth residing in the United States became classified as enemy aliens.

The historical precedent for the treatment of enemy aliens had been codified with the Alien and Sedition Acts of 1798, a collection of four bills signed under President John Adams during the "Quasi-War," a two-year period of naval conflicts between France and the United States. These were signed at a time when it was thought by the Federalists that "the greatest *internal* danger facing the nation was the rapidly growing foreign-born population," a sentiment that has been felt in waves during our American history, especially near wartime.[2]

Of these four, the Alien Enemies Act stipulated that in the event of war, internment of resident aliens of hostile countries, now considered enemy aliens, was allowed.

> Full authority to control "all natives, citizens, denizens, or subjects" of the enemy [aged fourteen years and upwards] within the United States rests in the hands of the President. When war is declared or invasion attempted or

threatened, he may proclaim "the manner and degree of the restraint to which they shall be subject, and in what cases, and upon what security their presence shall be permitted . . . and. . . establish any other regulations which shall be found necessary in the premises and for the public safety."[3]

This Act allows for "citizens from enemy foreign countries who were thought to present a danger, but who could not be charged with a crime [to be] interned as enemy aliens."[4]

Prior to World War II, the Alien Enemies Act had been invoked twice in U.S. history—once in 1812 and then again in 1917 with America's entrance into World War I. It was during World War I that President Wilson sanctioned the detention and internment of over 2,000 German civilians residing in the United States as enemy aliens through the authority of the Alien Enemies Act.[5]

In addition to authorizing the arrest and internment of Japanese aliens, Proclamation 2525 also handed down strict regulations regarding the conduct of enemy aliens. Enemy aliens could not board flights, move to a different home, change jobs, or even travel "without full compliance with any such regulations" set forth by either the Attorney General or Secretary of War, depending upon their location.[6] The Attorney General was given oversight of regulations for the continental United States, Alaska, and Puerto Rico while the Secretary of War was given the Canal Zone, Hawaiian Islands, and the Philippines.[7] Enemy aliens were also prohibited from having in their possession the following items:

> Firearms; weapons or implements of war or components thereof; ammunition; bombs; explosives . . .; short-wave radio receiving sets; transmitting sets; signal devices; codes or ciphers; cameras; and papers, documents or books in which there may be invisible writing; photograph, sketch, picture, drawing, map or graphical representation of any military or naval installations or equipment or of any arms, ammunition, implements of war, device or thing used or intended to be used in the combat equipment of the land or naval forces of the United States or any military or naval post, camp or station.[8]

With the declaration of martial law in Hawai'i, Governor Poindexter handed over the reins to Army General Walter Short who then:

> directed that all Japanese alien enemies possibly dangerous in view of prior investigations be taken into custody . . . A three-by-five card had previously been prepared on each individual to be apprehended, this card showing his name, address and citizenship status . . . Within three hours most of the apprehensions had been effected and those arrested delivered to the Immigration stations.[9]

Reverend Miyamoto was one of the men identified on a three-by-five card. By the evening of December 7, 1941, he was picked up under the auspices of previous suspicion. He was now considered an enemy alien. More specifically, he was now designated as a "Group A" enemy alien or those "individuals believed to be the most dangerous and who in all probability should be interned in event of War."[10]

Reverend Miyamoto's wife, Fumi, was now considered an enemy alien as well. After Reverend Miyamoto's arrest, she would not know her husband's whereabouts for some time. The Miyamotos were like other Japanese families who had fallen under suspicion by the FBI. "In many cases, the head of the family simply disappeared, and several weeks passed before his family learned he had been interned."[11] Fumi's cousin through marriage, Mrs. Saki Kohara, living what seemed a world away in Alexandria, Louisiana, had also become an enemy alien in the eyes of the U.S. government.

All three—Reverend Miyamoto, Fumi Miyamoto, and Saki Kohara—would have different experiences during the coming war years, but all were enemy aliens in the eyes of the U.S. government because of their place of birth and their inability to become citizens of the United States. Each had been relegated to perpetual resident alien status prescribed by U.S. laws that were mired in anti-Asian sentiment and bias.

Proclamation 2525's ban on enemy aliens having restricted items in their possession affected both families very differently. Clifford Miyamoto recalled that the family had no photographs from the war years. He said, "As far as photos taken during the war in Hawai'i there are none. The government confiscated our camera, standing short wave radio, and binoculars and never returned them after the war ended."[12] Standing in stark contrast to the confiscation of items from the Miyamoto family, the Kohara family in Alexandria did not have any of their photography equipment confiscated. After a short investigation into their photography business, the Koharas were allowed to continue operating their photography studio mere miles away from numerous military garrisons.

On February 24, 1942, just five days after FDR signed Executive Order 9066, the War Department placed an official order with Barber Brothers Company of Baton Rouge and Perrilliat-Rickey Construction Co., Inc. of New Orleans to construct, "in the shortest possible time . . . one Alien Concentration Camp at Camp Livingston, Alexandria, Louisiana."[13] The construction of this enclosure on the south-west corner of Camp Livingston was completed on April 15th, less than two months after construction had begun.[14] It was built to hold 5,000 enemy aliens and the Military Police that would stand guard over them. By that summer, hospital facilities for the enemy alien camp had been completed within the grounds as well. The costs for the construction of this camp totaled $1,576,281 and utilized a total of 346,439 man-hours, with 1,060 men working at the peak of construction.[15]

The initial letter sent on February 24th also stated that "The Secretary of War finds that it is in the interest of the National Defense that this work be not delayed."[16] This push for a quick turnaround from the War Department was because the would-be first occupants of the camp, Japanese enemy aliens, had already been arrested and were being held in temporary facilities around the nation.[17] One such future internee, Reverend Miyamoto, was being held in a temporary detainment facility in Hawai'i.

NOTES

1. Presidential Proclamation Aliens, No. 2525, Alien Enemies—Japanese.
2. Geoffrey R. Stone, *Perilous Times: Free Speech in Wartime* (W.W. Norton and Company, 2004), 30.
3. Quoted in "Alien Enemies and Japanese—Americans: A Problem of Wartime Controls," *The Yale Law Review* 51, no. 8 (1942): 1318–1319. Originally the Enemy Aliens Act of 1798 only pertained to males, but it was revised in 1918 to include women. (J. Edgar Hoover, "Alien Enemy Control," *Iowa Law Review* 29, no. 3 (March 1944): 398).
4. Jennifer K. Elsea, "Presidential Authority to Detain 'Enemy Combatants,'" *Presidential Studies Quarterly* 33, no. 3 (2003): 569.
5. Arnold Krammer, *Undue Process: The Untold Story of America's German Internees* (London: Rowman & Littlefield Publishers, Inc., 1997), 14. Even with the thousands that had been interned during World War I, the breadth of the internment and incarceration experienced by Japanese and Japanese Americans has remained unmatched.
6. Presidential Proclamation Aliens, No. 2525, Alien Enemies—Japanese.
7. Presidential Proclamation Aliens, No. 2525, Alien Enemies—Japanese.
8. Presidential Proclamation Aliens, No. 2525, Alien Enemies—Japanese.
9. Hoover, "Alien Enemy Control," 402.
10. Buntetsu Miyamoto FBI File No. 97-42, 1941, RG 389, Box 2626, National Archives, College Park, Maryland. As explained previously, the signing of Proclamation 2525 and the arrest and internment of enemy aliens is a different program than the more generally known camps overseen by the War Relocation Authority. The internment of enemy aliens was legally permissible because of the legal precedent set by the Alien Enemies Act of 1798. The forced removal of over 110,000 Japanese and Japanese Americans authorized with Executive Order 9066 is covered in more detail in Greg Robinson's *By Order of the President: FDR and the Internment of Japanese Americans* (2001), Michi Weglyn's *Years of Infamy: The Untold Story of America's Concentration Camps* (1976), and *Personal Justice Denied: Report of the Commission on Wartime Relocation and Internment of Civilians* (1982). Although different in their methods and practice of incarceration, both programs are tragedies of justice and have left legacies of trauma in their wake.
11. Harry N. Scheiber and Jane L. Scheiber, *Bayonets in Paradise: Martial Law in Hawaii During World War II* (Honolulu, HI: University of Hawai'i Press, 2016), 47.

12. Clifford Miyamoto, written correspondence with authors, 2016.

13. Completion Report, 1942, Alien Internment Camp and Hospital, Camp Livingston, LA, Volume 4; Construction Completion Reports 1917–1943, RG 77; National Archives at College Park, Maryland.

14. Completion Report, 1942, Alien Internment Camp and Hospital, Camp Livingston, LA, Volume 4; Construction Completion Reports 1917–1943, RG 77; National Archives at College Park, Maryland.

15. Completion Report, 1942, Alien Internment Camp and Hospital, Camp Livingston, LA, Volume 4; Construction Completion Reports 1917–1943, RG 77; National Archives at College Park, Maryland.

16. Completion Report, 1942, Alien Internment Camp and Hospital, Camp Livingston, LA, Volume 4; Construction Completion Reports 1917–1943, RG 77; National Archives at College Park, Maryland.

17. Though Camp Livingston would only hold Japanese enemy alien men at its outset and later German and Japanese Prisoners of War, in a letter dated March 27, 1942, between the Provost Marshal General and the Quartermaster General, a preference for Italians to populate this camp is noted in discussions for the planning of a special shoe repair shop dedicated to repairing Class B Army shoes. "It is believed by this office [Provost Marshal General] that of the nationalities classed as enemy aliens, Italians would be most adaptable to the labor involved in the operation of the special shoe repair shop recommended. At the present time there is an insufficient number of Italian internees to provide the personnel required for the operation of this shop. Further order of internment and transfers of internees from the Department of Justice to the War Department undoubtedly will increase the number of Italian internees to a sufficient number." The letter goes on to say that while they would like Italian nationals to be transferred to Camp Livingston for the proposed shoe repair shop, it is understood that "it is impossible to reserve this camp for Italians." Further consideration is given to the fact that shoe repair is labor that was approved in the Geneva Convention. The Camp Livingston shoe repair shop run by internee labor would not materialize. (Letter from B.M. Bryan, Chief Aliens Division to The Quartermaster General, March 27, 1942. Camp Livingston Louisiana, Construct; Prisoner of War Operations Division, Subject Correspondence File 1942–1946, RG 389 Provost Marshal General at National Archives College Park, Maryland).

Part III

WARTIME EXPERIENCES

Chapter 11

ISN-HJ-131-CI

Around noontime on December 7th, Colonel Bicknell of the Army, Robert Shivers of the Federal Bureau of Investigation (FBI), and the head of the Espionage Bureau of the Honolulu Police Department, John A. Burns, met to figure out how to proceed in the wake of the attack on Pearl Harbor. During this meeting, they decided they needed to begin detaining all the suspects on file to "remove any chance of them doing any damage, even though it might unjustly deprive them of their liberty for awhile."[1] In order to facilitate the mass apprehension of so many civilians, Burns requested of the police chief 100 cars and 100 men to start the process. Typically, there were two men assigned to pick-ups. There was a policeman (or reserve policeman) and a federal agent, but there could sometimes be three men assigned. Each group of men was given a set of cards with names and addresses of individuals to apprehend.[2]

Reverend Buntetsu Miyamoto was no different than the other men arrested on Oahu during those first days. Reverend Miyamoto checked off three of the most popular categories for arrest. He was a Buddhist priest. He was a Japanese language schoolteacher, and he had been a *toritsuginin*. Reverend Miyamoto was brought to the Honolulu Immigration Station with two other individuals from Waialua, a fellow minister and a newspaper bureau chief.[3] The drive from Waialua to Honolulu typically took only an hour and a half, but on that night, the drive took five hours.

> The car the three men were riding in passed the devastated Pearl Harbor naval port. At the sound of cannon fire, their guards would stop the car and dive under it. They arrived at the Immigration Office later that night, badly shaken.[4]

The men were packed into the small holding cell of the Immigration Station like sardines. A room meant to hold 80 people held 180 by the following morning.[5]

That night, Reverend Miyamoto was processed, and a Basic Personnel Record was created for him (see figure 4). In this record, he was described as follows: 5 feet 2 ½ inches tall, 130 pounds, 53 years old with a scar under his chin and birthmark on the inside of his right bicep, brown eyes, yellow skin, and slightly gray hair. He was fingerprinted; a mugshot was taken, and he signed his apprehension document. At that time, all valuables were seized from Reverend Miyamoto's person. He had $15.94 in cash. He was searched for contraband, such as possible lethal weapons, medicines, or foodstuffs. The property controller also suggested that Reverend Miyamoto appoint someone to act as his attorney-in-fact to handle his affairs. As part of his questioning by authorities, Reverend Miyamoto was asked for the first time if he wanted to be repatriated to Japan.[6] This is a question that would be repeatedly asked of him.

Two days later, Reverend Miyamoto was transferred to Sand Island Detention Center. A tiny coral island inside of Honolulu Harbor, Sand Island was originally known as Quarantine Island during the nineteenth century where ships believed to be carrying contagious passengers were quarantined. Immediately after Pearl Harbor, Sand Island was converted into a U.S. Army internment camp and served as the main transfer and holding site in Hawai'i for the following fifteen months. Sand Island was a five-acre camp enclosed by a fifteen-foot high barbed wire fence. Kumaji Furuya, an Issei arrested on December 7th, recalled arriving at Sand Island:

> I looked around, wondering where they were going to put us. I could see some structures that looked like a mess hall and latrines in a large field surrounded by barbed wire. We were told to go into the fenced area, put up tents, assemble army cots, and set them up eight to a tent according to the soldiers' instructions. These were to be our temporary accommodations. Although each of us got a pillow and blanket, we were not given pajamas. We were expected to lie down as we were dressed.[7]

The men detained at Sand Island would spend about a month with only the clothes on their backs and no other provisions provided by the government.[8] It would take two months before barracks were built.[9] In addition, there was no visitation, radio, or newspapers allowed, so the detainees lived without any knowledge of what was going on in the world around them.[10]

On December 30, 1942, at 1:30 p.m., Reverend Miyamoto and fellow detainees were weeding the lawn of Sand Island Barracks when three names were called to report to the guards: Kashiwa, Kusao, and Miyamoto. The three Waialua men, who had made the five-hour journey to detainment on December 7th together, were told they were to be taken to the FBI office in downtown Honolulu. Stricken with fear and trepidation of being interrogated, the men were transferred to the Dillingham Building, the location of the FBI offices. After waiting, they were shocked to discover they had a visitor: Mr. John H. Midkiff, manager of Waialua Sugar. Midkiff made the journey to Honolulu to bring newspapers, magazines, gum, candies, cigarettes, and most importantly information on the families of the three men. Midkiff assured them he would do everything he could to assist the men and that he would protect their families left behind with every power at his command. For Miyamoto, Kashiwa, and Kusao, this pledge by the inimitable Midkiff meant more than they could articulate. Midkiff's appearance in this nightmare situation felt like they had "met God in Hell."[11] The pledge overcame Reverend Miyamoto with emotion. He could feel a hot lump swell within his throat, and his eyelids became hot.[12] It also moved him to share that very day was, in fact, the sixth birthday of his youngest daughter, Keiko. When Midkiff returned to Waialua, he visited Reverend Miyamoto's home to tell the Miyamoto family that he had seen their husband and father in Honolulu and assured them that he was in fine shape. Midkiff then presented a doll to Keiko and told her that it was a birthday present he was delivering from her father. Midkiff did what he knew Reverend Miyamoto would have done if he had the money and freedom to do so: honor his daughter and celebrate her birth.[13]

Reverend Miyamoto recalled that many prominent Japanese were held at Sand Island, and they all claimed to have social relationships with influential white people. None of those men, however, ever received a visit such as Reverend Miyamoto and his fellow Waialua residents. Reverend Miyamoto stated that it took "daring beyond comprehension of laymen" for Midkiff to put himself at risk by associating with the Japanese and acting in support of them.[14] Reverend Miyamoto recognized the strength of Midkiff's character when he wrote, "The world ever needs a man with far-reaching knowledge of human relations and a man who can love all beings regardless of race, color, or creed."[15]

While at Sand Island, the government did visit Reverend Miyamoto to request permission to use the temple, and Reverend Miyamoto denied the request.[16] This battle for the temple would continue throughout his internment. The men awaited nonlegal hearings by a Board of Officers and Civilians or the Alien Enemy Hearing Board appointed to try detainees and determine if they should be released, paroled, or interned. Each board was comprised of three citizens and one Army officer. Typically, the president of the board was an attorney, and the Army officer acted as the recorder.[17] During this hearing, evidence gathered by the FBI was presented to the board. Detainees could testify on their own behalf, call witnesses to testify, and could obtain counsel.

Reverend Miyamoto was called to the Immigration Station on January 13, 1942, to begin his hearing process and was asked to name any witnesses he would summon in preparation for his hearing. He named Mr. John H.

Midkiff recalling Midkiff's pledge to help in any way possible during his visit. Immediately after uttering his name, Reverend Miyamoto hoped that he had not overstepped any boundaries by not consulting with Midkiff before naming him as a witness. After all, Reverend Miyamoto realized that he had been branded an enemy alien and Midkiff was an important figure in the community. The immigration official inquired as to whether this witness was a white man, and if he was, would he *really* come as a witness if requested to do so? Reverend Miyamoto replied that Midkiff would come. The questions continued. The immigration official derisively asked how Reverend Miyamoto would request Midkiff's presence. Reverend Miyamoto replied, "By telephone." Reverend Miyamoto, however, like all the other men arrested, had no money to make the call. Knowing the predicament that Reverend Miyamoto was in, the immigration official pressed further, asking how he expected to make this call with no money. Without hesitation, Reverend Miyamoto replied that he would reverse the charges. Trusting in the relationship built over many years, Reverend Miyamoto hoped that he had not abused his friend's pledge to help, but he had no other alternative. Interviews of both the detainee and any witnesses called were set to begin the very next day.[18]

At 11:10 a.m., the facts gathered during the investigation were presented to the Hearing Board. John Harold Hughes, special agent of the FBI, was called as a witness. During his testimony, he recited to the board all the information that had been collected on Reverend Miyamoto. From the hearing transcripts, Agent Hughes testified:

> This is the case of Buntetsu Miyamoto. He is a consular agent, and was appointed as such on January 1st, 1939, to serve for a period of two years, and he has served as such for a number of years.
>
> He is a Japanese alien, and arrived in Honolulu on July 9th 1915,[19] from Japan, and first became associated with the Haleiwa Jodo Mission, where he has since continually been a priest and principal of the Japanese language school.
>
> He has been a Jodo priest since he was 11 years old, in Japan, and has followed no other occupation than that of priest and school teacher.
>
> He has no known military service in Japan.
>
> Since his first arrival he has made only one trip to Japan, and that was for a period of six months, in 1920.
>
> The recorder asked: You speak of him as having no military training or service. Do you take the Navy in on that, as well as the Army?
>
> Hughes answered: Well, yes, we include all of them: the Army, the Navy, and the Air Service.
>
> I don't think I gave you the date of his birth. It was September 3rd, 1888. He has five children, all of whom are citizens of the United States.
>
> That is the substance of our information on Miyamoto.[20]

From the time the board convened at 11:10 a.m. to hear the evidence presented by the FBI on Reverend Miyamoto until the conclusion of the presentation of evidence, a whopping five minutes had elapsed. With that brief summary of information on Reverend Miyamoto, the board was dismissed at 11:15 a.m. and the hearing continued until the following day.

Reverend Miyamoto arrived at his hearing the following morning, January 14th, with swirling emotions of hope, doubt, assurance, and apprehension all whipping through his body as he waited in the yard of the immigration facility for his hearing to begin. Then, word came. Midkiff had, in fact, come to serve as a witness. Beyond that kindness, Midkiff also brought the Miyamoto family with him in the hopes that Reverend Miyamoto might visit briefly with them that day. Midkiff requested special permission of the board to allow Reverend Miyamoto to see his family, but one board member was reluctant to grant the request, so it was denied. Reverend Miyamoto recalled:

> At a time of tense feelings a thing of this sort was not unusual and I felt it could not be helped. I was more than grateful for what Mr. Midkiff had done for me, busy as he was, and moreover to try to let me have just a glimpse of my family, if worst came to worst—my deepfelt gratitude and respect to one who could understand the feelings of a person in distress as we were then in 1942.[21]

The Hearing Board convened soon after at 11:00 a.m., and Reverend Miyamoto was called as a witness. Because of his limited English-speaking ability, a Japanese interpreter was sworn in so Reverend Miyamoto could testify. This was not uncommon as many of the Issei men detained as enemy aliens had limited fluency in English. John Grote,[22] a Marianist Brother who previously spent time in Japan as a missionary, was paid during this period to act as an interpreter.[23]

The board began their questioning. Reverend Miyamoto testified to his name, address, occupation, nationality, date of birth, and arrival and duration in Hawai'i. He was asked if he received his education in Japan, whether he had any military service in Japan, and if he had any relatives that presently served in the Army or Navy. Reverend Miyamoto testified that he had worked as a consular agent and reported information concerning births and deaths of the Japanese population.

The board then asked Reverend Miyamoto about his children. He testified that he had five children, all American citizens. He had three boys, the oldest of whom had returned to Japan in 1938 to attend the Buddhist University and was still in Japan receiving his education. He testified that one of his sons was serving in the Hawaiian Territorial Guard. The board further asked if Reverend Miyamoto had expatriated his children to which he replied that he had not. He went on to explain that he thought it was best to wait until the children were twenty-one and let them make the decision for themselves.

The board recorder then asked Reverend Miyamoto to whom did he owe his allegiance.

Reverend Miyamoto:

> I am a Japanese, and I cannot possibly forget Japan, of course, but as far as direct loyalty, since I have been living all these years in America, Hawaii, and my children are all here, my feelings are for America, but I cannot forget Japan.

The recorder:

> In case of Japanese invasion, would you assist in fighting them away from our shores?

Reverend Miyamoto:

> I am living in America, and my children are here, and I would certainly help America, but it is very painful for me to think that we would have to work against the Japanese here.

The board persisted:

> Would you or would you not help fight them from our shores, yes, or no?

Reverend Miyamoto:

> I am a Buddhist, and as such, we want peace. In that case I would help America.[24]

The board excused Reverend Miyamoto and called Mr. John H. Midkiff as a witness. Midkiff testified that he had known Reverend Miyamoto for about eighteen years and was familiar with Reverend Miyamoto's activities as a teacher and Buddhist priest as he serviced a school near Midkiff's plantation. Midkiff testified that he never had any reason to question Reverend Miyamoto's loyalty to the United States. Midkiff detailed how he had meetings with leaders in the Japanese community several months prior to the outbreak of war to discuss the escalating situation between the United States and Japan and the things that he and the FBI thought the Japanese community should do in order to put themselves in the right position should war break out. Reverend Miyamoto was one of those leaders. Midkiff further described how the messages he asked the leaders to relay to the Japanese community were shared as he instructed. Additionally, Midkiff referenced an event held in March 1941 for the selectees called into service from the community.

Reverend Miyamoto addressed the crowd at the event, and Midkiff wanted to read the speech that Reverend Miyamoto gave to the selectees. Midkiff (reading from a speech transcript):

> We, the first generation, are very envious of you young men. (This is to the draftees who were going away). Although we have lived here and tried to assimilate the American ways, and enjoyed every protection of your country, we cannot become American citizens. We deplore this fact very much.
>
> You young Americans, by your birth right are Americans, and it is your solemn duty to preserve, protect and defend your country, the United States of America, against any encroachment, and it is your right to do this. Needless to say, in the performance of your duties it may be necessary to make a great sacrifice; may be necessary to lay down your lives to accomplish this.
>
> It is our sincerest desire that you do this un-hesitatingly and willingly. It is your sacred duty to take and protect these United States whose principles and ideals are embodied in the Constitution of the United States of America, as represented by your flag, with the stars and stripes.[25]

Asked if this speech represented Reverend Miyamoto's composition, Midkiff replied that he believed it did and that he found no one within the Waialua community that had any reason to feel that it did not represent Reverend Miyamoto's ideals.

Midkiff also informed the board that Reverend Miyamoto had rescinded his role as a consular agent prior to the outbreak of war as he recognized the relationship between Japan and the United States was declining rapidly. Midkiff agreed to be responsible for Reverend Miyamoto if he was paroled and felt that he could be a help as a leader within the community and that he could be relied upon.

Midkiff was excused. The investigative portion of the case was closed, and the board deliberated. The board listed six findings:

1. That Buntetsu Miyamoto is an alien, born in Japan; resident in Hawaii since 1915.
2. The internee states that he is loyal to the United States, and reliable statements and testimony showed nothing to the contrary.
3. The internee has acted as a consular agent, stating that his activities consisted of reporting vital statistics.
4. No information was presented connecting this internee with subversive activities.
5. Reliable testimony indicated that the internee had advocated loyalty and service to the United States, on the part of Americans born of Japanese ancestry.
6. The internee has taken no steps toward the expatriation of his own children, leaving that entirely to their own initiative.[26]

The board's recommendations followed the findings. It was recommended by the majority that Reverend Miyamoto be released on parole to Mr. John Midkiff's custody. One board member dissented and felt that Reverend Miyamoto should be interned for the duration of the war. With the recommendation of the Hearing Board complete, the board adjourned at 11:50 a.m. on January 14, 1942. The process to decide the fate of Reverend Miyamoto took the board just fifty minutes from start to finish that day.

Even though the board made its recommendation, it wouldn't be until February 26, 1942, that Reverend Miyamoto's fate would ultimately be decided. A second panel composed of FBI, Military Intelligence (G-2 Section of the Hawaiian Department), and the Office of Naval Intelligence representatives reviewed the Hearing Board's recommendation. Oftentimes, this second panel overruled the Hearing Board's recommendation for parole or release which meant continued internment.[27] On February 26, 1942, the Intelligence Bureaus submitted their opinion of Reverend Miyamoto's case. The Intelligence Bureau Board did not concur with the Hearing Board. Internment for the duration of the war was recommended. For men like Reverend Miyamoto who were detained due to their participation in certain religious, social, or community organizations, proving their innocence and loyalty was almost impossible. The government declared involvement in these organizations as dangerous and that point could not be disputed.[28]

The next day, February 27, 1942, Reverend Miyamoto was processed into the enemy alien internment system. He was assigned a number: ISN-HJ-131-CI.[29] With this number, he ceased to be Reverend Buntetsu Miyamoto and no longer had a name. This number was his identification. As one internee recalled, "As long as I have a name, I can feel confident, but when it is changed to a number—well, no good can come of it."[30]

With no idea of what was to happen next, Reverend Miyamoto waited at Sand Island for approximately a week and a half before being put on the second transfer boat that would deliver him to the mainland. The second transfer boat departed on March 19, 1942, carrying 166 men and set course for California.[31]

十日あまり空を仰がず海を見ず恨めしきかな牢獄の船　　　　　　ろせい

Over ten days
without seeing sky
nor sea
imprisoned on this ship
I am bitter

Rosei[32]

The journey by the *Grant* military ship to the mainland tested the internees. Kept in the hold in the bow of the ship, in quarters converted into prisoner cells, as many as fourteen men could be forced to share one cabin hold.[33] The men were only permitted to use the restroom once every three hours as they remained behind locked doors the remainder of the time. When allowed to have a restroom break, the lines formed instantly and were long. The men used garbage cans placed in the hallway to urinate into.[34]

Once the men made it to the mainland, they would be shuffled around the United States during their period of internment and never really knew why or when they would be moved. The constant movement of men from one camp to the next served many purposes, but official reasons for transfer were vague. Governmental memos stated, "Such transfer may be made to preserve the health of the internees, to maintain discipline, and to make better use of an internee's talents."[35] Probable unofficial reasons for transfers included keeping internees occupied with the moving and adjustments to new environments and making internee socialization and attachments with guards or personnel difficult. Additionally, camps often became crowded or needed to close or other administrative reasons caused the internees to be moved.[36]

Fort McDowell, California:

March 30, 1942, to April 6, 1942

Fort McDowell was an Army post located on the east side of Angel Island, a 740-acre island in the middle of San Francisco Bay. Originally opened in 1910 as an immigration station, Angel Island served as the primary processing center for all Asian immigrants entering the United States. Known as the "Ellis Island of the West," Angel Island detained an estimated 175,000 Chinese and 60,000 Japanese immigrants under oppressive conditions between 1910 and 1940.[37] When the Hawai'i internees arrived at Angel Island, they were relieved to finally be able to breathe fresh air after their eight-day journey locked inside ship cabins. While at Fort McDowell, the men exercised and were able to walk outside and could see the Bay Bridge and towns across the water. One internee recalled seeing poems carved by Chinese immigrants detained at Angel Island during its days as an immigration station. He recounted one of the poems:

A thousand sorrows and a hatred ten-thousand-fold burns between
    my brows.
Hoping to step ashore the American continent is the most difficult of
    difficulties.
The barbarians imprison me in this place.
Even a martyr or hero would change countenance.[38]

Internees spent little time here as the facility functioned primarily as a processing center that would check-in internees for their mainland detention camps. On April 6, 1942, 167 men boarded a Southern Pacific Line train that would travel 2,000 miles to Lawton, Oklahoma.[39] The train windows were stained black, and the glass had wire mesh in it so that the internees could not see out of the windows. The train was slow, and one internee recalled the "koton koton" noise the train made all the way to Oklahoma.[40]

Fort Sill, Oklahoma:
April 9, 1942, to May 29, 1942

The men reached Lawton, Oklahoma, on April 9, 1942. Upon arrival at Fort Sill, internees prepared for a medical check. Gathered in a makeshift clinic, the internees were stripped naked and told to hold out their chests on which a number was written in red ink. Ozaki, an internee transferred to Fort Sill in the same group as Reverend Miyamoto, recalled having the number written upon his body.

> An overwhelming sense of anger came over me. Large numerals written directly on my skin in red as though I am an animal—how can a civilized country like America do such a thing? It made me feel very sad.[41]

"Here at Fort Sill, Oklahoma, where glittering heat waves rise and peak as far as the eye can see" internees struggled with see-sawing environmental conditions as well as contended with the psychological toll of internment.[42] Harsh and fast-changing conditions marked Fort Sill. One internee described the environment stating:

> There is not a tree to be seen. Tents stand in rows. The heat. As though the wind is dead. Just as a breeze brings cooling relief, dust clouds cover the entire desert in a spectacular display and a sandstorm sweeps over the land. Everything disappears in a dense, shroud-like fog. When I lick my lips, I can feel the particles of sand. In time, the sandstorm moves on and crisscrossing flashes of lightning race across the entire sky like a whip rope.[43]

Internees would pick stones and rocks along the barbed wire fence in order to have some type of activity to relieve their boredom. Kaetsu Furuya remembered the guards watching from the watchtowers that loomed over the men, and he likened them to the "kind they use for 'bon odori.'"[44] The watchtowers were reminiscent of the central tower called a *yagura* that was used during the bon odori ceremony. The *yagura* was a symbol of celebration of life and a source of connection to family and community. The watchtower, manned with guards and guns, turned a symbol of religious, cultural, and community strength and joy into a menacing tower from which one's life could end in an instant.

Being removed from their families with little to no news about their well-being or news of the outside world created negative emotions within many of the internees.

> We become irritable. Eat. Sleep. Wake up. Eat. Sleep. Wake up. A life cut off from everything in the world. The unbearable monotony of a life without variation seems to slowly warp our minds. The crazy weather and tent life—one cannot help but begin to lose one's mind.[45]

The term "barbed wire disease" became used to describe the loss of sanity and purpose due to confinement, boredom, and monotony experienced within the internment camps.[46]

On the morning of May 12, 1942, internee Kanesaburo Oshima was shot dead by guards who claimed he was trying to escape.[47] An internee from Hawai'i recounted the horrific event:

> Mr. Oshima suddenly started to climb up the wired fence at the left side of the camp's main entrance. Fellow internees at the scene tried to pull him down. But, he climbed so fast and they could not catch him. He jumped down on the other side of the fence that was about ten feet high. A guard on duty standing nearby ordered him to stop, but he started running away southward. The guard chased him with a pistol in his hand. Watching the guard chase him, fellow internees ran together with the guard along the fence, shouting, "Don't shoot! He is insane." The guard seemed to be slightly hesitant, but he tried to shoot Mr. Oshima two or three times. Bullets did not hit him. Mr. Oshima, horrified by the sound of pistol, ran toward the foot of a guardpost tower where machine guns were positioned thereupon. He started to climb the barbed wire and reached the top of the fence, then he stopped there for awhile. At that moment, a guard who came running shot Mr. Oshima from the back. Unfortunately, one bullet got through his head. He fell down on his back. Mr. Oshima died on the spot.[48]

Oshima succumbed to the despair that a life of confinement, uncertainty, and worry was feared to bring about within the men. Oshima, fifty-eight years old, was arrested as an agent of the Japanese consulate and left behind his wife and eleven children and multiple business responsibilities in Kona, on the Big Island, where he had lived for over forty years. The internees were overcome with indignation over the incident. Seven hundred internees attended the funeral held for Oshima, and the internees vowed:

> We have every intention of having the Spanish consul, who represents the Japanese government, make restitution to Mr. Oshima's family. We are determined

to pursue this course and will not be deterred with any splendid funeral arranged by the authorities.[49]

Oshima was the first death experienced in this internee group.

Shortly after Oshima's cruel death, rumblings began to spread among the internees that they would be moved yet again. The prospect of leaving the hostile environs of Fort Sill behind for an unknown location was, at once, both comforting and unsettling. Unable to control their own fate, the men didn't dare to imagine where they would be sent next. Instead, thoughts of their families and the outside world consumed their daydreams allowing them momentary respite from their feelings of being lost in a perpetual state of limbo. The men could only guess at the reality that existed beyond their barbed wire confines.

NOTES

1. John A. Burns, Transcript of an oral history conducted in 1975 by Paul Hooper (Tape 4), in *John A. Burns Oral History Project, 1975–1976*, Hawn Collection, University of Hawai'i at Mānoa Library.

2. John A. Burns, Transcript of an oral history conducted in 1975 by Paul Hooper (Tape 4), in *John A. Burns Oral History Project, 1975–1976*, Hawn Collection, University of Hawai'i at Mānoa Library.

3. Yasutaro Soga's memoir detailed that Reverend Miyamoto was brought in with Ryuten Kashiwa and Takegoro Kusao. Ryuten Kashiwa was the priest of Waialua Hongwanji Mission. Takegoro Kusao was the Bureau Chief, West Oahu, *Nippu Jiji* newspaper.

4. Yasutaro Soga, *Life Behind Barbed Wire* (Honolulu, HI: University of Hawai'i Press, 2008), 27.

5. Miyamoto, *Hawaii*, 306.

6. In the early days of World War II, the United States and Japan came to an agreement in which officials and civilians of each respective nation, caught behind enemy lines, could be exchanged or repatriated to their country of birth. Neutral countries in the conflict acted as emissaries or Protectorate Powers for each country. In the case of Japan, Spain acted in the interests of Japanese on the U.S. mainland while Sweden was tasked with overseeing the interests of Japanese in Hawai'i. The U.S. government began asking those imprisoned as enemy aliens if they were interested in repatriation, and eventually even those held in the WRA camps would be surveyed. From letters we have found between men and their families, this was a question not taken lightly. It left some feeling torn, while others were eager to be repatriated. For some that had been separated from their families with no reunion in sight, repatriation seemed a solution if the family could be repatriated to Japan as well, despite many of their children being American citizens because of their place of birth. Despite many Japanese Issei willing to return to Japan, the United States felt that it did not

have enough for reciprocal exchanges. Their solution to this issue was to negotiate the removal (it was more akin to kidnapping) of over 2,000 Japanese living in Latin America that were then brought to the United States and kept in camps run by the Immigration and Naturalization Service to "expand the hostage pool." (Evelyn Iritani, "The Gripsholm WWII Exchanges," *Densho Encyclopedia*, August 24, 2020, https://encyclopedia.densho.org/The_Gripsholm_WWII_Exchanges/).

7. Suikei Furuya, *An Internment Odyssey: Haisho Tenten* (Honolulu, HI: Japanese Cultural Center of Hawai'i, 2017), 11.

8. Furuya, *An Internment Odyssey,* 31.

9. Alan Rosenfeld, "Sand Island (Detention Facility)," *Densho Encyclopedia*, https://encyclopedia.densho.org/Sand%20Island%20(detention%20facility)/ (accessed November 17, 2019).

10. Rosenfeld, "Sand Island (Detention Facility)."

11. Miyamoto, "Memories of Sand Island."

12. Miyamoto, "Memories of Sand Island."

13. Miyamoto, "Memories of Sand Island."

14. Miyamoto, "Memories of Sand Island."

15. Miyamoto, "Memories of Sand Island."

16. Clifford Miyamoto, summary of oral history conducted by Melvin Inamasu and Marilyn Higashide on January 19, 2015, Voice of Internment Project, Japanese Cultural Center Hawai'i, Honolulu, HI.

17. "Chapter V, Collection and Custody of Enemy Aliens," History of Provost Marshall Office, Part 2; Japanese Internment and Relocation Files, The Hawai'i Experience, University of Hawai'i at Mānoa Libraries.

18. Miyamoto, "Memories of Sand Island."

19. Miyamoto's hearing transcript has his date of arrival to Hawai'i as July 9, 1915. His internment file and alien registration file, however, list his arrival date as July 19, 1915.

20. Buntetsu Miyamoto, Record of the Hearings of a Board of Officers and Civilians, December 19, 1941, RG 389, National Archives at College Park, Maryland.

21. Miyamoto, "Memories of Sand Island."

22. Bro. John Henry Grote, SM taught in Japan from 1916 to 1931, spending 1921 to 1931 at Bright Star Commercial School in Osaka, Japan. He was later assigned to St. Louis College in Honolulu from 1934 to 1945. Facilities at this school were converted into an Army Hospital after the attack on Pearl Harbor in 1941. According to an account of his life written by a fellow Marianist, Bro. Grote spoke fluent English, French, and Japanese. Courtesy of the National Archives of the Marianist Province of the United States.

23. Eugene Paulin and Joseph Becker, *New Wars: The History of the Brothers of Mary (Marianists) in Hawaii, 1883–1958* (Milwaukee: Catholic Life Publications and Bruce Press, 1959), 115.

24. Buntetsu Miyamoto, Record of the Hearings of a Board of Officers and Civilians, December 19, 1941, RG 389, National Archives at College Park, Maryland.

25. Buntetsu Miyamoto, Record of the Hearings of a Board of Officers and Civilians, December 19, 1941, RG 389, National Archives at College Park, Maryland.

26. Buntetsu Miyamoto, Record of the Hearings of a Board of Officers and Civilians, December 19, 1941, RG 389, National Archives at College Park, Maryland.

27. Rosenfeld, "Sand Island (Detention Facility)."

28. Kashima, *Judgment Without Trial,* 59.

29. Each component of the internment number had a specific meaning. ISN stood for internment serial number. HJ denoted a Hawaiian Japanese. The numeral was the consecutive internment number. CI meant that the person was a civilian internee.

30. Gail Honda, ed., *Family Torn Apart: The Internment Story of the Otokichi Muin Ozaki Family* (Honolulu: Japanese Cultural Center of Hawai'i, 2012), 46.

31. Soga, *Life Behind Barbed Wire,* 226.

32. Original Writing 4th Poetry Reading and Critique Session, August 1942, held in Camp Livingston, AR1, Box 9, Folder 15, Ozaki Collection, Japanese Cultural Center of Hawai'i. All translations and notes on translations of poems from the 4th Poetry Reading are courtesy of the Japanese Cultural Center of Hawai'i volunteer: Yoko Waki, with volunteers Jean Toyama, Florence Sugimoto, and Sheila Chun.

33. Furuya, *An Internment Odyssey,* 45.

34. Furuya, *An Internment Odyssey,* 44–45.

35. Quoted in Kashima, *Judgment Without Trial,* 114.

36. Kashima, *Judgment Without Trial,* 114–115.

37. J. Wallenfeldt, "Angel Island Immigration Station," *Encyclopedia Britannica,* https://www.britannica.com/topic/Angel-Island-Immigration-Station (accessed August 7, 2022).

38. Furuya, *An Internment Odyssey,* 53.

39. Honda, *Family Torn Apart,* 46–47.

40. Kaetsu Furuya, Japanese Internment and Relocation Files, The Hawai'i Experience, Box 4, Folder 233 University of Hawai'i at Mānoa Libraries.

41. Honda, *Family Torn Apart,* 47.

42. Honda, *Family Torn Apart,* 66.

43. Honda, *Family Torn Apart,* 66.

44. Kaetsu Furuya, Japanese Internment and Relocation Files, The Hawai'i Experience, Box 4, Folder 233 University of Hawai'i at Mānoa Libraries.

45. Honda, *Family Torn Apart,* 66.

46. Gail Y. Okawa, "Putting Their Lives on the Line: Personal Narrative as Political Discourse among Japanese Petitioners in American World War II Internment," *College English* 74, no. 1 (September 2011): 56. See also: A.L. Vischer, *Barbed Wire Disease: A Psychological Study of the Prisoner of War* (London: John Bale, Sons and Danielsson, Ltd., 1919).

47. Tetsuden Kashima, "Homicide in Camp," *Densho Encyclopedia,* https://encyclopedia.densho.org/Homicide%20in%20camp/ (accessed November 18, 2019).

48. "'A' Death of Mister Oshima," Radio Script, June 3, 1950; Otokichi Ozaki collection, Japanese Culture Center of Hawai'i.

49. Honda, *Family Torn Apart,* 69.

Chapter 12

Let Photographs Tell the Story

Reverend Miyamoto was not the only resident alien in his family to be classified as an enemy alien, though the consequences of this classification for his Louisiana cousin would be much less dire.[1] Within the first week of the attack on Pearl Harbor, there were already six names of Japanese aliens residing in Louisiana on the Custodial Detention List that had been identified for immediate arrest and internment.[2] Mrs. Saki Kohara was not one of these six. Despite this, she was still considered an enemy alien by the happenstance of her birth in Japan. And so, on December 9, 1941, the Kohara Photography Studio was closed for investigation by the FBI and the Treasury Department.[3] Alexandria chief of police, George Gray, received a telephone call from the Treasury Department with orders to close the studio so Treasury Department agents could investigate the studio's finances due to the federal regulation freezing all Japanese assets in the country. In addition to closing the studio, city police were posted at both the studio and the Kohara family home. Sammy Kohara, the oldest son at only twenty-six years old, had just taken the helm of the family business due to his father's recent passing, and he worked tirelessly with the agents to facilitate their investigation. The investigation made headlines in the local newspaper, the *Alexandria Daily Town Talk*. In the article announcing the studio's temporary closure to the community, Sammy made it clear that this closure and investigation had come during the studio's busiest season and asked that customers please be patient. Sammy stressed that all Christmas orders would be processed in earnest as soon as the studio was cleared. Showing a surprising amount of support for the family given the general anti-Japanese sentiment that had reached fever pitch around the rest of the country, the newspaper article went on to emphasize that all the Kohara children were U.S. citizens, practicing Christians, and none of the children spoke Japanese. None of the family were removed from their home and detained, but they did stay under house arrest during the investigation.[4]

Marion, the youngest Kohara child and a teenager during that time, recalled her family being put under house arrest.

> Right after Pearl Harbor, the FBI put our family under house arrest because my mother wasn't a citizen, and at that time, they weren't allowed to become citizens . . . I can remember the sheriff apologizing to my mother for having to put her under house arrest . . . he said, "The FBI is making me do it and I have to do it. So sorry about that, Mrs. Kohara." But he was very nice about it. Most of the people that I came into contact with were. They treated me like we treated the Italians and Germans, who were in the same position but weren't being relocated.[5]

Mrs. Kohara, still grieving the loss of her husband, remained stoic in the face of the investigation and took the process in stride.

The family matriarch also recounted the FBI investigation.

> Because we were a photo shop, the FBI must have thought that we had files of secret photographs. They ferreted through every negative and every scrap of paper at the store and at our house but did not find anything in the way of contraband. Our shop was closed about a week or so and that was the end of the investigation.[6]

In a story passed down through the family, it was told that Mrs. Kohara directed the FBI and Treasury agents as they examined every piece of paper. She told them which pieces of paper to throw away and which to keep as they were going through the house—effectively having the agents clean her entire home for her.[7] Marion vividly remembered the two FBI agents who stayed at the Kohara home during the investigation who played poker with her two older brothers and would send her next door to the drugstore for ice cream.[8] The FBI agents quickly realized that the Kohara family was sending two kids to college, one to medical school, and no money was being sent to Japan.[9] On December 20, 1941, the investigation was completed, and the studio reopened with no evidence of wrongdoing found.[10]

Following the results of the investigation, the *Daily Town Talk* ran a story touting the "American-ness" of the Kohara family on January 13, 1942 (see figure 5). The article opened by stating that all the Kohara children were American citizens, and none of them had traveled outside of the United States. After listing the places of birth of the Kohara children, the article noted, "This makes them pretty good American citizens, and if you will just visit the Kohara Studio and talk with them a few minutes you will realize they are as thoroughly American as one whose forefathers landed at Plymouth Rock."[11] The article stated that during the investigation of the studio and the family "not one shadow of doubt regarding their patriotism was found."[12] Further driving home their "American-ness," the article remarked that:

> the forefathers of all persons, except those of Indian descent, now living in this nation came from some country across the sea, so did those of the Kohara children, but the sons and daughters have the same patriotic feeling toward the United States as do all who were born here and glory in a democratic nation.[13]

This stance taken by the local paper was one of great support for a minority family within their midst. It turned a blind eye to the more widely held ideals that permeated much of the United States that equated "Americanism" with a White Anglo-Saxon Protestant ideal.

With the support of community members and the threat of internment removed, the Kohara family continued to operate their photography studio as normal. Despite the prohibition against resident enemy aliens owning or operating cameras,[14] they even provided photography services to the surrounding Army camps. In fact, the studio became so busy with work at this time that twenty employees worked to fulfill all the orders.[15] They were also able to freely visit two nearby War Relocation Authority incarceration camps in Arkansas: Jerome and Rohwer. According to Marion, visits to these incarceration camps, which were not uncommon, were viewed as social outings. Given their isolation as the sole Japanese family in the center of the state, the ability to travel a few hours to socialize with other Japanese was a rare and welcome opportunity for the Kohara family. For Marion, she could interact with other Japanese children for the first time. For her mother, Saki, it was an opportunity to speak Japanese.

A mere twelve miles away from the Kohara home in Alexandria, Camp Livingston operated as a bustling Army base. Central Louisiana was a confluence of military activity at that time with several military installations operational. Because of the Koharas' proximity to Camp Livingston and the fact that they were the sole Japanese family in the area, the Kohara family quickly became known throughout various Nikkei communities. The first person to stay at the Kohara family home was a young woman who was attending college in Chicago. She attempted to get a hotel reservation in Alexandria, but there was not a room to be had in the city due to all the individuals who had descended upon Alexandria for military-related business. Desperate to find accommodations, the young woman wrote to the Alexandria Chamber of Commerce seeking guidance. Someone there, knowing the Kohara family, gave the woman the family's address, and she wrote a letter to Mrs. Kohara to ask if the family could provide accommodations. The answer was swift, and the family welcomed her into their home. From that point forward, the Kohara address became a stopping point for numerous Nikkei who were visiting loved ones held at Camp Livingston and the two nearby War Relocation Authority camps in Arkansas.

In a 1949 *Pacific Citizen* article, the author interviewed Mrs. Kohara and mentioned the visitors the Koharas hosted.

> During the war years, the Koharas of Alexandria served as a one-family USO for which many Nisei were ever grateful. There were times when as many as a dozen trainees stayed at the Kohara home over the week-ends. Some slept on the floor, ate off the mantle, all enjoying their brief furloughs which reminded them of "back home."[16]

While many Nisei GI soldiers stayed at the Kohara home during furlough, the Kohara family also housed individuals visiting Japanese men held in Camp Livingston's enemy alien internment camp. Marion remembered:

> I didn't really think too much about it, but evidently, it did not have a big population of prisoners, although there were several because besides my father's first cousin, we had at one time a young man who brought four ladies there to visit their husbands. They were from another camp out west somewhere and they hired this young man, who was also an internee, to escort them because they didn't speak English well enough. But those are the only people that I know of personally. There were some more who were visited by people from the Arkansas camps.[17]

Mrs. Kohara explained to Marion why these men were being held at Camp Livingston.

> At the time, I didn't really understand why they were visiting Camp Livingston. But my mother told me that they had some Japanese prisoners, she referred to them, there who were considered a threat or might be considered a threat.[18]

She would discover in conversations with her mother that the family had a personal tie to the camp. The husband of her father's first cousin, Buntetsu Miyamoto, was being held there. Her mother explained that he was a Buddhist priest brought all the way from Hawai'i, although he had been interned at other camps along the way. Marion learned:

> they didn't relocate all the Japanese from the Hawaiian Islands. They just picked certain ones that they considered as leaders who might incite a rebellion or encourage sabotage or spying or something like that. He was just a Buddhist priest.[19]

This was a hard lesson for anyone to learn. The reality of the war had come to Alexandria with the arrival of both servicemen and internees.

The Kohara family's experience during this time is an anomaly and an important representation of another type of Nikkei experience during World War II that is often overlooked. While most only associate Japanese Americans and World War II with the forced removal from the west coast to incarceration camps, there were individuals, like the Koharas, who had to carefully navigate the landscape of the United States at war in a different manner altogether. They remained situated in a strange no-man's-land living mere miles away from a largely unknown internment site of Japanese civilian men, hours away from two family incarceration camps in Arkansas, and yet able to provide services to the Army as well as Japanese individuals affected by the government's policy of internment and incarceration. The Kohara's experience was in stark contrast to the harrowing journey their extended family in Hawai'i were about to embark upon.

NOTES

1. The title for this chapter comes from the advertisements in local newspapers of the Kohara Photo Studio. "Let Photographs Tell the Story" and "Photographs of Distinction" were two of their prominent taglines.

2. Their names were as follows: Tsuneze Haruzana, Zengi Imakura, Ichiziro Kamo, Gange Kugchi, Shiro Metsukawo, and Iwakichi Nakashima. ("Custodial Detention (Arrest Warrants), Japanese 1941," FBI File Number 100-2-60, Section 30, [p. 23], https://www.foitimes.com/internment/Arrest30.pdf).

3. According to J. Edgar Hoover, "From January 28, 1942, to the present time, 25,881 dwellings and premises of alien enemies were searched for prohibited articles by Special Agents of the FBI and cooperating local law enforcement officers." (Hoover, "Alien Enemy Control," 405).

4. "Kohara Studio Closed by U.S. Here," *Weekly Town Talk* (Alexandria, LA), December 13, 1941.

5. Marion Kohara Couvillion, interview with authors, July 12, 2016.

6. Roku Sugahara, "The Koharas of Louisiana: Story of Nisei Family in the South," *Pacific Citizen* (Los Angeles, CA), December 24, 1949.

7. Kohara, "Growing up Asian in Louisiana."

8. Marion Kohara Couvillion, interview with authors, July 12, 2016.

9. Kohara, "Growing up Asian in Louisiana."

10. "Kohara's Studio Open for Business," *Daily Town Talk* (Alexandria, LA), December 20, 1941.

11. "Kohara Studio Operated by Americans," *Alexandria Daily Town Talk* (Alexandria, LA), January 13, 1942.

12. "Kohara Studio Operated by Americans."

13. "Kohara Studio Operated by Americans."

14. Presidential Proclamation 2525.

15. Sugahara,"The Koharas of Louisiana."

16. Sugahara, "The Koharas of Louisiana."
17. Marion Kohara Couvillion, interview with authors, July 12, 2016.
18. Marion Kohara Couvillion, interview with authors, July 12, 2016.
19. Marion Kohara Couvillion, interview with authors, July 12, 2016.

Chapter 13

"Koton, Koton"

After weeks of waiting, the internees at Fort Sill prepared to leave for their next destination, Camp Livingston, located almost 500 miles away near Alexandria, Louisiana.[1] On May 29th around 9:00 a.m., 700 internees lined up in groups of five on the main road of the base, roll was called, and the men gathered their baggage for the three-mile walk to the train station.[2] The day was cool, so the walk to the train was pleasant. The men took seats on the train in alphabetical order for the trip to Louisiana.

As the train pulled away from the station, the familiar sound of the wheels slowly laboring on the tracks—"koton, koton"—began and served as a constant accompaniment to their thoughts. While the act of riding in the train cars was restrictive and dull, the world outside of the cars was expansive and captivating with views stretching out unrestricted for "1000 miles in this Louisiana Territory for days and days."[3] There were no mountains to block their views, and the great expanse of the country was laid out before the eager eyes of the men. Gihachi Yamashita recorded the journey in his journal:

> May 29: I didn't see a single mountain. And in terms of crops even I recognize potato and corn but I couldn't tell what the other crops were. Near Dallas, Texas, see a lot of rice, truly startling. Since this is about rice, we Japanese were very happy. On the way we see Dallas and Fort Worth, even though we were seeing them from inside of the train, [we could tell] they were truly grand.[4]

As the train entered Louisiana, the men noticed the groves of pine. Yamashita recalled:

> There are pine trees on both sides of the railroad tracks, and the train runs through a pine forest. The trees appear to be 15-30 years old and they had grown well. They are from 50-70 feet and like *sugi* pines in Japan.[5]

May 30: At 8:30 in the morning, we arrived in Ft Livingston. Again we lined up in five rows and walked the roughly five-mile road to camp. This day was very hot and the walk was quite difficult. But since all the ill were transported by bus there wasn't a single person among those who walked who had to drop out. We arrived at the camp at 11.[6]

NOTES

1. "Koton, Koton" is how Furuya described the noise of the slow-moving trains that transported internees from camp to camp. (Kaetsu Furuya. Japanese Internment and Relocation Files, The Hawai'i Experience, Box 4, Folder 233 University of Hawai'i at Mānoa Libraries).

2. Yamashita Diary Vol. 1, Japanese American National Museum (Gift of Gihachi and Tsugio Yamashita Family, 94.166.29).

3. Yamashita Diary Vol. 1, Japanese American National Museum (Gift of Gihachi and Tsugio Yamashita Family, 94.166.29).

4. Yamashita Diary Vol. 1, Japanese American National Museum (Gift of Gihachi and Tsugio Yamashita Family, 94.166.29).

5. Yamashita Diary Vol. 1, Japanese American National Museum (Gift of Gihachi and Tsugio Yamashita Family, 94.166.29).

6. Yamashita Diary Vol. 1, Japanese American National Museum (Gift of Gihachi and Tsugio Yamashita Family, 94.166.29).

Figure 1. Miyamoto Family Circa 1930. The photo features Buntetsu and Fumi along with their children: Osamu, eldest son; Terufumi, third son; Taeko, eldest daughter; and Kanji, second son. Hoji Shinbun Digital Collection, Hoover Institution Library & Archives. Photo taken from book titled Dendō kinen yōjō no hikari = Jodo mission of Hawaii.

Figure 2. Kohara Family Circa 1925. Featured from left to right: Kay, Sammy, Jackie, Saki, Manabu, and Tommy. Courtesy of Kohara family.

Figure 3. Kohara Studio in Alexandria, Louisiana. Courtesy of Kohara family.

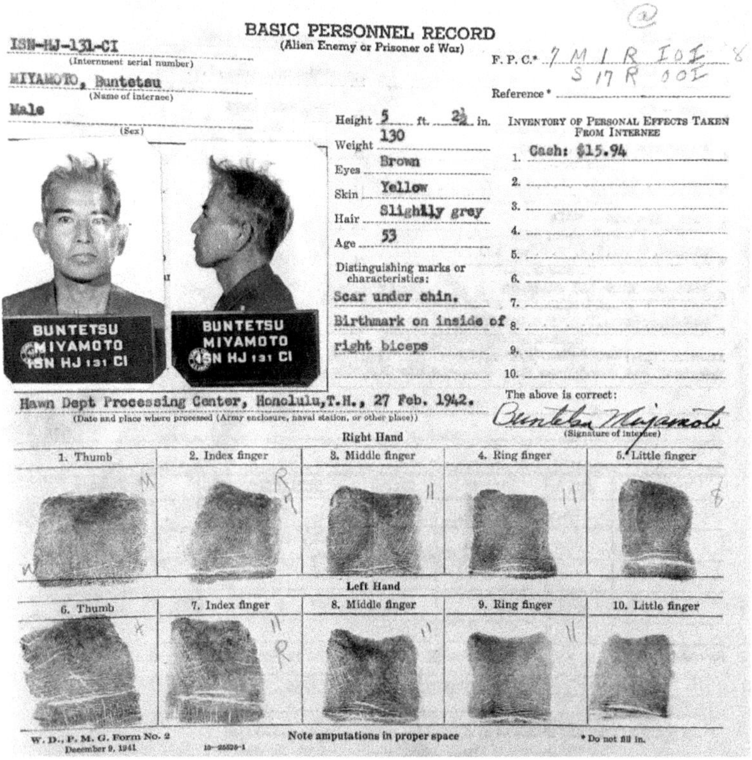

BASIC PERSONNEL RECORD
(Alien Enemy or Prisoner of War)

ISN-HJ-131-CI
(Internment serial number)

MIYAMOTO, Buntetsu
(Name of internee)

Male
(Sex)

F. P. C.* 7 M 1 R IOI 8
S 17 R OOI

Reference *

Height 5 ft. 2½ in.
Weight 130
Eyes Brown
Skin Yellow
Hair Slighlly grey
Age 53
Distinguishing marks or characteristics:
Scar under chin.
Birthmark on inside of
right biceps

INVENTORY OF PERSONAL EFFECTS TAKEN FROM INTERNEE
1. Cash: $15.94
2.
3.
4.
5.
6.
7.
8.
9.
10.

The above is correct:
Buntetsu Miyamoto
(Signature of internee)

Hawn Dept Processing Center, Honolulu, T.H., 27 Feb. 1942.
(Date and place where processed (Army enclosure, naval station, or other place))

Right Hand

1. Thumb	2. Index finger	3. Middle finger	4. Ring finger	5. Little finger

Left Hand

6. Thumb	7. Index finger	8. Middle finger	9. Ring finger	10. Little finger

W. D., P. M. G. Form No. 2
December 9, 1941

Note amputations in proper space

* Do not fill in.

Figure 4. Reverend Miyamoto's Personnel Record, Highlighting His Mugshot, Taken on the Night of His Arrest. Miyamoto FBI File, National Archives at College Park, Maryland.

Figure 5. Kohara Family. First row from left to right: Kay, Saki, Marion. Second row from left to right: Sammy, Jackie, Tommy. Courtesy of Kohara family.

Figure 6. Entrance to Camp Livingston's Enemy Alien Internment Camp. Camp Livingston Construction Completion Report, National Archives at College Park, Maryland.

Figure 7. War 1939–1945. Louisiana, Livingston. Japanese civilian internee camp. Group of internees. Dated: 11/21/1942. ICRC Archives (ARR), Reference V-P-HIST-03413-10.

Figure 8. War 1939–1945. Louisiana, Livingston. General view of Japanese civilian internee camp. Dated: 11/24/1942. ICRC Archives (ARR), Reference V-P-HIST-03390-34A.

Figure 9. War 1939–1945. Louisiana, Livingston. Japanese civilian internee camp. ICRC Archives (ARR), Reference V-P-HIST-03413-30.

Figure 10. War 1939–1945. Louisiana, Livingston. Japanese civilian internee camp. Internees in a vegetable garden. ICRC Archives (ARR), Reference V-P-HIST-03413-11.

Figure 11. War 1939–1945. Louisiana, Livingston. Japanese civilian internment camp building. ICRC Archives (ARR), Reference V-P-HIST-03390-34.

Figure 12. War 1939–1945. Louisiana, Livingston. Buildings of the Japanese civilian internment camp. ICRC Archives (ARR), Reference V-P-HIST-03390-35.

Figure 13. War 1939–1945. Louisiana, Livingston. Japanese civilian internee camp. Clearing land. ICRC Archives (ARR), Reference V-P-HIST-03415-08.

Figure 14. World War II. Livingston. Camp for civilian internees. ICRC Archives (ARR), Reference V-P-HIST-03332-13.

Figure 15. War 1939–1945. Louisiana, Livingston. Japanese civilian internee camp. Sawing wood. ICRC Archives (ARR), Reference V-P-HIST-03415-07.

Figure 16. War 1939–1945. Louisiana, Livingston. Japanese civilian internee camp. Baseball game. ICRC Archives (ARR), Reference V-P-HIST-03412-25.

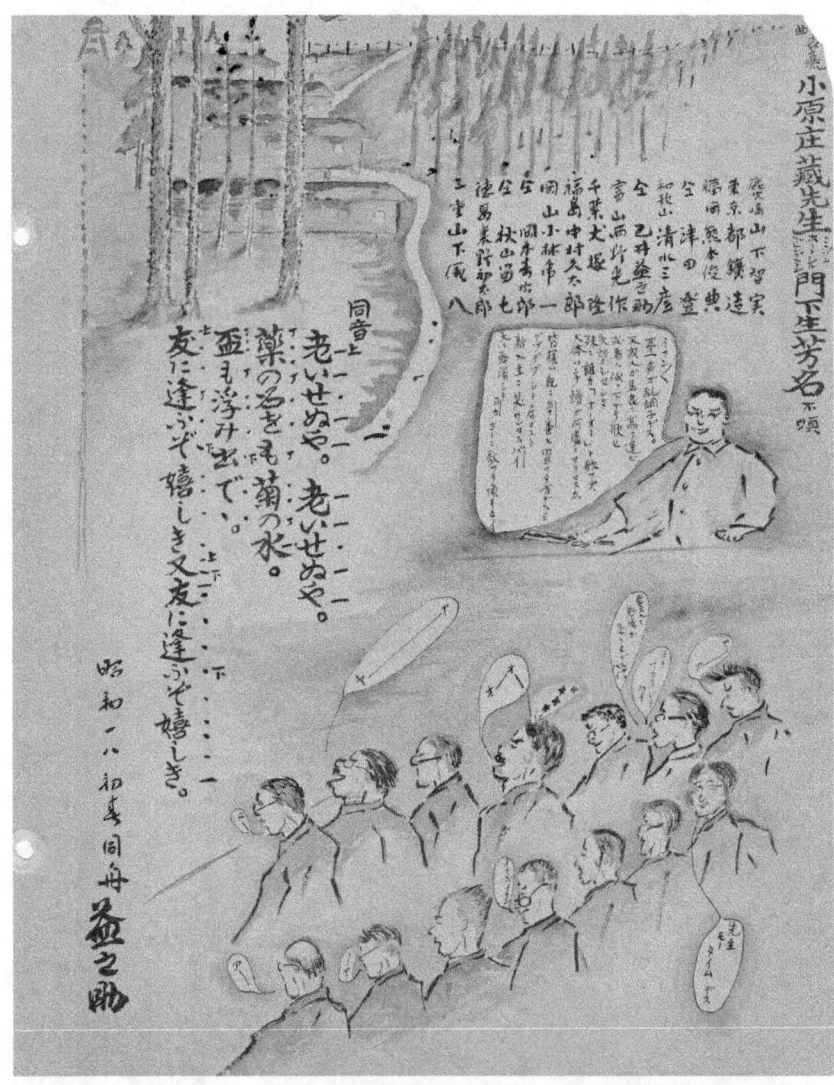

Figure 17. Illustration of *Utai* (Noh Singing) Class, Contributed to Gihachi's Scrapbook by a Classmate, While Both Were Interned at Camp Livingston. Courtesy of Japanese American National Museum (gift of the Gihachi and Tsugio Yamashita Family, 94.166.29).

Figure 18. War 1939–1945. Louisiana, Livingston. Japanese civilian internee camp. The governor and the director of the museum. Dated: 11/1942. ICRC Archives (ARR), Reference V-P-HIST-03412-23.

Figure 19. War 1939–1945. Louisiana, Livingston. Japanese civilian internee camp. Museum objects. ICRC Archives (ARR), Reference V-P-HIST-03412-26.

Figure 20. "Kyampu Ningyo" or Camp Doll. Handcarved nude of Japanese woman standing with arms raised and hands at back of head; her weight is on proper left leg while other leg is bent. Made from a single block of wood. Camp Livingston, Louisiana. Courtesy of Japanese American National Museum (Gift of Ryo Munekata, 2003.82.1a).

Figure 21. War 1939–1945. Louisiana, Livingston. Japanese civilian internee camp. The director of the museum showing a carved cane. Dated: 11/1942. ICRC Archives (ARR), Reference V-P-HIST-03412-22.

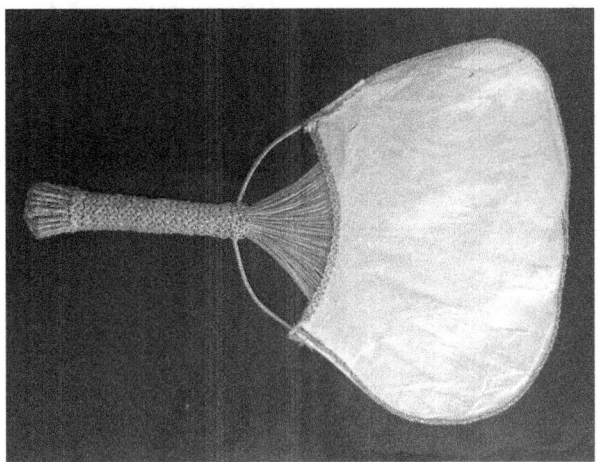

Figure 22. A Surviving Incomplete *Uchiwa* Fan of Reverend Kunio Ohta. This photo illustrates how the long pine needles were used and covered with *hanshi* paper. *Uchiwa* fan made by Reverend Kunio Ohta in Camp Livingston, Louisiana circa 1942/43. Courtesy of Ella Miyeko Tomita, née Ohta.

Figure 23. War 1939–1945. Louisiana, Livingston. Japanese civilian internee camp. Panels at the museum. ICRC Archives (ARR), Reference V-P-HIST-03412-27.

Figure 24. Christmas Card Designed by a Camp Livingston Internee. Courtesy of Japanese American National Museum (Gift of Gihachi and Tsugio Yamashita Family, 94.166.164).

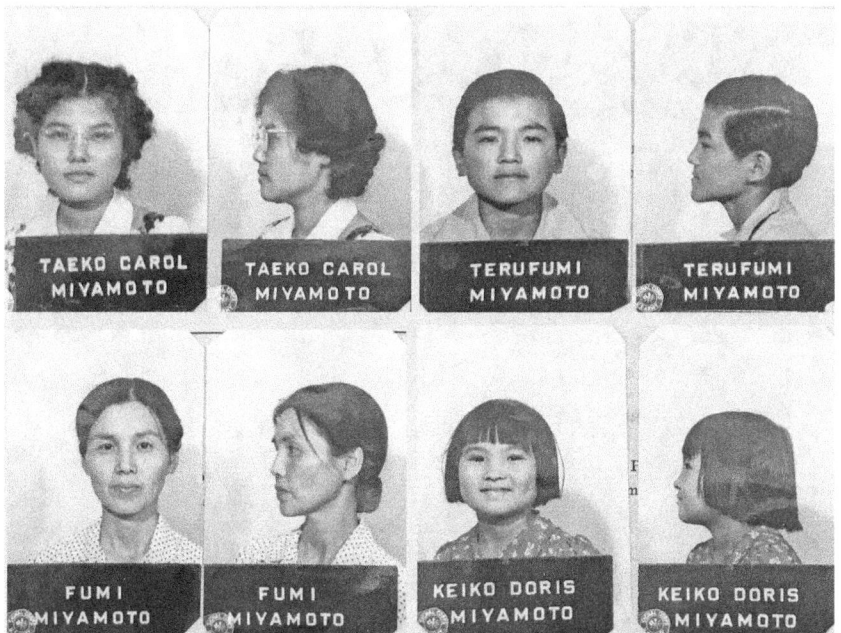

Figure 25. Mugshots Taken of Fumi, Carol, Clifford, and Keiko Before They Set Sail on the SS *Republic* Bound for the Mainland. Miyamoto FBI File, National Archives at College Park, Maryland.

Figure 26. Carol, Fumi, Clifford, and Keiko at the Grove Park Inn in Asheville, North Carolina. Courtesy of Miyamoto family.

Figure 27. Fumi and Carol's Visit to Alexandria, Louisiana, in 1945. Courtesy of the Kohara family.

Figure 28. Among the 910 Hawaii Residents, Who Returned from Mainland Relocation Camps Were Terufumi and Carol Miyamoto of Waialua, Oahu. Typical of the job of family reunions was this scene when David embraced his sister, Carol, at the wharf, while brother Terufumi looks on. Courtesy of the Hawaii Hochi, Ltd.

Figure 29. Miyamoto Family on the Steps of the Haleʻiwa Jodo Mission. Courtesy of the Miyamoto family.

Figure 30. Archbishop Miyamoto in Japan. Courtesy of Miyamoto family.

Figure 31. Saki Kohara Fishing in Louisiana. Courtesy of Kohara family.

Figure 32. Reverend Kano Returning to Visit Camp Livingston in 1969. © The Town Talk – USA Today.

Part IV

CAMP LIVINGSTON

Chapter 14

Life in Camp Livingston

In this camp among the pine trees
We finally settle down

—Suikei Furuya writing in Camp Livingston (Louisiana)[1]

On May 29, 1942, officers of the medical detachment at Camp Livingston were alerted to the arrival of a train to the Camp Livingston Railroad Station expected the following day. This train was carrying some very intriguing human cargo. Aboard were enemy aliens en route to the internment camp on site. Not all the men on board were in good health, however, and it was instructed that Ward 9 be made available for "three litter patients and a number of others of lesser degree of disability requiring medical care" to be taken to the hospital.[2] Four ambulances were ordered to meet the train to transport the men, each with a Military Policeman and orderly. The next day word spread quickly of their arrival, and as the Ward was being prepared to intake their newest patients, two majors stationed at the camp sped to the railway station to see the enemy aliens that everyone was talking about. What they saw was an "unusual sight"—700 Japanese males considered enemy aliens disembarked from the train.[3] "They were all dressed in khaki breeches (dyed green), blue denim jackets and fatigue hats except for a few who wore their own clothing. Most of them were unshaven."[4] The four sick men—two of which had tuberculosis, one recovering from gall bladder surgery, and another with hypertension—were loaded into the ambulances and taken to the waiting staff at Ward 9.[5] The rest of the men were forced to walk five miles to the internment camp that would be their home and prison for the next ten months. Reverend Miyamoto had arrived in Louisiana.

As Reverend Miyamoto and his fellow internees exited the train, they were told to leave their larger suitcases and only carry their smaller luggage with them. Many, however, disregarded this directive, not knowing the distance before them, nor familiar yet with the Louisiana heat. Weighed down by luggage and exhaustion, the men walked two-by-two escorted on all sides by armed military police.[6] Due to the long distance, the men had to take frequent rests in the shade offered by the pine trees that lined the road.[7] Reverend Miyamoto, however, had no larger baggage beyond his Army-issued clothing and toiletries because his personal baggage never made it across the ocean from Hawai'i. Word had spread through Camp Livingston and "Nurses of the hospitals and soldiers idling in camp" all came to see "this strange procession."[8] Many of the bystanders tried to take pictures of the newly arrived prisoners but were thwarted in their efforts by the guards escorting the men to their camp.[9]

> Baggage hanging over our shoulders
> We trudge toward summer clouds
>
> —Suikei Furuya[10]

As Reverend Miyamoto and the internees slowly approached the alien internment camp, they were met by an eleven-foot-tall hog wire fence topped with double arms of barbed wire.[11] They would proceed through two sentry stations, each with an armed guard, and just beyond, they could see it was divided into ten sectors, each enclosed by seven-foot-tall barbed wire fences making each sector double-fenced throughout the camp (see figure 6).[12] Each of these fenced areas contained thirty-four barracks raised off the ground and covered in tar paper.[13] Newly constructed, these barracks were like those found in the main camp that housed the soldiers garrisoned for training. Each barrack held between ten and fifteen men, so each section could hold a little over 500 men at any given time. A familiar sight for the internees by this time—watchtowers with spotlights—could be found inside and outside of the camp; a total of nineteen guard towers loomed over the camp, each manned by military police armed with machine guns.[14] The camp was further divided into four sections—J1, J2, K1, and K2—or the J area and K area. Each section would hold Japanese men from different parts of the world. J area held mostly men from Hawai'i and Panama, while K area held men from the mainland.[15] Reverend Miyamoto was housed in J-2, Barrack 1923 within the Fourth Internment Company.[16] Others would soon follow.

The alien camp was built below an embankment ringed with pines. When constructing this camp, many of the pines had been spared the saw so there was an abundance of pine throughout the grounds of the camp.[17] The pines of Camp Livingston had few branches and were "as straight as telephone poles" with grass like Japanese *kaya* found beneath the pines.[18] The raised barracks, tall pine trees, and long grass underfoot gave the men some respite in the still and merciless heat (see figures 8, 9, 11, and 12). For the men, to be able to "live among these trees, listening to the whirring sound of the leaves" and the thick humidity of the Louisiana summer was reminiscent of Japan.[19] One internee noted that Camp Livingston's setting among the pines was like staying in a "sanitorium or park" and was "quite comfortable."[20] In comparison to the other camps that this internee had been in thus far, Camp Livingston was declared the camp with the "best location," though better amenities were found at Missoula.[21]

The first group of internees to arrive with Reverend Miyamoto had been transferred from Fort Sill, Oklahoma. This first group consisted of 400 men from the mainland, 150 men from Hawai'i, and 160 men from Panama and Costa Rica who had been summarily kidnapped from their homes to be used in a prisoner exchange program between the United States and Japanese governments.[22] A contingent of Japanese nationals from Peru was also held in Camp Livingston. Tensions between the internees from Hawai'i and those from the mainland were common in camp and often resulted from their very different lived experiences. One internee, Masayuki Chikuma from Hawai'i, recalled how the mainland internees would tease the internees from Hawai'i by calling them a *konseki*, meaning very tiny or just a trace, group of men.[23] Chikuma believed that this "trace group" were some of the elites of Hawai'i and important members of the community. He recalled, "People in the outside [in Hawaii] are thankful for your sacrifice . . . that should be of some comfort. I may be *konseki,* but I'm not the only one. There are plenty of Japanese on the outside [in Hawaii]."[24]

For the second group of men who arrived shortly thereafter, they were welcomed into camp by the first contingent with "huge characters *Kwangei* or 'Welcome' written on wrapping paper and there came a tremendous outburst of shouts in unison, *Banzai.*"[25] One of the men in this second group was Reverend Hiram Hisanori Kano,[26] an Episcopalian minister from Nebraska who had been picked up as an enemy alien, along with thousands of others, on December 7, 1941. A fastidious journal keeper, Reverend Kano wrote daily entries about life in the camp.[27] As the Japanese men held in camp were taken from so many varying places—the mainland, Alaska, Hawai'i, Central and South America—Reverend Kano "felt as though [he] was attending a conference of Japanese from the Americas at government expense."[28] Reverend Kano even broke down the group of men into percentages describing age ranges and occupations (see figures 7 and 10). According to his tallies:

> Most (41 percent) were in their fifties; 24 percent were in their sixties; and 14 percent were in their forties . . . The oldest of the internees, Matsuoka-kun from Alaska who came originally from Yamaguichi Prefecture, was eighty.

Most internees were connected with farming—28 percent . . .; 25 percent were businessmen; 15 percent were in fishing; 9 percent had religious careers; and 4 were newspapermen. Among the religious were 77 Buddhist priests, 32 Shinto priests, and 15 Christian pastors. There were 53 instructors of Japanese language schools and 14 medical doctors.[29]

During the roundups of enemy alien men, some Nisei were also arrested in the dragnet that began on December 7th. These men were eventually sorted out of the DOJ/Army camp system and either allowed to return to Hawai'i or sent into the War Relocation Authority family incarceration camps. On August 1, 1942, Reverend Kano noted that the internees hosted a farewell party in honor of eighteen interned Nisei who were leaving the camp on August 3rd by order probably to head to Sand Island and back to Honolulu.

INTERACTIONS WITH GUARDS AND MEN STATIONED AT LIVINGSTON

The military personnel who oversaw the internee camp included the 251st and 252nd Military Police (MP) Companies as well as the 304th, 327th, and 328th Military Police Escort Companies.[30] They were tasked with assuring adherence to the provisions laid out in the Geneva Convention relative to the Treatment of Prisoners of War (POWs) (1929) regarding the treatment of the internees and POWs being held in the internment camp at Livingston. The first to oversee the camp was Colonel John Dunn, a Brooklynite, whose initial assignment at Camp Livingston had been as Camp Inspector in January 1942 but was soon appointed Commanding Officer of the Alien Camp on May 16th—just two weeks before the arrival of the first group of men.[31] Dunn served as Commanding Officer until early 1943 when the post was taken over by Colonel Weaver. Weaver was a man torn. He lost his brother when the Japanese sunk the USS *Astoria,* but he also remembered his brother's love for the "land of cherry blossoms" and the "fine treatment" his brother received from the Japanese people before the war broke out when he and the men of the *Astoria* returned the body of Ambassador Saito home to Japan.[32] Weaver told the men in camp:

> I cannot like the Japan that caused the death of my brother, but I would not forget the things he said about your country and people. You can rest assured that I will do my duty as the commander of this camp to the best of my ability.[33]

The MPs at Camp Livingston had their own recreation hall called "Kindergarten Inn," held holiday dances and dinners, and most of all, had freedom of movement and choice.³⁴ They could leave camp and its barbed wire fences behind them, unlike the men held inside.

> ガードは親しく吾に語らへどあな腹立たし敵兵彼は
> The guard talks to me
> So friendly
> How maddening
> that he is a soldier
> of the enemy³⁵

Interactions with the Army guards and camp commanders were a routine part of life for the internees. In fact, the internees elected men to serve as their representatives and leaders who could bring various issues, complaints, and wants to the attention of the camp commanders, Spanish Embassy officials, and the Red Cross. Although Colonels Dunn and Weaver were remembered fondly in the memoirs of Japanese internees at Camp Livingston, some of the men entrusted with guarding the internees viewed them as nothing more than "Japs." The letters of Richard K. Leary, a POW Escort Guard for the Eighth Corps, speak to this attitude. Leary wrote numerous letters home to his wife in Laconia, New Hampshire, about his time in Camp Livingston. In one letter dated April 30, 1943, he wrote that they had been "on the alert" because civilians from the nearby town had come near camp and "were going to try to kill these Japs." But in the end, "they didn't try."³⁶ He also requisitioned gifts for his wife that were crafted by the men in camp which he called "Jap trinkets"—a pocketbook and a hand-painted pair of shoes.³⁷ One of the men making the pocketbook was in and out of the alien internment hospital which Leary lamented in two letters dated April 10 and 16, 1943. Leary himself had to take the man to the hospital at one point on account of his failing eyesight.³⁸ For Leary, the worry was not for the man, but rather for when the pocketbook would be completed.

Many of the men in the camp did not speak English, or they did not speak English well. Others, like the Panamanians, only spoke Japanese and Spanish.³⁹ In order to facilitate communication between the Japanese internees and those guarding them, enlisted Nisei men, like William Oshita, who were serving in the Army in different capacities, were tapped to also act as translators. Oshita, and others like him, had background checks done on their service and personal history, and all that served in this position were marked as "character excellent."⁴⁰ The men they were translating for were the same ages as their fathers and grandfathers, and this was possibly something they had done previously in civilian life for the older members of their family.

PRISONER OF WAR, NUMBER ONE

Also being held in the alien internment area of Camp Livingston was POW Number One—Kazuo Sakamaki—the man who had piloted one of the midget submarines during the attack on Pearl Harbor. Having washed up on shore after the attack, he was arrested and held in various detention and internment facilities across the country—first at Sand Island on Oahu, then Angel Island in San Francisco Bay. From California, he was put on a train headed for Camp McCoy in Wisconsin, then Camp Forrest in Tullahoma, Tennessee, before reaching Camp Livingston on June 30, 1942.[41] He was held separately from the rest of the men in a "hut near the entrance of the camp," but was allowed to fraternize unguarded during the day with the civilian internees, even attending classes at the internee-run "Internment University."[42] In November, Sakamaki was moved from his hut to another area within the internment camp where he was joined by fifty other Japanese POWs—men captured during the Aleutian Campaign and at the battles of Wake Island and Midway.[43] Three officers, one warrant officer, and thirty-eight seaman, all Japanese Naval POWs, were transferred to Camp Livingston because it was "thought that the facilities at Livingston are better suited to segregate prisoners of the war from the Internees."[44]

Even though separated by barbed wire fences, the POWs still interacted with the internees, especially in cultural matters. Bunyu Fujimura, a Buddhist priest from California, wrote about interacting with the Japanese Imperial Navy POWs during his time as an internee at Camp Livingston. The POWs learned that many of the internees were Buddhist priests and, knowing this, disclosed that they possessed the *ihatsu* or hair of their fallen comrades. The POWs were carrying the *ihatsu* wrapped in pieces of paper but did not feel this showed the proper reverence to their fellow fallen soldiers. To rectify this, they requested that the Buddhist priests assist them in dedicating their *ihatsu* in front of a *butsudan* or Buddhist altar. Not having an altar, however, the priests approached a fellow internee who was teaching sculpture and carving. His name was Nakashima, and he was from Peru. To begin work, Nakashima and his students purified themselves in the shower. Nakashima took on the job of carving the statute of Kwannon Bosatsu. Students created the altar, *rosokudate* (candle holder), *kabin* (flower vase), *koro* (incense burner), and the other implements necessary, including a drawer to hold the *ihatsu*.[45]

LIVING CONDITIONS IN CAMP

For the internees, every day of camp life could be physically and emotionally taxing with its constant undercurrent of loneliness and tedium embedded in their days. In that way, Camp Livingston was not fundamentally different than the other Department of Justice or Army camps in which the men were held. On the door to each hutment were listed the names of the men who were occupying it; however, the guards did not refer to the men by name—only by the number assigned to them at the time of their processing into the internment system.[46] This dehumanizing tactic had been the norm in each camp they had entered.

The structure of a typical day in camp started with reveille around 5:30 a.m. each morning. The men performed their assigned duties within camp such as KP duty, camp maintenance, or authorized outside work. They attended meetings, classes, or visited other barracks. On certain nights, there was a movie shown in the evening, and taps was at 10:00 p.m. every night. One day a week was dedicated to rest, which was usually on a Sunday.

Self-governance among the internees was a constant in each camp where the men were held, and Camp Livingston's environment proved no different. The men were required by the internment camp regulations to select leaders from their respective companies. If the men did not or could not select a leader, the camp or company commanders would appoint an internee to serve as the leader until someone was chosen from within the internee group. Internee company leaders were responsible for overseeing the maintenance and cleanliness of the quarters within their units. The leaders were also utilized in the relay of orders from camp officials to their fellow internees. These internee associations were mini-governmental units within camp that administered their own self-government and liaised between the internees and company and camp commanders as well as to those international organizations that were tasked with overseeing the fair treatment and well-being of the internees. This liaison role extended to requests and complaints of internees as well. Internee leaders were responsible for collecting requests and complaints from their units and presenting those to the company or camp commander as the authorized representatives of the internees.[47] Typical officer roles that needed to be filled included: group leader, assistant group leader, consulting, secretary, detail and supply, office clerk, chief cook, boiler room supervisor, latrine supervisor, recreation, library, sports director, physicians, canteen, and school instructor.[48] In addition to managing the life of the internment camp through the maintenance of duties and overall administration, self-governance within the camp also extended to the resolution of disputes among internees. One such dispute occurred in August of 1942 when a conference was held in Barrack 1925 and 1903 to settle trouble that had arisen in connection with an image of the Buddha that had been carved by Mr. Kusuda. Reverend Kano did not share what the trouble was about exactly, only that through a quick conference among the internees it was resolved, as Reverend Kano never mentioned this trouble again.

The natural environment of Camp Livingston was simultaneously comforting and jarring for the internees. While the pine trees of Camp Livingston and its environs reminded the internees of Japan and conjured happy memories of days gone by, the reality of Louisiana oddities often either fascinated or unsettled the men. The presence of poisonous snakes was noted by the internees. One account detailed how an internee from Maui preserved a coral snake in formalin and showed it to the other internees who were both curious but also fearful of the existence of the poisonous reptiles throughout the camp.[49] Some of the men even made pets of the local wildlife, including a group of men who were able to catch seventeen turtles. These new and "very cute" companions were kept in an area specially constructed for them and fed with worms.[50] When the men went out on nature classes, led by Reverend Kano, the men saw eels with fins that looked like feet, which one internee described as enabling the eels to navigate the shallow creeks and surrounding grass. He described one eel that was caught on their outings as being creepy, quite fat, and more than two feet long.[51] Capturing these eels was a popular pastime as was preserving snakes, spiders, and scorpions. Some of the preserved wildlife was even gifted to the POWs who were held nearby.[52]

> Under the blazing sun
> The camp sleeps
>
> —Suikei Furuya[53]

Intense heat during the days, coupled with suffocating humidity, only led to swarms of mosquitoes in the evenings. The bugs and heat led to fan-making among the internees.[54] Some internees asked their families to send mosquito netting for use "outside of barrack to protect [themselves] from the flies which sting so bad."[55] Reverend Kano recorded temperatures and weather in his journal. In late September 1942, Reverend Kano documented the temperature fluctuation that occurred on a single day. September 23, 1942: 9:00 a.m. 68°; 3:00 p.m. 90°; 8:00 p.m. 80°. Suikei Furuya, a Honolulu store owner, recounted some of the ways the men tried to cope with the intense Louisiana heat. He recalled:

> It was very hot in the barracks and in the pine forest, as well. Someone dug a hole in the ground and found it was more comfortable to be in there, lying down and reading books. I visited the hole and found it to be much cooler indeed. [. . .] These holes were very comfortable—cool in the summer and warm in the winter. Perhaps this is how the gods taught primitive man to protect himself from heat and cold.[56]

Reverend Kano noted one evening in September that he retired to bed at 9:00 p.m. and many of the men were taking naps under the floor because it was cooler than in their beds. It wasn't just heat the men suffered. In the winter months, the temperatures dipped below freezing—a type of cold, which paired with the Louisiana humidity, one feels in their bones. The coldest day in camp, though sunny and bright, bottomed out at 17°. Despite the heat emanating from the firewood they had cut, the men were fighting a losing battle against the cold because of the tar paper that covered the outer walls. Even with the oftentimes extreme and uncomfortable conditions, the internees still found beauty in the environment of the camp. Gihachi Yamashita, an internee from California, recalled "at night you can see lots of fireflies come out of the grass and jump around in the trees—this must be a miracle under heaven."[57]

The internees were issued "renovated" clothing—old G.I. shirts and pants. These uniforms were dyed and marked in white with the internment serial number of the internee across his back, on the outside of the article of clothing, "with letters at least two inches high midway between the shoulders."[58] The dye used on the uniforms caused them to shrink, which meant those that were tall "found it difficult to get wearable clothing."[59] The Quartermaster Corps provided a set of stencils for each company of men in order to keep their clothing marked with their internment serial numbers.[60] Because these uniforms were previously worn and dyed cheaply, the color of the uniforms began to fade on the shoulders and back returning them to the original light brown color. Furuya noted that the general feeling in camp was that the internee's clothing did not look good. Unsatisfied with their appearance, one internee purchased dye and began re-dying his uniform. Soon, the rest of the camp followed. In reference to the men who followed suit and began dyeing their clothes, Furuya wrote:

> In our normal life, most of us had considered it shameful to copy others as monkeys do. Now, behind barbed wire, we tended to be childish. We copied one another and kept an eagle eye on food. Camp life had made us abandon our pride as men.[61]

The men wore wooden shoes, called *geta,* which they fashioned themselves using small tools which were allowed in camp. As the Louisiana summer approached, many of the men took to wearing just a "sport pant and geta" in response to the unrelenting heat and humidity.[62] The popularity of crafting and wearing *geta* in camp provided a tangible link to the men's Japanese culture as well as a quick solution to both the heat and the Army's lag in the production of appropriate footwear.[63]

Even though the Army provided clothing and other essentials, Reverend Miyamoto actively worked to have his personal luggage found and returned to him. Throughout September, October, and November of 1942,

Reverend Miyamoto wrote letters and prompted communications between the various internment centers where he was previously held in order to locate the one piece of luggage he was able to bring when he left Hawai'i. Locating this baggage was especially important to Reverend Miyamoto, since he had received word on September 7, 1942, that his request for repatriation had been approved. He was desperate to have his personal items retrieved before leaving for Japan. Reverend Miyamoto's efforts to reclaim his lost baggage and discarded property were one way that he could regain a sense of power and control in a situation where he had lost autonomy.

Food for the internees was given at the same ration as prescribed for U.S. troops. According to the internment camp regulations, the rations could "be altered to suit the needs of the various racial groups but in no case will the money value of the ration exceed that prescribed for soldiers."[64] Even so, one internee, reflecting upon the differences between the internment camps he had been held in up to this point, remarked that Livingston was remarkable for serving the least amount of food.[65] Reporters from the *Alexandria Weekly Town Talk* noted on a visit to the camp that the men:

> were pouring into the mess halls in quiet, orderly lines, [and] served rice, ham, potatoes, and fresh beans with ox heart cherries for dessert. They have milk three times a week. They want rice three times a day and fish is a big item on the menus which are printed and distributed.[66]

Heavy wines or spirituous liquors were forbidden. Internees could, however, purchase beer or light wine at their own expense, but no man was allowed more than one pint of either, or both, in twenty-four hours. Internees received a camp canteen allowance of ten cents per day in the form of canteen coupons.[67] As time wore on, the food in camp became more palatable to the internees. "Our foods here are 1st class now that fresh milk, vegetables, fruits, melons, ice cream, bacons, ham, 2 eggs, fishes rice, and all kind of meats. Now we have ice water & tea at drinking place all day."[68] In celebration of Christmas and the New Year, the men were given "wonderful yong & tender turkey dinner[s] . . . in addition [to] all sorts of Japanese New Year delicacies including mochi (rice cake) and good things."[69] These "good things" might have been a reference to ozoni, a Japanese soup served at the New Year. Gihachi Yamashita, an internee from Los Angeles, wrote to tell his daughter that he had "invited 30 people in my barrack to eat the zoni, but we had another zoni a day before yesterday in our messhall."[70]

In this foreign environment where Japanese food staples were rare, men often had to get inventive with leftover foodstuffs. One internee recalled receiving a rice ball from the head cook that was made by scraping the burnt rice from the bottom of a pot. He:

> added raw onions sliced very thin, on which I poured some precious soy sauce sent by a family in Denver. I have never eaten anything more delicious than that. Once I get out of camp, I thought, I must eat my fill of this great delicacy.[71]

And while basic necessities such as food, shelter, and clothing were provided to the men, camp life and the uncertainty surrounding their futures took a toll on them. This life behind barbed wire often brought out their base desires of survival and self-preservation. An apple was typically set out each morning for breakfast. Some of the apples were large, and others were small. Bunyu Fujimura recalled the social dance that would happen each morning between the internees who always waited patiently to be seated at a table.

> When they came to a setting were the apple was small, however, they became excessively polite. "After you," they would say, giving up their seat for the next person. When they came to a setting with a large apple, however, their attitude changed completely. Then, it was a scramble to, "Let me have this seat . . ." They used much more polite language, of course, but you cannot say such things other than politely in Japanese, but everyone knew what was meant. Education, culture, reasoning power, everything seems to disappear when it comes to self survival.[72]

But what does survival in a constant state of limbo look like?

NOTES

1. Furuya, *An Internment Odyssey*, 123.
2. Andrew Chesson, "History of the Surgical Service Station Hospital Camp Livingston, Louisiana," History of the Surgeon's Office 1941–1942, US Army Operational, Tactical, and Support Org. (WWII and Thereafter), Posts, Camps, and Stations 1905–1954, RG 338, National Archives at College Park, Maryland.
3. Chesson, "History of the Surgical Service Station Hospital Camp Livingston, Louisiana."
4. Chesson, "History of the Surgical Service Station Hospital Camp Livingston, Louisiana."
5. Chesson, "History of the Surgical Service Station Hospital Camp Livingston, Louisiana."
6. Miyamoto, *Hawaii*, 384.

7. Miyamoto, *Hawaii*, 384.
8. Miyamoto, *Hawaii*, 384.
9. Miyamoto, *Hawaii*, 384.
10. Furuya, *An Internment Odyssey*, 123.
11. Completion Report, 1942, Alien Internment Camp and Hospital, Camp Livingston, LA, Volume 4; Construction Completion Reports 1917–1943, RG 77; National Archives at College Park, Maryland.
12. Ralph Brewer, "Japanese Captured at Pearl Harbor Held at Livingston Camp," *Alexandria Daily Town Talk* (Alexandria, LA), July 14, 1942; Completion Report, 1942, Alien Internment Camp and Hospital, Camp Livingston, LA, Volume 4; Construction Completion Reports 1917–1943, RG 77; National Archives at College Park, Maryland.
13. "First Enemy Alien, All Japanese, at Livingston Internment Camp," *Alexandria Daily Town Talk* (Alexandria, LA), June 6, 1942.
14. Brewer, "Japanese Captured at Pearl Harbor Held at Livingston Camp."
15. Furuya, *An Internment Odyssey*, 99.
16. "List of Member of Hawaii Group," Folder 2, Box 10, AR1, Otokichi Ozaki Collection, AR 1, Japanese Cultural Center of Hawai'i.
17. "Operations Branch Inspection of Prisoner of War Camps," Camp Livingston, Louisiana—Construct; Prisoner of War Operations Division, Subject Correspondence File, 1942–46; RG 389; National Archives at College Park, Maryland.
18. Yamashita Diary Vol. 1, Japanese American National Museum (Gift of Gihachi and Tsugio Yamashita Family, 94.166.29).
19. Miyamoto, *Hawaii*, 386.
20. Yamashita Diary Vol. 1, Japanese American National Museum (Gift of Gihachi and Tsugio Yamashita Family, 94.166.29).
21. Yamashita Diary Vol. 1, Japanese American National Museum (Gift of Gihachi and Tsugio Yamashita Family, 94.166.29).
22. The internment of Japanese Issei from Central and South America had been in negotiations as a possible security measure as the relationship between the United States and Japan worsened in 1941. By January 1942, delegates attending a Conference of Foreign Ministers and of the American Republics in Rio de Janeiro agreed to a proposal submitted by the U.S. Department of Justice calling for the arrest and internment of dangerous Axis nationals; however, if unable to detain in their own country, signatories could deport these individuals to the United States for internment—at the United States' expense no less. (Weglyn, *Years of Infamy*, 58–60). These so-called dangerous men would be arrested and sent to the United States by boat. On arrival at a state-side port, they would be arrested by the Immigration and Naturalization Service and sent into the enemy alien internment system. Some were kept in Army camps, while others were sent to the Department of Justice camp in Crystal City. In the end, approximately 2,300 Japanese alien residents from Central and South America were sent to the United States for internment. Another 700 alien residents who were Italian or German by birth were also deported from Latin America to the United States and interned. As was the case in the United States, fears of Japanese aggression and attack mixed with "cultural prejudice and antagonism based on

economic competition . . .," fueled the deportations and internment. (*Personal Justice Denied*, 305). For more information, please see *Years of Infamy* (Weglyn), *Personal Justice Denied* (Commission on Wartime Relocation and Internment of Civilians), *Pawns in a Triangle of Hate* (Gardiner), *America's Japanese Hostages* (Connell), and *Adios to Tears* (Higashide).

23. Masayuki Chikuma, Transcript of oral history interview by Rev. Ryokan Ara, July 6, 1979, Japanese Cultural Center of Hawai'i, https://jcch.soutronglobal.net/Portal/Default/en-US/RecordView/Index/8373.

24. Masayuki Chikuma, Transcript of oral history interview by Rev. Ryokan Ara, July 6, 1979, Japanese Cultural Center of Hawai'i, https://jcch.soutronglobal.net/Portal/Default/en-US/RecordView/Index/8373.

25. Miyamoto, *Hawaii*, 385.

26. Life in camp was something that internees documented either while in camp or later in their lives. One internee that did both was Reverend Hiram Hisanori Kano. Reverend Kano was an Episcopal minister in Nebraska. Born "the second son of Viscount Kano, prince of Ichi-no-Miya," he left his noble beginnings to pursue a life of missionary work (Soga, *Life Behind Barbed Wire*, 137). Out of 5,000 Japanese living in Nebraska, Colorado, and Wyoming, Reverend Kano claimed in his memoir to be the only one to be interned (Hiram Hisanori Kano, *Nikkei Farmer on the Nebraska Plains: A Memoir* (Lubbock, TX: Texas Tech University Press, 2010), 110). According to Wegars, there was one other man interned from that area: Sancho Kamesaka from Denver, Colorado (Priscilla Wegars, *Imprisoned in Paradise: Japanese Internee Road Workers at the World War II Kooskia Internment Camp* (Moscow, ID: University of Idaho, 2010), 204). According to Soga, Kano's internment may have been the result of his involvement with the Japanese Ministry of Agriculture. Having received an agricultural degree from Tokyo Imperial University, he was well suited to report on issues related to farming "and other related matters" within the United States (Soga, *Life Behind Barbed Wire*, 137). While being detained as an enemy alien, Reverend Kano kept daily journals of his life in various internment camps. Reverend Kano's journals concerning Camp Livingston span the period of June 1942 to June 1943 and give a daily snapshot of his life there. A typical entry begins with a 5:30 a.m. reveille followed by morning prayer and various camp meetings throughout the day. These seemingly small insights into what daily life looked like in the camp coincide with other oral history accounts that men gave later in life about their time at Camp Livingston. Copies of Reverend Kano's personal journals are in the authors' possession.

27. Reverend Kano counted 2,500 Japanese internees at Camp Livingston already there when he arrived, and his recorded numbers would eventually grow to a total of 4,000 Japanese men. The official rosters for Camp Livingston record at least 1,171 Japanese alien internees, but Reverend Kano wrote that "about 2,500 were listed on the roster." The difference in numbers is confusing, as Reverend Kano was incredibly detailed in his entries and not prone to exaggeration. An additional and very important note about the official rosters for Camp Livingston: we have in our possession four out of what we believe were five rosters created for Camp Livingston in 1942 that were found at the National Archives—there appears to be one missing. When originally compiling these names, our tally came to 1,264, but through the gracious and diligent

work of Duncan Ryūken Williams, the list of names actually comes to 1,171. Through his expertise, Dr. Williams was able to remove duplicates of names that appeared due to spelling differences or even spelling errors that were found within the documents.

28. Kano, *Nikkei Farmer on the Nebraska Plains*, 128.

29. Kano, *Nikkei Farmer on the Nebraska Plains*, 129.

30. Completion Report, 1942, Alien Internment Camp and Hospital, Camp Livingston, LA, Volume 4; Construction Completion Reports 1917–1943, RG 77; National Archives at College Park, Maryland.

31. "He Watches the Japs," *The Communique* (Camp Livingston, Louisiana), August 6, 1942.

32. Sakamaki, *I Attacked Pearl Harbor*, 64.

33. Sakamaki, *I Attacked Pearl Harbor*, 64.

34. "New Recreation Hall Opened for Internment Camp Troops," *The Communique* (Camp Livingston, LA), October 15, 1942; "Troops of Intern Camp Hold Halloween Dance at USO Club," *The Communique* (Camp Livingston, LA), November 5, 1942; "Internment Camp Bids Officers Farewell," *The Communique* (Camp Livingston, LA), December 3, 1942.

35. Original Writing 4th Poetry Reading and Critique Session, August 1942, held in Camp Livingston, AR1, Box 9, Folder 15, Ozaki Collection, Japanese Cultural Center of Hawai'i. All translations and notes on translations of poems from the 4th Poetry Reading are courtesy of the Japanese Cultural Center of Hawai'i volunteer: Yoko Waki, with volunteers Jean Toyama, Florence Sugimoto, and Sheila Chun.

36. Richard K. Leary, "April 30, 1943," Series II: Letters from Richard Leary, December 1942–June 1943, Louisiana State University Special Collections.

37. Richard K. Leary, "April 10, 1943," Series II: Letters from Richard Leary, December 1942–June 1943, Louisiana State University Special Collections.

38. Richard K. Leary, "April 10, 1943," Series II: Letters from Richard Leary, December 1942–June 1943, Louisiana State University Special Collections; Richard K. Leary, "April 16, 1943," Series II: Letters from Richard Leary, December 1942–June 1943, Louisiana State University Special Collections.

39. Miyamoto, *Hawaii*, 386.

40. Message from Headquarters Camp Livingston, Camp Livingston, Louisiana, "Information on Enlisted Personnel of Japanese Ancestry," November 24, 1942, http://www.javadc.org/java/docs/1942-11-24%20MSG%20from%20HQ%20Camp%20Livingston,%20LA,%20to%20The%20Adj%20Gen,%20Wash%20DC,%20re%20Info%20on%20JA%20EM_Pg2_ay.pdf.

41. Sakamaki, *I Attacked Pearl Harbor*, 49–59; "Weekly Report of Change of Internees," found in folder titled June (Camp Livingston Internment Camp) Box No 1541, Prisoner of War Operations; RG 389, Provost Marshal General; National Archives at College Park, Maryland.

42. Sakamaki, *I Attacked Pearl Harbor*, 60–61.

43. Sakamaki, *I Attacked Pearl Harbor*, 62.

44. Letter from Brigadier General Guerre to the Provost Marshal General, "Transfer Japanese Prisoners of War," October 29, 1942, RG 389; National Archives at College Park, Maryland. A May 11, 1943, memo noted that there were approximately sixty-two

Japanese POWs being held at Camp Livingston that were being transferred to Camp McCoy in Sparta, Wisconsin. (Transfer of Japanese Prisoners of War, May 11, 1943, RG 389, Provost Marshal General; National Archives at College Park, Maryland).

45. Bunyu Fujimura, *Though I be Crushed: The Wartime Experiences of a Buddhist Minister* (Los Angeles: Nembutsu Press, 1985), 79–80.

46. Brewer, "Japanese Captured at Pearl Harbor Held at Livingston Camp."

47. Internment Camp Regulations, Headquarters, Camp Livingston Internment Camp, Camp Livingston, Louisiana (ca. 1942), 2010 JARP Collection, Kasai Family Papers (Collection 2010). UCLA Library Special Collections, Charles E. Young Research Library.

48. "List of Officers of 4th Intern. Co.," Folder 2, Box 10, AR1, Otokichi Ozaki Collection, Japanese Cultural Center of Hawai'i.

49. Miyamoto, *Hawaii*, 387.

50. Letter from Gihachi Yamashita to Yetsuko Yukiko Yamashita, August 29, 1942, Yamashita Family Collection, Japanese American National Museum (Gift of Gihachi and Tsugio Yamashita Family, 94.166.147-154). Note: A difference in the writing style of Yamashita can be clearly seen between his diary entries (which were translated from Japanese by staff at the Japanese American National Museum) versus his own English writing which is featured in his letters.

51. Furuya, *An Internment Odyssey*, 108.

52. The internees at Camp Livingston were not the only ones new to the area's flora and fauna. Since many of the Army men stationed for training at Livingston were not from Louisiana or even the South for that matter, a "snake house" was constructed in an effort to teach the men all the varieties of poisonous snake one could find in the pine forests (William H. Collier, *The 106th Cavalry's Story* (Bloomington, IN: Trafford Publishing, 2012), 16). Some Army men even tried to domesticate them. In addition to snakes, Livingston's soldiers kept a variety of pets. "A soldier likes friends and pets. This can be seen by driving through army camps, and ours is no exception. In our street alone, you can find a pig, rooster, goat, many snakes, and one good Chow named Pal. Pal is the official mascot of Company F. We awoke one morning and found him wandering up and down our street. He is still here, sole boss and undisputed ruler." (Arthur G. Kroos, "Sergeant Reports on Life with Company F and Tells of Problems in the Army," *The Sheboygan Press* (Sheboygan, Wisconsin), June 3, 1941).

53. Furuya, *An Internment Odyssey*, 124.

54. Howard Fields, *First Taken Last Released: Overlooked WWII Internment* (Lahaina, HI: Setting the Record Straight Books, 2015), 141.

55. Letter from Gihachi Yamashita to Lillian Yamashita, June 16, 1942, Yamashita Family Collection, Japanese American National Museum. (Gift of Gihachi and Tsugio Yamashita Family, 94.166.127–138).

56. Furuya, *An Internment Odyssey*, 102.

57. Yamashita Diary Vol. 1, Japanese American National Museum (Gift of Gihachi and Tsugio Yamashita Family, 94.166.29).

58. Internment Camp Regulations, Headquarters, Camp Livingston Internment Camp, Camp Livingston, Louisiana (ca. 1942), 2010 JARP Collection, Kasai Family

Papers (Collection 2010). UCLA Library Special Collections, Charles E. Young Research Library; Furuya, *An Internment Odyssey*, 106.

59. International Committee of the Red Cross, *Report of the International Committee of the Red Cross on its Activities During the Second World War (September 1, 1939–June 30, 1947), Volume 1: General Activities* (Geneva, 1948), 590.

60. Internment Camp Regulations, Headquarters, Camp Livingston Internment Camp, Camp Livingston, Louisiana (ca. 1942), 2010 JARP Collection, Kasai Family Papers (Collection 2010). UCLA Library Special Collections, Charles E. Young Research Library.

61. Furuya, *An Internment Odyssey*, 106.

62. Letter from Gihachi Yamashita to Angela Yamashita, June 22, 1942, Yamashita Family Collection, Japanese American National Museum (Gift of Gihachi and Tsugio Yamashita Family, 94.166.127-138).

63. International Committee of the Red Cross, *Report of the International Committee of the Red Cross on its Activities During the Second World War (September 1, 1939–June 30, 1947), Volume 1*, 590.

64. Internment Camp Regulations, Headquarters, Camp Livingston Internment Camp, Camp Livingston, Louisiana (ca. 1942), 2010 JARP Collection, Kasai Family Papers (Collection 2010). UCLA Library Special Collections, Charles E. Young Research Library.

65. Yamashita Diary Vol. 1, Japanese American National Museum (Gift of Gihachi and Tsugio Yamashita Family, 94.166.29).

66. Brewer, "Japanese Captured at Pearl Harbor Held at Livingston Camp," 1942.

67. Internment Camp Regulations, Headquarters, Camp Livingston Internment Camp, Camp Livingston, Louisiana (ca. 1942), 2010 JARP Collection, Kasai Family Papers (Collection 2010). UCLA Library Special Collections, Charles E. Young Research Library.

68. Letter from Gihachi Yamashita to Lillian Yamashita, August 6, 1942, Yamashita Family Collection, Japanese American National Museum (Gift of Gihachi and Tsugio Yamashita Family, 94.166.147-154).

69. Letter from Fred Toyota to Kame Toyota, January 28, 1943, Toyota family papers (Collection 2010). UCLA Library Special Collections, Charles E. Young Research Library, UCLA.

70. Letter from Gihachi Yamashita to Angela Yamashita, January 13, 1943, Yamashita Family Collection, Japanese American National Museum (Gift of Gihachi and Tsugio Yamashita, 94.166.167-170).

71. Fujimura, *Though I be Crushed*, 78–79.

72. Fujimura, *Though I be Crushed*, 78.

Chapter 15

Prisoners under the Pines

Camp life was a life of contrast. There were days marked by seeming nothingness. Days spent laboring on the orders of Army commanders. Days filled with exercise. Days turned inward toward faith and religion. But all days started and ended behind barbed wire. Life for the men in Camp Livingston was difficult as they contended with inclement weather, labor disputes, and an overwhelming sense of limbo as they awaited word on their and their families' fates.

LABOR IN CAMP

Labor was an expectation and often harsh reality for the men in camp. While labor assignments did offer some respite from the despair and monotony that camp life offered so freely, working conditions were often especially difficult for the men as they were advanced in age and had never been exposed to manual labor due to their religious and vocational callings.

Labor in camp was divided into two classes. The men were designated as to the type of work they were capable of doing based on their physical condition and age. Class One labor consisted of work that was necessary for the maintenance or repair of the internment camp. This included the barracks, roads, walks, sewers, sanitary facilities, water piping, or fencing. It also comprised all labor that led to improving or providing for the comfort and health of the internees, such as work connected with the kitchen, canteen, fuel, garbage disposal, hospitals, or camp dispensaries. Internees worked as cooks, cooks' helpers, barbers, tailors, cobblers, or other positions connected with the interior economy and maintenance of their companies. A man's skillset and training were taken into consideration when being assigned to these jobs. Deemed necessary for the internment camp upkeep and continued operation, Class One labor was unpaid. However, men who performed overly large amounts of Class One labor, making them unable to participate in Class Two labor, could be paid at the discretion of the camp commander. Class Two labor meant that the internee was employed by the War Department upon any work not directly connected with military operations. This work had to be approved by the Provost Marshal General and had to occur within the vicinity of the internment camp. Internees earned ten cents an hour for this labor, and the money earned was credited to their accounts.[1]

Some, like Gihachi Yamashita, tried to find the good in the labor required of him. Writing to his daughter he said:

> I am working too but just a half a day in a week for which I will be paid 10 cents for an hour. It is very cheap but it is better than get nothing. We have to work in our mess hall and around barrack without any pay. I am trying to do some little work that will help keep me in good health.[2]

Mitsuhiko H. Shimizu found the hard work manageable because of the freedom it allowed the men to be outside (see figure 13). Recalling the work that the men were required to do in camp he stated:

> They were poor jobs like raking the ground in the forest. But I thought it was good for us to do that. We could go outside and eat lunch. It's better than being confined all the time. But people felt bad about undertaking jobs that were forced work.[3]

Kaetsu Furuya, a principal from Kauai, recalled memories of internees having to clean the internment camp premises, prepare their own food while at Camp Livingston, and even having to cut their own firewood indicated that not all work was viewed in the same positive light (see figures 14 and 15).

> They had us go outside the barbed wire fence and told us, "Cut your own firewood" so, having no choice, we went out to chop down trees. We took sickles. But the way we cut trees was different from the way they wanted us to. They wanted us to cut even the large trees straight through instead of circling it—this we thought was strange. On top of this, they wanted us to build a crematory (*kasoro*). We were appalled (thought it was "*keshikaran*") and complained to the Spanish consul about this.[4]

These complaints to the Spanish consul were commonplace as Spain, who remained neutral during World War II, acted as the representative for Japanese interests when negotiating with the United States. These interests included the men in camp who were Japanese resident aliens, now being held as enemy aliens. The clearing of ground was addressed by the U.S. Department of State to the Spanish Embassy. The State Department noted in its 1944 report that internees were, in fact, required to cut grass outside of the camp:

> within a hundred feet of the fence, without pay, as this was considered camp maintenance. Internees were permitted to voluntarily cut grass outside of the compound beyond this point, but within the limits of Camp Livingston, and payment was made to them for this work.[5]

But sometimes, tensions around working conditions in camp erupted before the consul could get involved. Two distinct labor disputes were documented involving the cutting and removal of pine logs outside of the camp. In one instance, internees were ordered to cut and move pine logs that were on a hill outside of the camp. The internees protested the order as they believed it went against the Geneva Convention because it was a job that was taking place outside of camp grounds. The camp authorities insisted the area was still in the camp compound and the logs would be used by the internees to keep themselves warm. The complaint of the men against leveling the ground for the airfield was deemed unfounded in a Department of State report to the Spanish Embassy. The report noted:

> In order to collect firewood for heating the quarters of the Japanese internees, wood was hauled from the vicinity of a nearby field, where a considerable number of pine trees had been felled. No airfield, runway, or any type of military construction has ever been installed on the site from which the wood was obtained.[6]

With this new understanding that the logs would be for their own use, the labor dispute ended, and the men cut and carried the logs. Another, more explosive, labor dispute erupted when internees were ordered to load pine logs two miles east of the camp. The ground was rumored to be cleared for a military airfield and the internees resisted the order. The Army did not back down and locked the gate to stop the internees from engaging in their recreational activities.

Suikei Furuya remembered:

> at the gate two armed guards stood by, and the machine guns in the watchtowers were pointed at us. The atmosphere of the camp became tense. Those internees who in the beginning had been strongly opposed to the order started to give in, and we finally conceded.[7]

Reverend Kano journaled about the closing of the gates after a Class Two labor dispute on October 7, 1942, and subsequent reading of the Geneva Convention concerning war prisoners and internees in the barracks on October 10,

1942. On the same day as the reading of the Geneva Convention, a mass meeting was held regarding both the labor and unspecified baseball controversy. Five months later, on March 11, 1943, Reverend Kano again noted a labor Class One and Two dispute which caused the gate to be closed and the regulations to be distributed in each barrack again as a way of reminding the internees of their duties within the camp. In a report from the Minister in Switzerland to the Secretary of State, it was alleged that "the Authorities of the Livingston internment camp decreased the amount of food of those who raised complaints about labour."[8] The memo also asserted, "Japanese nationals interned at the internment camps at Uption, Ellis Island, Livingston, and Sand Island suffered from weakening eyesight, their weight decreased, and the number of people requiring eye glasses increased on account of malnutrition."[9] The United States responded to the allegations of withholding food in a response to the Spanish Embassy. The Department of State wrote, "The United States affirms that Japanese nationals in that camp [Livingston] were never placed upon a restricted diet as a disciplinary measure for that or for any other reason."[10]

These tense disputes exemplify the strong will of the men interned in camp and the knowledge of their rights as stipulated in the Geneva Convention, a document with which those on both sides of the barbed wire fence were well acquainted.

> Machine guns atop the guard tower
> Sounds from a radio drift down
>
> —Suikei Furuya[11]

Many of the men were quite unused to manual labor. The majority of internees were educated men who had spent their whole lives in pursuit of their vocations. Bunyu Fujimura, a Buddhist minister, was only thirty-three years of age when he was held in Camp Livingston. Manual labor was something he had never experienced as he said, "I had never in my life until then lifted anything heavier than a sutra-book."[12] He described the areas where the men worked clearing the burned logs. Men stripped to their waist in the unforgiving Louisiana heat and since all the trees had been burned down, there was no shade under which to find a moment of solace. He wrote:

> Sweat poured off of me. The carbon from the burned tree trunks blackened my body, and my skin was never without scratches from which blood flowed freely. My abdominal area where I clutched the log sections for dear life became red and swollen. And yet there was no stopping the work of repeatedly loading one heavy piece of timber after another onto the truck bed.[13]

The work of removing stumps in the military aviation field was noted in a 1944 memo from the Minister of Switzerland to the U.S. Secretary of State. The memo stated, "The Authorities of the Livingston internment camp subjected the Japanese to the work of removing stumps in the military aviation field, infested with poisonous snakes adjacent to the United States military barracks."[14]

The lives of the men within Camp Livingston were monotonous, strenuous, and devoid of fulfilling intellectual and leisure pursuits. However, many of the men had been leaders in their life before camp. They were used to planning, organizing, and advocating for their wants and needs, and this had not changed with their internment. To combat the grueling and tedious days of labor and uncertainty under the searing Louisiana sun, the men within Camp Livingston took the utmost advantage of the privileges afforded to them under the Geneva Convention. The men found creative ways to persevere under the adversity they faced daily, fashioning lives within the confines of Camp Livingston that aimed to replicate as much normalcy as they could manage during their dreary imprisonment among the pines.

CAMP ACTIVITIES

Activities, of both the physical and intellectual varieties, were strongly encouraged by the Army, international organizations, and among the internees themselves. The act of occupying one's time within camp cannot be undervalued in helping the men to cope with their confinement.

The Army camp commander supported and encouraged the internees' participation in sports as it was believed to assist in both the psychological and physical well-being of the internees. A corporal in charge of recreational activities took two internees to purchase sporting equipment, even allowing them a highball beverage during their outing.[15] Internment camp regulations stated that athletic and sports contests could be sponsored by the internee associations, and internees wasted no time in negotiating with the camp administration to have certain facilities built. Mitsuhiko H. Shimizu recalled, "I played golf often. Spending days in camp is no good for health. So, I negotiated with the administration people to get permission to establish a golf course, which they permitted."[16] Many men took advantage of the golf course. Katsuma Mukaeda remembered it, saying "We had a sand green golf course in the camp. We used to play golf in a pine forest. We managed to play all right. Our stay at Livingston, Louisiana was pretty fair. We got by all right."[17] Kazuo Miyamoto wrote about the golf course in his book as well. "A nine hole golf course was constructed in an empty area and enthusiasts began practicing daily with capable instructors like Mr. Uyeda from St. Louis who was a semi-professional."[18]

Beyond golf, the men also participated in other physical activities such as judo and sumo, which were extremely popular among the men. Judo, a Japanese martial art, requires both physical and mental prowess making it a good way for the men to exercise their minds and bodies simultaneously.

> The army provided a barrack with mattresses to cover the floor. Judo classes were started and there was ample opportunity to improve in this art as there were many third, fourth, and fifth class men who were entitled to wear the black belt, to act as teacher.[19]

Sumo, a form of Japanese wrestling, was popular with many of the younger men in camp.

> Most of the men from the West coast and Hawaii were in the fifth or sixth decade of life, but those from Panama were younger. These men decided to have wrestling matches. An earthen outdoor ring was constructed according [to] the regular Japanese *dohyo* [sumo] or wrestling area on the slope of a small gully between the two adjoining enclosures. When this arena was built and ready for use, Reverend Miyao of Izumo Taisha Shrine of Honolulu conducted the purification ceremonies. Reverend Tatsuguchi . . . became the coach and every evening for one-and-a-half hours there was a great throng to enjoy the rough and tumble of this very fast competitive game which is the perhaps cleanest of all sports.[20]

Sumo tournaments were commonly held in the evenings and would last for around three hours. *Kendo*, a Japanese martial art derived from swordsmanship, was prohibited even with wooden weapons, as "these wooden swords in capable hands could be just as destructive in hand to hand combat as the steel of the *samurai* swords."[21]

Baseball was an extremely popular physical recreation for the internees (see figure 16). Initially, there was only one baseball field, but as demand for play and the number of internees grew, a second baseball field was constructed within the internee camp. The lively and competitive baseball games were played under the watch of internment camp guards with Colonel Dunn and other camp officers often attending the games as spectators. Katsuma Mukaeda remembered playing baseball at Camp Livingston. He stated:

> We had the prisoners of war from the Midway naval battle, the Japanese sailors taken in there. They were quite a few blocks away but they were in the area. So we used to play baseball games between the internees and the navy war prisoners. We had to have some kind of recreation.[22]

In his journal, Reverend Kano noted the first time the POW baseball team faced off against the internee baseball team on January 17, 1943, from 1:00–3:30 p.m. Quite the match, nearly the whole camp turned out to witness that first game.

According to the internment camp regulations, the moral and intellectual needs of the internees needed to be provided for just as their physical well-being. If instructors were available, internees were allowed to hold classes on topics considered suitable such as languages, history, mathematics, or other subjects that met the approval of the Provost Marshal General.[23] In response to this, the internees formed an "Internee College" helmed by Reverend Kano. An agriculturalist by training, Reverend Kano instituted a Biology and Agriculture class that would go outside of the camp gates on field trips which proved to be so popular that Reverend Kano was required to break the class into two days per week to accommodate the number of men wanting to participate. On January 5, 1943, Reverend Kano noted that his largest class ever was taken out on the field trip— thirty-two men participated. During these field trips, the men found eels, turtles, bamboo, holly, and many other Louisiana native plants and animals. Other internee college classes were held in English, carving, calligraphy, Noh chant, music, Spanish, and even dance and were held in different areas of camp. The internees also had a library located in Barrack 1924 that contained approximately 1,500 books that the internees could check out. Dance classes were given by Michio Ito, a famous dancer and choreographer.[24] In a letter to his daughter, internee Gihachi Yamashita wrote about these classes. He wrote:

> I have learned the dance very good but have to practice more to dance gracefuly, soon get cooler we start practice the dance that what my teacher Mr. Ito. Michio said I can have any body as partner but some people has stincky breath and some people step on toe all time. So Mr. Sakakura is my best partner for it.[25]

The internee college even had college terms or semesters with new schedules of classes debuting at the start of a new semester. The numerous benefits afforded by the internee college were readily apparent to both the men in camp and the camp administrators, especially in the promotion of the men's mental health. The student body grew to approximately fifty men who excitedly expressed their appreciation to the faculty by hosting tea parties to honor the internee college faculty and their efforts.

The *utai* or Noh singing class, seen in figure 17, was yet another way that the men channeled their energies into creative pursuits. The drawing depicts the disciples of Mr. Shōzō Ohara. The small characters on the top right are the names of the students and their prefectures. The chant inscribed in this drawing done at Camp Livingston is a scene from a *noh* drama titled *Shōjō Midare*. This drama is known for its celebratory and auspicious atmosphere.

老いせぬや。老いせぬや
Eternal youth, eternal youth.

薬の名をも菊の水
The water of chrysanthemum has been called the medicine of eternal youth.

盃も浮み出でて
The moon is floating in a cup floating in the liquor. I myself am floating out tonight.

友に逢うぞ嬉しき
It is such a pleasure to encounter a friend.

また友に逢うぞ嬉しき
It is a pleasure to meet with a friend.

The men in camp were extremely organized which was undoubtedly owed to their backgrounds as ministers, teachers, and businessmen. Bulletin boards were available where they could post announcements of new committees such as the ministerial association, musicians' meetings, various *kenjinkai*[26] as well as the meetings of internee governmental associations. Different areas of the camp also organized entertainment events. The Panama internees held musical concerts often. For example, on August 20, 1942, the first musical conference was held in Panama Park[27] from 7:30–8:30 p.m. with Mr. Hashimoto presiding over the concert. An orchestra and corresponding music classes were organized on October 23, 1942. Days later on October 27th, the first music class was held with Reverend Shoshin Toda, a Buddhist priest, serving as instructor. There were approximately a dozen students registered. Special lectures would be given by internees in the evenings on a wide variety of subjects. The men would hold social gatherings with one another, and soda parties were a frequent occurrence. During these soda parties, an internee would invite others to his barracks to partake in soda water, which the host purchased from the canteen, and they would socialize with one another. The men were extremely resourceful when undertaking their recreational activities. Some of the Hawaiian internees taught the Peruvians how to perform kabuki. Masayuki Chikuma recalled the men putting on a performance of *Dan-No-Ura*, a kabuki play about a famous warrior. To create the costumes, one internee from Maui obtained a tent from the camp office, washed it, and even attached stage names to it to create the costume. As this kabuki was about a warrior, suits of armor, known as *yoroi*, were also necessary for the stage production. The men found a material that was "like a tar paper for roofing [tinplate]. It glittered like silver. We cut the plate to make beautiful *yoroi* to be worn by the young men from Peru."[28] The Peruvian men performing in the play even made their own wigs, known as *chonmage*, out of loosened hemp rope.²⁹

Hungry for any word from the outside world, news of global affairs was of the utmost importance to the men; internal camp goings on came in at a close second. To keep abreast of both external and internal news, the internees created their own forms of communication. Beginning in late December 1942, meetings began between some of the men regarding creating a camp paper publication. Reverend Kano met with Mr. Asami, who had served as the editor of the *Nippu Jiji* newspaper in Honolulu, about the suggestion of starting the paper, probably to get his expert advice and guidance. Three days later, an internee's executive or leader's meeting was held wherein Reverend Kano was asked to speak on the matter of creating a camp paper. The group requested that Reverend Kano convene a special journalist conference in order to start the camp paper. By December 30, 1942, the group had met and elected Michio Ito to serve as the chief editor of the Livingston Camp Paper. By mid-January of 1943, the camp paper was up and running, and Reverend Kano submitted several articles on topics such as truck crop farming and pine woods. The men also held their own news broadcasts where they would take news published in English newspapers and then translate it into Japanese for their broadcast. This was "by far the most popular program in the camp."³⁰

In a May 6, 1943, letter, Shigeo Soga, the editor and general manager of *The Hawaii Times, LTD.*, sent a letter to Lt. C. J. Cavanaugh, the U.S. District Postal Censor in Honolulu, regarding the apparent ban on Japanese language newspapers at the internment camps on the mainland. In December 1942, permissions were received that the receipt of the papers had been approved by the War Department. With the approval, papers were mailed weekly to internee subscribers. Soga noted in his letter that the internees at Camp Livingston stopped receiving the newspapers in February. Soga continued to explain that the internees were anxious to receive the papers as that was the only way many of them could get news of Hawai'i as many were unable to read English.³¹ Hungry for news, and using any avenue possible, one internee was even a subscriber to the local paper, the *Alexandria Town Talk*.³²

FAITH, RITUAL, AND RELIGION

The faiths of each internee must have been tested during this time of incredible and seemingly endless burden of imprisonment. Buddhist, Shinto, and Christian priests, ministers, and practitioners all faced the same daily "moment[s] of dislocation."³³

Given that many of the internees in Camp Livingston were religious figures, it is no surprise that many religious services and meetings were held.

After the men arrived, a ministerial association was soon formed that met once per week and even had elected officers. Conferences with the Army chaplains assigned to the camp were also a common occurrence. Weekly pastoral calls to the hospital were made by religious figures. The camp commander even issued special passes to those religious figures visiting the sick so they could get to and from the hospital with ease. The internees submitted petitions to Colonel Dunn regarding creating a camp chapel as well as a Buddhist temple installation in the E area of camp.

Reverend Kano often preached during the Christian services held at camp with sermons on "Christian Immigrant Philosophy," "Where is God?" and "My 25 Years in America." He even performed baptisms at Camp Livingston. In a November 15, 1942, journal entry, Reverend Kano noted that he conducted the baptismal service for Ryuichi Kashima to which sixty men attended. It was the first baptism Reverend Kano had officiated since his internment. Duncan Ryūken Williams, in *American Sutra,* shares the effects of internment on those of the Buddhist faith.

> For the interned Buddhist priests, incarceration often served as muddy water. Their American sutra was written not in a realm of purity and formality but in the swamps of Louisiana and deserts of New Mexico. The internment camps became new arenas for deepening religious practice for those whose mission it was to offer valuable Buddhist teachings to America.[34]

Reverend Seytsu Takahashi used his experience in the deadening heat of the camp to "[connect] to others in Buddhist history who had transmitted the religion while overcoming various obstacles."[35] In a letter he wrote:

> I have thought that this lengthy internment life has been provided to me by Heaven and the Buddhas as an opportunity for years or months of Buddhist practice. I return to the quiet and supreme life of walking alongside the Kōbō Daishi. As if trying to practice meditation under the moonlit pine, I have been viewing the guard's searchlights as the Buddha's sacred light and have been practicing Kōmyō meditation.[36]

Reverend Takahashi took every opportunity afforded him to reflect on his Buddhist practice. When trying to copy a Buddhist sutra (known as *shakyo*) he found that "the swampy heat inside the barracks caused his sweat to drip onto the paper as he tried to copy Buddhist scriptures using the traditional calligraphic style."[37] Instead of surrendering to the heat's persistence, Reverend Takahashi employed the use of "a handkerchief to lock his elbows into a position that prevented sweat from dropping onto the paper, [and] managed to perfect the writing of the sacred script despite the awkward posture."[38] As Williams reminds us, "this act of reiterating the teachings of the Buddha, however hostile the situation, was a way to maintain one's traditions and simultaneously to inscribe one's faith onto a new landscape."[39]

As life went on inside of camp, so too did life progress outside the barbed wire confines. Even though the men were physically separated from their families with scant and erratic mail communication, they maintained their emotional connections through celebrations of milestone life events they were not able to be physically present for. Men would routinely hold birthday celebrations in honor of a child's birthday and invited their fellow internees to their barracks for a soda water treat. The birth of a grandchild would also be feted via a celebratory gathering. Weddings were also cause for joyous festivities. Writing to his wife Sada about his daughter Yoshiko's upcoming nuptials, Tetsuo Toyoma told her that "on that joyful and memorable day [August 16, 1942], I shall invite intimate friends and barrack mates to party serving ice cream & soda water."[40] Just a few months later, on December 14th, another wedding celebration party was held in the K area to celebrate the marriage of Mr. T. Chino of San Diego's son, Thomas Toyoo Chino, to Mrs. Mary Chiyoko Sugahara of Seattle. Reverend Kano attended this camp celebration and said a prayer for the newly married couple. We might imagine that lurking under the surface of these celebrations was a deep pain and frustration, possibly even anger or resentment, at having been forcibly separated from their families and being made to miss these special familial milestones.

As life was celebrated, death was remembered within Livingston. On November 1, 1942, Jihei Kuga, an internee in Barrack 1910, passed away. Reverend Kano gave a short sermon to the congregation of 200 men assembled to honor Mr. Kuga. The camp's interned religious figures, in addition to providing worship services and pastoral counseling, held memorial services for those men who died while being held at Camp Livingston as well as the loved ones of internees that passed away outside of camp. Gihachi Yamashita received a telegram on June 28, 1942, informing him that his brother, with whom he was especially close, had passed away suddenly. Grief-stricken, he was at a loss as he couldn't do the things he normally would in the event of the passing of a relative such as send money, be with them, and offer words of comfort to his family. He could only send condolences to his sister-in-law through telegram.[41] His journal entry encapsulated this tragedy when he wrote, "I truly resent this."[42] After discussing his situation with several fellow internees, it was decided that a memorial service would be held for his brother. Yamashita and Reverend Takahashi wanted to have the service in the evening to avoid the stifling June weather, but the hall where the service was to be held was already bookmarked for use. It was decided to move forward with an afternoon service "in spite of [the] heat."[43] For the memorial service, the men decorated the barrack space with Yamashita's bed sheets, an embroidered tablecloth his daughters had sewn for him, and a tin cup as a candle holder. The men also gathered wild flowers and *warabi* (Fiddlehead or bracken fern).[44] These flowers, along with an orange and *yokan* (red bean sweets), were placed in front of the Buddha as offerings. Seventy-two men attended the service, a testament to the sense of community among the men in camp.[45] Pooling two friends' coupons as well as one of his own for $1.50, Yamashita purchased soda water for the attendees. In a letter to his wife describing the service, Yamashita wrote, "It was very successful services as to the condition. The spirit of my brother must glad for the services I held for him."[46] Thoughts of his brother's spirit were never far from Yamashita's mind. Six weeks after the memorial service, writing to his daughter, Yamashita described the recent Urabon, or Obon, service held in camp. "On Aug 16 we had urabon, decoration day here made a little stage among the pine trees & had several programs too. I bet my brothers spirit was here then & he must enjoyed in having good time with me & every body."[47] While this Obon celebration would have been markedly different than the large festivals the men had attended before camp, the description that Yamashita shared with his daughter points to certain traditions of the Obon being honored in camp, such as the men possibly celebrating by circling the stage among the pines during Bon Odori ("Bon Dance") or even celebrating with song.

In moments of quiet contemplation, thoughts often turned toward their families, the days apart, what the future held, and what was awaiting them in the afterlife. Writing to his wife, Tetsuo Toyama mused:

> Today we had quiet & steady rain like May rain in Japan. Under a big pine tree, various flowers are blooming, which I had taken care of last seventy days. When breeze comes, vines and blossoms waves . . . Recently I am filled with inspiration. I believe I got an Eternal life. "Even I die here physically, you and I are wife & husband forever in the presence of our Lord, and live happily together in Heaven."[48]

No matter the faith of the men in camp, it helped sustain them when things seemed hopeless and days separated from their families turned to weeks, then months, and for many, eventually years.

NOTES

1. Internment Camp Regulations, Headquarters, Camp Livingston Internment Camp, Camp Livingston, Louisiana (ca. 1942), 2010 JARP Collection, Kasai Family Papers (Collection 2010). UCLA Library Special Collections, Charles E. Young Research Library.

2. Letter from Gihachi Yamashita to Lillian Yamashita, September 10, 1942, Yamashita Family Collection, Japanese American National Museum. (Gift of Gihachi and Tsugio Yamashita Family, 94.166.147-154).
3. Clark, "Those Other Camps," 108.
4. Kaetsu Furuya, Japanese Internment and Relocation Files, The Hawai'i Experience, Box 4, Folder 233 University of Hawai'i at Mānoa Libraries. *Keshikaran* is a Japanese word meaning that something is disgraceful, shameful, or outrageous.
5. *Foreign Relations of the United States*, Diplomatic Papers, 1945, Volume VI, The British Commonwealth, The Far East (Washington, DC: Government Printing Office, 1945), Document 249, https://history.state.gov/historicaldocuments/frus1945v06/d249 (accessed December 5, 2020).
6. *Foreign Relations of the United States*, Diplomatic Papers, 1945, Volume VI, The British Commonwealth, The Far East (Washington, DC: Government Printing Office, 1945), Document 249, https://history.state.gov/historicaldocuments/frus1945v06/d249 (accessed December 5, 2020).
7. Furuya, *An Internment Odyssey*, 112.
8. *Foreign Relations of the United States,* Diplomatic Papers, 1944, Volume V, The Near East, South Asia, and Africa, The Far East, Document 994, https://history.state.gov/historicaldocuments/frus1944v05/d994 (accessed December 5, 2020).
9. *Foreign Relations of the United States,* Diplomatic Papers, 1944, Volume V, The Near East, South Asia, and Africa, The Far East, Document 994, https://history.state.gov/historicaldocuments/frus1944v05/d994 (accessed December 5, 2020).
10. *Foreign Relations of the United States*, Diplomatic Papers, 1945, Volume VI, The British Commonwealth, The Far East (Washington, DC: Government Printing Office, 1945), Document 249, https://history.state.gov/historicaldocuments/frus1945v06/d249 (accessed December 5, 2020).
11. Furuya, *An Internment Odyssey*, 123.
12. Fujimura, *Though I be Crushed*, 81.
13. Fujimura, *Though I be Crushed*, 81.
14. *Foreign Relations of the United States,* Diplomatic Papers, 1944, Volume V, The Near East, South Asia, and Africa, The Far East, Document 994, https://history.state.gov/historicaldocuments/frus1944v05/d994 (accessed December 5, 2020).
15. Furuya, *An Internment Odyssey,* 100.
16. Clark, "Those Other Camps," 108.
17. Clark, "Those Other Camps," 77.
18. Miyamoto, *Hawaii*, 388.
19. Miyamoto, *Hawaii*, 388.
20. Miyamoto, *Hawaii*, 387–388.
21. Miyamoto, *Hawaii*, 388.
22. Clark, "Those Other Camps," 77.
23. Internment Camp Regulations, Headquarters, Camp Livingston Internment Camp, Camp Livingston, Louisiana (ca. 1942), 2010 JARP Collection, Kasai Family Papers (Collection 2010). UCLA Library Special Collections, Charles E. Young Research Library.
24. Ito is known today as the "forgotten pioneer of modern dance."

25. Letter from Gihachi Yamashita to his daughter Lillian, June 20, 1942, Yamashita Family Collection, Japanese American National Museum (Gift of Gihachi and Tsugio Yamashita Family, 94.166.54A-54B).

26. Associations based on what prefectures the men were from in Japan. (Kelli Nakamura. "Kenjinkai," *Densho Encyclopedia*, https://encyclopedia.densho.org/Kenjinkai/ (accessed December 18, 2019)).

27. Panama Park is what the internees called the section of camp that housed the Japanese internees who were taken from Panama and elsewhere in South America.

28. Masayuki Chikuma, Transcript of oral history interview by Rev. Ryokan Ara, July 6, 1979, Japanese Cultural Center of Hawai'i, https://jcch.soutronglobal.net/Portal/Default/en-US/RecordView/Index/8373.

29. Masayuki Chikuma, Transcript of oral history interview by Rev. Ryokan Ara, July 6, 1979, Japanese Cultural Center of Hawai'i, https://jcch.soutronglobal.net/Portal/Default/en-US/RecordView/Index/8373.

30. Furuya, *An Internment Odyssey,* 111.

31. Shigeo Soga to Lt. C.J. Cavanaugh, May 6, 1943, Folder 15, Box 1, AR 9 Nippu Jiji/Hawaii Times/Yasutaro Soga, Japanese Cultural Center of Hawai'i.

32. Brewer, "Japanese Captured at Pearl Harbor Held at Livingston Camp."

33. Williams, *American Sutra*, 96.

34. Williams, *American Sutra*, 86.

35. Williams, *American Sutra*, 95.

36. Quoted in Williams, *American Sutra*, 95.

37. Williams, *American Sutra*, 96.

38. Williams, *American Sutra*, 96.

39. Williams, *American Sutra*, 96.

40. Letter from Tetsuo Toyama to Sada Toyama, August 12, 1942, Tetsuo Toyama papers. 2000.366, Japanese American National Museum. Los Angeles, CA.

41. Letter from Gihachi Yamashita to Tsugio Yamashita, June 30, 1942, Yamashita Family Collection, Japanese American National Museum (Gift of Gihachi and Tsugio Yamashita Family, 94.166.127-138).

42. Yamashita Diary Vol. 1, Japanese American National Museum (Gift of Gihachi and Tsugio Yamashita Family, 94.166.29).

43. Letter from Gihachi Yamashita to Tsugio Yamashita, June 30, 1942, Yamashita Family Collection, Japanese American National Museum. (Gift of Gihachi and Tsugio Yamashita Family, 944.166.127-138).

44. Letter from Gihachi Yamashita to Tsugio Yamashita, July 8, 1942, Yamashita Family Collection, Japanese American National Museum. (Gift of Gihachi and Tsugio Yamashita Family, 94.166.139-146).

45. Yamashita Diary Vol. 1, Japanese American National Museum (Gift of Gihachi and Tsugio Yamashita Family, 94.166.29).

46. Letter from Gihachi Yamashita to Tsugio Yamashita, July 8, 1942, Yamashita Family Collection, Japanese American National Museum. (Gift of Gihachi and Tsugio Yamashita Family, 94.166.139-146).

47. Letter from Gihachi Yamashita to Lillian Yamashita, August 20, 1942, Yamashita Family Collection, Japanese American National Museum. (Gift of Gihachi and Tsugio Yamashita Family, 94.166.147-154).

48. Letter from Tetsuo Toyama to Sada Toyama, September 16, 1942, Tetsuo Toyama Papers, 2000.366.47-51, Folder 10 September 1942, Japanese American National Museum.

Chapter 16

Art, Community, and Resistance

Art can be viewed as an expression of spirituality manifesting in some form of physicality—through movement, words, objects, the list goes on. It can be therapeutic as well as an act of resistance. The internees in Camp Livingston created art that took a variety of forms, from the written word to the painted board. The creation of art by the Japanese community can be found in internment and incarceration camps across the United States—symbolic of the shared sense of community behind the barbed wire. As the men settled into their lives among the Louisiana pines, they began creating art that not only reflected this new locale but also helped combat the monotony of imprisonment.

By July 18, 1942, a camp art exhibit was proposed, and Reverend Kano, as the cultural program director of the camp, was asked by the various artists in the camp to organize it. For the next week, Reverend Kano threw himself into organizing the event writing in his journal that it was consuming all his time. At one point during the preparation, he was allowed to leave the camp gates under guard to gather pine logs to make a gate. On July 26th, the art exhibit opened in Barrack 1902 to great fanfare, including visits from ten Army officers and thirty soldiers. Reverend Kano noted that the exhibit was quite a good exposition of internee work and even Colonel Dunn attended the art exhibit on its second day. A suggestion box had been included to collect feedback from visitors. Confirming Reverend Kano's opinion on the caliber of work included in the exhibit, the suggestion box was filled with multiple notes of admiration and compliments on the exhibit.

The popularity of the art exhibit could not be denied, and on August 3, 1942, Colonel Dunn requested of Reverend Kano that another art exhibit be organized to coincide with the visit of the Spanish Consul of New Orleans to Camp Livingston happening in two days' time. With such short notice, preparations began the following day with the consul touring the exhibit in Barrack 1913 on August 5th, a testament to Reverend Kano's efficiency. Another exhibit was planned for late October/early November as well. Gihachi Yamashita, in a letter to his daughter Lillian, wrote that he had spent the last two weeks preparing for an exhibit of which he was not only on the planning committee, but also had shown some of his work.

> I exhibited two writing which was very good . . . The exhibition was so gorgeous and was success. The exhibition hall is closed now but things are still displayed yet as we got to show for army's big men who are coming soon to see them.[1]

These exhibits continued throughout the men's tenure at Camp Livingston, and their popularity grew so much that by November 1942, Reverend Kano visited all three camp areas to gauge the sentiment toward a proposed museum. He then conferred with camp officials regarding the creation of this museum that would house internee art.

As opposed to a general showing of internee art, museum exhibits were themed. Themed exhibits included "Stone Art" and "Root and Stump Art" highlighting the use of materials from nature. Some men would take tree roots and carve them into shapes, while others made walking sticks from a rattan-like plant they called the *sankirai*, carving elaborate designs on the ends. Utilizing materials from the natural world around them allowed the men to delve into their creativity as well as their practicality during their time in camp (see figures 18, 19, 20, 21, and 23). These pieces serve to illustrate the connection these men had to nature. Besides museum displays, the men also held at least two auctions of their creations. The first auction, held on November 16, 1942, included thirty articles for sale and garnered $60 in proceeds.[2] Another held on December 4th garnered $70 in proceeds.

While the men who were held as internees, as well as the men who guarded them, noted the presence of the pine trees that transported them to another time and place, the pine trees were not only a visual escape. For the internees, the endless supply of pine needles provided material to use in the creation of various crafts. The most popular type of craft utilizing the pine needles was constructing fans. The men made *sensu* (folding hand fans) and *uchiwa* (fixed or non-folding hand fans) as both decorative objects and as implements to use during hot summer days to cool oneself off.

> In the pine forest, fireflies everywhere
> An evening sky in a foreign land
>
> —Suikei Furuya[3]

Reverend Kunio Ohta, an artist and calligrapher, made both *sensu* and *uchiwa* fans to occupy himself during his long hours confined while interned at Camp Livingston. Reverend Ohta would paint the fans in watercolor depicting varied views of Camp Livingston such as the pine trees, various camp scenes, and the watchtowers. The fans were given to some of his friends in camp to help them tolerate the summer heat. When the Ohta family was preparing to return to Hawai'i after the war in December 1945, Reverend Ohta threw several *uchiwa* that he was unable to complete during his time in Camp Livingston into the trash. Reverend Ohta's daughter, Ella Miyeko Tomita, née Ohta, unknown to her father, rescued these from the trash and carefully packed them between the few items of clothing that she had.[4] Therefore, there are no paintings on the surviving fan (see figure 22).

POETIC EXPRESSIONS: HAIKU AND TANKA

Haiku and tanka were popular artistic pursuits for many of the men interned at Camp Livingston. Poetry became a mechanism for expression of emotions that may have been too difficult to verbalize otherwise. This type of poetry had long been a tradition in Japan, and "these short poems, being less cumbersome than long diaries were ideal forms for those internees to express their pent-up emotions in view of the scarcity of writing paper."[5] Hisashi Fukuhara, an internee at Camp Livingston, taught haiku classes while in camp. He noted:

> Haiku become your personal records of that moment or day. If you write another one next month, it'll be different. That becomes haiku. When we were in camp, it was the experience of camp life. You can't write haiku from something else that someone else wrote. It has to come from your own head.[6]

With this emphasis on haiku being representations of feelings as they are experienced, the focus of haiku written by men changed from what they would have written prior to their internment. Fukuhara continued:

> When we were confined, we would construct the feelings that we were experiencing then. We didn't know what was happening outside. Just the feelings while we were confined. Our universe was different then. If it is now, we know of world events and write about them. But back then, we didn't go out, so we didn't know them. Just the thoughts within the camps. As a result, there is a lot of suffering that comes out of the haiku. There are things like when one is separated from one's family. Separated from one's children. You can't see them. Since we can't see them, we don't know. You can't write haiku about things

you can't see. Only things that are felt in the soul. So, being confined, we only knew of what we saw in the camps. We didn't know what was going on outside.[7]

Fourth Poetry Reading and Critique Session, August 1942[8]

At Camp Livingston, there were poetry readings and critique sessions of the poetry written by the men, a twisted version of the salon-like sessions they had had in their normal lives before Pearl Harbor and before being held behind barbed wire. One session, held in August 1942, was the fourth such reading and critique session held since arriving in Louisiana.[9]

These poems remain today as the expression of the innermost thoughts and feelings of the internees as they sat behind barbed wire at Camp Livingston and underscore their connection to and the importance of the towering Louisiana pines in the everyday lives of the men in camp.

思ひ出の配所の松に日は落ちて別れ名残るか蝉しきりなく

—かつろく

Remembering the pines
as the sun sets
in my place of exile,
the cicadas singing
as if in farewell

—Katsuroku

なびき来る煙に脂の香して松の古株焼き居り暮る々

—しうんほう

The smell of resin
in the smoke wafting
from the burning
old pine
as darkness falls

—Shiunhou

さみどりのながながし葉の松直ぐにのびそろひたる森の下道

Green pine leaves
grow straight and long
along the path
in the woods

アメリカの南の果てに廻り来て松の林に蛍飛ぶ見る

—すいけい

Having gone around
the farthest tip
of the South American continent
I now see fireflies
in the pine forest

—Suikei

GAMAN: AN ACT OF RESISTANCE, CONNECTION, AND SOLIDARITY

In Japanese, *gaman* is a term meaning "to endure, persist, persevere, or to do one's best in times of frustration and adversity."[10] *Gaman* connotes the practice of suppressing emotion, specifically anger, and is the practice of endurance in the face of adversity and hardship. It is important to stress that *gaman* is not a passive act. The use of *gaman* during World War II "is mistaken by many non-Japanese to indicate a lack of assertiveness or initiative rather than strength in the face of difficulty and suffering."[11] The communal creation and subsequent sharing of art can be viewed as a manifestation of the practice of *gaman*.

The definition of what constitutes art is something that is always under debate. Art is defined as, "a visual object or experience consciously created through an expression of skill or imagination."[12] For the men in Camp Livingston, art took on a variety of forms including wooden carvings, ikebana, calligraphy, and haiku. Many times, these items were not created for the men themselves, but as objects they could send to their families, wherever they might be. Gihachi Yamashita often wrote of making *geta* (a type of Japanese sandal) to send to his family and friends as gifts. Writing to his daughter Lillian, he said:

> Within 2 weeks I will send you about 9 getas which are beautiful that not only painted nice but my friend painted a nice picture on it, some micky mouse, butterfly, and flowers the picture will be finished in few days but I have to make hanas (string) by the clothe you sent to me.[13]

As we can see from this letter, men in camp used their artistic talents to complement each other's work. In this case, Yamashita made the *geta* and his unnamed companion painted them with beautiful scenes that would appeal to Yamashita's daughters and wife. "Employing camp-made art to re-form family connections was especially significant in the context of internment when we recall that dramatic changes occurred within the family, between husbands and wives, and children and parents."[14] The most significant change faced by the men in Livingston and other enemy alien holding facilities was their separation from their wives and children, a separation with no end in sight. The children of these men also created art that they sent to their fathers held in camp. This reciprocal creation of art and exchange between the men and their families was another way they were able to connect to the outside world. Further, this art created a tangible object of connection that went beyond the words contained in letters, their only other means of communication. Yamashita's daughters, Lillian and Angela, while being held at the Santa Anita Assembly Center before being sent to a War Relocation Authority family camp in Arkansas, mailed a tablecloth to their father that they had decorated with hand embroidered birds and colorful flowers. Writing a letter of thanks to his youngest daughter, Angela, upon receipt of the embroidered tablecloth, Yamashita remarked:

> I don't know how I thanks for the pretty embroidery which is surprized me in fact. I received it on 19th at the office and is opened by inspectors; not only 3 inspector in the office but many office worker and bystanders who saw the cloth are amazed for its wonderful work. Lots people envy me that I have nice children. I am sure I will keep it for forever for memory.[15]

This handmade creation was so beautiful and dear to him that Yamashita used this same embroidered tablecloth as decoration for his brother's memorial service that was held in the camp barracks.

The coming together of internees to create works of art as well as a venue for their display can be viewed in several ways. First, it was a communal activity that promoted interaction and cooperation among the men. It promoted bonding and forging together of talents to reach a common end goal. Additionally, the art served as an important medium through which the men could express their thoughts and feelings in a constructive way. The production, display, and community building centered on art forms is a way for the men within Camp Livingston to reclaim their identity, autonomy, form solidarity, and collectively resist their internment. The artwork produced in Camp Livingston is the internees' own practice of *gaman*. Solidarity and communication through artistic expression allowed the men to cope with their status as interned enemy aliens. And the *gaman* practiced among the pines in Louisiana was not exclusive to Camp Livingston; other Japanese communities forced to endure behind barbed wire fences also partook in the practice.[16] In addition to the larger War Relocation Authority camps, there are examples of *gaman* being practiced by those with enemy alien status being held at the Santa Fe Internment Camp run by the Department of Justice as well as Lordsburg Internment Camp, an Army camp similar to Livingston.[17]

As impressive and popular as the internee museum was at Camp Livingston, it could only last as long as the internees who filled the barrack halls with heartfelt art were held in the confines of camp. Beginning in the late spring and early summer months of 1943, sections of the internee camp were vacated as the men were sent to other camps around the country. The internee museum at Camp Livingston closed on April 11, 1943, when the H area of the camp was evacuated. The men soon left the pine woods of Louisiana for other camps, but some of their art has survived through the decades since. These pieces are a testament to the skill, strength, and solidarity of these men and have had a lasting impact on any who views them.

NOTES

1. Letter from Gihachi Yamashita to Lillian Yamashita, November 12, 1942, Yamashita Family Collection, Japanese American National Museum. (Gift of Gihachi and Tsugio Yamashita Family, 94.166.155-166).

2. This auction may have been for the "big army men" that Yamashita mentions in his letter to his daughter Lillian. (Letter from Gihachi Yamashita to Lillian Yamashita, November 12, 1942, Yamashita Family Collection, 94.166.155-166, Japanese American National Museum).

3. Furuya, *An Internment Odyssey,* 124.

4. Ella Miyeko Tomita, née Ohta, discussions with authors, December 2019.

5. Susan Yim, "The Poems That Won't Let us Forget," *Honolulu Star-Bulletin,* October 5, 1982.

6. Hisashi Fukuhara, Japanese Internment and Relocation: The Hawai'i Experience, Box, Folder 232, University of Hawai'i Mānoa.

7. Hisashi Fukuhara, Japanese Internment and Relocation: The Hawai'i Experience, Box, Folder 232, University of Hawai'i Mānoa.

8. Original Writing 4th Poetry Reading and Critique Session, August 1942, AR1, Box 9, Folder 15, Ozaki Collection, Japanese Cultural Center of Hawai'i. All translations and notes on translations of poems from the 4th Poetry Reading are courtesy of the Japanese Cultural Center of Hawai'i volunteer: Yoko Waki, with volunteers Jean Toyama, Florence Sugimoto, and Sheila Chun.

9. The themes of this session were "ship" or "separation," and the eight internees who participated rose to the call writing a total of twenty-eight pieces. Please see appendix II for the twenty-eight poems in their entirety.

10. Brian Niiya, ed., *Japanese American History: An A-to-Z Reference from 1868 to the Present* (New York: Facts on File, 1993), 143.

11. Niiya, *Japanese American History,* 143.

12. Art. (2017). In Encyclopaedia Britannica, *Britannica concise encyclopedia* (Chicago, IL: Britannica Digital Learning), http://libezp.lib.lsu.edu/login?url=https://search.credoreference.com/content/entry/ebconcise/art/1?institutionId=463.

13. Letter from Gihachi Yamashita to Lillian Yamashita, October 27, 1942, Yamashita Family Collection, Japanese American National Museum. (Gift of Gihachi and Tsugio Yamashita Family, 94.166.155-166).

14. Dusselier, *Artifacts of Loss,* 94.

15. Letter from Gihachi Yamashita to Angela Yamashita, June 22, 1942, Yamashita Family Collection, Japanese American National Museum. (Gift of Gihachi and Tsugio Yamashita Family, 94.166.127-138). As promised, Gihachi Yamashita did keep the tablecloth for memory. This beautifully embroidered piece is currently held in the Yamashita Family Collection at the Japanese American National Museum in Los Angeles, California. In addition to the hand-embroidered birds and bright bursts of flowers, they have embroidered their names in cursive, as well as the date and place of its creation (June 21, 1942, Santa Anita Assembly Center).

16. As noted previously, the practice of *gaman* was a staple in the War Relocation Authority camps.

17. Lordsburg Internment Camp, located deep in the barren desert of southwest New Mexico, was an Army-run internment camp like Livingston. In celebration of the "2,306rd anniversary of Emperor Jinmu's accession" to the Japanese throne, the internees displayed the artwork created in camp as part of the festivities. (Soga, *Life Behind Barbed Wire*, 104). Another two "handicraft exhibitions" were held in Lordsburg. One exhibition, held in observance of their internment, included almost 700 items such as paintings, caricatures, calligraphy, poetry and other literary works, crafts, carved walking sticks and other wooden handiwork, and "collections of rare stones from Missoula, insects, and grasses." (Soga, *Life Behind Barbed Wire*, 110). It must be remembered that "All of these had been made with the simplest tools and materials." (Soga, *Life Behind Barbed Wire*, 110). A second exhibition was held just a few days later where "Many of the items were made from stone and wood." (Soga, *Life Behind Barbed Wire*, 110). The exhibitions were open to more than just the men being held in camp—guards, officers, and other military personnel in the camp often attended these arts and crafts shows. At the urging of the officers in charge of Lordsburg, a third exhibition was held and "Many Americans came to see it, not only from Lordsburg and the surrounding area, from as far away as El Paso. They were quite impressed, and many newspapers and magazines reported on the exhibition." (Soga, *Life Behind Barbed Wire*, 110). The Santa Fe Detention Center, where many of the men who were held in Camp Livingston were eventually transferred, is another prime example. Here, an exhibition was held under the auspices of an "exhibition committee" wherein about 130 paintings were displayed: pastels, watercolors, oils, and some in the "Japanese-style." (Soga, *Life Behind Barbed Wire*, 155). Those in attendance were encouraged to share their thoughts of the art using the comment box. As refreshments were served, the comments were read, resembling a critique session the men might have attended in their pre-internment lives. (Soga, *Life Behind Barbed Wire*, 155).

Chapter 17

Connections to the Outside World

The moment the men held in Camp Livingston were arrested as enemy aliens and taken from their homes, their sole mode of communication with loved ones became the written word. Contact with their families was strictly through telegrams or letters until they were reunited in some capacity—whether in a War Relocation Authority (WRA) or Department of Justice family camp, or those lucky few who were visited by family members while interned in Louisiana. Through these letters, we become witness to the heartache these men felt at being separated from their families. It would be months or even years before they heard the laughter of their children again. Gihachi Yamashita, in a letter to his wife, Tsugio, inquired about his two daughters writing, "Hope they are good children as same as I left you 10 months ago."[1] Likewise, the loving voices and faces of their wives were relegated to dreams during their separation. Tetsuo Toyama tenderly wrote to his wife, "I dream of you nearly every night, but I believe, you are fine as silk under God's protection and care."[2]

During the months and years the men were interned behind barbed wire, life on the outside marched on. There were births and deaths. Children got married or volunteered their service and, for many, their lives for the U.S. military. For any of these momentous life occasions, the men relied solely on telegrams and letters to communicate their hopes, dreams, advice, or concern to their families. While Tetsuo Toyama was interned, his daughter, Yoshiko, became engaged to marry. Testuo first approved of this match via wire sent from the internment facility at Camp Forrest, Tennessee.[3] A few weeks later after he had settled into his new camp barrack at Camp Livingston he wrote to his wife:

> Really this is the first Japanese letter from home since I was detained, which made me happy and sentimental extremely. I love to read mother's Japanese Letter and English letter from Yoshiko because I am studying English steadily here in camp. I have already approved the marriage between Yoshiko and Mr. Sato by sending you telegram and letter. Hope you can let me know the date of the wedding three weeks ahead . . . If you have anything important to consult with me quickly, don't write, wire.[4]

This momentous occasion would be the subject of conversation in ensuing letters and wires between Tetsuo and his family. The competing emotions of joy and sadness in this moment—happiness for his daughter and yet grief at his absence—must have been hard for Tetsuo to reconcile. It was also during his internment that Tetsuo's son, Sadao, volunteered his service to the U.S. Army. During Sadao's training, Tetsuo would write letters to his son, never sure if he would receive them. Writing to his wife about their son, Tetsuo said:

> I am going to write to Sadao today although I don't know his exact address. He may be sent to [illegible] army battle front. I consider it is quite honor and I pray that he's always a faithful and brave soldier of Uncle Sam.[5]

Tetsuo's pride as a father and concern for his son are evident, but his situation as an internee made it impossible for him to express those words to his son in person. Tetsuo, like so many other men in Camp Livingston, could only hope that one day they might have the opportunity to express all they wanted to their loved ones face-to-face. Until that day, news of family and friends, connections with their children, and the comforting words of a spouse would come only through the mail.

For many of the men in camp, letter writing in English was either not a skill they possessed or was something they were trying to better master as can be deduced from the high level of participation in the various English class offerings. In order to have their mail processed quickly, the letters needed to be in English. To this end, men, like Reverend Kano, offered their time and English skills to many men in the camp. Many of Reverend Kano's evenings were dedicated to writing English letters for others, a task which took him a considerable amount of time. There were many varied and changing rules regarding internee mail; therefore letters and postcards from internees instructed family and friends on how to ensure mail reached the internment camp. These included how to properly address mail to internees,[6] not writing about other internees' affairs,[7] and how many letters one was allowed to send from camp.[8] According to a letter written in July 1942, the men were limited to writing only "2 letters [and] 1 post card weekly."[9] The mail leaving camp was sent to different censorship offices where the letters were read to remove instances of geographic location, number of men, and other classified information that the Army would not want shared outside of the confines of camp. The censoring process took time, and many of the men complained to the International Committee of the Red Cross (ICRC) of the delay of communication.[10] The men's families often received letters that were unintelligible due to the amount of pieces cut from the letters as part of the censoring process. In addition to letters, the men could also receive care packages, documents, and even newspapers. Men were able to send handmade gifts to their families and could even receive packages from friends and relatives containing items like food supplies which were usually shared among fellow internees. All items were appreciated, but the handwritten letters with news from home were the most longed for. Weeks could go by where the men might not receive letters from their loved ones sparking feelings of isolation, loneliness, and worry. Writing to his wife, Tetsuo Toyoma said:

> I can't understand this silence . . . yet I am very desirous to hear from home directly. Probably the delay is due to censorship. I haven't heard anything about even Yoshiko's happy wedding by letter. Anyhow, it is almost our anguish that our correspondence doesn't run smoothly at this time . . . When we miss your mail more than two months, we naturally begin to worry.[11]

Six weeks later the silence was deafening. Tetsuo still had not received a letter from his wife. "Haven't heard from you quite awhile. Your letter of 8/28 was last one. I am kind envious of my friends who are receiving lots of mails. When mail doesn't come, I become gloomy too."[12] Her letters would eventually arrive, and despite the lag in delivery, Tetsuo continued to write faithfully. His longing possibly abated with the connection that putting thoughts and feelings to paper allowed him.

待てど待てど家の音信（おとずれ）絶えてなき日のみ続きて今日も暮れ行く
—ろせい

> Waiting and waiting
> day after day
> yet no letter comes
> and the sun sets
> today again
>
> —Rosei[13]

While serving as a basic means of communication, the mail also allowed internees to communicate with their families to execute legal documents that would ensure their assets would be protected during their internment.

Reverend Miyamoto executed several powers of attorney during his time in internment. In December 1942, a power of attorney was executed to Ryuzo Oka and several church members giving them authority over the Hale'iwa Jodo temple's assets. In March 1943, Reverend Miyamoto executed another power of attorney to Lewzo Oka, an employee at the Bishop National Bank in Waialua. The persistent need to change powers of attorney in order to maintain and protect their assets and lives back home was something that every internee had to contend with. For Reverend Miyamoto, these powers of attorney were extremely important in safeguarding the temple and school that he desperately hoped to be able to return to one day. Ever since he was detained at Sand Island, the Army and other powerful interests continually sought to wrest control of the temple, school, and its valuable land from Reverend Miyamoto.

In addition to the execution of powers of attorney to keep their affairs in order, internees at Camp Livingston also filed legal affidavits in the parish of Rapides in which Camp Livingston was located in the hopes that they could be reunited with their families in the various WRA camps. These affidavits all followed similar formats. They began by listing pertinent information about the interned man, including his occupation and how long he had resided in the United States. The affidavits went on to declare the man was a law-abiding resident, never engaged in any activities that could be deemed un-American or subversive, his children were U.S. citizens, and that the affiant was loyal to the United States. The affidavits ended with the formal request to allow the man to join his family at their WRA camp. These affidavits were yet another way the men fought against their internment and attempted to be reunited with their families.

While news from the outside world mostly trickled in through letters and newspapers, the men did have visitors in camp, both from official representatives and, in some joyous cases, from members of their family.

Reverend Kano's journals indicated that the International Red Cross visited the camp; this would have been to ensure that the Geneva Convention's stipulations regarding the treatment of alien internees was being upheld. On November 24, 1942, Reverend Kano did what he did for hundreds of days before and hundreds of days after, he wrote down the day's events. This day, however, stood out with the mention of receiving visitors to Camp Livingston. The day began as usual with a 5:30 a.m. reveille followed by *chowado*[14] and prayers. Reverend Kano then noted, "Red Cross representative Mr. Cardinaux (Swiss) and Mr. Young, the State Department representative visited our camp. Inspected art exhibit took pictures of exhibit." The report from the International Committee of the Red Cross representative, Alfred Cardinaux, regarding this same trip mentioned in Reverend Kano's journals, commented first on the location of the camp and that it "sits in a beautiful forest of fir trees and [has] an excellent climate." The report went on to say:

> The cooks, nurses, and the internees who work in the forest, earn a daily pay of 80 cents. Japanese gardens and *objets d'art* created by the interns themselves make the camp appear pleasant. Various classes of study with libraries have been organized and the internees have two golf courses and a baseball field; they indulge themselves with these games. The living conditions are generally satisfactory . . . no complaints were passed along to the delegate, save for remarks related to delays in the censorship of the distribution of the mail.[15]

The International Red Cross, in conjunction with the U.S. State Department, often sent delegates to Camp Livingston to check on the well-being of the internees by holding meetings with representatives of the men so they could ask questions, voice grievances and concerns, and learn more about other topics like repatriation, mail services, and requests for hearings and release.

During this same November visit, the representatives also held an interview with the men in the library of J2 barrack #1924.[16] During this meeting, several internees from Hawai'i were able to pose questions specific to their unique situation which differed from the mainland men being interned. For the men of Hawai'i, their top priority and inquiry to officials was how they could be reunited with their families who were left behind and separated from them by an ocean.

The representatives learned from some of the men from Hawai'i that their families were being held at the Assembly Inn in North Carolina, and the men hoped to gain some information on how their families were faring. The representatives vowed to visit the Assembly Inn as soon as possible to investigate the situation under which the families were living. The representatives were also going to put in a request to help with the sending of clothing to the families to protect them from the cold weather there.

Communication concerns were also brought forward by the men. They complained about the communication systems in place to which the representatives informed them that the system is "currently most needed and used by the military. We regret that there is a fact of inconvenience put upon the general public, but we are unable to do much now."[17] As far as the delay or non-delivery of telegrams, the military stipulated that was the responsibility of Western Union Company. The representatives even discussed a way in which the internees could communicate with their families for Christmas. Three sample cards would be made within the Livingston enemy alien internment camp and sent to the YMCA. The YMCA would then choose one of the designs, print it, and distribute to the internees to send to their families (see figure 24). The representatives cautioned that they were unsure of how many cards would be distributed, however.

The lost and confiscated items the men were living without was also a topic during the interview. The military authorities were continuing to investigate those items, but if they were unable to be located, "Lieutenant Colonel Dunn personally consider[ed] that the military should be responsible for them after both internee representatives and military representatives duly discuss the value of the items."[18] Other necessities such as dentures and reading glasses were asked about. The representatives let the men know that the military was trying to provide these items, but there was a lack of materials. The men also asked about the showing of movies within the camp and getting Japanese tea sent. The response of the representatives to many of these inquiries indicated the bureaucratic nature of these visits as no definitive answers were given in the moment—they would instead have to "return to Washington D.C. and discuss with the authorities."[19]

Herbert V. Nicholson, a Quaker missionary to Japan from 1915 until he returned to America in 1940, became one of the prominent white defenders of alien Japanese and Japanese Americans during World War II. A man of "exceptional energy and vitality" with "a great love for people,"[20] Nicholson offered spiritual support and aid to the families as well as defended prisoners in speeches and advocated for their release.[21] Mitsuhiko Shimizu recalled of Nicholson:

> He did many things to help the internees when nobody turned to us. He did things that ordinary people didn't do. I really felt that way . . . He did liaison work between the internees and society. They asked him to do things that they wanted him to do. Once he promised them to do something, he carried it out without fail. He negotiated with the administration people, and he looked into things outside if they asked him to do so. He truly did many kindness for them.[22]

On September 21, 1942, Nicholson visited Camp Livingston. In a report bearing his initials found in the Camp Livingston, Louisiana, Construction file, Nicholson relayed the following about his visit:

> On one edge of a large military camp, in a beautiful pine grove, is situated [a] Japanese internment camp . . . It is a beautiful location with regular type army barracks—those for the guarding soldiers being of the same type as those holding the internees. The M.P.s were largely from Scranton neighborhood in Pennsylvania and were very friendly. Lt. Col. Dunn did all he could to make my visit worth while turning me over to Captain Ichter, who gave himself entirely to me the four days I was there. It was impossible for me to go inside the enclosure without a special pass from the Provost Marshal General's office in Washington, but they brought out groups of men for me to visit in the visitor's room.
>
> I had very satisfactory visits with 150 men in small groups. With but one exception they were in fine spirits and very happy in the camp because they are

treated like human beings. Food was reported excellent and the treatment very satisfactory. They do all the work within the barracade [sic] and if they wish to are allowed out in groups with armed guards to work on the camp grounds outside. The hospital was fine and I had two good visits there to see sick men on my list. I saw the head chaplain of the camp and chaplain Appleton who had special charge of the Japanese camp. They were high calibre [sic] men and did all they could to aid me in my work. The only problem with the interned men was that they wished to be back with their families. They had been assured by the Spanish Consul that arrangements were being made to do this, so that they all had that hope![23]

While the purpose of Nicholson's visit was to observe and report on the well-being of the men interned, his visit perhaps had an even greater effect on the soldiers tasked with overseeing the alien internment camp. Over his four-day visit to Livingston, Nicholson had a chance to interact with Colonel Dunn and the guards:

[The colonel] said, "Boy, that's going to take a long time. You're allowed to see only one at a time, and you must have an official with you, and you can talk only in English." I said, "I've got only four days here. Mr. Collaer in Missoula let me go in and talk to them freely." "Oh, you can't! These are dangerous men!" I said, "Now, just wait a minute, Colonel. There's not a single dangerous man there. They're all loyal Americans. They would be citizens if they were allowed to be. The FBI picked the cream of the Japanese American community to arrest, and they're wonderful people. Have you noticed—haven't they organized already? Don't they have a mayor? Don't they have a city council?" "Sure," he said, "they're well organized. They got together and have a little town of their own inside." The internees had divided up the work and they were all doing their part. I said, "Don't you see that?" He said, "Yes. Ok then, you can go and see as many as you can this morning and then have lunch with me." So I had lunch with him and we talked more. He said "You can go in the hospital and visit all of them in there." So I did that and then came back the next day. He didn't actually get me inside, but he let me get a whole bunch together and talk freely with them. So I saw all I had wanted to see. Before we got through, he shook my hand and said, "Nicholson, I'm so glad you came. I realize these are decent people. They're not dangerous, you're right." Wasn't that great? It was just a wonderful thing.[24]

With Nicholson's visit, he was able to open the minds of the guards who were overseeing the internees and assist them in realizing that the men they were charged with guarding were not dangerous and were simply victims of circumstance.

Other officials and aid agencies came to check on the welfare of the men as well. Two representatives from the YMCA, Mr. Hibbard and Dr. Fischer, visited the camp for four days in October 1942. They had a meeting at "Panama Park" where men from three areas of the camp attended. Reverend Kano presided over the meeting and acted as interpreter between the delegates and the men and was even invited to dine with the two visitors and Lt. Schmidt.[25]

In the international arena, Spain, as a neutral country in the global conflict, acted on behalf of Japanese interests, which included determining the welfare of Japanese aliens interned in the United States. In this capacity, representatives of the Spanish consul would visit various internment camps, including Camp Livingston. Their visit was to ensure the health, welfare, and safety of the men, as well as gather any complaints they might have as to their treatment and report these to the Japanese government. Writing to his daughter Angela, Gihachi Yamashita recalled one such visit.

> Yesterday Aug 5, we were visited by Spanish consul at New Orleans. We asked him lots thing and were told lots good thing because the consul is take all Japanese interests in U.S. He told us as follow (1) He will take into consideration of joining families and there is possibility of we can live together (#2) We people in here can write to Japan in Japanese once a month. #3 The ship fare to Japan will be paid by U.S. He told more thing for those go to Japan but it is not concern on us much so I don't write you about. I by myself am going to make a application to authority expressing my desire of joining family in few days; and I advise you that you better do same thing I do to authority to live together. It will have better results if you & families ask U.S. government about. These are told by the Spanish consul when he was here.[26]

Mr. Garay, a representative of the Spanish Embassy, and Mr. Herrick, of the State Department, would also visit the camp again on December 17, 1942.

The men continually petitioned for themselves and their treatment while interned. In a document found in Otokichi Ozaki's papers from 1942, a list from Company 4 Area J-2 (Hawaiian section) in Camp Livingston included requests for improvements such as having the kitchen mess kits changed to Chinaware; more fresh vegetables, cereals, and fruit as well as a daily supply of fresh milk; the prompt supply of raincoats, underwear, socks, pillow cases and sheets; prompt delivery of all mail; improvement to the internment camp area itself including better lighting, roof repairs, and an increase in laundry soap; the establishment of a recreation center and play grounds; a way to purchase goods from outside of camp; wanting family and dependents to be able to accompany the men if repatriated, or join them in Japan; and investigations into issues of money being held for the men as well as articles sent by their families in Hawai'i that had been lost in transit.[27] It is unclear to which official these demands were given; however, this example demonstrates a consistent theme in the men's requests: better treatment during their internment and concern for their families and repatriation. Visitations to camp weren't limited to just international aid groups or officials, they could be much more personal. The 442nd Regimental Combat Team was a segregated unit comprised of Japanese Americans who became the most decorated unit in U.S. military history for its size and length of service. On July 15, 1946, at a White House ceremony in honor of the 442nd, President Harry Truman said, "You fought not only the enemy, but you fought prejudice—and you have won."[28] Katsugo Miho served in the 442nd and visited his father, Katsuichi Miho, a Japanese language schoolteacher and store manager, who was being detained at Camp Livingston. Of the visit, he recalled:

> So I ended up with about five of us. And there was just enough time from Camp Shelby [in Mississippi][29] to get to (Camp Livingston,) [Louisiana], call in the officer of the day, two o'clock in the morning, tell him to get our parents ready, and that we go down there . . . by taxi . . . And from about five o'clock to six o'clock or six-thirty, I think it was, that we were allowed the visitation, in the . . . visitor's quonset hut for prisoners of war. And as prisoners of war, there were all kinds of signs. "Speak English Only," and visitors on one side of the table and the POWs [prisoners of war] on the other side of the table. But this officer of the day, when he saw us in uniform, his jaws dropped, and he told the two guards, "You get out of the quonset hut, leave these people alone." And so we had freedom of visitation for about an hour and a half in [Louisiana].
>
> And my dad was taking it very nicely. All the Japanese isseis, I think, were being treated really nice because by physical appearance, there was no way they could run away. So they would give you a lot of freedom. And they had a lot of outings that they would go out to, one, two guards instead of being, you know, looked over by four or five guards, or forty or fifty people could go out with one guard or two guards. And I think the Japanese people there, actually, they don't complain. And so, I think the American security was more lenient to them.[30]

Tetsuo Toyama's son, Sadao, had enlisted in the Army in November 1941 just a few weeks before his father would be arrested as an enemy alien in the wake of Pearl Harbor. During his father's internment, Sadao was in Army training at Camp McCoy, Wisconsin, and then at Camp Savage in Minnesota as part of the special Military Intelligence Service Language School.[31] These Nisei volunteers were being trained to serve as translators both on and off the battlefield. Sadao was never far from his father's thoughts. In a letter to his wife, Tetsuo asked, "Do you hear from Sadao lately? I haven't gotten any reply yet. There were a few soldiers of McCoy who called on their fathers here, they said Sadao is getting along nicely. I, as his father, am praying for him constantly."[32] Throughout his internment at Camp Livingston (and even prior), Tetsuo wrote letters to his son that would often go unanswered.

Finally, in November 1942, Sadao was able to visit his father in Camp Livingston. Tetsuo immediately wired and then wrote his wife to say:

> Informed you already by telegram and letter that Sadao called on me here. After his return to Camp McCoy safely, he wrote me a fine letter which excited me greatly with gratitude and thankful heart as this was really first letter he gave me since his enlistment to army.[33]

These letters and memories serve as picture windows to these cherished moments, at once beautiful and heart-wrenching, but also unsettling as the painful irony of the situation seeps through—a father imprisoned due to his enemy alien status while his son fights for the country that imprisoned him.

While the idea that a man serving in the U.S. military would need to visit his father being held as an enemy of the very United States that he was fighting to defend seems preposterous, this was actually a very common situation encountered by Nisei soldiers. This situation underscored an invisible divide that existed between the Issei fathers and their American-born sons, a divide that made the former an enemy and the latter a citizen and patriot of the very same country through a simple accident of birth. This invisible divide completely changed the trajectory of each father and son's life and forced them to reckon with unfair and life-altering consequences.

兵となって下のデッキに子は乗れり父なる人は囚はれにして

—無音

> The son rides below the deck,
> a soldier
> His father,
> a prisoner,
> aboard the same ship
>
> —Muin[34]

In addition to enlisted sons visiting their fathers, other men were especially lucky to receive visits from other members of their families as well. For Gihachi Yamashita, the joyous yet brief visitation from his wife and daughters was due in some part to their new proximity to Camp Livingston. After Yamashita was arrested, his wife and daughters in Los Angeles were forced by the government to relocate, eventually being placed into the Rohwer WRA camp located in Arkansas about 200 miles from Camp Livingston. Upon learning of his family's forced removal to Arkansas, Gihachi wrote to his daughter Angela with fatherly advice for the long train ride from California, a journey he had already taken as an internee.

It be quite a long trip that will take 4 days at least. I hope the train go through Salt Lake so it has more beautiful scenery you will see in Ut. The trip by train won't be so bore at all because the scenery is changing all time. On the train you may need some medicine such as first aid measures. More people will have trouble of constipation (bowel stoppage) so better prepared something for that even there are some doctor on the train. One thing I want you prepared before the trip is to get some medicine for skin eruption being poisoned of poisoned oak, grasses or itching caused by insects, mosquitos; but mosquito be gone the time you come, but you may suffer the itching caused by insects which can't see by naked eye. So you better buy something for quick relief for itching caused by insects bites bruises and similar minor ailment.[35]

With only 200 miles standing in the way of the possibility of a brief family reunion, Gihachi's wife and daughters were able to obtain leave and make the trip to visit him in February 1943. Writing in his diary, he said of the visit:

Even though I'd received notice that my family was coming, until we actually were reunited, I felt that it wasn't really happening and seemed like a dream. On the day, when I received an order from the military administrators to report to the reception area, I was overjoyed. This was the happiest day since my children were born. I put on my suit that had gotten all wrinkled from being shoved in my trunk since Los Angeles. There are around 50 yards to the reception area but I reached it in a moment. The first thing to enter my vision was Yukiko [Angela], then my wife, and because Yetsuko [Lillian] was so much bigger than I expected I didn't recognize her at first.

We are fortunate that my wife was able to come here to visit from a place 180 miles away, since including with the expense it was not easy; when I think of the other people in the camp I was truly fortunate. We were able to visit for two days, and parted at 3pm on the 17th. I wonder when we will be able to meet next.

My wife brought gifts/souvenirs—we had Mr Yamamoto cook the snapper and shrimp and invited about 30 friends to an eventful evening (with 48 bottles of beer) and food. For almost everyone this was the first time they had snapper sashimi. Of course it was a first for me as well.[36]

The thrill of this visit stayed with Yamashita even after his family left to return to Rohwer. Writing to Lillian about their recent visit, he said:

The Feb 16-17-1943 was happiest and historical day. For us that have met in such place after 14 months . . . Especially I was glad and happy to see my 2 dearest daughters were grown so big, healthier, and prettier more than I expected. Of course Mamasan looks fine too.[37]

Yamashita was very lucky that his family could afford to visit him in camp. The costs associated with making the trek to see a loved one being held at

Camp Livingston were quite high; for many families, it proved too high. While interned at Camp Livingston, Fred Toyota wrote to his family in McGill, Nevada asking them not to come to visit him. He wrote, "You says wants come to see me, but that is too far too much expense and just meet only a few hours, so you and Toshiko don't need come over here."[38]

Despite her father's protests, just a few weeks later Toshiko did make the long train ride to see her father after receiving her permit for visitation from officials in the Army.[39] In a letter to his wife, Toyota described their visit:

> I am very well and doing nice. Toshiko visit me day before yesterday morning and glad to talk with her all forenoon, then she went back to Alexandria and that after noon she had shopping. Yesterday morning she visit me again, and try to visit all our friend [being held in camp], but she couldn't, because changed rule over here that must have a permit for each person. We have talked two morning each other all about home and our condition, and was very much satisfied every things.[40]

At only twenty-three, Toshiko had made this journey to see her father on her own—a fact which made her father very proud.[41]

逢ひに来し末の娘の唯だぼつねんともの言ひ得ぬ姿目にしむ

—かつろく

> My youngest daughter visits,
> a lonely figure
> unable to say a word
> My eyes begin to tear
>
> —Katsuroku[42]

Even with the letters from home and the respite of these family visits, the men in camp longed to be with their families again. Gihachi Yamashita's sentiments of hope at a reunion with his daughter Lillian echoed the feelings of many in camp. "No matter wherever and how humble it be I like to live together with you."[43] Soon the time would come for the men to leave Camp Livingston providing a chance for some to reunite with their families. For others, their solitary internment journey would continue.

> We leave tomorrow
> I water the grasses and flowers
> On this last evening
>
> —Suikei Furuya[44]

All the men who were held in the alien internment camp within Camp Livingston as Japanese enemy aliens were transferred to various other camps around the country by June 1943.[45] Some of these men joined their families in WRA camps; others were sent on to Department of Justice facilities like the Santa Fe Internment Camp or Fort Missoula in Montana. A handful volunteered to be sent to the Kooskia workcamp in Idaho,[46] while still others were sent to the Department of Justice family internment camp at Crystal City, Texas, for a chance at reuniting with their families and the possibility of repatriation to Japan. Each was being sent to another camp, and it did not matter if it was run by the WRA or the Department of Justice. It was still, in the end, surrounded by barbed wire.

In total, Reverend Miyamoto spent 305 days among the central Louisiana pines; 305 days behind barbed wire fences dreaming of home.

Reverend Miyamoto left Camp Livingston on March 30, 1943, but he was not yet heading home. He was moved westward to Crystal City, Texas, where he was received by INS in the early morning hours. There, Reverend Miyamoto was among families again, but he was still alone waiting for *his* family to join him. Fumi, Carol, Clifford, and Keiko were on their own journey of repatriation that would take them across the ocean to the mainland in the hopes of joining together as a family once again.

NOTES

1. Letter from Gihachi Yamashita to Tsugio Yamashita, October 29, 1942, Yamashita Family Collection, Japanese American National Museum. (Gift of Gihachi and Tsugio Yamashita Family, 94.166.155-166).

2. Letter from Tetsuo Toyama to Sada Toyama, September 24, 1942, Tetsuo Toyama papers. 2000.366, Japanese American National Museum. Los Angeles, CA.

3. Wire from Tetsuo Toyama to Sada Toyama, June 26, 1942, Tetsuo Toyama papers. 2000.366, Japanese American National Museum. Los Angeles, CA.

4. Letter from Tetsuo Toyama to Sada Toyama, July 7, 1942, Tetsuo Toyama papers. 2000.366, Japanese American National Museum. Los Angeles, CA.

5. Letter from Tetsuo Toyama to Sada Toyama, July 21, 1942, Tetsuo Toyama papers. 2000.366, Japanese American National Museum. Los Angeles, CA.

6. Postcard from Fred Toyota, February 1, 1943, Toyota family papers (Collection 2010). UCLA Library Special Collections, Charles E. Young Research Library, UCLA.

7. Postcard from Yotaro Yamamoto to Mrs. Kame Toyota, Fred Toyota, October 1, 1942, Toyota family papers (Collection 2010). UCLA Library Special Collections, Charles E. Young Research Library, UCLA.

8. Letter from Fred Toyota to Kame Toyota, July 22, 1942, Toyota family papers (Collection 2010). UCLA Library Special Collections, Charles E. Young Research Library, UCLA.

9. Letter from Fred Toyota to Kame Toyota, July 22, 1942, Toyota family papers (Collection 2010). UCLA Library Special Collections, Charles E. Young Research Library, UCLA.

10. International Committee of the Red Cross, *Report of the International Committee of the Red Cross on its Activities During the Second World War (September 1, 1939–June 30, 1947), Volume 1*, 583.

11. Letter from Tetsuo Toyama to Sada Toyama, October 9, 1942, Tetsuo Toyama papers. 2000.366, Japanese American National Museum. Los Angeles, CA.

12. Letter from Tetsuo Toyama to Sada Toyama, November 14, 1942, Tetsuo Toyama papers. 2000.366, Japanese American National Museum. Los Angeles, CA.

13. Original Writing 4th Poetry Reading and Critique Session, August 1942, held in Camp Livingston, AR1, Box 9, Folder 15, Ozaki Collection, Japanese Cultural Center of Hawai'i. All translations and notes on translations of poems from the 4th Poetry Reading are courtesy of the Japanese Cultural Center of Hawai'i volunteer: Yoko Waki, with volunteers Jean Toyama, Florence Sugimoto, and Sheila Chun.

14. "'Chowa' means harmony and 'do,' road or morals, being the same character as [the 'to'] in Shinto and ['Tao'] in Taoism. Chowado may thus be translated as the road of harmony. It indicates the attempt by the founder to reconcile the utilitarian with the sacred by a system of physical exercises merged with religious or spiritual exercises ... According to the Reverend Reisai Fujita, its founder, physical health is the basis of everything in this world. For any kind of physical activity as well as for religious and spiritual activity, health is an essential ingredient. Thus, it is permissible for an individual to practice a set of physical exercises devised by him for health, which he calls Chowaho, without belonging to the church itself. On the other hand, no one may become a member of his church unless he has practiced and mastered the health engineering system, for according to him, a healthy body is an essential component of a truly religious individual." (Evelyn Yama and Agnes Niyekawa, "Chowado," *Social Process in Hawai'i* 16 (1952): 48).

15. Le Comité International de la Croix-Rouge et la Guerre, "Delegations du Comite International Dans Les Cinq Continents," *Revue Internationale de la Croix-Rouge*, Bulletin 289 (January 1943): 8. Translation provided by Allen LeBlanc.

16. A Report of Summary of Interview with Mr. Young of the Department of State, and Mr. Gardiner (?), a representative of International Red Cross dated November 24, 1942, AR1, Box 10, Folder 2, Ozaki Collection, Japanese Cultural Center of Hawai'i. All translations from this interview are courtesy of the Japanese Cultural Center of Hawai'i volunteers. Translation in authors' possession.

17. A Report of Summary of Interview with Mr. Young of the Department of State, and Mr. Gardiner (?), a representative of International Red Cross dated November 24, 1942, AR1, Box 10, Folder 2, Ozaki Collection, Japanese Cultural Center of Hawai'i. All translations from this interview are courtesy of the Japanese Cultural Center of Hawai'i volunteers. Translation in authors' possession.

18. A Report of Summary of Interview with Mr. Young of the Department of State, and Mr. Gardiner (?), a representative of International Red Cross dated November 24, 1942, AR1, Box 10, Folder 2, Ozaki Collection, Japanese Cultural Center of Hawai'i. All translations from this interview are courtesy of the Japanese Cultural Center of Hawai'i volunteers. Translation in authors' possession.

19. A Report of Summary of Interview with Mr. Young of the Department of State, and Mr. Gardiner (?), a representative of International Red Cross dated November 24, 1942, AR1, Box 10, Folder 2, Ozaki Collection, Japanese Cultural Center of Hawai'i. All translations from this interview are courtesy of the Japanese Cultural Center of Hawai'i volunteers. Translation in authors' possession.

20. Letter from R.E. Heywood to Virginia Nicholson, January 23, 1984, Herbert V. Nicholson Papers, 2003.1, Japanese American National Museum.

21. In the introduction to *Valiant Odyssey: Herbert Nicholson in and out of America's Concentration Camps,* Michi Weglyn says of Nicholson: "What is especially unusual about the near-legendary wartime service Herbert Nicholson rendered is the way he stood up for the rights of the Issei—the immigrant Japanese denied United States citizenship—then totally powerless as 'enemy aliens.' Here was a man of scant means who, steeled by the determination to undo, or at least mitigate, the grotesque governmental injustices then perpetrated amidst the deliberately whipped-up racism in the wake of the Pearl Harbor attack, raced about and wrestled near-single-handedly with authorities of a world in which everything was going wrong. Nor did he ever despair in his efforts, or slow down one iota, until he confronted policy makers at the highest levels of government—speaking truth to power." (Michi Weglyn and Betty E. Mitson, eds., *Valiant Odyssey: Herbert Nicholson in and out of America's Concentration Camps* (Upland, CA: Brunk's Printing, 1978), vi–vii).

22. Clark, "Those Other Camps," 114.

23. "Brief Report of Internment Camps Visited by H.V.N., September, 1942," Camp Livingston, Louisiana—Construction, Operations Branch Subject Correspondence File 1942-46, RG 389 (Provost Marshal General) Prisoner of War Operations Division, National Archives at College Park, Maryland.

24. Weglyn and Mitson, *Valiant Odyssey,* 18–19.

25. Dr. Fischer of the YMCA would visit again from January 14–16, 1943.

26. Letter from Gihachi Yamashita to Angela Yamashita, August 7, 1942, Yamashita Family Collection, Japanese American National Museum. (Gift of Gihachi and Tsugio Yamashita Family, 94.166.147-154).

27. "Company 4, Area J-2," Folder 2, Box 10, AR1, Otokichi Ozaki Collection, AR 1, Box 10 Folder 2, Japanese Cultural Center of Hawai'i.

28. Greg Robinson, "Harry S. Truman," *Densho Encyclopedia,* https://encyclopedia.densho.org/Harry_S._Truman/#cite_note-ftnt_ref4-4.

29. Depending on the route taken, the distance between Camp Shelby in Mississippi and Camp Livingston in Louisiana would have been between 240 and 280 miles.

30. Katsugo Miho, Transcript of interview by Michi Kodama-Nishimoto and Warren Nishimoto conducted in 1989, Hawaii Political History Documentation Project, University of Hawai'i at Mānoa, http://hdl.handle.net/10125/29923.

31. Sadao Toyama's training at Camp McCoy in Wisconsin is taken from references in his father's letters; "Sadao Toyama," Japanese American Military Experience Database, Discover Nikkei, http://www.discovernikkei.org/en/resources/military/13708/ (accessed December 5, 2020).

32. Letter from Tetsuo Toyama to Sada Toyama, September 24, 1942, Tetsuo Toyama papers. 2000.366, Japanese American National Museum. Los Angeles, CA.

The irony of being held in an internment camp (Camp McCoy) near the location of where his son was training for the military was not lost on Tetsuo as he writes to his wife, "It is quite interesting to know that Sadao station where I spent nearly three months." (Letter from Tetsuo Toyama to Sada Toyama, July 14, 1942, Tetsuo Toyama papers. 2000.366, Japanese American National Museum. Los Angeles, CA).

33. Letter from Tetsuo Toyama to Sada Toyama, November 14, 1942, Tetsuo Toyama papers. 2000.366, Japanese American National Museum. Los Angeles, CA.

34. Note Courtesy of JCCH: Translations of this poem also appear in Jiro Nakano and Kay Nakano, *Poets behind Barbed Wire* (Honolulu: Bamboo Ridge Press, 1983), 29 and Honda, *Family Torn Apart*, 73. Also see this latter citation for a description of the circumstances of this poem. Original Writing 4th Poetry Reading and Critique Session, August 1942, held in Camp Livingston, AR1, Box 9, Folder 15, Ozaki Collection, Japanese Cultural Center of Hawai'i. All translations and notes on translations of poems from the 4th Poetry Reading are courtesy of the Japanese Cultural Center of Hawai'i volunteer: Yoko Waki, with volunteers Jean Toyama, Florence Sugimoto, and Sheila Chun.

35. Letter from Gihachi Yamashita to Angela Yamashita, August 31, 1942, Yamashita Family Collection, Japanese American National Museum. (Gift of Gihachi and Tsugio Yamashita Family 94.166.147-154).

36. Yamashita Diary Vol. 1, Japanese American National Museum (Gift of Gihachi and Tsugio Yamashita Family, 94.166.29).

37. Letter from Gihachi Yamashita to Lillian Yamashita, March 4, 1943, Yamashita Family Collection, Japanese American National Museum. (Gift of Gihachi and Tsugio Yamashita Family 94.166.171-176). Interestingly, not just the difference in the flora and fauna were noticed by the Yamashita family. It must be remembered that at this time the South was still practicing segregation. This was even the case within Camp Livingston as well. Writing to Lillian, Gihachi brings this to her attention. "Although you had hard time through the trip & spent lots money you have gained lots knowledges of the nature and Louisiana. Especially the public is divided to two races not only public uses like drink fountain, waiting room but some cities has two side walks for white, black people . . . I have never experienced in anything like these of Southern States." (Letter from Gihachi Yamashita to Lillian Yamashita, March 11, 1943, Yamashita Family Collection, 94.166.171-176, Japanese American National Museum).

38. Letter from Fred Toyota to Kame Toyota, July 28, 1942, Toyota family papers (Collection 2010). UCLA Library Special Collections, Charles E. Young Research Library, UCLA.

39. The permit needed for a visit to camp was actually first received by Fred Toyota who then mailed it to his daughter. In a postcard dated August 1, 1942, he informs his wife, "Today I have receipt permit for Toshiko from army authority, which she can visit me during week of August 16. Therefore I will send it to her tomorrow." (Postcard from Fred Toyota to Kame Toyota, August 1, 1942, Toyota family papers (Collection 2010). UCLA Library Special Collections, Charles E. Young Research Library, UCLA).

40. Letter from Fred Toyota to Kame Toyota, August 22, 1942, Toyota family papers (Collection 2010). UCLA Library Special Collections, Charles E. Young Research Library, UCLA.

41. Letter from Fred Toyota to Kimiko Toyota, September 4, 1942, Toyota family papers (Collection 2010), UCLA Library Special Collections, Charles E. Young Research Library, UCLA.

42. Original Writing 4th Poetry Reading and Critique Session, August 1942, held in Camp Livingston, AR1, Box 9, Folder 15, Ozaki Collection, Japanese Cultural Center of Hawai'i. All translations and notes on translations of poems from the 4th Poetry Reading are courtesy of the Japanese Cultural Center of Hawai'i volunteer: Yoko Waki, with volunteers Jean Toyama, Florence Sugimoto, and Sheila Chun.

43. Letter from Gihachi Yamashita to Lillian Yamashita, December 21, 1942, Yamashita Family Collection, Japanese American National Museum. (Gift of Gihachi and Tsugio Yamashita Family 94.166.155-166).

44. Furuya, *An Internment Odyssey*, 126.

45. Letter from Daniel Byrd to Provost Marshal General, "Transfer of Internees from Camp Livingston Internment Camp," June 12, 1943, Records of the Provost Marshal General, RG 389; National Archives at College Park, College Park, Maryland. These transfers were in response to the Army's concern that it could not properly care for the individuals being held as enemy alien internees as well as the influx of prisoners of war from Germany, Italy, and Japan as outlined in the 1929 Geneva Convention (Kashima, *Judgment Without Trial,* 117). It should also be noted that when the men left, they did not take everything with them. Some left behind books, while others left behind instruments. When readying the newly deserted alien camp for incoming German and Italian POWs, it was reported that "six musical instruments were left by the Japanese" ("Operations Branch Inspection of Prisoner of War Camps, Prisoner of War Division, Provost Marshal General's Office," August 6, 1943, Camp Livingston, Louisiana, Construct; Prisoner of War Operations Divisions, RG 389, National Archives at College Park, Maryland).

46. A secret memo to the Commanding Officer and Transportation Officer at Camp Livingston, dated June 9, 1943, announced the departure of "14 Japanese" on June 2, 1943, to Kooskia, Idaho ("Headquarters, Camp Livingston Internment Camp, Office of the Commanding Officer (June 9, 1943)," Jack and Aiko Herzig Papers (Collection 451). UCLA Library Special Collections, Charles E. Young Research Library, University of California, Los Angeles). Through the seminal scholarship of Priscilla Wegars in her 2010 book *Imprisoned in Paradise: Japanese Internee Road Workers at the World War II Kooskia Internment Camp*, we believe we have been able to identify the fourteen individuals who are mentioned, but nameless, in this memo. They are: Tokuhei Akena, Louis or Luis Yorikatsu Kakiyama, Katushi Koba, Takeshi Miya, Kizaemon Ikken Momii, Kokichi Nakamura, Kyutaro Nakamura, Teiji Nakamura, Kosaku Sato, Ryohei Tanaka, Seichi Tokuda, Sokan Raymond Ueoka, Motoharu Umeda, and Ichita Yoshida (Wegars, *Imprisoned in Paradise,* 201–213). The authors would like to note that Kooskia was unique among the internment camps in its complete lack of barbed wire. In fact, it had no fence at all!

Part V

A FAMILY REUNITED

Chapter 18

The Road to Repatriation

A Hawaiian paradise—
Yesterday's dream.
Robbed of father, torn from husband,
Wife and children view the moon
Through tears.

—Shoichi Asami writing in Camp Livingston (Louisiana)[1]

Left behind in the wake of sudden arrests and swift removals of fathers and husbands, entire families lived in uncertainty and fear and struggled to survive. The reality that the majority of community leaders and the elite of the Japanese community in Hawai'i had been taken away so swiftly was a shock that reverberated throughout the Islands. While the men taken away as enemy aliens faced a long road of uncertainty and hardship, their families fared little better. Families went from prominent members of their communities to outcasts overnight with no head of the household to provide for them in their time of need. Many of the Japanese families who did not have someone interned were afraid to associate with the families of those that did. They feared that, by association, they too could become a target of the U.S. government. Without Reverend Miyamoto, Fumi and the children were left with no income and searching for support.

With Reverend Miyamoto gone in what felt like an instant, the Miyamoto family struggled to try and make ends meet. Clifford, only thirteen at the time, had to take on physically demanding work in the Dillingham Farm banana fields to earn money to help support the family.[2] David Kanji, who was in his first semester as a freshman at the University of Hawai'i, was a member of the ROTC and became a part of the Hawaiian Territorial Guard.[3] Eventually, David Kanji was released from the Guard and was forced to leave college to work at a nearby bank in order to have an income for the family. Clifford recalled that time:

> We were ordered eventually to move inland to a vacated old house which was owned by one of the church members. Some members of the church brought goods, but many were afraid to do so. It was a difficult time.[4]

The struggles that Clifford remembered were echoed in a January 29, 1942, report made by the FBI. In this report, Special Agent G.L. Lewis documented the receipt of information that soldiers had looted the Miyamoto home after Reverend Miyamoto was arrested. The report also noted that Reverend Miyamoto's wife did not speak English, and the family was "in desperate circumstances."[5] When Reverend Miyamoto was arrested and throughout his time in internment, he continually executed powers of attorney to protect the temple and school. One of the men designated to safeguard the properties, Dr. Seiichi Miyasaki, recalled that the temple and school buildings were occupied by the Army and military officials during the war. At one point, the men entrusted with safeguarding the temple were pressured by the Army to deed over the temple and land to them. The men refused to acquiesce to the Army's demands. Dr. Miyasaki recalled the destruction the Army caused as well.

> During their [Army] occupation, they destroyed practically all the desks used in the school and took many contents and also the bell and the shrine of the temple. The bell was later found in Mr. John Midkiff's yard, which, too, was occupied by the Army. It was used to inform them of their meal times.[6]

Even in the extremely difficult situation the family found themselves in, they still supported the war efforts. The Waialua plantation employees formed a Victory Unit and raised funds for the Red Cross in the amount of $4,800. Fumi was a donor to the cause.[7]

Since the family was under duress, Fumi and Reverend Miyamoto decided to apply for repatriation. If the family repatriated, they could rejoin Osamu who had left for Japan prior to the outbreak of war for his schooling. In the case of the Miyamotos and other Japanese families with similar circumstances, Issei parents, guardians, or heads of households harangued by the U.S. government, repatriation meant to return to the land of their birth which seemed a welcome alternative to being held behind barbed wire. Repatriation provided the one chance at family reunification. During the war, a total of 1,050 Japanese family groups were sent to relocation centers on the mainland. These families all volunteered themselves for relocation with the expectation of being repatriated to Japan. Typically, the decision was made with the hope that moving to the mainland would result in the family being reunited with the fathers and husbands who had been taken away.[8]

Fumi (age 41), along with Carol (age 16), Clifford (age 13), and Keiko (age 7), began their journey to the mainland in the hopes of being reunited with Reverend Miyamoto. David Kanji, the oldest son, stayed behind as he was of age and could continue working to assist in supporting the family and could watch over the family's possessions and temple. On August 16, 1942, Fumi, Carol, Clifford, and Keiko were processed at the Alien Processing Center in Honolulu (see figure 25). Two days later, the family sailed on the military ship USS *Republic* bound for California. In total, the USS *Republic* carried 133 evacuees—thirty-seven adult females and ninety-six children ultimately bound for New York and the M.S. *Gripsholm* for their repatriation voyage to Japan via Singapore.[9]

The trip to the mainland took eleven days. During the voyage, the families were instructed to remain inside the ship's hold and were not allowed to stay on deck. The families were told this was for their own safety for fear of submarines that could be lurking in the waters.[10] For protection, their ship was escorted by two destroyers. The voyage was especially hard on Fumi, Carol, and Keiko as each suffered from seasickness, so Clifford helped by fetching food for them and other items as needed.[11] The USS *Republic* landed at the port of embarkation at Fort Mason in San Francisco, California, on August 26th at approximately 9:30 a.m. Upon arrival, the repatriates were put onto a ferry boat to cross the bay and brought to the Oakland Port of Embarkation where they boarded a train to travel across the country to New York. A "Supervisory Party" of civilian personnel served as guards. Seven men, Interior Security Police, were employed by the WCCA (Wartime Civilian Control Agency). These guards were assisted by four American Red Cross aides. Two male civilian guards were assigned to each train car along with one Red Cross aide who could assist the male guards in caring for the repatriates. A doctor, along with his wife, and two nurses were also hired and would be dispatched according to the Train Commander's orders as needed throughout the train cars.[12]

Train No. 21737, consisting of four passenger cars, two baggage cars, and one dining car, departed the train depot at 3:55 p.m. on August 26, 1942, with all the window shades drawn shut. The train took the following route: Western Pacific Railroad to Salt Lake City; Union Pacific Railroad to Denver; Santa Fe Railroad to Kansas City; and CB&Q Railroad to Chicago. In Chicago, the train came to a stop. According to Ella Ohta Tomita, née Ohta[13] the repatriates were informed that due to heightened war activity in Singapore, where the *Gripsholm* was to originally drop them, they were being rerouted to North Carolina rather than traveling onward to New York to board the ship.[14] Mitsuko Masaki, wife of Reverend Jikyo Masaki, a priest at the Makiki

Jodo Mission, recalled being told the news that the exchange ship would not be in New York to reunite her and her children with Jikyo. They too were now on a path of internment. Frustrated and feeling deceived by the government, Mitsuko remembered, "We cried, you know, we say how come we are treated like this? They kind of deceived us, you see."[15] With heavy hearts, the families sat contemplating their fates as the train left Chicago taking the Pennsylvania Railroad to Cincinnati and arriving via Southern Railway to Asheville, North Carolina. During their journey, the repatriates were not able to exit the train at any point unless there was an emergency.[16] All in all, it took about a week for the Pullman train to make the journey from Oakland to North Carolina.[17]

The State Department, through its Special War Problems Division, established and ran its own internment centers at several resort locations in the Appalachian Mountains. The hotels housed Axis diplomats, businessmen, and consular corps staff, affiliates, and their families who were awaiting repatriation.

On September 2, 1942, the Miyamoto family, together with the rest of the families that had set out from Hawai'i weeks prior, arrived at the first of these hotels, the Grove Park Inn in Asheville, North Carolina (see figure 26). Built in 1913, the Grove Park Inn was a grand resort hotel nestled among the trees on Sunset Mountain. Cutting a striking figure, with its facade of granite boulders, the State Department paid to house the Japanese families in their care at a daily rate of $8 per adult and $5 per child.[18] Clifford recalled that the children spent a lot of free time playing pool while at Grove Park.[19] Even though there were no fences or guards keeping them in one spot at the hotel, no one in the group ventured outside of the hotel—not even to take advantage of the inn's swimming pool.[20] After almost two months there, the German and Japanese internees were transferred to another location because the Navy had leased the Grove Park Inn to serve as a rest and recreation center for naval officers. Internee families were bussed to the Assembly Inn at Montreat, North Carolina, on October 29, 1942. Six National Trailways buses left the Grove Park Inn flanked by automobiles of the state highway patrol, U.S. marshal's office, and the Immigration and Naturalization Service with border patrolmen in the group as guards.[21] This second stone "mountain retreat" was managed by the Presbyterian Church of the United States and only cost the State Department a daily rate of $2.80 per voluntary repatriate.[22] Montreat was located about sixty miles northeast of Asheville on the banks of Lake Susan. The Assembly Inn was a three-story retreat with about 130 rooms described as "a first-class hotel with elevators, a large lobby, and [where] most of the rooms have baths."[23] In order to keep a sense of normalcy and continuity among the younger children, basic classes were taught by the teenagers from Hawai'i who had already graduated from high school.[24]

Although the scenery surrounding the hotel was new and beautiful, Fumi, Carol, Clifford, and Keiko were in limbo living out of hotel rooms and being watched by guards while anxiously waiting to hear if and when they would be reunited with Reverend Miyamoto and sail to Japan to escape this prison disguised as a mountain retreat. The fight to reunite as a family was constant. While in Montreat, Fumi continued to petition for repatriation so she and the children could be reunited with Reverend Miyamoto. On January 11, 1943, Fumi completed a Petition for Repatriation form for herself, and if it was granted, she requested for Reverend Miyamoto and her three children that had made the journey to North Carolina with her to be repatriated as well.[25] While Fumi and Reverend Miyamoto would be returning to their "native land," Carol (17), Clifford (14), and Keiko (8) were American citizens by birth and had never set foot on Japanese soil. While in Montreat, the International Red Cross, having learned from the men in Camp Livingston that their families were being held there, made good on their vow to inspect the Assembly Inn. In January 1943, two months after visiting Camp Livingston, Alfred Cardinaux along with other International Red Cross representatives inspected where the mothers and children were staying. In a report, he wrote about his visit.

> A winter resort, organized at Assembly Inn Montreat [sic] (in North Carolina) accommodates 133 German men, women and children from South America, and 135 Japanese women and children from the Hawaiian Islands; all are waiting for their repatriation, but they have made no complaints.[26]

The Miyamotos and other families at Montreat would wait in vain for their repatriation to occur. Instead of boarding a ship bound for Japan, four months later, on April 30th, Fumi, Carol, Clifford, and Keiko would board a train bound for Texas and a family internment camp. Though this was not the freedom through repatriation they had originally signed up for, the much hoped-for reunion of the Miyamoto family was close at hand.

NOTES

1. Claire Sato and Violet Harada, *A Resilient Spirit: The Voice of Hawai'i's Internees* (Honolulu, HI: Japanese Cultural Center of Hawai'i, 2016), 18.
2. Clifford Miyamoto, summary of oral history conducted by Melvin Inamasu and Marilyn Higashide on January 19, 2015, Voice of Internment Project, Japanese Cultural Center Hawai'i, Honolulu, HI.
3. The Hawai'i Territorial Guard was called to action within hours of the attack on Pearl Harbor. Members of the ROTC from the University of Hawai'i were the first group to be deployed to strategic civilian points around Oahu to stand guard and act as an "anti-sabotage force." Initially comprised of a small group of officers and men (35 and 370, respectively), by December 31st numbers had swelled to include

"89 officers and 1,254 men on guard at 150 posts" with many coming from local high school ROTC units. Disbanded on January 21, 1942, many of the men went on to serve as laborers in the Varsity Victory Volunteers, the Corps of Engineers Auxiliary unit at Schofield Barracks. Eventually, many served as members of the famed 442 Regimental Combat Team, or in some cases as translators for the Military Intelligence Service. (Kelli Y. Nakamura, "Hawaii Territorial Guard," Densho Encyclopedia, https://encyclopedia.densho.org/Hawaii_Territorial_Guard/ (accessed August 19, 2022); Frank Odo, "Varsity Victory Volunteers," Densho Encyclopedia, http://encyclopedia.densho.org/Varsity_Victory_Volunteers/ (Last modified December 29, 2021)).

4. Clifford Miyamoto, interview with authors, October 10, 2016. Clifford recalled in another interview as well that "Japanese were not allowed to live on the shoreline." Therefore, the family was ordered to move inland. (Clifford Miyamoto, summary of oral history conducted by Melvin Inamasu and Marilyn Higashide on January 19, 2015, Voice of Internment Project, Japanese Cultural Center Hawaiʻi, Honolulu, HI.)

5. Buntetsu Miyamoto, FBI File No. 97-42, 1941, RG 389, Box 2626, National Archives, College Park, Maryland.

6. Clark, *Guardian of the Sea*, 85.

7. "Plantation People Team Up to Raise Large Contribution," *Honolulu Star Bulletin* (Honolulu, HI), September 15, 1942.

8. "Chapter IX, Prisoners of War and Internees," History of Provost Marshal's Office, Part 2; Japanese Internment and Relocation Files: The Hawaiʻi Experience, University of Hawaiʻi, Mānoa.

9. Kendall J. Fielder to Chief, Military Intelligence Service, "Repatriation of Japanese Families," August 17, 1942, Box 1, Folder 133, RG 107, Japanese Internment and Relocation Files: The Hawaiʻi Experience, University of Hawaiʻi, Mānoa.

10. "Japanese American Internment Unit for Modern History of Hawaiʻi (2008)," Japanese Cultural Center of Hawaiʻi, 55, https://www.hawaiiinternment.org/sites/default/files/Modern%20History%20of%20Hawaii_0.pdf.

11. Clifford Miyamoto, summary of oral history conducted by Melvin Inamasu and Marilyn Higashide on January 19, 2015, Voice of Internment Project, Japanese Cultural Center Hawaiʻi, Honolulu, HI.

12. "Transportation of Hawaiian Evacuees (133 persons) from San Francisco to Ashville, North Carolina," August 25, 1942, Japanese Women and Children to be Repatriated (133); RG 107, Japanese Internment and Relocation Files: The Hawaiʻi Experience; University of Hawaiʻi, Mānoa.

13. Ella Miyeko Tomita, née Ohta was from Laupahoehoe on the Big Island. She was traveling with her mother and siblings, alongside the Miyamoto family and others from Hawaiʻi, seeking to be reunited with her father, Reverend Kunio Ohta, a Buddhist minister. Ella recalled the Miyamoto family during a phone interview conducted with the authors. The Ohta and Miyamoto families followed the same repatriation journey from Hawaiʻi all the way to Crystal City, Texas. The two family patriarchs, Reverend Miyamoto and Reverend Ohta, also traveled together during their internment journey. After the war, Reverend Miyamoto became bishop of the Jodo Mission

on Makiki Street in Honolulu and Reverend Ohta was one of the ministers who would serve under Bishop Miyamoto. ("Jodo Buddhists are Celebrating Anniversary with Colorful Fete," *Honolulu Star-Bulletin*, September 2, 1950.)

14. "Japanese American Internment Unit for Modern History of Hawai'i (2008)," 56.

15. Mitsuko Sumida and Dorothy Murakami, transcript of oral history interview by Ted Tsukiyama, August 6, 1997, Japanese Cultural Center of Hawai'i, https://jcch.soutronglobal.net/Portal/Default/en-US/RecordView/Index/4654.

16. "Transportation of Hawaiian Evacuees (133 persons) from San Francisco to Ashville, North Carolina," August 25, 1942, Japanese Women and Children to be Repatriated (133); RG 107, Japanese Internment and Relocation Files: The Hawai'i Experience; University of Hawai'i, Mānoa.

17. Clifford Miyamoto, interview with authors, October 10, 2016.

18. Landon Dunn and Timothy Ryan, *Axis Diplomats in American Custody: The Housing of Enemy Representatives and Their Exchange for American Counterparts, 1941–1945* (Jefferson, NC: McFarland & Company, Inc., 2016), 60.

19. Clifford Miyamoto, summary of oral history conducted by Melvin Inamasu and Marilyn Higashide on January 19, 2015, Voice of Internment Project, Japanese Cultural Center Hawai'i, Honolulu, HI.

20. Clifford Miyamoto, summary of oral history conducted by Melvin Inamasu and Marilyn Higashide on January 19, 2015, Voice of Internment Project, Japanese Cultural Center Hawai'i, Honolulu, HI.

21. "Enemy National Moved From Here to Montreat," *The Asheville Citizen* (Asheville, North Carolina), October 30, 1942.

22. Dunn and Ryan, *Axis Diplomats in American Custody*, 110.

23. "Montreat Inn Leased for Aliens," *The Asheville Citizen* (Asheville, North Carolina), October 21, 1942.

24. "Japanese American Internment Unit for Modern History of Hawai'i (2008)," 56.

25. "Petition for Repatriation," January 11, 1943; Records Relating to Japanese Civilian Internees During World War II, 1942–1946; RG 389: Records of the Office of the Provost Marshal General; National Archives at College Park, Maryland.

26. Le Comité international el la guerre, "Delegations du Comité Internationale dans les Cinq Continents," *Revue International de la Croix-Rouge*, Bulletin 289 (January1943): 9. https://international-review.icrc.org/fr/articles/le-comite-international-et-la-guerre-delegations-du-comite-international-dans-les-cinq-0. Translation provided by Hayley Johnson.

Chapter 19

Reunited Behind Barbed Wire

It was a few days' journey by train for Fumi and the children from North Carolina to the Crystal City Family Internment Camp just on the outskirts of Crystal City, Texas. Located approximately 110 miles southwest of San Antonio, Texas, the Crystal City Camp was surrounded by sagebrush and sand—a far cry from the lush landscape of the Hawaiian Islands, the tall pines of central Louisiana, or the misty mountains of North Carolina. It was hot and flat. Temperatures could soar into triple digits, a heat that would only allow cacti to grow.

> There were only skinny, poor-looking cactuses... And the cactuses were pitch-black... They changed to a nice green in the evening when the temperature cooled down. The reason was that flies couldn't fly and just hung on to the cactuses to look for a bit of shade.[1]

In the sixteenth century, the intrepid Spanish explorer Cabeza de Vaca called the area "El Desierto de los Muertos, The Desert of the Dead."[2] Three hundred years later, the American colonists dubbed it "heartbreak country."[3] But for Fumi, Carol, Clifford, and Keiko, the barren desert landscape didn't matter; all that mattered was seeing Reverend Miyamoto again.

Crystal City Family Internment Camp opened in December 1942 as a site to house the families of individuals who had been arrested as enemy aliens in the aftermath of Pearl Harbor. In an effort to be reunited with the male heads of their households who were being held in Army or Department of Justice camps scattered across the United States, many wives and their children had opted for repatriation which resulted in internment-by-default when exchange ships were not available. Other families included those who had been kidnapped and deported from Latin American countries under the U.S.

Department of State's Special War Problems Division prisoner exchange program. Still others would come from War Relocation Authority camps like Poston, Gila River, Heart Mountain, and Tule Lake. Crystal City was believed to be only a temporary stop on their journey toward repatriation.

The land on which the Crystal City Camp was located had been previously owned by the Farm Security Administration as a housing site for migratory agricultural workers during the Great Depression. When it became clear to authorities that a family internee camp would be needed, this location was chosen because of the existing buildings on the property (41 three-room cottages, 118 one-room shelters, and other service buildings), the availability of utility services for a 2,000 person camp, and mild winters.[4] The Farm Security Administration transferred their holding of 240 acres of land to the U.S. Department of Justice Immigration and Naturalization Service (INS), the government agency that would now oversee the building, expansion, and daily operations of the Crystal City Family Internment Camp.[5] The INS immediately purchased an additional 50 acres of land making the camp a total of 290 acres.[6]

Joseph L. O'Rourke oversaw the daily operations of the entire camp as the Officer in Charge of Camp.[7] Described as "a jolly Irishman," his magnetic personality led to him being considered the "Pied Piper of Crystal City," so great was his popularity in camp, especially with the children.[8] According to O'Rourke, "this being the first venture in the internment of family groups, no precedent for operations existed. The Administration could only apply and temper basic regulations existing for the detention of male internees and prisoners of war."[9] The regulations that O'Rourke was referring to are from the 1929 Geneva Convention that also regulated the treatment of the interned alien populations at U.S. Army and Department of Justice camps, such as Camp Livingston. In order to facilitate aid and compliance with these guidelines, the YMCA and International Committee of the Red Cross shared a liaison office on-site and entertained visiting officials from these agencies when they would inspect the camp conditions and treatment of internees.[10] When originally conceived as a family internment camp, Crystal City had been slated to hold only Japanese internees and their families. This aligned with the 1929 Geneva Convention to "as far as possible avoid bringing together in the same camp prisoners of different races or nationalities."[11] However, the first internee residents who arrived at camp in December 1942 were 35 German families, consisting of 115 individuals, previously held at Ellis Island Detention Station and Camp Forrest, Tennessee. This first group was only to be housed temporarily at Crystal City until appropriate accommodations were made available at the Seagoville Internment Camp outside of Dallas.[12] Before coming to Crystal City, this first group of Germans had promised to help build parts of the camp, "but immediately began to object to such work because it would benefit only the Japanese—so very little constructive assistance was rendered by them."[13] More Germans arrived throughout February 1943, including a large group (131 persons) from Costa Rica.[14] It wasn't until March 10, 1943, that the first group of Nikkei arrived at camp—fourteen women and fourteen children.[15] On March 17, 1943, the first group of Japanese male internees from Camp Livingston arrived, followed a week later by male internees from the Lordsburg Internment Camp in New Mexico.[16] They had been brought ahead of their families so they could continue to help build out the internment camp including the housing units that they and their families would occupy during their stay.[17] As more internees arrived, the "original idea that Crystal City would be strictly a Japanese camp had been abandoned, and plans from that time forward contemplated a mixed nationality group," which made the Crystal City Family Internment Camp unique.[18]

On March 30, 1943, Reverend Miyamoto arrived at Crystal City—the same day he left Camp Livingston. He, like the other men in camp, arrived ahead of his family to help with the construction of the camp's housing. At this point, Reverend Miyamoto had been an enemy alien internee in the custody of the U.S. government for over a year. Unbeknownst to him however, J. Edgar Hoover was still in pursuit of prosecuting him for his role as a consular agent. Through continued correspondence with Assistant Attorney General Wendell Berge the matter was *finally* settled on June 11, 1943, with a memo from Berge to Hoover stating:

> the facts in this case are not sufficient to warrant prosecution, particularly in view of the fact that the War Department opposed proceeding against so-called "consular agents" and since the subject is now interned by the military authorities for the duration of the war.[19]

In the memo, Berge described the role of the consular agent as "engaged in functions commonly performed by a notary public,"[20] a statement both refreshing and upsetting as this final understanding of the role of a *toritsuginin* had come so long after the start of Reverend Miyamoto's internment odyssey.

A month after Reverend Miyamoto's arrival to Crystal City, on April 30th, the Japanese and German families being held at the Assembly Inn, including Fumi and the children, began their journey to reunification with their husbands and fathers.[21] Fumi, Carol, Clifford, and Keiko arrived in Crystal City on May 2nd to be greeted by Reverend Miyamoto. The family was finally reunited after one year, four months, and twenty-five days apart.

As families and their sizes varied throughout the camp, so too did housing units. Single-family units, duplexes, triplexes, and a type of Quonset hut "often called the 'Kamaboko' house due to its shape" were some of the variety of housing that could be found throughout the camp.[22] The Miyamotos lived on "Arizona Street" in Q-59, a duplex housing unit with two bedrooms and a kitchen-living room.[23] There were no doors within their new housing unit, and so there was no privacy for the five newly reunited family members. The family had to share a latrine with their neighbors in the duplex unit, and they had to shower in a public bath facility shared by many. Water that was cool and refreshing in the summer months turned frigid in the winter months, making showering a brief and difficult affair.[24] Despite the lack of privacy within their unit, officials overseeing the camp respected the "privacy of the home . . . and never entered without just cause."[25] Although each unit, save for the Victory Huts, was "arranged for family style cooking," when internee families first arrived at the camp, they were "fed in a common mess hall," while they got their bearings, arranged their dwellings to their liking, and received their "subsistence allowances."[26] These allowances could be used to purchase food at the general store, which was comprised of a central grocery and meat market, while milk and ice were delivered to the internees' housing units, with internee labor being used for these deliveries.[27]

The grocery store came to fruition when it was noticed that the original system of issuing food without regard to need or taste was not working. Food was going to waste and made the camp feel more like a prison.[28] So, a grocery store was created where internees could come and shop like they had done before camp and choose foods that suited the family's palates.[29] Soon, "the morning shopping tour of the housewives" was a daily event at the marketplace, where the women of the household would bring homemade grocery carts and line them up in front of the store—"literally scores" of them, according to O'Rourke. Often they would bring their young children and leave them in the cart while they shopped inside.[30] The "money" used to purchase items in camp, including food from the market and items from the camp clothing store, was red and green plastic or pressed paper tokens, called camp scrip.[31] There was also a ration system in place that used coupons for items like milk, eggs, butter, and bread. Rations would sometimes be traded among the internees as demonstrated by Carol Miyamoto's acquired taste for sauerkraut resulting from one such trade with some of the German internees in camp. Fumi was able to cook for the family in their housing unit's kitchen which even had an ice box that kept items cool from the block of ice that was placed on top.[32] Items for the home—cooking utensils, furniture, bedding, and the like—were provided by the Internal Relations Division of the camp and could only be replaced if the used item was returned.[33] Food items particular to Japanese cuisine were made available including "miso paste, soy sauce, rice, noodles, seaweed, dried shrimp, adjinimoto seasoning, tofu, etc."[34] After numerous requests from the Japanese internees, a "Tofu Factory" was established in a newly erected Victory Hut wherein the appropriate equipment was provided for the making of tofu. Families could purchase tofu using camp scrip, and each family made their own container from tin cans to carry the tofu back to their homes.³⁵

As internees became acclimated to their new homes and settled into camp life, they began to beautify their surroundings. Many families built porches and additional rooms onto their housing units and created gardens—all with their own money. It was estimated that internees spent $50,000 out of their own pockets on these projects.³⁶ This added greenery helped not only with enriching the desolate landscape but also provided a respite from the heat. According to a scrapbook compiled by Mary F. Clark, head nurse at Crystal City, "by 1944 almost every building in camp was hidden by a mass of Greenery. Little bridges, rock gardens, gold fish ponds were everywhere. As were all kinds of flowers, vines, shrubs and quick growing trees."³⁷ Reverend Kyōdō Fujihana³⁸ recalled the ingenuity of those in camp:

> there is always a way when you're at your wits' end. Someone got hold of beans from a castor oil plant somehow some place. So we planted the beans. It was a great success. The beans grew to be like large trees in half a year. The whole camp became a cool place.³⁹

Designed by the INS as a self-contained community, the camp also had:

> food stores, auditoriums, warehouses, administration offices and a 70-bed hospital, places of worship, post office, bakery, barber shop, beauty shop, school system, a Japanese Sumo wrestling ring, and a German *beer garten*.⁴⁰

There was also a print shop that supported the printing of four camp newspapers, each representing the language of an internee group held in camp—English, Japanese, Spanish, and German.⁴¹ The German beer garden was named Café Vaterland and was the result of the German internees refurbishing part of their recreation building and pooling their rations together to host an "old style German Beer Garden and eating house on Saturday nights."⁴² There was also a clothing store on-site that allowed internees to choose their clothes as opposed to having them issued (where oftentimes the clothing would not fit or be the wrong color or style), with the latter process helping build camp morale. Much like a regular clothing store, items were placed on shelves for purchase, and "there were bargains, sales, displays as in any small town store. The display windows were kept lighted at night for the benefit of the strollers and window shoppers."⁴³ Next to the Miyamoto home was the camp's library which contained 3,500 volumes—1,400 in German, 200 in Japanese, and 100 in Spanish—donated by the YMCA, National Catholic Welfare Conference, and American Friends. If the library did not have a book the internee needed, they could borrow a book from the University of Texas library for up to three weeks.⁴⁴ On a map of Crystal City, the recreation hall located near the center of the camp was earmarked as a multi-faith chapel where internees could practice their faith freely, welcoming Buddhist, Catholic, Konko, Lutheran, and Shinto practitioners; however, Mary F. Clark noted that buildings had been set aside for practitioners—"one for the Christians and one for the Shinto and Buddhist faith."⁴⁵ On the eastern edge of camp was a 4.2-acre citrus orchard, peppered throughout with beehives, as well as two basketball courts and football, soccer, and baseball fields.⁴⁶

In an attempt to beat the heat of the brutal summers, an agreement was reached between the internees, German and Japanese, and the camp's administration whereby the internees could use the camp's reservoir as a swimming pool if they agreed to dredge the existing pond—overrun with snakes and water hyacinths, and too small to irrigate the farming activities of the camp and surrounding land—and line the new, larger reservoir with concrete. When completed, the "pool" was a 250-foot wide circular structure. The deep end was approximately fifteen feet and had three diving platforms. It was separated from the shallow end, filled with tadpoles, by a cable.⁴⁷ It was said that the "swimming pool/irrigation reservoir was the camp's largest defining feature."⁴⁸ Clifford was nicknamed "Hawaiian Shark" because of his natural swimming abilities, no doubt honed by swimming regularly in the waters just steps from the family's home and temple.⁴⁹ For many children interned in Crystal City, camp life was permeated with both recreational activities and school. Clifford remembered:

> attend[ing] English school as well as Japanese school. At the English school, we had proms, graduation, and the cheering section for the football team and other school activities were baseball, basketball, track, swimming. We had a large irrigation ditch reservoir. And sumo, Boy Scouts,⁵⁰ judo and outdoor movies once a week.⁵¹

There was also a Japanese Young People Division that would sponsor events like a "spring occasion" where girl scouts and boy scouts would present their troop flag, have a "grand athletic meeting" between them, and finally a prize trophy would be presented to the winners by camp commander O'Rourke.⁵² Through the monotonous days, children acted as children do, regardless of their surroundings. Clifford recalled one incident when some of the children began loudly singing "Don't Fence Me In." While the children found it humorous, Clifford was glad that there was no recourse and "nobody got shot."⁵³

War had interrupted the lives of everyone. But the forced removal, incarceration, and/or internment of fathers, mothers, and whole families had stopped normal life in its tracks for those affected. Many children of those interned, like the Miyamoto children, had not been able to attend school or continue their studies on the long and arduous journey to Crystal City. This changed once they entered the family camp. Within the barbed wire fences of Crystal City, three types of schooling were available to students: German, Japanese, and Federal (or American style). The German and Japanese schools focused on cultural and linguistic education and utilized teachers, including Reverend Miyamoto, from within the internee community at Crystal City to instruct students.[54] According to Alfred Cardinaux, who also visited Crystal City as a representative of the ICRC, the:

> Japanese kindergarten class comprises 58 little ones, and 150 students at the primary school, 50 at secondary . . . [He] attended a Manners class in which the Japanese demonstrated to their daughters habits from their country: how to serve tea according to Japanese custom, for example.[55]

The language schools were especially appealing to those whose future appeared to be repatriation so that students could become familiar with the language and customs of their future home.

Even though some of the other children who had journeyed with the Miyamotos to Crystal City elected to attend the Japanese school exclusively, Reverend Miyamoto insisted that his children attend the American school as their main source of schooling. After their regular school day, they would then attend the Japanese school—much like what they had done in Hawaiʻi.[56] The American schools—Federal Elementary and Federal High School—were open to all interned children in camp, regardless of nationality. Despite this, most students in the American schools were Japanese. Overseen by the Texas Board of Education, the Federal schools provided a typical public school curriculum that could be found elsewhere in Texas.[57] Faculty for the Federal schools was difficult to come by during wartime. There was a shortage of teachers, the length of employment was uncertain, and the location was remote.[58] When Miss Mabel B. Ellis of the YWCA wrote about the family camp she remarked, "Because of the isolated location of Crystal City, the employees of the internment camp have relatively little more freedom than the internees behind the fence."[59] Despite this, qualified and dedicated faculty were found and brought in from around the country. According to Ella Miyeko Tomita, née Ohta, these teachers, all Caucasians, did not live in camp with the interned families and had to go through armed checkpoints every time they entered Crystal City. Ella thought "they were terrific! They really dedicated themselves to us."[60] In 1945, the graduating class from Federal High School numbered thirty-six students, one of which was Carol Miyamoto. Some of these students went on to various colleges in the United States including such schools as Texas University and Wayne

State University.⁶¹ The following year's graduation class would also be its last. Federal High School only has four recorded names for the graduating class of 1946—Henry Horie, Barbara Minner, Sachiko Sasaki, and Yukio Tsuchitani—a reflection of the war's end.⁶²

Despite the apparent harmony within the camp, an incident in 1944 stemming from a proposed high school dance does give insight into cultural clashes that could occur in a camp with such a varied populace. A proposal for a springtime prom for the juniors and seniors at the Federal High School was met with backlash from some in the Japanese community. Demanding the dance be canceled, a spokesman for the Japanese community stated:

> According to time-honored Japanese customs, social dance has been condemned morally and religiously, and *prohibited by law* . . . The most deplorable event in many Relocation Centers is that many girls and boys have been demoralized through social dance which are held as often as they want.⁶³

O'Rourke, however, persisted and the social was held; in attendance were "approximately thirty teenagers from the Japanese group and about a dozen more from the German community."⁶⁴ In response, a short-lived strike occurred when the Japanese language school closed and the Japanese teachers retaliated against those who attended the dance by refusing to teach them.⁶⁵ Reporting the event to W. F. Kelly, the assistant commissioner for Alien Control Office, O'Rourke wrote:

> . . . and [they] request that you [Kelly] advise me not to take steps which endanger the moral life of their children. The Japanese have been permitted to hold their celebrations and athletic events regularly, but when the American School scheduled the dance, the Japanese opposed to it, proposed a secret move against the dance being held by their group as a whole . . . This instance regarding the dance is just a small one, in which an attempt is made by the older Japanese to force upon the generation born in the United States, the customs and culture of Japan.⁶⁶

This situation is interesting as the use of striking as a means of achieving desired outcomes has, as we have seen, roots in the Hawaiian labor strikes as well as strikes held by the men in other internment camps prior to their internment at Crystal City.

While the children in camp were occupied with school or found diversion in recreational activities, the older internees could choose to work at various jobs supporting the operations of the camp, such as the market, mess halls, warehouses, garbage detail, farming assistance, or even the hobby shop. Others were allowed to run their own camp-sanctioned businesses such as barber or beauty shops or acting as canteen managers for the German

General Store or Japanese Union Store.[67] The canteens sold items like toiletries and tobacco that the government purchased and then sold "to the internee stores who in turn sold them for the token money. The token money was returned to the officials, who purchased new merchandise for whatever amount had been returned."[68] Many internees took up work they had done before internment—"butchers became butchers"[69] and those trained in the medical field were tapped to work at the seventy-bed hospital located in the southwest section of the camp, just feet from the barbed wire fences.[70] The hospital employed forty-nine internees as physicians, dentists, pharmacists, and support staff, in addition to the small team of official hospital staff from the U.S. Public Health Services Department.[71] Some of the young women in camp, a few still teenagers, were allowed to train under the nurses at the camp hospital to become nurses' aides—no easy feat as many of the young trainees were still in high school. These young women would go to school during the day and then report for their shift from 3:00 p.m. to 11:00 p.m. or even work the night shift from 11:00 p.m. to 7:00 a.m.[72] The first group of nurses' aides graduated on June 30, 1943, and were celebrated in camp.[73] Joining the ranks of the other internees employed at the hospital, these new nurses' aides could assist with almost anything, including emergency delivery and even surgery.[74] But no matter the position, from doctor to nurses' aide to store clerk, each internee received an hourly rate of ten cents an hour for their work, with most working eight-hour days.[75]

Life in the camp was more than just work or school. Holidays and birthdays were celebrated with zeal. German internees were noted to observe May Day, Christmas, and Easter, while the Japanese internees celebrated New Year's Day as well as *Hinamatsuri* (Girl's Day or Doll's Day) in March.[76] There may have even been a summer Bon dance in the Japanese community to honor the ancestors' spirits.[77] For many internees, this was the first time in a long time that holidays and other special occasions were spent together as a family, giving it special significance. There were other cultural pursuits available to internees as well. The continued creation of poetry and art, as was seen in Camp Livingston and other internment and incarceration camps across the nation, found a welcome home in Crystal City. One of the internee physicians employed at the camp hospital was none other than Dr. Motokazu Mori, the prolific tanka poet and Honolulu surgeon.[78] Writing under the pen name *Taisanboku*, before the outbreak of the war, he was one of the founding members of the Honolulu tanka club *Choonshisha,* or the Sound of the Sea. His wife, Dr. Ishiko Mori, also wrote tanka poetry with the pen name *Shakunage*. Between treating patients at Crystal City, Dr. Motokazu Mori cofounded the *Tekisesu-shisha* or the Texas Poetry Club. In October 1945 while still in camp, Dr. Mori edited a collection of over 300 tanka poems from internees in Crystal City that would be published as a mimeographed collection titled

Nagareboshi or Shooting Stars.[79] Additionally, the Japanese community at Crystal City held exhibitions showcasing artistic works like drawings, paintings, fans, flower arrangements, calligraphy, crafts, and needlework.[80] Each exhibition included numerous pieces. Photographs show them clustered together tightly, but orderly, on the walls, almost hiding the tar paper of the barracks and the grim reminder of where these exhibitions were being held. *Gaman* was not just found among the men held at Camp Livingston; here at Crystal City, we can see that *gaman* was practiced by all ages. The essence of *gaman* was a common binding thread within and between camps.

Crystal City as a designated family camp strived to normalize this new life for internees as much as possible. "There were births, deaths, love affairs, marriages, love triangles, the ups and down of any community life."[81] But even though Crystal City was built to resemble a community, for those held inside the constant reminder of imprisonment was ever present. Surrounding the camp was a ten-foot-high barbed wire fence and six watchtowers with armed guards. An armed guard patrolled the fence line and internal security guards patrolled interior areas within the camp.[82] "At night, the searchlights from the camp could be seen across the border in Mexico," thirty-five miles away.[83] Clifford recalled that life in Crystal City was fine, "even though we were caged in like criminals."[84] The security, censorship of mail, and other restrictions would have come as a shock to those who had voluntarily or in some cases inadvertently chosen internment to bring their families together once again, namely the women and children who had left their homes to join their husbands and fathers behind barbed wire. This new life as a prisoner was a hard pill to swallow for many in the camp.

Upon entering Crystal City, they were no longer free to come and go as they pleased. In an effort to combat this feeling of isolation and imprisonment, the camp administration allowed for groups of internees to picnic down the road from camp on the Nueces River as a morale-building exercise, including school groups and those that worked together. This was a popular pastime for many in camp, but it was temporarily stopped because the Surveillance and Internal Relations personnel soon became overwhelmed with requests (including one in which a group of 600 Germans requested permission for a "mass picnic at the same time").[85] Family and friends were permitted supervised visits with internees in the visitation building near the main entrance. Only the children of internees, visiting their parents during their school's summer or winter break, could cross over into the camp.[86]

It was possible, however, for internees to petition the camp administration to be allowed to travel outside of the camp confines for a designated period of leave to visit family. As Fumi was catching up with a friend who recently returned from a leave period, she learned about a Japanese family in Alexandria who frequently hosted fellow Nikkei on their journeys to visit friends and family. Intrigued by this family and their generosity, Fumi asked her friend the family's name. Her friend answered "Kohara."

Fumi was stunned by the name she heard. Kohara! As in her cousin Manabu Kohara? She couldn't quite believe the strange coincidence and geography of chance that had reconnected the Miyamoto and Kohara families. As Reverend Miyamoto would say, "There is nothing more mysterious than destiny, after all." Unable to pass up the opportunity to reconnect with her family, Fumi wrote to the Kohara family address and arranged to visit them. In the late summer of 1945, Fumi and Carol made the trek from Crystal City, Texas, to Alexandria, Louisiana. Carol served as Fumi's translator on the journey, but once Fumi was reunited with Saki, they were able to converse easily in their native Japanese. Fumi and Carol were able to pay their respects at Manabu's gravesite, a moment captured by a photograph—the quintessential Kohara way (see figure 27).

Fumi and Carol stayed with Saki for 3 ½ weeks before returning to Crystal City with neither Fumi nor Saki knowing what the future held for their families. Would the Miyamoto family finally be chosen for repatriation? Many had already left Crystal City and been repatriated back to Japan, among them were people they had known in Hawai'i or had come to know during their internment journey, but the Miyamoto's names had never been called to board one of these exchange ships.[87] Was repatriation their fate or was it something they even wanted anymore? It was during Fumi and Carol's trip that Reverend Miyamoto submitted a non-repatriation request asking that the family be released at the conclusion of the war to return to Hawai'i "for the benefit of my children's education. Also because I have a son in Hawai'i [David Kanji]; he wants the family to come back."[88] This request was reviewed in the Internal Relations office at Crystal City by E. D. Alexander who noted that the application "has little or no merit" because Reverend Miyamoto had "always demonstrated a very pro-Japanese attitude and [had] repeatedly requested to return to Japan until termination of war."[89] Reverend Miyamoto submitted his non-repatriation request just three weeks after the last atomic bomb had been dropped on Nagasaki signaling the end of the war, and consequently, the end of the need to be repatriated as a means to escape the family's imprisonment. Again, Reverend Miyamoto would be marked as "other" simply for attempting to work the internment system in favor of his family and their freedom. Despite the reviewing officer's suspicion around Reverend Miyamoto's non-repatriation request, three months after the chance reunion between Fumi and Saki, the Miyamotos were released from Crystal City to begin their journey home to Hawai'i.[90] Fumi and Saki would never meet again; however, the two families would remain forever linked through this shared time of hardship.

Even though the Miyamotos left Crystal City after the conclusion of the war in 1945, the camp would continue to operate as a center of internment until the summer of 1947 when its last inhabitants, mostly Japanese Peruvians, were either repatriated to Japan or Hawai'i, released to the care of sponsors, or departed to work at Seabrook Farms in New Jersey.[91] "In general the internment ended very slowly and tortuously."[92] When writing his report recounting the history of the camp, O'Rourke stated: "from its inception through June 30, 1945 the Crystal City camp inducted 4,751 internees (including 153 births)."[93] The majority of those held in camp were Nikkei, and over half (52.4 percent) were children—either Latin American or U.S. citizens by birth, some even born in camp.[94] By the time the camp officially closed on February 27, 1948, it had grown to encompass 694 buildings.[95] Like Camp Livingston, nothing substantial remains of the Crystal City Family Internment Camp today save two historical markers, some slabs of concrete, a flag pole, and memories.[96]

NOTES

1. Reverend Kyōdō Fujihana, interview by Ichigūkai members [Names unknown], May 6, 1978, Japanese Cultural Center of Hawai'i, Honolulu, HI, https://jcch.soutronglobal.net/Portal/Default/en-GB/RecordView/Index/6381. Despite the heat and barren landscape, Crystal City farmers were able to grow spinach and other winter vegetables. With the introduction of railway lines to the area, the production and shipment of spinach became so great that the town was dubbed the "Spinach Capital of the World." To celebrate this new moniker, a statue of Popeye, still standing today, was erected in downtown Crystal City in 1937, and the town's yearly spinach festival still takes place in the fall. Some internees, like Hideo Kaneshiro, even remember seeing the Popeye statue on their way to the Crystal City Family Internment Camp.

2. Jan Jarboe Russell, *The Train to Crystal City: FDR's Secret Prisoner Exchange Program and America's Only Family Internment Camp During World War II* (New York: Scribner, 2015), 35.

3. Russell, *The Train to Crystal City*, 36.

4. Joseph O'Rourke, "Historical Narrative of the Crystal City Internment Camp," a report to W.F. Kelly, Assistant Commissioner for Alien Control Office, Immigration and Naturalization Service, Crystal City Internment Camp, RG 85, 101/161, 32, National Archives, 1, https://gaic.info/history-of-crystal-city-internment-camp-now-online/. There is no mention in O'Rourke's report of consideration at the time regarding weather conditions, namely heat, in the summer months. Additionally, this original number projection of individuals to be held in Crystal City was grossly underestimated. During 1945, Crystal City's internment population peaked to 3,374 individuals. (United States Department of Justice, Immigration and Naturalization Service, "United States Family Internment Camp, Crystal City, Texas," https://www.foitimes.com/CampHousing.pdf).

5. O'Rourke, "Historical Narrative of the Crystal City Internment Camp," 5. As the camp grew, it began to become more self-sufficient. Case in point, at a certain point a sewage plant was built on site to "take care of excess" and this became "colloquially known as Lake O'Rourke," after the camp's commander. (Mary F. Clark, "The Camp" in "Before I Forget, 1942–1947," California State University, Sacramento, Department of Special Collections and University Archives, https://cdm16855.contentdm.oclc.org/digital/collection/p16855coll4/id/10934)

6. O'Rourke, "Historical Narrative of the Crystal City Internment Camp," 5.

7. O'Rourke became Officer in Charge of Camp at Crystal City in June 1943, replacing Mr. N.D. Collaer. Before taking the position at Crystal City, O'Rourke had previously directed the Seagoville Internment Camp in Seagoville, Texas. (O'Rourke, "Historical Narrative of the Crystal City Internment Camp," 3.)

8. Clark, "Those Other Camps," 128. According to Jerre Mangione, "The children were his [O'Rourke's] primary concern; he was determined to imbue them with the sense of freedom being denied to their parents. Looking ahead to the time when the camp would be shut down, he wanted the children to have happy memories of the place so that 'they can grow up to be good American citizens.' It was a matter of pride with them that many of the children seemed unaware that they were imprisoned; they were under the impression that the fence around them was intended for the people on the other side of it. 'Of course, sooner or later they'll find out the truth but meanwhile it's something that doesn't have to prey on their minds.'" (Jerre Mangione, *An Ethnic at Large: A Memoir of America in the Thirties and Forties* (New York: G.P. Putnam's Sons, 1978), 332).

9. O'Rourke, "Historical Narrative of the Crystal City Internment Camp," 3.

10. United States Department of Justice, Immigration and Naturalization Service, "United States Family Internment Camp, Crystal City, Texas," https://www.foitimes.com/CampHousing.pdf. This document has informed much of our understanding of the general layout of Crystal City, the functions and locations of buildings and services, as well as specific dwellings in which families were housed.

11. International Committee of the Red Cross, *Convention Relative to the Treatment of Prisoners of War. Geneva, 27 July 1929,* Part III, Section II, Article 9. https://ihl-databases.icrc.org/applic/ihl/ihl.nsf/ART/305-430010?OpenDocument

12. O'Rourke, "Historical Narrative of the Crystal City Internment Camp," 6.

13. O'Rourke, "Historical Narrative of the Crystal City Internment Camp," 7.

14. O'Rourke, "Historical Narrative of the Crystal City Internment Camp," 7.

15. O'Rourke, "Historical Narrative of the Crystal City Internment Camp," 7.

16. O'Rourke, "Historical Narrative of the Crystal City Internment Camp," 7.

17. O'Rourke, "Historical Narrative of the Crystal City Internment Camp," 7.

18. O'Rourke, "Historical Narrative of the Crystal City Internment Camp," 7.

19. Buntetsu Miyamoto, FBI File No. 97-42, 1941, RG 389, Box 2626, National Archives, College Park, Maryland.

20. Buntetsu Miyamoto, FBI File No. 97-42, 1941, RG 389, Box 2626, National Archives, College Park, Maryland.

21. "Japs, Germans to be Sent to Camp in Texas," *Asheville Citizen-Times* (Asheville, North Carolina), April 28, 1943.

22. "Japanese American Internment Unit for Modern History of Hawai'i (2008)," 57; United States Department of Justice, Immigration and Naturalization Service, "United States Family Internment Camp, Crystal City, Texas," https://www.foitimes.com/CampHousing.pdf. According to O'Rourke, because it was thought that the first group of German internees were to be living at Crystal City only temporarily, they were given access to the best quarters and other facilities available in camp, including housing with indoor bathrooms. As the population of German internees grew paired with the way the camp was to be segregated by nationality, it did not make sense to move them. "[T]he Germans enjoyed favor until a repatriation in January 1945, when it became necessary to reclaim an entire German section having toilet facilities in the buildings for assignment to additional Japanese who arrived." (O'Rourke, "Historical Narrative of the Crystal City Internment Camp," 7).

23. United States Department of Justice, Immigration and Naturalization Service, "United States Family Internment Camp, Crystal City, Texas," https://www.foitimes.com/CampHousing.pdf; Clifford Miyamoto, summary of oral history conducted by Melvin Inamasu and Marilyn Higashide on January 19, 2015, Voice of Internment Project, Japanese Cultural Center Hawai'i, Honolulu, HI.

24. Clifford Miyamoto, summary of oral history conducted by Melvin Inamasu and Marilyn Higashide on January 19, 2015, Voice of Internment Project, Japanese Cultural Center Hawai'i, Honolulu, HI.

25. Mary F. Clark, "Family Life" from the scrapbook titled "Before I Forget, 1942–1947," California State University, Sacramento, California State University Japanese American Digitization Project, https://cdm16855.contentdm.oclc.org/digital/collection/p16855coll4/id/10942.

26. O'Rourke, "Historical Narrative of the Crystal City Internment Camp," 10–11.

27. O'Rourke, "Historical Narrative of the Crystal City Internment Camp," 11; Mary F. Clark, "The Grocery Store" from the scrapbook titled "Before I Forget, 1942–1947," California State University, Sacramento, California State University Japanese American Digitization Project, https://cdm16855.contentdm.oclc.org/digital/collection/p16855coll4/id/11016.

28. According to Kenko Yamashita, there was an abundance of meat and milk served to the Japanese, neither of which are staples of Japanese daily diets. Often, they would just leave the meat and the officers and guards stationed at the camp would bring it home to their families who were experiencing war time rationing of such food. One sergeant brought a cake that his wife had baked in return for the meat he had been able to take home to her. As for the milk, one internee used it to water their morning glories and ivy. A notice was sent out soon after that read, "Milk is not a good fertilizer for plants" in the hopes of deterring any further gardening experiments with their milk supply. (Clark, "Those Other Camps," 194.)

29. Mary F. Clark, "The Grocery Store" from the scrapbook titled "Before I Forget, 1942–1947," California State University, Sacramento, California State University Japanese American Digitization Project, https://cdm16855.contentdm.oclc.org/digital/collection/p16855coll4/id/11016.

30. O'Rourke, "Historical Narrative of the Crystal City Internment Camp," 12.

31. "Japanese American Internment Unit for Modern History of Hawai'i (2008)," 58.

32. Clifford Miyamoto, summary of oral history conducted by Melvin Inamasu and Marilyn Higashide on January 19, 2015, Voice of Internment Project, Japanese Cultural Center Hawai'i, Honolulu, HI.

33. O'Rourke, "Historical Narrative of the Crystal City Internment Camp," 11.

34. O'Rourke, "Historical Narrative of the Crystal City Internment Camp," 18.

35. O'Rourke, "Historical Narrative of the Crystal City Internment Camp," 18.

36. O'Rourke, "Historical Narrative of the Crystal City Internment Camp," 12.

37. Mary F. Clark, "Landscaping at Crystal City Department of Justice Camp" from the scrapbook titled "Before I forget, 1942–1947," https://cdm16855.contentdm.oclc.org/digital/collection/p16855coll4/id/10947/rec/12. Gardens created by those interned and incarcerated can be found in other camps as well, even being the subject of Ansel Adams' Manzanar photographs of Merritt Park, created and maintained by those incarcerated in the WRA camp. Other photographic examples can be found in Jerome and Minidoka, but "camp gardens numbered in the thousands" throughout the WRA camps. (Anna Hosticka Tamura, "Gardens Below the Watchtower: Gardens and Meaning in World War II Japanese American Incarceration Camps," *Landscape Journal* 23, no. 1 (2004): 3). In addition to larger gardens, the beautifying of the landscape around a family's hutment was popular. Much like the practice of *gaman*, creating gardens while interned or incarcerated have undercurrents of "power, defiance, and resistance" surging through them. (Tamura, *Gardens Below the Watchtower*, 2). The Nikkei who created these artful landscapes showed an "extraordinary level of agency . . . [and] successfully buffered the severity and monotony of the military-issued barracks, barbed wire, and structured layouts of the camps . . . [as well as buffering] the psychological and physical trauma of the incarceration experience." (Tamura, *Gardens Below the Watchtower*, 2).

38. Reverend Fujihana, a Buddhist priest from Maui, was held alongside Reverend Miyamoto at Camp Livingston.

39. Reverend Kyōdō Fujihana, interview by Ichigūkai members [Names unknown], May 6, 1978, Japanese Cultural Center of Hawai'i, Honolulu, HI, https://jcch.soutronglobal.net/Portal/Default/en-GB/RecordView/Index/6381.

40. Texas Historical Commission, "Crystal City (Family) Internment Camp," https://www.thc.texas.gov/preserve/projects-and-programs/military-history/texas-world-war-ii/world-war-ii-japanese-american-2.

41. Texas Historical Commission, "Crystal City (Family) Internment Camp," https://www.thc.texas.gov/preserve/projects-and-programs/military-history/texas-world-war-ii/world-war-ii-japanese-american-2.

42. Mary F. Clark, "Recreation" from the scrapbook titled "Before I Forget, 1942–1947," California State University, Sacramento, California State University Japanese American Digitization Project, https://cdm16855.contentdm.oclc.org/digital/collection/p16855coll4/id/11033.

43. Mary F. Clark, "The Clothing Store" from the scrapbook titled "Before I Forget, 1942–1947," California State University, Sacramento, California State

University Japanese American Digitization Project, https://cdm16855.contentdm.oclc.org/digital/collection/p16855coll4/id/11011.

44. "Missions du Comité international de la Croix-Rouge," *Revue International de la Croix-Rouge,* Bulletin 307 (July 1944): 531. Translation provided by Hayley Johnson; O'Rourke, "Historical Narrative of the Crystal City Internment Camp," 14.

45. United States Department of Justice, Immigration and Naturalization Service, "United States Family Internment Camp, Crystal City, Texas," https://www.foitimes.com/CampHousing.pdf; Mary F. Clark, "Religion" from the scrapbook titled "Before I Forget, 1942–1947," California State University, Sacramento, California State University Japanese American Digitization Project, https://cdm16855.contentdm.oclc.org/digital/collection/p16855coll4/id/11039.

46. United States Department of Justice, Immigration and Naturalization Service, "United States Family Internment Camp, Crystal City, Texas," https://www.foitimes.com/CampHousing.pdf.

47. O'Rourke, "Historical Narrative of the Crystal City Internment Camp," 12; Texas Historical Commission, "Crystal City (Family) Internment Camp," https://www.thc.texas.gov/preserve/projects-and-programs/military-history/texas-world-war-ii/world-war-ii-japanese-american-2.

48. Texas Historical Commission, "Crystal City (Family) Internment Camp," https://www.thc.texas.gov/preserve/projects-and-programs/military-history/texas-world-war-ii/world-war-ii-japanese-american-2. In the summer of 1944, the pool was also the site of one of the most tragic events in camp when a young Japanese Peruvian girl drowned after she slipped into the deep end. Bessie Masuda tried to form a human chain with six or seven other children to reach her, but their efforts were in vain. Her death reverberated throughout the camp. (Bessie Masuda, transcript of oral history by Lara Newcomer, July 22, 2011 Texas Historical Commission, https://www.thc.texas.gov/public/upload/Bessie%20Masuda%20Transcript.pdf).

49. Clifford Miyamoto, summary of oral history conducted by Melvin Inamasu and Marilyn Higashide on January 19, 2015, Voice of Internment Project, Japanese Cultural Center Hawai'i, Honolulu, HI.

50. The troop was originally overseen by the principal of the Federal High School, Mr. R.C. Tate, considered a fine scoutmaster and kind person by his troop. Eventually, another internee who had served in the Japanese army insisted that the Japanese boys join his Boy Scouts of Japan troop—a much more militant troop that practiced marching and corporal punishment and treated the children like little soldiers. (Clifford Miyamoto, summary of oral history conducted by Melvin Inamasu and Marilyn Higashide on January 19, 2015, Voice of Internment Project, Japanese Cultural Center Hawai'i, Honolulu, HI.)

51. Clifford Miyamoto, interview with authors, October 10, 2016.

52. Mary F. Clark, "Invitation from Motokazu Mori" from the scrapbook titled "Before I Forget, 1942–1947," California State University, Sacramento, California State University Japanese American Digitization Project, https://cdm16855.contentdm.oclc.org/digital/collection/p16855coll4/id/11046.

53. Clifford Miyamoto, summary of oral history conducted by Melvin Inamasu and Marilyn Higashide on January 19, 2015, Voice of Internment Project, Japanese Cultural Center Hawai'i, Honolulu, HI.

54. Clifford Miyamoto, summary of oral history conducted by Melvin Inamasu and Marilyn Higashide on January 19, 2015, Voice of Internment Project, Japanese Cultural Center Hawai'i, Honolulu, HI.

55. "Missions du Comité international de la Croix-Rouge," *Revue Internationale de la Croix-Rouge,* Bulletin 307 (July 1944): 531. Translation by Allen LeBlanc.

56. Clifford Miyamoto, summary of oral history conducted by Melvin Inamasu and Marilyn Higashide on January 19, 2015, Voice of Internment Project, Japanese Cultural Center Hawai'i, Honolulu, HI.

57. Texas Historical Commission, "Crystal City (Family) Internment Camp," https://www.thc.texas.gov/preserve/projects-and-programs/military-history/texas-world-war-ii/world-war-ii-japanese-american-2.

58. O'Rourke, "Historical Narrative of the Crystal City Internment Camp," 26.

59. O'Rourke, "Historical Narrative of the Crystal City Internment Camp," 5.

60. "Japanese American Internment Unit for Modern History of Hawai'i (2008)," 57.

61. O'Rourke, "Historical Narrative of the Crystal City Internment Camp," 29.

62. United States Department of Justice, Immigration and Naturalization Service, "United States Family Internment Camp, Crystal City, Texas," https://www.foitimes.com/CampHousing.pdf.

63. Quoted in Clark, "Those Other Camps," 33.

64. Clark, "Those Other Camps," 33.

65. Clark, "Those Other Camps," 33.

66. Quoted in Clark, "Those Other Camps," 33.

67. O'Rourke, "Historical Narrative of the Crystal City Internment Camp," 13–16.

68. Mary F. Clark, "Canteen Tokens" from the scrapbook titled "Before I Forget, 1942–1947," California State University, Sacramento, California State University Japanese American Digitization Project, https://cdm16855.contentdm.oclc.org/digital/collection/p16855coll4/id/11017.

69. Carolyn Shizuko Izumo, transcript of oral history by Florence Sugimoto, May 16, 2007, Japanese Cultural Center of Hawai'i, https://jcch.soutronglobal.net/Portal/Default/en-US/RecordView/Index/4563.

70. United States Department of Justice, Immigration and Naturalization Service, "United States Family Internment Camp, Crystal City, Texas," https://www.foitimes.com/CampHousing.pdf.

71. O'Rourke, "Historical Narrative of the Crystal City Internment Camp," 22.

72. Carolyn Shizuko Izumo, transcript of oral history by Florence Sugimoto, May 16, 2007, Japanese Cultural Center of Hawai'i, https://jcch.soutronglobal.net/Portal/Default/en-US/RecordView/Index/4563.

73. O'Rourke, "Historical Narrative of the Crystal City Internment Camp," 22.

74. Carolyn Shizuko Izumo, transcript of oral history by Florence Sugimoto, May 16, 2007, Japanese Cultural Center of Hawai'i, https://jcch.soutronglobal.net/Portal/Default/en-US/RecordView/Index/4563.

75. O'Rourke, "Historical Narrative of the Crystal City Internment Camp," 15.

76. O'Rourke, "Historical Narrative of the Crystal City Internment Camp," 12.

77. At the time of Carolyn Shizuko Izumo's oral history interview about her life in the Crystal City Family Internment Camp, over sixty years had passed. Relying on her

memory about this juncture in her life, she said, "we even had a bon dance, I think, over there." (Carolyn Shizuko Izumo, transcript of oral history by Florence Sugimoto, May 16, 2007, Japanese Cultural Center of Hawai'i, https://jcch.soutronglobal.net/Portal/Default/en-US/RecordView/Index/4563). The likelihood of a Bon celebration at Crystal City is high as confirmed by the Urabon celebrated in Livingston described by Gihachi Yamashita in a letter to his daughter as well as the account of a Bon dance in the Santa Fe internment camp shared by Yasutaro (Keiho) Soga. Soga wrote, "A Buddhist *bon* service was held on July 15 at the open-air theater. Unfortunately it rained, but the service went on as scheduled. As soon as the weather cleared, the *bon* dance began. It was like a scene in Honolulu before the war. Quite a few of the men dressed in women's costume, and the dance was a big success. Many beautiful *bon* lanterns were hung around the theater." (Soga, *Life Behind Barbed Wire*, 155).

78. Motokazu and Ishiko Mori, a husband and wife team of practicing physicians, were also the subjects of the infamous "Mori Call." To learn more about the Mori Call, visit the article referenced in note 79.

79. Sheila H. Chun, "Motokazu Mori," *Densho Encyclopedia*, 2017, https://encyclopedia.densho.org/Motokazu%20Mori/.

80. Mary F. Clark, "Japanese Art and Flower Exhibit," from the scrapbook titled "Before I Forget, 1942–1947," California State University, Sacramento, California State University Japanese American Digitization Project, https://cdm16855.contentdm.oclc.org/digital/collection/p16855coll4/id/11060; Mary F. Clark, "Exhibit of Japanese 'Brush' Writing" from the scrapbook titled "Before I forget, 1942–1947," California State University, Sacramento, California State University Japanese American Digitization Project, https://cdm16855.contentdm.oclc.org/digital/collection/p16855coll4/id/11061; Mary F. Clark, "Japanese Carnival" from the scrapbook titled "Before I Forget, 1942–1947," California State University, Sacramento, California State University Japanese American Digitization Project, https://cdm16855.contentdm.oclc.org/digital/collection/p16855coll4/id/11054/rec/48.

81. Mary F. Clark, "Family Life" from the scrapbook titled "Before I Forget, 1942–1947," California State University, Sacramento, California State University Japanese American Digitization Project, https://cdm16855.contentdm.oclc.org/digital/collection/p16855coll4/id/10942.

82. Texas Historical Commission, "Crystal City (Family) Internment Camp," https://www.thc.texas.gov/preserve/projects-and-programs/military-history/texas-world-war-ii/world-war-ii-japanese-american-2.

83. Russell, *The Train to Crystal City*, xvi.

84. Clifford Miyamoto, interview with authors, October 10, 2016.

85. O'Rourke, "Historical Narrative of the Crystal City Internment Camp," 13.

86. O'Rourke, "Historical Narrative of the Crystal City Internment Camp," 14.

87. According to Carolyn Izumo, as soon as her family arrived at Crystal City numbers were pulled for who would be on the next exchange ship. To determine what families would be on the following ship, straws were pulled. (Carolyn Shizuko Izumo, transcript of oral history by Florence Sugimoto, May 16, 2007, Japanese Cultural Center of Hawai'i, https://jcch.soutronglobal.net/Portal/Default/en-US/RecordView/Index/4563). Despite the many exchanges that occurred at Crystal City,

the Miyamoto family's name never made it on a ship's final manifest. As we will see in a coming chapter, reflecting on this chance occurrence decades later, Reverend Miyamoto would understand the dire consequences that could have befallen both Clifford and himself if they had been chosen for one of these exchange ships.

88. Buntetsu Miyamoto Alien File, RG 566, Series: Alien Case Files, 1944–2009, National Archives, San Francisco, CA.

89. Buntetsu Miyamoto Alien File, RG 566, Series: Alien Case Files, 1944–2009, National Archives, San Francisco, CA. This is an interesting snapshot of what must have been going on in Reverend Miyamoto's mind at this moment in time as the non-repatriation request is signed on August 30, 1945—just three weeks after the last atomic bomb had been dropped on Nagasaki and just days before Japan officially surrendered aboard the USS *Missouri*, the document of that surrender signed by none other Mamoru Shigemitsu, Fumi's distant cousin through her father. Reverend Miyamoto's last request for repatriation had been on February 4, 1944—what must have seemed a lifetime ago at the time. According to Clifford Miyamoto, it was also possible that the chances of repatriation for the family had been diminished as the U.S. government was afraid that the Hawaiian internees were too knowledgeable about the military outposts on Oahu—information that could be valuable to the Japanese military. (Clifford Miyamoto, interview by Melvin Inamasu and Marilyn Higashide, January 19, 2015, interview summary by Carolyn Okinaga, Voice of Internment Project, Japanese Cultural Center of Hawai'i, Honolulu, HI).

90. Mary F. Clark notes her scrapbook that "On December 1, 1945—101 internees started on their way to Germany. 162 Japanese internees left for Hawai'i. 1236 Japanese began the long journey back to Japan on December 2, 1945. These were all voluntary repatriates, thus within twenty-four hours we lost almost half our camp population." ("Repatriation" from the scrapbook titled "Before I Forget, 1942–1947," https://cdm16855.contentdm.oclc.org/digital/collection/p16855coll4/id/11071).

91. After the conclusion of the war, Peru refused to allow the Japanese Peruvians who had been taken for internment and repatriation, to return. Because of "hastily-written wartime agreements . . . the United States had not exacted initial guarantees defining the deportees' postwar fate." (*Personal Justice Denied*, 312). Some Japanese Peruvians voluntarily repatriated to Japan, while others were sent to Hawai'i. Others still wanted to remain in the United States. It wasn't until 1953 that the Japanese Peruvians who still remained, having now lived in a state of uncertainty in the United States for over seven years, were given a reprieve from deportation by Congress. (*Personal Justice Denied*, 314).

92. *Personal Justice Denied*, 312.

93. O'Rourke, "Historical Narrative of the Crystal City Internment Camp," 8.

94. Kashima, *Judgment Without Trial*, 120.

95. O'Rourke, "Historical Narrative of the Crystal City Internment Camp," 2.

96. In Mary Clark's scrapbook is a page with an inlaid poem titled "Hell in Texas"—underneath she has written the following: "'Hell in Texas' it was those first two years, what Texas didn't do to your disposition, the internees did. Anyone who can live through life in an Alien Internment Camp in Texas, need never fear they will ever meet a problem in life they cannot surmount." While she is writing

about her own experience as a non-interned civilian nurse who was free to leave the camp whenever the mood struck, this is an applicable statement to those held behind the barbed wire fences and in the heat of south Texas for years. The harsh reality of internment can be summed up in her second sentence—for anyone who was forced to endure this, the reserves of strength and hope needed to survive would most likely have stayed with them throughout their entire life and used to face obstacles outside of camp. ("Hell in Texas" as found in Mary F. Clark's from the scrapbook titled "Before I Forget, 1942–1947," https://cdm16855.contentdm.oclc.org/digital/collection/p16855coll4/id/10933).

Part VI

AFTER WAR

Chapter 20

Life beyond War

The world needs the light (teachings) that Buddha attained under the Bodhi (type of banyan) tree that day 2,500 years ago to guide us in this troubled world today.
  Let Buddha kindle a light within you to help bring more light to others.[1]

—Bishop Buntetsu Miyamoto, 1956

With Japan's official surrender on September 2, 1945, aboard the USS *Missouri*[2] docked in Tokyo Bay, the war had finally come to an end. The Miyamoto and Kohara families, like all others whose lives had been interrupted, faced a new and unknown future. An order from the Military Commander of the Territory of Hawaiʻi would not be issued until October 22, 1945, in which all individual internment orders pursuant to Presidential Proclamations issued December 7th and 8th of 1941 would be rescinded which in effect would allow the Hawaiian internees and their families to return home.[3]

The Miyamoto family returned home to Hawaiʻi in December of 1945, a full three months after the conclusion of World War II. The emotional reunion between David Kanji and two of his siblings, Carol and Clifford, was captured by a *Hawaiʻi Herald* photographer and featured on the front page of the December 11, 1945, issue (see figure 28). Almost four years had passed since the family left Hawaiʻi—in handcuffs or voluntarily—but always surrounded by guards. For Carol (now 20), Clifford (now 17), and Keiko (almost 11), they set off with their mother as children, but they returned to David Kanji as two young adults and a budding teenager. The Miyamoto children were forced to grow up during their time behind barbed wire. They had lived in a constant state of "'not knowing [which] is one of the most depressing feelings one gets."[4] But they had finally made it home. Clifford recalled being greeted by his brother and community at the dock in Honolulu. The large reception, which community members traveled an hour to attend, was unexpected after the Miyamotos' long absence but very moving for the family to arrive home to such support.

The family quickly settled back into their lives in Hale'iwa with Reverend Miyamoto eagerly resuming his role as the minister and leader of the temple and school that he loved so dearly (see figure 29). Within five years of returning home, Reverend Miyamoto had risen up the ranks of the Jodo Mission to become the ninth Bishop of the Hawai'i Council of Jodo Missions in 1950. His popularity as Bishop was exemplified when in 1960, the Hale'iwa Jodo named their newly built student dormitory Miyamoto Hall, after Bishop Buntetsu Miyamoto.

Some of Reverend Miyamoto's post-war writings and sermons survived giving us a glimpse into his view of the world and the past. In 1963 while still serving as Bishop of the Honolulu Jodoshu Betsuin located on Makiki Street in Honolulu, Bishop Miyamoto wrote a reflective piece titled "The Blessing of Adversity." In this piece, Bishop Miyamoto contemplated the difficulties of life once he and his family were able to return to Hawai'i.

> *While many of my comrades had quite difficulties upon returning to Hawaii after four years of internment without places to live, I was quite fortunate because I could live in a house that was well renovated after my original temple, Haleiwa Jodoin, was confiscated during the war and returned afterward by the US Military. In addition, while I came back to Hawaii preparing for hardships, the actual life here was quite blessed and enjoyable, contrary to my expectations.*
>
> *Probably because I came back from a long life of internment, most every Japanese in and around Haleiwa came to visit and see me. In particular, numerous, pure-hearted considerations by my students before the war made me feel like crying. One of them left a paper bag saying "Mister, this is a token of my sympathy," and I was quite surprised when I opened it later. Inside, there were bills worth $200. Just like that, I enjoyed a very blessed life.*
>
> *Nevertheless, in our world, "Great things don't last long," or "No one knows what's around the corner." Only four months after I came back to Hawaii, or on April 1, 1946, a huge tidal wave that suddenly swiped Hawaii demoted me a poor homeless in a second. Indeed, that downfall happened quite suddenly, and it was literally "Yesterday's edge became shallows of today."*
>
> *The only fortunate matter was that all of my family members were safe because my wife remembered the experience of the tidal wave some years ago, sensed its coming just beforehand, and made us evacuate.*
>
> *It happened to be April Fool's Day, and we had pulled various jokes, some funny, some not. Nonetheless, the tidal wave was an actual reality, not a joke, and I was just completely stunned looking at the site of atrocious damages.*
>
> *During the period of quandary, devastated by this unexpected natural disaster, we received a notification from one of my masters in Japan on our*

oldest son, Osamu, on whom we made an inquiry with the help of my student who was serving in the Occupation Forces in Japan. First coming to my eyes after opening the letter was heartbreaking news of Osamu killed in action. Oh what a grief. He had been killed in the Philippines in 1944. Ignorance is bliss, indeed. My wife and I have been praying for his safety every day and night since we received a notice of "Osamu enlisted" in the Internment Camp.[5] Oh what a remorse despite our hope! The proverb, "It never rains but it pours," was the most suitable statement of myself at that time. Being a very strong-willed person, even I got completely knocked out this time. My wife understandably became a complete invalid.

Come to think of it, when he graduated from Pacific College in 1939, I coaxed and sent him to Japan to become a Buddhist monk even though he was reluctant. My remorse is deepened further when I think about it.

Day and night, my thought strayed here and there, wandered on the verge of despair, even swore at Buddha, "Oh, I wonder if there is no God or Buddha. This ordeal is too much to overcome for this old monk with the night fallen and still having a long way to go," and felt like abandoning everything in this world where everything is painted black. Still, while mourning my son's death, holding a grudge and crying, with bowing my head to the floor saying a prayer to Buddha with tear, he made me realize that my prayers in the past were all empty and then I clearly felt inspiration. "Yes, the ordeal given by Buddha is invaluable after all. He gave me that ordeal as a means to bestow a true prayer on me." I couldn't help but joining my hands with prayer for the grace of adversity which I realized for the first time.

Because of this experience, my desperate feeling was gradually calming down, and, though one slow step after another, I could concentrate on restoration of the damages caused by the tidal wave, being able to complete first the temple and residence, the school in the second stage, and stone wall in the third stage, one after another. The stone wall on the oceanside, in particular, I had really wanted to build from the time I had first moved here but couldn't do so until this day. The misfortune this time gave us an opportunity and I felt absolutely grateful that a very sturdy one with 220 feet long, 9 feet high, and 2 feet thick was completed with five Sundays, thanks to everyone's contribution.

Thus, everything was perfectly furnished more than before, but this was indeed an infinite virtue of Buddha for me to obtain a blessing of adversity when I got used to an easy way of life and started to lose the determination of the time when I came back to Hawaii. Joining hands in prayer.[6]

While the Miyamoto family was fortunate to have a home and temple to return to, their life after internment was not without challenges and struggles. The loss of Osamu during the war weighed heavily upon the Miyamoto family and was a pain carried within them always, even more acute and persistent than the experience of internment.

Typically, within Buddhist traditions, the lotus flower must transcend the muddy water from which it grows in order to achieve enlightenment. The lotus represents rebirth, purity, and transcendence over obstacles. Japanese Buddhist traditions tend to view the lotus and its environment differently. According to scholar Duncan Ryūken Williams, "most Japanese Buddhist traditions emphasize that for the lotus flower to exist, the nutrients from the muddy waters are essential. It is a metaphor that emphasizes how the karmic obstacles of this world are interconnected with liberation and enlightenment."[7] Bishop Miyamoto's account of his struggle with Osamu's death and his subsequent realization that it was only through the tremendous adversity and hopelessness he faced while submerged in the dark waters of his despair and grief that he was able to obtain a sense of grace, liberation, and true enlightenment. For the first time, Bishop Miyamoto truly recognized the power inherent in growing from the teachings of the muddy waters in order to break through the surface toward a more grateful and understanding self. Bishop Miyamoto emerged from the muddy waters of his grief with a renewed resolve and determination that helped him continue to serve his community until his retirement.

In 1966, Bishop Miyamoto was summoned out of retirement and was asked by the Jodo sect headquarters to serve as the Archbishop of Zendōji Temple in Fukuoka, Japan (see figure 30). This posting was especially meaningful as it placed Archbishop Miyamoto into one of the highest roles within the Jodo church rewarding his lifelong dedication, service, and sacrifice.

Many years after the war, Archbishop Miyamoto was visiting his children and grandchildren in Hawai'i from his posting in Japan and asked his granddaughter to drive him to the Punchbowl.[8] He wanted to pray for all the soldiers who had lost their lives during the war, never forgetting the tragedy that had befallen so many others. Archbishop Miyamoto had been involved in honoring the soldiers who died in battle since his return to Hawai'i from the mainland in 1945.[9] As important as it was to him to praise the young men going off to war in March 1941 and encourage them to do their duty as American citizens, so too was it important that Archbishop Miyamoto continue to honor their sacrifices all those decades later. The speech he had given those young men in 1941 that was cited in his internment hearing as they were going off to war was not composed of empty words. Archbishop Miyamoto had been put between an impossible rock and hard place. The U.S. government may have labeled Archbishop Miyamoto as pro-Japan and a threat to the United States, but there is no doubting his support of the brave men who served and paid the ultimate sacrifice in defense of their country which was the country where Archbishop Miyamoto made a life, raised a family, and immersed himself into the service of his community.

Just four years prior to his death, ninety-year-old Archbishop Miyamoto created a calligraphy piece for his granddaughter. The character he drew was *yume*. Translated, *yume* means dream, vision, transiency. Through this calligraphy piece, Archbishop Miyamoto reminded his granddaughter to set lofty but realistic goals and strive to attain them through diligence and perseverance, a lesson that Archbishop Miyamoto had learned and practiced throughout his life.

Through his own diligence, perseverance, and dedication, Archbishop Miyamoto had attained a position of honor within his sect. He started at a small, rural temple on the North Shore of Oahu and earned the position as Archbishop of the Daihonzan Zendoji, one of the largest Pure Land temples in all of Japan. All this occurred despite the tremendous adversity he and his family faced during World War II.

Unlike the Miyamoto family who were part of a large group of Japanese in Hawaiʻi deemed suspicious and a threat, the Kohara family, as the sole Japanese family in their area, did not pose the same threat because they had fully integrated into the community through their Christianity coupled with the lack of other Japanese families with which to form a perceived subversive group. They had been spared the trauma of being interned, though they had seen firsthand the suffering that internment could inflict on families, especially the agony of separation. The Kohara family continued to operate their photo studio with Saki working alongside her sons to keep her husband's business a success. It was "almost second nature with her to see that every department of the store [was] running in perfect order."[10] The studio continued to be an Alexandria mainstay.

> A few doors off the main shopping artery of Alexandria is Kohara's—a handsome modernistic photo studio. During the day, native Alexandrians stream in to have their pictures developed or to make an appointment for a family picture. At night a large prominent neon signs keeps blinking, "Kohara."[11]

Marion remembered that at some point the floor of the entryway to the photo studio had been inlaid with mosaic tile that read "Kohara"—a testament to how the studio and the Kohara family were embedded into the Alexandrian community.[12] Saki enjoyed her life outside of the photo studio too. She watched over her grandchildren, and in true Louisiana fashion, would go fishing on Sundays because that was how she felt close to God (see figure 31).

The ties to Camp Livingston and the Kohara family resurfaced in a surprising encounter nearly twenty-five years after the end of World War II. In preparation for writing his memoirs, Reverend Kano, the organizer of Camp Livingston's Internee University and the fastidious journaler through whom we learned so much about Camp Livingston, visited all the locations where he had been interned during World War II. Upon his return to Camp Livingston, where he had spent over a year of his life, Reverend Kano was interviewed by Tommy Kohara for the *Alexandria Daily Town Talk,* where Tommy served as the chief photographer for twenty-five years (see figure 32). This chance meeting and interview was not lost on Tommy. He noted in his article that there was a personal connection between the Koharas and Reverend Kano. Tommy's parents, Manabu and Saki, had known Reverend Kano from their days living in the Midwest before they made the move to Louisiana. Unfortunately, Saki would not get to see this moment come full circle. She passed away on October 3, 1969, only twenty-two days before her son's article was printed.

On October 25, 1969, Tommy Kohara reported, Reverend Kano:

> found the wooded Camp Livingston a far cry from the bustling army camp of the early 1940's and was not sure that he could identify the building foundations, all that is left of the compound where he was interned.[13]

But Camp Livingston had stayed with Reverend Kano as we can see in his memoir, when he wrote, "when I went back to see three of the old camps, they had been removed and there were forests and woods in their place. The pine, oak, and walnut trees brought back many memories."[14] These steadfast wooden sentries serve as a visual representation of the memories of these men and their time in Camp Livingston; they still stand today.

While Fumi and Saki were never to meet again after that fateful visit in 1943, members of the Kohara and Miyamoto families would form a connection and bond over the ensuing decades and would meet again in all the locations which shaped their lives. In 1960, Keiko made a visit to Louisiana to see Saki and the Kohara family in Alexandria. Then in 1975, members of the Kohara family traveled to Honolulu to visit the Miyamotos. The families would continue the tradition of meeting in various locales throughout the following decades ensuring they remained in touch.

In 1976, members of the Kohara family visited Archbishop Miyamoto and Fumi at his temple in Fukuoka, Japan. There, the Miyamotos lived within the historic temple complex. Even today, the impression that Archbishop Miyamoto left on the Koharas is especially strong. The Koharas recalled being struck by Archbishop Miyamoto's demeanor which they remembered as calm and Buddha-like. From his person, he radiated a gentleness and beatitude of spirit with a soft and sweet smile. Even Archbishop Miyamoto's earlobes reminded the Koharas of the Buddha statutes they saw throughout their visit in Japan. He even made a calligraphy piece for them of the character for happiness.[15]

Archbishop Miyamoto represented how an individual could transcend beyond the hardship, struggle, and racism of wartime. The trauma of the internment experience affected him as well as his whole family, but their collective strength in rising above is exemplified through what the entire family was able to accomplish with their lives after this unjust experience.

Ultimately, despite the tragedy of internment, being racially and religiously othered during a time of crisis, the children of both the Miyamoto and Kohara families were able to find success in their chosen professions. Among the children and grandchildren are engineers, bank managers, doctors, artists, news reporters, photographers—the list goes on. The descendants of Reverend Miyamoto and Fumi Miyamoto as well as Manabu and Saki Kohara are today spread across the globe, but the memories of the strength of their ancestors live on in them.

NOTES

1. "1,500 Oahu Buddhists Celebrate Annual Observance of Bodhi Day," *Honolulu Star Bulletin* (Honolulu, HI), December 10, 1956. Reverend Miyamoto gave a speech during the annual gathering in observance of Bodhi Day which is the day celebrating when the Buddha attained enlightenment.

2. Mamoru Shigemitsu, the Japanese Minister of Foreign Affairs, signed the documents of surrender on behalf of Japan aboard the USS *Missouri*. Shigemitsu served as a Japanese diplomat and politician in the Empire of Japan, as well as the Japanese minister of foreign affairs at the end of World War II and later as the deputy prime minister of Japan. Shigemitsu is most famously known as one of the signers of the Japanese Instrument of Surrender on September 2, 1945. The other signer was General Yoshijirō Umezu. According to an *LA Times* article, "Shigemitsu hobbled up the starboard gangway of the U.S. battleship Missouri . . . wearing a top hat, morning coat, and striped pants. He leaned on a black cane, balancing unsteadily on the peg-leg he acquired after a terrorist bombing in Shanghai." But apart from cutting such a dashing, or should we say interesting, figure, his connection to our story hits closer to home as he and Fumi Miyamoto were distant cousins by way of their fathers. We know that Fumi and Mamoru were aware of their status as relatives and that Fumi visited Mamoru when he stopped over in Hawai'i on his travels. She is noted twice in the *Honolulu Star Bulletin's* newspaper coverage of his visits in 1955 and 1956. ("Japan Foreign Minister Seeks Peace in All Asia," *Honolulu Star-Bulletin,* August 24, 1955; "Shigemitsu," *Honolulu Star Bulletin,* December 14, 1956.) (David Lamb, "Aug. 14, 1945: the Day the Fighting Stopped . . ." *Los Angeles Times*, August 14, 1995, https://www.latimes.com/archives/la-xpm-1995-08-14-mn-35013-story.html).

3. Order to the Office of Internal Security, Iolani Palace Grounds, October 22, 1945; Folder 10, Box 8, AR 1, Otokichi Ozaki Collection, Japanese Cultural Center of Hawai'i.

4. "Japanese American Internment Unit for Modern History of Hawai'i (2008)," 55.

5. Many Nisei had returned to Japan prior to the outbreak of war, like Osamu, for schooling. When war erupted, these Nisei were trapped in Japan. If the young men were of age, they could be conscripted into serving in the Japanese Imperial Army

or Navy. Such was the case with Osamu. He was conscripted into Japanese military service and was utilized for his English language skills.

6. Courtesy of Jodo Mission of Hawai'i; Translation provided by Yoshinori Kamo, PhD, Louisiana State University.

7. Williams, *American Sutra*, 86.

8. Punchbowl Cemetery is the informal name for the National Memorial Cemetery of the Pacific located at Punchbowl Crater in Honolulu, HI.

9. "Former Chaplain of 442nd RCT is Honored Guest," *Honolulu Star-Bulletin*, September 26, 1947; "Memorial Services Set for Pacific War Dead," *Honolulu Star-Bulletin*, May 22, 1953; Richard Gima, "Club 100 Veterans Honor Wartime Dead," *Honolulu Star-Bulletin*, September 29, 1958.

10. Sugahara, "The Koharas of Louisiana."

11. Sugahara, "The Koharas of Louisiana."

12. Marion Kohara Couvillion, interview with authors, July 12, 2016.

13. "Japanese Priest Revisits Louisiana," *Alexandria Daily Town Talk* (Alexandria, LA), October 25, 1969.

14. Kano, *Nikkei Farmer on the Nebraska Plains*, 128.

15. Personal correspondence with Kohara family, September 2019.

Chapter 21

Mysterious Memories

A Remembrance of Those Who Did Not Return

Camp Livingston was rendered inactive as an Army base in November of 1945.[1] From late May of 1942 to June 1943, it held over 1,100 men of Japanese nationality within its confines, men classified as "enemies" because of their place of birth and their position within their communities. All we have left are the pine trees that still grow on site and the memories of the men who were held there. The men held in the internment camp have long since passed, but in some instances their time in camp was recorded in journals, oral histories, and even books. Others who guarded the camp or visited have left letters, memos, reports, and photographs of what they saw there. This one spot in the central Louisiana pine forests touched the lives of thousands, and these stories and documented histories are scattered across the world.

In 1980, Reverend Miyamoto, then the Archbishop at the Zendoji Temple in Fukuoka, Japan, gave a sermon looking back on his experience during World War II titled "A Mysterious Memory." In it, he shared his experiences of being arrested, his internment journey, and, most strikingly, his time in Crystal City and the disappointment at not finding his name on the final list of people who were to be repatriated. But where the absence of his name was the source of frustration at the time, what we learn is that this simple twist of fate probably saved both his life and that of his son Clifford. The following is a translation of what he shared:

> There is nothing more mysterious than destiny, after all. While I have various memories, I will hereby present one of the most mysterious ones.
> Memories usually tend to fade in their impressions as we age years after years and some of them eventually disappear leaving nothing, but this memory of mine is nothing but opposite.

> I was dispatched to Haleʻiwa Jodoin as a chief priest when the Japan-US War broke out on December 7, 1941. Because of that, on the same day as the war broke out, I was arrested by United States authorities and incarcerated in the internment camp in Honolulu. Afterwards, I was transferred to other internment camps in the mainland and went through four internment camps in total. The first was in San Francisco, California, the next was Fort Sill, Oklahoma, then it was Livingston, Louisiana, and the last was Crystal City, Texas. The War ended when I was there, and I was sent back to my old home at Haleiwa Jodoin on December 10, 1945, after four years and two days.
>
> The first thing I was interrogated in the internment camp was "If you want to return to Japan." I of course answered, "Yes." My intention was passed on to my family in Hawaii, so that my wife was sent to the mainland along with our boy and two girls and waited in another camp for the day to be sent back to Japan with me.
>
> No matter which camp, the first question was "Do you want to return to Japan," as I wrote above. This question was asked primarily to make a list of prisoners of war for an exchange, and the exchange was made based on this list. While my name was on the first three lists, my return didn't materialize. My name was not on the fourth and final list of Crystal City. I wondered why and went to the office to ask for that, only came back disappointed with the rude response, "Nothing there means nothing."
>
> On the other hand, those people whose names were on the list gleefully left out of the gate of the internment camp. Several days later, they got on the ship to exchange POWs to Japan, but left off in Singapore to work for the military. With the situation of war getting worse, it was finally decided that they were sent back to Japan, and Awa-Maru was chosen as the safest ship. It was because the U.S. Navy assured that they would not attack this ship. Their condition was that no women should be on the ship and it departed only with men on board. It was, however, attacked and sank off Taiwan on the way back, and two-thousands and more souls were drowned at sea with deep-seated grudges. It was way more than miserable and indeed extremely tragic.
>
> I shed my tears again when the wives and daughters of those victims perished on Awa-Maru came back to Hawaii several years after the war and told me the details. And I couldn't help wondering why my name was not on the list of Crystal City while it was on the three previous lists. Had it been there, I was 57 years old and my son, Terufumi [Clifford], was 12 years old when we both perished drowning at sea. In reality, what a blessing that I lived long to be 92 years old and was made into a head priest of Daihonzanzendoji; I am just so thankful for the gods and Buddha, and keep chanting the name and praying to Amida Buddha.[2]

Although the Miyamoto family was forced to endure the trauma of internment during World War II, they were allowed to eventually return to their home at the Haleʻiwa Jodo Mission. There were others who would be deprived of this fortune and would be dealt further misery at the hands of the United States.

The sinking of the Japanese relief ship *Awa Maru*, mentioned here in Reverend Miyamoto's sermon, is a tragedy unto itself.

After delivering two thousand tons of Red Cross relief supplies for prisoners of Japan—both military and civilian—to various ports on the South China Sea, the *Awa Maru* began her voyage back home to Japan.[3] On the way, she docked at Singapore and took on around 1,700 additional passengers clambering to return to Japan.[4] Over 2,000 passengers set sail on the *Awa Maru*. Many of the passengers were noncombatants who consisted of merchant marines, businessmen, engineers, scientists, diplomats, military and government officials, and "ordinary working men."[5] At least two men, who had been identified as candidates for the repatriation efforts and prisoner exchange program between the United States and Japan, boarded the *Awa Maru* with their young sons in Singapore. These two Japanese men were considered enemy aliens in the United States and had been taken from their homes within hours of the attack on Pearl Harbor and had been interned in various camps throughout the United States during the war. Each man had been interned at Camp Livingston. Neither they nor their sons would make it to their new home in Japan.

Despite the bright navigation lights on her deck illuminating the white crosses that had been painted all over the ship signifying it was a Red Cross relief vessel and was permitted "safe passage" through the war-plagued waters of the South China Sea, the submarine USS *Queenfish* fired four torpedoes at the *Awa Maru* through the dense fog on the evening of April 1, 1945. The *Queenfish* had not taken the time to properly identify the ship when they fired and did not know that it was the *Awa Maru*—a ship ordered to "let pass safely."[6] All four torpedoes met their mark, slamming into the hull of the *Awa Maru*. She split in two and sunk within four minutes. So quickly did the attack come that no distress signal was sent.[7] The *Awa Maru* sank with over 2,000 individuals on board. Only one man survived—Kantaro Shimoda—picked up by the *Queenfish* in the oil-slick waters littered with the debris from the explosion. The fate of the *Awa Maru* would not be known to Japan for ten days. The Japanese government in Tokyo sent out radio requests for information on her whereabouts as she had never arrived at her planned destination. At this, the United States finally "acknowledged responsibility for the wrongful sinking" of the relief ship.[8] This "ship of hope" had become a ship of sorrow.[9]

Mitsuko Sumida was born in Haleʻiwa in 1915 and received her formal education in Japan where she met and married her husband, Jikyo Masaki. Upon moving back to Hawaiʻi, they had two children, their son Takashi and daughter Akiko, or Dorothy. Reverend Masaki became a priest at the Jodo Mission in Honolulu, and on the night of December 7, 1941, he was arrested and interned as an enemy alien for the duration of the war. Like the Miyamoto family, Mitsuko and her children were eventually reunited with Reverend Masaki in Crystal City after being forcibly separated with his internment. A contingent of Hawaiians made the trek to Crystal City together, including Mitsuko and Fumi, both with their children in tow. Mitsuko was "very, very close" to the Miyamoto family, and because they were there with her, people she knew from her community in Haleʻiwa, Mitsuko "felt brave."[10] She wanted to join her husband and be repatriated back to Japan "because [she] wanted him to be a free man."[11] After being reunited as a family in Crystal City, they soon departed on the *Gripsholm* in August 1943, to make the long journey to Japan. At the port of Goa in India, they transferred to another boat but disembarked at Singapore because it felt like a safer place to live than Japan. They stayed for almost a year and half until the United States began to bomb Singapore in a military campaign beginning in 1944. By April 1945, the Masaki family decided it was time to leave for Japan because Singapore had become too dangerous. On April 1, 1945, the family lined up together to board the *Awa Maru,* but at the last minute, they were told that Mitsuko and her daughter could not board the boat and would have to take another. Reverend Masaki and his seven-year-old son, Takashi, boarded the *Awa Maru* expecting to be reunited in Japan in a few days' time. Mitsuko and Dorothy (Akiko) boarded another ship one week later, and after disembarking in Japan, they took a train to Hiroshima to Reverend Masaki's parents' home. No one met them at the train station, and so Mitsuko carried Dorothy, exhausted from the travel, to her father-in-law's home, a forty-five-minute walk. Mitsuko began to have a "funny feeling" the closer they got to the home when her son did not come out to greet them as he normally would.[12] As they entered the home, Reverend Masaki's parents asked where Jikyo and Takashi were—why weren't they with her? Mitsuko responded that they were supposed to have already been there as they had left on the *Awa Maru* a week before. Reverend Masaki's parents told her that it had been announced on the news the day prior that the *Awa Maru* had sunk after being bombed. At that moment, they realized that Reverend Masaki and seven-year-old Takashi had perished in the attack. The reunion and the safety they had so longed for were not to be.[13]

Another father boarded the *Awa Maru* in Singapore—Shoichi "Seiha" Asami, editor-in-chief of the *Nippu Jiji,* the Hawaiian-based newspaper written in Japanese and English. With him was his eleven-year-old son Harold. Asami's story was similar to those of the Miyamotos and Masakis. He was picked up by FBI agents the night of December 7, 1941, and his parting words to his wife were, "Don't worry. . . everything will be all right. . . take care of the children."[14] Separated from his family for almost a year and a half, his family traveled to other camps and temporary relocation centers across the United States in the hopes of being reunited with him. Their happy reunion finally came in 1943 in Crystal City. They too boarded the *Gripsholm*, making the arduous journey to India. There, they boarded the *Teia Maru* and eventually made it to Singapore where "Japanese officials urged persons who could speak English to get off there because help was needed."[15] The Asami family, as well as twenty others, disembarked to live for a time in Singapore. Their eldest son, Kinichi, was soon conscripted into the Japanese Army.

> I didn't want to go, but if I opposed, I knew I would be put into prison or something. The army was the boss. I could have resisted no matter what the consequences. But I gave in and kept my mouth shut.[16]

As the United States bombed Singapore and her armed forces advanced ever closer in March 1945, the evacuation of civilians in Singapore was ordered by the Japanese military. Shoichi Asami put his wife and daughters on a hospital ship bound for Japan. It was to be only a temporary separation for they would see each other soon as he and their youngest son Harold were scheduled to leave shortly on the *Awa Maru*. But fate dealt a mighty blow. His wife and daughters would not know of the fate of the *Awa Maru* until they reached Japan.[17] Asami was a writer by nature, not only as an editor for a newspaper, but also as a poet. Writing under the pen name "Seiha," which translates to Blue Wave, he was actively engaged in the tanka critique sessions at Camp Livingston, submitting three poems to the poetry reading in August 1942 alone. Each of the poems he shared for that session detailed the longing he had for his freedom and his family. Reading the poems again, knowing now the tragedy that would befall the Asami family, the grief is almost tangible. A fellow Livingston internee, Itsuo Hamada, vividly remembered Shoichi Asami and his poetry during their time together in camp. Hamada recalled a poem that Asami had written:

> *Frenzy storm! I pray that it will pull me down to the bottom of the sea.*[18]

Hamada said, "As his pen name Seiha (Blue Wave) shows, he loved the sea, but when I read the above poem, 'Frenzy Storm!,' I cannot but feel his strange destiny."[19]

The tragedy of the *Awa Maru* is not widely known in the United States. It has "vanished from American public memory."[20] This can be said for the Japanese and Japanese American experience in the United States during World War II as well. Most aren't aware of the forced removal and imprisonment of 120,000 Japanese and Japanese Americans in incarceration camps in the United States. Even less is known about the internment of enemy aliens during this time. Camp Livingston is gone. The men held in these camps are gone. It is only through sharing these stories of the men and their families—members of marginalized groups within society that were affected by a program of surveillance, suspicion, and isolation—that we can ensure this history will not be repeated.

NOTES

1. "Livingston, Beauregard Go on Inactive List," *Alexandria Daily Town Talk* (Alexandria, LA), November 7, 1945.
2. Courtesy of Jodo Mission of Hawai'i; Translation provided by Yoshinori Kamo, PhD, Louisiana State University.
3. Roger Dingman, *Ghost of War: The Sinking of the Awa Maru and Japanese-American Relations, 1945–1999* (Annapolis, MD: Naval Institute Press, 1997), 42, 48.
4. David Miller, *Mercy Ships* (London: Bloomsbury Publishing, 2008), 136.
5. Dingman, *Ghost of War*, 46.
6. Dingman, *Ghost of War*, 70; Richard Speer, "Let Pass Safely the Awa Maru," *Proceedings of the United States Naval Institute* 100, no. 4 (April 1974): 72.
7. Miller, *Mercy Ships*, 141.
8. Dingman, *Ghost of War*, 101.
9. Dingman, *Ghost of War*, 41.
10. Mitsuko Sumida and Dorothy Murakami, Transcript of an oral history interview by Ted Tsukiyama, August 6, 1997, Japanese Cultural Center of Hawai'i, https://jcch.soutronglobal.net/Portal/Default/en-US/RecordView/Index/4654.
11. Mitsuko Sumida and Dorothy Murakami, Transcript of an oral history interview by Ted Tsukiyama, August 6, 1997, Japanese Cultural Center of Hawai'i, https://jcch.soutronglobal.net/Portal/Default/en-US/RecordView/Index/4654.
12. Mitsuko Sumida and Dorothy Murakami, Transcript of an oral history interview by Ted Tsukiyama, August 6, 1997, Japanese Cultural Center of Hawai'i, https://jcch.soutronglobal.net/Portal/Default/en-US/RecordView/Index/4654.
13. Mitsuko Sumida and Dorothy Murakami, Transcript of an oral history interview by Ted Tsukiyama, August 6, 1997, Japanese Cultural Center of Hawai'i, https://jcch.soutronglobal.net/Portal/Default/en-US/RecordView/Index/4654.
14. Tomi Kaizawa Knaefler, *Our House Divided* (Honolulu: University of Hawai'i Press, 1991), 46.
15. Knaefler, *Our House Divided*, 49.
16. Knaefler, *Our House Divided*, 49.
17. Knaefler, *Our House Divided*, 46–50.
18. Itsuo Hamada, "The Outbreak of the Pacific War and the Detention of Representative Japanese," Folder 9, Box 6 Series: Other Writings, Otikichi Ozaki Collection, Japanese Cultural Center of Hawai'i.
19. Itsuo Hamada, "The Outbreak of the Pacific War and the Detention of Representative Japanese," Folder 9, Box 6 Series: Other Writings, Otikichi Ozaki Collection, Japanese Cultural Center of Hawai'i.
20. Dingman, *Ghost of War*, 177.

Chapter 22

What Remains

Nearly eighty years after the last World War II internment camps closed, the exact number of individuals affected by the enemy alien internment measures remains unclear. Numbers that include Japanese, Italians, and Germans vary between 11,000 and 31,899 persons.[1] A constant found among these tallies, however, is that persons of Japanese descent make up the majority of those interned—between 54.8 and 72.7 percent.

The other constant in this matter is the use of lists to identify the "dangerousness" of an individual. By 1943, use of these types of lists was being questioned in some of the highest offices of the U.S. government. In July of that year, the U.S. attorney general wrote a strongly worded memo to the assistant attorney general and J. Edgar Hoover effectively ending the practice as it was "a mistake that should be rectified."[2] He went on to say:

> After full re-consideration of these individual danger classifications, I am satisfied that they serve *no useful purpose* . . . The Special Case procedure has been found to be *valueless* . . . it is now clear to me that this classification system is *inherently unreliable*. The evidence used . . . was *inadequate*; the standards applied to the evidence . . . were *defective*; and finally, the notion that it is possible to make a valid determination as to how dangerous a person is in the abstract and without reference to time, environment, and other relevant circumstances, is *impractical, unwise, and dangerous*.[3]

The attorney general then directed that a copy of the memo should be included "in the file of each person who has hitherto been given a classification."[4] Furthermore, a stamped statement was to be placed on each person's classification card that said: "This classification is unreliable. It is hereby cancelled, and should not be used as a determination of dangerousness or of any other fact."[5] What purpose could this serve for those who had already experienced almost four years of internment? This would not change history or the trauma that these men, women, and children experienced because of their race or place of birth. To those who view the files now, it is a sobering reminder that these individuals, guiltless of any transgressions, were interned based on an unfounded categorization.

> It was a label born from a chilling assumption of racial guilt rather than any military or other intelligence . . . "based on a twisted notion of 'guilt by reason of race.' Not on any actual evidence of pro-Japan, anti-U.S. activity."[6]

It should be noted, however, that this does not mean that the loyalty of the Issei is a simple or clear-cut issue. It could never be, especially in Hawai'i.

> It is hard to believe that any Japanese-American in Hawai'i felt 100 percent loyalty to Japan or to the United States in the 1930s if such loyalty meant the exclusion of emotional feelings and respect toward one or the other country. Available evidence and common sense suggest that a majority felt an attachment to both countries. The proportions of this attachment, of course, varied from individual to individual . . . an intricate web of human ties bound Hawai'i to both sides of the Pacific. The eastern and western strands of this web could be severed only at the cost of considerable pain and disorientation. The situation of many Hawai'i Japanese in 1941 was not unlike that of a child of divorced parents, where each parent castigates the other and demands the child's undivided love.[7]

While in Camp Livingston, Gihachi Yamashita wrote about this dichotomy to his daughter. He wrote, "I always said that Japan is my natural mother and this county is foster mother that I owe this country debt of gratitudes."[8] But to love two countries—the one of your birth and the one you have chosen to make your home—is not a crime. The internment of these individuals for years, away from their homes and families, is a failure of the U.S. government that must be acknowledged and remembered to prevent xenophobic hysteria and racism from winning the day again.

Today, Camp Livingston survives as a footnote within history books. Often only discussed as the setting for the World War II Louisiana Maneuvers, there are no surviving physical structures where the camp once stood. The thousands of acres of land where Camp Livingston was built have long since returned to a dense forest of pine trees. No markers exist. Only the heavy pines, a cover under which these men expressed their longing, sadness, as well as their eternal hope, remain as a testament to the fascinating and tragic history that occurred beneath the needle-filled canopy of an isolated Louisiana forest. At the publishing of this book, it will be almost eighty years that this history of internment in Louisiana will have gone largely unrecognized in both the scholarly and popular literature.

The Louisiana Maneuvers and Military Museum at Camp Beauregard in Pineville, Louisiana, is the only institution dedicated to covering the famous Louisiana Maneuvers. In addition to highlighting the Maneuvers, the museum also recognizes the operations of U.S. military forces. Since its opening, a hand-crafted wooden podium on display in its galleries had always been attributed to a Japanese Prisoner of War (POW) held at Camp Livingston. Comparison of the name from the podium plaque to the Camp Livingston alien internee rosters showed that, in fact, its creator was an enemy alien internee, not a POW. Yonezo Sueyasu, the maker of the podium, was born on March 15, 1887, in Japan and was living in Honolulu with his family when he was interned. He was a carpenter and Shinto priest. In addition to Camp Livingston, he was also held in Jerome in Arkansas and Tule Lake in California. While discovering that this podium was made by an enemy alien internee rather than a POW may not seem groundbreaking, it is what this discovery and podium represent that make it so special: the history of enemy alien internment at Camp Livingston, recorded in a physical artifact and the recognition of its creator's journey—a reattribution of a lost memory.

By sharing the lives and experiences of the Miyamoto and Kohara families, we have been able to not only explore enemy alien internment and Camp Livingston's place in this program but have seen the effects of discrimination based on ethnicity or religion that occurred during World War II against individuals of Japanese descent. Reinstating these memories to their rightful place is especially important in today's political climate as issues of democracy, civil rights, intolerance, and xenophobia still persist as evidenced by the public outcry against a growing list of "others"—specifically immigrants such as Syrian and Honduran refugees and the resurgence of immigrant detention facilities. This rhetoric has been used before resulting in the incarceration of over 120,000 American citizens and permanent resident non-citizens as well as 31,000 legal aliens of Japanese, Italian, and German ancestry. Dillon S. Myer, the man in charge of the ten War Relocation Authority camps, upon reflecting on this wartime policy said, "It is not easy to raise good Americans behind barbed wire."[9] The purpose of this book is aligned with Myer's statement—by othering our neighbor, by putting those seeking a better life here in America in the cross hairs of fear-inspired hate, we will find ourselves on the wrong side of historical memory. The current climate calls for a remembrance of these past mistakes in the hopes of charting a better course for the future.

Through this book and our research, we have returned these men back from a historical void where they were simply ghosts of the past. We have been able to find the names of the men held at Camp Livingston, discover where they built their lives prior to the war, uncover correspondence from their time in camp, journal entries, and even artwork created during their time of internment. We are giving humanity back to these men who had been stripped of it simply for being Japanese in wartime.

Unfortunately, the history of Camp Livingston as a site of enemy alien internment is not unique. The book serves as a representation of the enemy alien program that was being conducted across the United States during World War II.

By 1948, the Department of Justice closed the last internment camp and released the remaining few internees. The internees returned to their lives and salvaged and rebuilt what they could. What seems almost universal, however, is the lack of discussion of their past and time in internment.

> Actually the internment was a painful, traumatic experience. It had a repressive impact on the character of the internees . . . The Japanese did not have a choice but to obey . . . Most internees had to accept the camp experience, so consequently, their defense mechanisms were repression, denial, and rationalization to keep from facing the truth.[10]

All the men who were interned have long since passed away, and their children are now elderly and left with few memories of their fathers' experiences. This book serves as a eulogy for those men who were held in Camp Livingston and lauds their trials, their strength, and their perseverance in the face of widespread discrimination and fear.

The words Camp Livingston internee Seikichi Arata spoke to his grandson, who was visiting from his training post at Camp Shelby with the 100th Division, are an emphatic summation of the Hawai'i Issei experience. Arata said:

> That is right. I am an alien. I am a Japanese national because I was born in Japan. But which country gave me most? I spent the first twenty years there, but the next forty mature years were in Hawaii. Citizen or no, I love Hawaii and that is my country and I'll be happy to be buried there. I am no longer swayed by the flag-waving patriotic songs or frenzied by the harangues of demagogues. I do my own picking.[11]

Arata recognized that he had a choice, and in that recognition, he gained power.

Choice is a powerful tool available to all of us. We have the choice to deny or "other" entire groups based on race or religion. We have the choice to embrace a country that doesn't embrace us. We have the choice to persevere. Most importantly, we have the choice to remember and to speak out.

This book is a product of choice. Our choice is to remember.

NOTES

1. In Roger Daniels' "Words Do Matter," he writes that J. Edgar Hoover reported the number of enemy aliens arrested and taken into custody by the FBI as 14,087

persons. Daniels' own total number for those enemy aliens interned is 11,000. Kashima, *Judgment Without Trial*, appears to be more inclusive of those *affected* by internment—those interned as enemy aliens, including Central and South Americans, as well as the families that chose "voluntary internment" so that they could be reunified as a familial unit. Kashima sources his number from the Justice Department's Alien Enemy Control Program. (Roger Daniels, "Words Do Matter: A Note on Appropriate Terminology and the Incarceration of the Japanese Americans," in *Nikkei in the Pacific Northwest*, ed. Louis Fiset and Gail M. Nomura (Seattle: University of Washington Press, 2005), 193); Kashima, *Judgment Without Trial*, 125.

2. Buntetsu Miyamoto FBI File No. 97-42, 1941, RG 389, Box 2626, National Archives, College Park, Maryland.

3. Emphasis authors' own. Buntetsu Miyamoto FBI File No. 97-42, 1941, RG 389, Box 2626, National Archives, College Park, Maryland.

4. Buntetsu Miyamoto FBI File No. 97-42, 1941, RG 389, Box 2626, National Archives, College Park, Maryland.

5. Buntetsu Miyamoto FBI File No. 97-42, 1941, RG 389, Box 2626, National Archives, College Park, Maryland.

6. Alice Hiraga, "The Price of Freedom," *Pacific Citizen*, December 16, 2016, https://www.pacificcitizen.org/the-price-of-freedom/.

7. Stephan, *Hawaii Under the Rising Sun*, 6–7.

8. Letter from Gihachi Yamashita to Lillian Yamashita, March 11, 1943, Yamashita Family Collection, Japanese American National Museum. (Gift of Gihachi and Tsugio Yamashita Family, 94.166.171-176).

9. "Interview of Dillon S. Meyer on the Relocation of Japanese Americans, Ca. 1943." Department of the Interior, War Relocation Authority, 1943, https://archive.org/details/OnTheRelocationOfJapaneseAmericans.

10. Ruriko Fukuhara, "The World War II Internment Camp Experience of the Japanese in Hawaii," MS Doc 141, Bernice Pauahi Bishop Museum.

11. Quoted in Miyamoto, *Hawaii*, 397.

Chapter 23

Talk Story

In Hawai'i, there is a phrase that one hears often when speaking with locals—"talk story." The first time we heard this phrase, we were speaking with our friend, Barbara Ritchie, our ebullient local historian and tour guide, who had just spent the day showing us around Hale'iwa and giving us a history of the town. While waiting with us to catch the bus back to Honolulu that evening, she said, "Let's talk story." While we had never heard the phrase before, we instinctively understood she meant to chat and share stories, and we settled into conversation like old friends not thinking about that phrase again until we were back home in Louisiana several weeks later. What we came to realize was this phrase perfectly encapsulated our approach to research, especially with this project.

From the outset of our journey into the history of Camp Livingston, we have been guided by our personal connections to this history and the stories of the Kohara and Miyamoto families. As librarians, people often assume we get excited by documentary evidence and the unearthing of old documents while doing research. While that is partially true, our real excitement and impetus behind our research and the writing of this book are only possible through the personal connections we have built.

Completing successful research of this type often necessitates the perfect balance of serendipity and grit. This magic combination of chance and determination requires the willingness to follow leads wherever they may take you as well as being open to taking chances in order to create those leads yourself. To create our own leads, one amazing resource we had at our disposal were the journals of Reverend Kano. Reverend Kano, who is cited throughout the Camp Livingston chapters, provided us with many insights into the daily lives of the men within Camp Livingston. His journal entries also left breadcrumbs that we followed in the hopes of gleaning more information about Camp Livingston.

One particular December 1942 entry stood out to us. In that entry, Reverend Kano detailed a visit to the camp by the International Red Cross. He wrote, "Pine board made by Mr. Shige [illegible] sent to Mr. Alfred L. Cardinaux, red cross representative, Washington, D.C., by parcel post as he wished to have it." This entry was striking as it was one of the few that had both an identified person from an organization and a follow-up action completed by the internees. Even though on the surface this didn't seem like a lot, it struck us as being important and worth pursuing.

Uncovering an individual from almost eighty years prior is a daunting task when your only information is a name and international organizational affiliation. Initially, trails for Alfred L. Cardinaux ran cold (see figure 23.1). Refusing to be deterred, our persistence and research efforts led to Emil Cardinaux, a prominent Swiss artist whose nephew turned out to be none other than Alfred Louis Cardinaux, a former commercial artist employed by the International Committee of the Red Cross. Combing through immigration records, census records, and finally public records yielded a lead to the Cardinaux family. We only had a mailing address, so we wrote a letter to a man we were hoping was Alfred Cardinaux's son without knowing if he would receive the letter, if he would respond, and, most importantly, if he was in fact the man we were looking for. Cardinaux's son received our "unexpected communication" and congratulated us on tracking him down—a feat he would ask for specifics on later. He told us a bit about his father in our initial communication and while

Figure 23.1 Alfred Cardinaux Looking Out of Window Overlooking an Internment Camp. Courtesy of Robert Cardinaux.

Figure 23.2 Carving Done in Camp Livingston by Reverend Nitten Ishida and Fellow Internee. Gifted to Alfred Cardinaux after his visit to the camp. Courtesy of Robert Cardinaux.

he didn't know about his father's work during World War II, he unequivocally recalled the wooden carving with Japanese characters, a treasured possession of his father's (see figure 23.2). It hung in the family home and moved with Cardinaux as he traveled the world after the war. His son was certain the carving was still among his father's possessions. Several months later, Cardinaux's son found the carving and wishing to know what was inscribed upon it, posted images of the carving to an online translation forum. As swiftly as the image was uploaded, a translation was posted.

簡易以為尊 (from right to left)
Simplicity is to be valued.
紀元弐千六百弐年十一月三日
November 3, imperial year 2602 (AD 1942)
於米國配所
At the place of exile in the United States
僧正日天 [kaō]
Sōjō Nitten[1]

Confirming the validity of the online translation was important, and so the next step was finding members of the Ishida family who would be able to confirm the calligraphy was done by Archbishop Ishida and the translation was correct. After more searching, we were able to contact Archbishop Ishida's daughter who confirmed the calligraphy on the board was indeed written by her father, Archbishop Nitten Ishida, a Buddhist priest and master calligrapher, who founded the Nichiren Temple in San Francisco in the 1930s (see figure 23.3).

Looking at her father's words, Ishida's daughter stated that they sounded "like a reflection."[2] Using his calligraphy, Archbishop Ishida expressed, in his own authentic voice, his inner truths, ways of thinking, and values. For Archbishop Ishida, he was always a priest first and artist second. The two

Figure 23.3 Archbishop Nitten Ishida circa 1960 in San Francisco, California. Courtesy of Renko Ishida Dempster.

roles may not have been as disparate as they would first appear. Ishida's daughter recalled, "When he did calligraphy, it was like a mediation. Breathing in and breathing out. His characters have vitality and energy."[3] The art of calligraphy helped to center both his thoughts and feelings and channel those into powerful expressions of art. For Archbishop Ishida, embracing simplicity while interned provided a powerful way to cope with his isolation and deprivation.

Creating such a beautiful and poignant expression of internment through the combination of words and carving resonated with Alfred Cardinaux, an artist himself. It moved him in a powerful way and forged a connection between himself and the internees—a connection that stretched beyond his role as an International Red Cross Representative tasked with reporting on the conditions of the camp and the men within. That personal connection was strong enough to move Alfred Cardinaux to attentively care for the carving for the remainder of his life—a prized possession that would, unfortunately, lose its significance and meaning due to the passage of time. Being able to reform this connection some seventy-eight years after the art was created has restored its story, importance, and created a new memory for both the Cardinaux and Ishida families and has helped to illuminate a small portion of the stories of the men held within Camp Livingston.

While the discovery of the artwork is but one example of how we were able to re-forge a connection to Camp Livingston, we found that the connections we were able to form personally and emotionally to both families and the physical site of Camp Livingston were especially poignant and integral in our research journey.

Being able to sit with Marion Kohara Couvillion, listen to her story, view her photographs, and connect with her on such a personal level would be the foundational connection that would underlie everything that happened from that first meeting onward. Eventually, we were able to connect with other members of the Kohara family, build personal relationships with them, and further discover this history through their generosity in sharing what they knew of their family history and connections to Hawai'i. We have spent many hours with the family, entered their homes and lives, and felt compelled to do justice to their legacy and history.

Richard Moran of the Louisiana Maneuvers & Military Museum graciously took us to the site of Camp Livingston outside of Alexandria. We drove there with only a World War II era camp map guiding us along the same Army roads that crisscrossed this part of the Kisatchie forest during the 1940s. The roads, unpaved and muddy from the wet winter weather, were straight and reminiscent of ancient Roman roads surrounded only by trees—the ever-present sentinels guarding the remains of what was once Camp Livingston. In our attempt to locate the internment camp site, we had to hike through the woods. The area now served as a favorite hunting location, so we were required to don orange safety vests for our trek through the forest while distant rifle shots echoed in the trees above us. The weather was cold and wet, and the underbrush was almost impossibly thick with thorns and vines sharply impeding the pace we were able to set. Richard guided us, but no physical structures remained for us to verify the site. Standing in the midst of the pine trees, however, we noticed a high bank of ground that was described in numerous letters written by men in the camp. Suddenly, we felt a gossamer-thin moment in time wash over us—the pine smell, the Louisiana cold seeping into our bones, the feeling of being far from home in that moment—over one thousand men nearly eighty years before this moment had also been here, maybe experiencing the same sensations that we were. This feeling of connection has not left us, even still.

In July of 2019, we traveled to Hawai'i to complete our research for the book. This time in Hawai'i, three weeks spent researching, altered both our perception and connection to the story that we have shared. Before embarking off the mainland, we only had the opportunity to research through documents we found or through brief phone calls with Miyamoto family members. But our time in Hawai'i, literally walking in the footsteps of Reverend Miyamoto at times, changed everything. The most momentous occasions were time spent with two of Reverend Miyamoto's sons, Clifford and David Kanji, and their families. Spending time with the Miyamotos, hearing memories of times past, looking at photographs—nothing can describe this feeling. It was and remains a deeply personal and emotional connection that we carry within us. We can only share our gratitude to the Miyamotos for welcoming us so warmly into their homes and hope that they are proud of the story we have been able to share honoring Reverend Miyamoto and his family's sacrifices, struggles, and perseverance. It is an honor to be allowed to share what we've learned here in this book.

While in Hawai'i, we made discoveries that we could have never imagined. While looking through a book on Hiroshi Honda's work at the University of Hawai'i Mānoa titled *Reflections of Internment: The Art of Hawaii's Hiroshi Honda*, we were struck by some of the artwork created by Honda and its similarities to the environs of Camp Livingston. Visually, we were struck by the pine trees he painted: the starkness and loneliness reaching out from the page. Emotionally, we were jettisoned back to our sojourn into the forest in central Louisiana just months prior. The images in the book were dated, but there was no indication of *where* they had been painted or *which* particular camp they might be from. From the camp rosters we found, as well as the impressive research done by the Japanese Cultural Center of Hawai'i in compiling the Hawai'i Internee Directory, we knew that some of these dates coincided with Honda's imprisonment at Livingston. This knowledge coupled with uncovered photographs of Camp Livingston and our recent trip to the cold pine forest of central Louisiana fresh in our minds, we were emboldened to reach out to the Honolulu Museum of Art to inquire whether we could view Honda's sketchbooks held in their collection in the hopes of discovering sketches of Camp Livingston. Having made a compelling case, we were graciously received and spent an afternoon surrounded by sketchbooks that had once been held by Mr. Honda as he painted his internment experience providing another gossamer-thin moment in our own research journey. As the pages were turned for us by a museum curator, we were able to identify sketches of Livingston by sight—the landscape chronicled before us through metered brush strokes, the words of the men resonating in our ears as they wrote to their families of what Livingston was like. The pines connecting us again through time (see figure 23.4).

We also found inspiration from researching at the Japanese Cultural Center of Hawai'i. There, we had the honor of meeting Jane Kurahara, a retired librarian with an enchanting smile, spirit, and magnetic personality. While helping us to locate documents and collections at the JCCH, Jane shared her own research story with us. Jane, along with fellow JCCH volunteer Betsy Young, uncovered the Honouliuli internment camp that had been lost to memory in the years since World War II. Like Camp Livingston, Honouliuli

Figure 23.4 Watercolor, Ink, Graphite Sketch Done by Hiroshi Honda (1910–1970). Courtesy of Honolulu Museum of Art Purchase, 1992 (21,434).

was a U.S. Army internment camp that was closed at the end of the war and quickly faded into obscurity. Listening to Jane share her experiences of uncovering this camp through pure happenstance, determination, and librarian know-how, we realized we had found a kindred spirit who further inspired us in our research journey to bring Camp Livingston's history as a site of internment back to the national consciousness as an act of reverence and remembrance.

On a warm summer night, we sat in Reverend Miyamoto's temple, the Haleʻiwa Jodo Mission, as the congregation were led in chants and incense slowly filled the air. As the sun set, we watched from the temple balcony as the Obon dance below reached a fever pitch. The sights, sounds, and scents were unlike anything we have ever experienced. Later that evening, we watched as hundreds of illuminated paper lanterns, inscribed with the names of those gone before us, were placed into the dark ocean waters just steps from the temple. As the lanterns floated out to sea, they slowly became lights flickering on the edges of waves as the Buddhist priests chanted and the crowd surged around them. The chanting felt tangible, like a warm embrace. While our feet sank into the cool sand of the beach, we had never felt closer to Reverend Miyamoto, who had overseen this same celebration several decades earlier. We could almost feel his presence there with us. That experience, one among many, exemplified our entire research journey of making connections—historical, personal, and even spiritual at times.

Back in Louisiana, we began to reflect on our journey and how the struggle of doing this type of research lies in the inherent disconnectedness of both the memories and documentary artifacts. The memories and artifacts exist in archives spread across the United States (and even Japan) as well as residing with the families of those who lived through this traumatic and trying experience. We thought of our friend, Barbara, who encouraged us to "talk story" with her. We realized that our whole research journey was one long conversation built upon the ability to compile these memories and documents and allow them to "talk story" with one another and form connections. It is through talking story that we were able to fully realize this project and bring the story of the Miyamoto and Kohara families and consequently the story of Camp Livingston to life.

Research is so much more than searching through archival records and reading historical accounts in books and scholarly journals. It is about connections; specifically, the personal connections that move you beyond the academic and often emotionally detached lens traditionally used to view and understand history and toward a more holistic and humanistic way to connect and examine the past. We hope that the stories of the Miyamoto and Kohara families and the history of internment at Camp Livingston have inspired you to "talk story."

NOTES

1. A note from the translator stated: His kaō looks like the character 石 (ishi), which may have been taken from his surname 石田 (Ishida).
2. Renko Ishida Dempster, interview with authors, October 18, 2019.
3. Renko Ishida Dempster, interview with authors, October 18, 2019.

Epilogue

Softening their blinding light, they mix with the dust; this is the beginning of their affinity [with the unenlightened].[1]

A pine tree is one of the most common and recognizable trees in the world. Upon it, numerous cultures place symbolism and meaning such as constancy, endurance, longevity, wisdom, and good fortune. In Japanese culture, pine trees often signify the connection between the real and spiritual worlds. Pine trees are planted around temples to mark the boundaries of sacred grounds and invite the gods inside. They are also often planted at the entryway of homes to serve as guardians. The Japanese word for pine, *matsu,* translates as "waiting for a god's soul to descend from heaven," which relates to the Shinto belief that pines are ladders used by *kami* (Shinto gods) to descend from heaven. The spirits of *kami* can also inhabit the trees.

In Japanese noh[2] theater, the story of *Takasago* is a beloved drama depicting the spirits of Sumiyoshi and Takasago, twin pines that are located many miles apart and are further separated by mountains and water. Each night the spirit of the Sumiyoshi Pine travels to visit his wife, the Takasago Pine. Their bond transcends both time and distance.

This is the story of *Takasago.*

A priest named Tomonari from the Aso Shrine in Kyushu decided to travel to the capital, Miyako, and wanted to do sightseeing at famous places along the way. Tomonari and his companions put on their traveling robes and boarded a ship to sail to Takasago where he heard tales of the famous twin pines, the Takasago and Sumiyoshi Pine, which were planted by the *kami* from the same seed. The spring winds were favorable, and the trip, which took several days, felt like it took no time at all. The ship arrived in Takasago

Bay in the Harima Province to the sounds of crashing waves and evening bells tolling from the mountaintop temple.

An old couple is on the beach raking needles from underneath a pine tree. The old man and woman share their inner thoughts while raking.

Whom, I wonder, do I really know, if Takasago's ancient pine
Is not my friend from long ago?
The time gone by piles age on age: white snow,
I do not know how deep,
But like the hoary crane, keep vigil,
Watching moonlight shine at dawn,
Cast upon the springtime rime night-shed, and from my bed
I hear the long familiar pine-blown wind. I take as friend my mind
And spread before it intertwined the sedge-mat weave of my
thoughts.[3]

The old man is the aged crane that wakes before dawn and sits in solitude looking at the moon and listening to the wind in the pines. This sound is a familiar friend that has followed him throughout his long life. The wind in the pines is the passing of time, the process of aging, and the solitude of inner thoughts.

Amid this reverie, Tomonari and his group disembark from the ship and encounter the old couple raking needles and wondering how much longer they will live like the ancient pine under which they work.

The coastal wind comes visiting,
Conversing with the pine and casting down a cloak of fallen
needles;
Sleeve next to sleeve
Let's rake away the litter underneath the tree,
Let's rake away the litter underneath the tree.[4]

Tomonari asks the old couple which of the trees before him is the venerated pine of Takasago. The old man answers, "The very one I am raking under is the Takasago pine."[5]

Confused, Tomonari says:

The pines of Takasago and Suminoe are said to be a pair (*aioi*) or have grown up together. But Sumiyoshi is in an altogether different province from this place. How then, can they still be called "the pines that grew up together"?[6]

The old man states that he is from Sumiyoshi province and the old woman is from Takasago. The old man tells Tomonari that he visits Takasago daily to see his love. Surprised, the priest sees the old couple together but cannot understand how that is possible since they live whole provinces apart, separated by land and sea taking a person three days to traverse, yet they are together in one place.

The old woman replies:

A man and his wife may be separated by mountains and rivers for a
full thousand leagues,
But as long as their thoughts run back and forth,
They are never far from each other.[7]

The old couple continue:

These pines of Takasago and Suminoe
Are nonsentinet beings, yet even they are known
As the pines that grew up together.
So all the more should we—we who have feelings,
We, who together have lived through all these years,
This old woman and I who am grown accustomed to visit her from
far-off Sumiyoshi—
There's all the more reason that we be known as the couple grown
old together,
Living to this great age with the pines.[8]

Being sentient beings, the old couple see themselves as more linked than the famous insentient pines planted by the *kami*. Distance cannot separate hearts that are joined nor dampen love tested by adversity. Unity in separation creates an unbreakable bond between the couple and the pines.

And yet this pine, for all eternity,
Stays green. Its needles and flowers make no discrimination of the
times,
And even when the seasons pass to winter,
Its millennial green glows deep in drifts of snow.
What's more, they say pine blossoms make ten appearances, once
every thousand years,
So, awaiting this occasion, the branches of the pine,
Bear leaves of poetry, shining with dewdrop gems,
Seeds to polish the mind's sensibility.
Each and every living thing
Draws under the shelter of Shikishima.[9]

At Takasago
From the peak of Onoe I hear the tolling bell,
Through the night till dawn;

Even though white frost covers each branch, the needles
Keep their constancy of deepest green.
In morning or at night, although we step into its shade
To rake the fallen needles, there is no end to them.
True indeed, the needles of the pine in falling
Never leave the tree completely bare;
Its color still increases, like the trailing laurel vine,
A symbol of our timeless generation.
The most illustrious of evergreens: this pine of Takasago,
An example to serve the ages to come,
Happy indeed, the pines that grew up together![10]

The pine is recognized as ancient and eternal. Its immortality is manifested by the never-ending supply of fallen needles at its base which the old couple continuously rake in an act of purification. The pine is also a source of poetry and beauty that serves as a standard for the ages.

Feeling satisfied that he has learned the past of the famous pines, Tomonari asks the old couple their names.

These are justly famous pine boughs.
These are justly famous pine boughs.
Reveal your past, as old as these great trees,
And let us know your names.[11]

The old couple reply:

What now do we have to keep concealed?
We are Takasago's, Suminoe's,
Spirits of the pines that grew up together,
Come here manifest as man and wife.[12]

The old couple reveal themselves to be the spirits of the pines made human for a short period of time. Their spirits inhabit the pine trees and communicate to each other through the wind that travels through the pine needles. Thus, even when they are no longer able to see each other in physical form, they are connected through the wind that tousles the everlasting and evergreen needles.

The tale of *Takasago* and the telling of the old couple's transformation reveal the pine to be a vessel of spirit, memory, and unbroken bonds. Perhaps the pines of Camp Livingston were the same type of vessel as in the tale of *Takasago*. Perhaps they are the reason that Reverend Miyamoto was able to keep his hope and endure in the face of unbearable adversity and uncertainty. Did he sit under those pines and listen to the rustling of the needles and hear

Figure E.1 Pine cone display made by Reverend Kunio Ohta in Camp Livingston, Louisiana, circa 1942/43. In addition to handcrafting fans, Reverend Ohta also collected large pinecones while at Camp Livingston. He placed the huge cones on simple stands he constructed. These served as "conversational pieces" as there are not such large pinecones in Hawaiʻi. Courtesy of Ella Miyeko Tomita, née Ohta.

the voices of his wife and children? Did the undulating branches conjure images of waves lapping at the sandy shore of his temple? While the exact thoughts, feelings, hopes, and fears that Reverend Miyamoto and the other internees felt while confined beneath the canopy of pines can never truly be known, the pines served as transportive vessels allowing the men to feel closer to home, to dare to hope, and rebelliously imagine a life outside of internment.

NOTES

1. Hare notes that this passage comes from the basic Tendai text, Makashikan (The Great [Treatise]) on Concentration and Insight. This line describes bodhisattvas that come to earth and mingle with the unenlightened souls of people as the first step in bringing those souls to enlightenment. Hare notes, "In Japan the Shinto gods were considered transformations of these bodhisattvas." (Thomas Blenman Hare, *Zeami's Style: The Noh Plays of Zeami Motokiyo* (Stanford, CA: Stanford University Press, 1986), 85).

2. Classical Japanese theater.
3. Hare, *Zeami's Style*, 75–77.
4. Hare, *Zeami's Style*, 78–79.
5. Hare, *Zeami's Style*, 81.
6. Hare, *Zeami's Style*, 81.
7. Hare, *Zeami's Style*, 81.
8. Hare, *Zeami's Style*, 81.
9. Hare, *Zeami's Style*, 89.
10. Hare, *Zeami's Style*, 91.
11. Hare, *Zeami's Style*, 94.
12. Hare, *Zeami's Style*, 94.

As Abraham Lincoln said that all men are created equal, well, so I say do not discriminate or criticize others because of their race or color of their skin.

—Clifford Miyamoto

So we bring to a close this story "Life in an Internment Camp" during World War II. We close with the hope that no gate will ever again close behind an internee of war, and that Old Glory will always fly over a nation at peace in a world at peace.

—Mary Frances Clark[1]

Figure C.1   Reverend Miyamoto at the Hale'iwa Jodo Mission. Courtesy of the Hale'iwa Jodo Mission.

NOTE

1. Scrapbook page containing a closing statement and reflection on World War II Department of Justice Internment Camps. From the Mary F. Clark scrapbook, "Before I Forget, 1942–1947," California State University, Sacramento, California State University Japanese American Digitization Project, https://cdm16855.contentdm.oclc.org/digital/collection/p16855coll4/id/11104

Appendix I

CAMP LIVINGSTON ROSTERS FROM 1942

This is a compilation of names found in rosters dated July 10, September 7, October 1, and December 1, 1942, numbered as List 1, 2, 3, and 5. Missing from this list is the fourth roster, which was not found at the National Archives.[1]

Names are listed as last name, first name.

Abe, Arakichi
Abe, Gisaburo
Abe, Tatsuo
Aihara, Seikichi
Aizumi, Susumu
Aka, Ryosei
Akashi, Kaoru
Akayama, Tomikichi
Akegarasu, Takeo
Akena, Sanra
Akena, Tokuhei
Akita, Uheiji
Akiyama, Tomekichi
Akizaki, Takeo
Akutagawa, Kiyoshi
Akutsu, Kiyonosuke
Ama, Takao
Amano, Yoshitaro

Amino, Inosuke
Aochi, Yasokichi
Aoki, Kamenosuke
Aoki, Kenji
Aoyama, Minoru
Araki, Kazuna Joseph
Araki, Kyushiro
Araki, Takuo
Arase, Shohei
Arima, Toun
Arita, Tamaki
Asaba, Kinzo
Asada, Tokiichi
Asaeda, Horyu
Asakawa, Hachisaku
Asakura, Junji
Asami, Shoichi
Asano, Kakusyo

Asano, Kamezo
Asano, Kintaro
Asano, Tameichi
Asanuna, Yonejiro
Asaoka, Kahuko
Asato, Eishu
Asayama, Sakuichi
Aso, Sanzo
Atsuumi, Noriaki
Azuma, Yu
Azumano, Hatsutaro
Baba, Tokuji
Ban, Takeshi
Bessho, Gentaro
Bunya, Shiro
Chiba, Magojiro
Chiba, Tatsushiro
Chikuma, Masayuki

Chino, Tsuneji
Daigo, Keitara
Date, Naminosuke
Deme, Josen
Doi, Kaizo
Doi, Kanichi
Edo, Kinjiro
Endo, Kakozo
Endo, Koshiro
Endo, Unosuke
Endow, Chosaku
Eto, Tameji
Fuchino, Hago
Fujihira, Shosuke
Fujie, Koju
Fujihana, Kyodo
Fujihira, Shosuke
Fujii, Seiichi
Fujii, Touroku
Fujii, Yosokichi
Fujiie, Eshobo
Fujikado, Hoshin
Fujimoto, Herbert Kenkichi
Fujimoto, Kanta
Fujimoto, Kikuhei
Fujimura, Bunyu
Fujinami, Tokujiro
Fujino, Hego
Fujino, Jisaburo
Fujino, Kiju
Fujino, Shigeo
Fujino, Takesaburo
Fujishiro, Utanosuke
Fujita, Masakatsu
Fujita, Masata
Fujitsubo, Hirao
Fujizawa, Shunan
Fukamaki, Inokichi
Fukawa, Inosuke
Fukayama, Tsutomu
Fukuda, Kentaro
Fukuda, Masami
Fukuda, Teiichiro
Fukuda, Yozo
Fukuhara, Hisashi

Fukuhara, Mitsuo
Fukunaga, Seichi
Furuguri, Kyutaro
Furukawa, Enta
Furusawa, Takashi
Furuta, Shiroichi
Furuta, Tomoki
Furuya, Kaetsu
Furuya, Kumaji
Gota, Fumio
Goto, Fusataro
Goto, Isao
Goto, Mankichi
Goto, Sotaro
Hama, Shinazo
Hama, Yosaburo
Hamada, Itaro
Hamada, Itsuo
Hamada, Jisaku
Hamada, Shigeichi
Hamada, Takae
Hamaguchi, Heizaburo
Hamamoto, Kiichi
Hamamoto, Sadasuke
Hamamura, Chiyomatsu
Hamamura, Koichi
Hamanaka, Taneo
Hanada, Tessui
Hanada, Toichi
Hanaki, Eizo
Handa, Itaro
Hara, Kojiro
Hara, Takuzo
Hara, Toyoyori
Harada, Takashi
Harada, Tsunetaro
Haragami, Nichizo
Haraguchi, Tome
Hasegawa, Kenryu
Hasegawa, Tzuruzo
Hasebe, Charles Ichitaro
Hashimoto, Kazuichi
Hashimoto, Manzuchi
Hasuike, George Susumu
Hata, Goro

Hatakeyama, Kikuji
Hatanaka, Sutegi
Hatanaka, Yoshisuke
Hatashita, Isohei
Hatashita, Teizo
Hattori, Masato
Hayase, Ryuzo
Hayashi, Akisuke
Hayashi, Kyuhichi
Hayashi, Tomoichi
Hayashi, Yoshio
Hidaka, Tsuguo
Hidano, Tetsushiro
Higashi, Hikozo
Higashi, Kyusaburo
Higashi, Toyokichi
Higashi, Unosuke
Higo, Seitaro
Himaka, Chosuke
Himeno, Masahiro
Hino, Shuzui
Hino, Yoshio
Hirabayashi, Hamao
Hirabayashi, Motoyoshi
Hiraga, Jusho
Hirama, Teruzo
Hirano, Naojiro
Hirano, Toshio
Hirao, Kengo
Hirao, Shinjiro
Hirao, Tomiji
Hiraoka, Mazumi
Hirashima, Masaichi
Hirata, Frank Kazuma
Hirayama, Bunjiro
Hirayama, Shinsei
Hiromoto, Seiroku
Hirose, Kosuke
Hirose, Magotaro
Hisatake, Itsuo
Honda, Eisaku
Honda, Hiroshi
Honda, Kaneki
Horagami, Nichizo
Hori, Isaburo

Hori, Kishiro
Hori, Minetaro
Hori, Sojiro
Horiuchi, Mitsutaka
Hoshiko, Hitoshi
Hoshiko, Iwao
Hosokawa, Yoshimoto
Hosono, Kiyozo
Iba, Shoichi
Ichiba, Isao
Ichikawa, Frank Kiyoshi
Ichikawa, Tatsuya
Ichimaru, Kakuzo
Ichiyasu, Hirotaka
Ida, T. William
Igarashi, Hisashi
Ige, Kamaroku
Iguchi, Soichi
Ihara, Tamotsu
Iida, Koichi
Iinuma, Toshio
Iizuka, Shotaro
Ikawa, Eiichi
Ikeda, Bunen
Ikeda, Kwando
Ikeda, Naoichi
Ikeda, Sukeo
Ikemiya, Guillermo
Ikeno, Masao
Ikeya, Kaiji
Ikezawa, Benjamin Shuntaro
Imada, Ikuichi
Imada, Kiyoshi
Imahashi, Shigeji
Imahashi, Torajiro
Imai, Seizo
Imai, Toyoji
Imaizumi, Yasugi
Imamoto, Jusako
Imamura, Tsutomu
Imamura, Yoneji
Imura, Koichi
Imura, Torakichi
Inaba, Heisaku

Inazaki, Itsuo
Inokuchi, Uyemon
Inoue, Tokuji
Inouye, Hikohachi
Inouye, Hisao
Inouye, Hokichi
Inouye, Jukichi
Inouye, Kikuji
Inouye, Kumaki
Inouye, Nobujiro
Inouye, Susumu
Inuyama, Gengo
Inuzuka, Takashi
Iseda, Gyosuke Joe
Iseri, Torao
Ishibashi, Naoichi
Ishida, Kyujiro
Ishida, Nitten Jiro
Ishida, Shotaro
Ishida, Tazo Tom
Ishii, Chuhei
Ishii, Tsurutaro
Ishikawa, Yassaku
Ishikawa, Yasuji
Ishikawa, Yoshizo
Ishima, Chiyohachi
Ishima, Kazuyoshi
Ishimoto, Sannosuke
Ishimoto, Masao
Ishiwata, Chozo
Ishizaki, Raiji
Ishizuka, Kunisaburo
Isobe, Misao
Isobe, Shigemi
Itahara, Kumashige
Itami, Asagora
Itanori, Kenji
Ito, Choichi
Ito, Hichijiro
Ito, Hosaku
Ito, Kiyoharu
Ito, Michio
Ito, Naotaro
Ito, Tokijiro
Iwahara, Taketo

Iwanaga, Tomoki
Iwasa, Sueji
Iwasaki, Tatsuji
Iwashima, Sokichi
Iwashita, Hiroki
Iwashita, Shigeo
Iwata, Kametaro
Iwata, Masayuki
Iwata, Ryoichi
Iwatsuba, Matsuo
Izuhara, Hiroshi
Izui, Mikisaburo
Izumi, Kakusho
Izumi, Kiyoto
Izumi, Kuichi
Izuno, Tokio
Kabashima, Suizo
Kadonaga, Hikoichi
Kadotani, Tommy Yoshito
Kagawa, Lawrence Takeo
Kagawa, Shotaro
Kai, Masajiro
Kajikawa, Iwanari
Kajiwara, Rinzaburo
Kajiwara, Taryo
Kajiwara, Tasuke
Kakiyama, Louis
Kamada, Kyohei
Kame, Kameniro
Kamegawa, Fujima
Kamei, Sadaichi
Kamibayashi, Hanbei
Kamiya, Harukichi
Kamiya, Masutaro
Kamon, Kazuo
Kan, Gunzo
Kan, Tatsumi
Kanagae, Katsuzo
Kanazawa, Ginjiro
Kaneko, Hatsuhei
Kaneko, Junji
Kaneko, Kurakichi
Kaneshima, Seisuke
Kanja, Yonezo
Kano, Hisanori

Karaki, Kakichi
Kariya, Hiroshi
Kasai, Henry Yoshihiko
Kasai, Umenosuke
Kasashima, Hatsutara
Kashihara, Ryuju
Kashima, Matsunosuke
Kashima, Ryuichi
Kashima, Takaichi
Kataoka, Ichiro
Katayama, Takeo
Kato, Keijiro
Kato, Sannosuke
Kato, Senya
Kato, Takichi
Kato, Tomosaburo
Kato, Toyataro
Kato, Yahichi
Katoda, Tetsuei
Kawabori, Jintaro
Kawada, Shigenaga
Kawaguchi, Asakichi
Kawaguchi, Hikotaro
Kawaguchi, Kinzo
Kawaguchi, Kumekichi
Kawaguchi, Sajiro
Kawaguchi, Shojiro
Kawahara, Koichi
Kawai, Hikoichi
Kawai, Hiromi
Kawai, Kingo
Kawakami, Jutaro
Kawakami, Shozo
Kawamoto, Katsuichi
Kawamura, Kiyoshi
Kawano, Antonio
Kawano, Junsaku
Kawano, Kazuo
Kawasaki, Kazowe
Kawauchi, Rinosuke
Kawauchi, Kichitaro
Kayahara, Chosuke
Kayano, Mitaro Harvey
Kikuchi, Chikyoku
Kimoto, Jutaro

Kimura, Akio Robert
Kimura, Dotatsu
Kimura, Muneo
Kimura, Tomiji
Kimura, Toraki
Kinoshita, Sadashichi
Kirita, Kamekichi
Kishida, Eiichi
Kishida, Jisaburo
Kishima, Shunichi
Kishishita, Yozo
Kiso, Iichi
Kita, Taiji
Kitajima, Shoyu
Kitajima, Yoshio
Kitamura, Kiyoharu
Kitamura, Mitsuo
Kitayama, Goro
Kiyama, Soshiro
Kiyohara, Tetsuei
Kiyosaki, Masato
Kizu, Yoshimatsu
Koba, Katsushi
Kobayashi, Enjo
Kobayashi, Hajime
Kobayashi, Makio
Kobayashi, Motoichi
Kobayashi, Nisshu
Kobayashi, Takio
Kobayashi, Toraichi
Kobayashi, Yoshio
Kobayashi, Toraichi
Kodama, Masayuki
Koga, Haruto
Koga, Yoshio
Kohara, Sadaji
Kohatsu, Yukihide
Kohno, Akeo
Koide, Shoichi
Koide, Taju
Koiso, Tetsunosuke
Kojima, Hikoji
Kojima, T. George
Kojima, Gitaro
Kokuma, Masao

Kokuzo, Zenkai
Komai, H. Toyosaku
Komatsu, Kumataro
Komatsu, Seisaku
Komatsu, Taichi
Komatsu, Kenzaburo
Komorita, Kenzo
Kondo, Saburo Hirashima
Konno, Ichiro
Kono, Isamu
Kono, Katsuya
Kono, Toraichi
Koshiba, Takeji
Koyama, Keizaburo
Koyama, Sankichi
Koyama, Shiroichi
Koyana, Keizaburo
Koyanagi, Yasukichi
Kubokawa, Kyokujo
Kubota, Fukujiro
Kubota, Fukumatsu
Kubota, Ryudo
Kubota, Saichiro
Kubota, Sakutaro
Kuchiba, Gikyo
Kudo, Isamu
Kuga, Jihei
Kuge, Naoyoshi
Kumamato, Shusuke
Kunitomo, Wakichi
Kuniyuki, Ikuzo
Kurachi, Sajuro
Kuranaga, Yeishiro
Kuranishi, Masaichi
Kurashita, Yukio
Kurata, Itsuo
Kuratomi, Rintaro
Kuroda, Katsuto
Kuroda, Keisei
Kurokawa, Tetsuji
Kusano, Yasutaro
Kusumoto, Joy Rokuichi
Kusuda, Kakushin
Kuwahara, Gunichi
Kuwahara, Shigeru

Appendix I

Kuwata, George Minori
Maeshiba, Naojiro
Maeda, Kametaro
Maekawa, Shigezo
Mamiya, Toshio Bino
Mamiya, Yoshigoro
Mamizuka, Matsujiro
Mano, Ichiro
Mano, Ichisaburo
Mano, Tokujiro
Marui, Motoichi
Marumoto, Minoru
Maruoka, Shigemitsu
Maruyama, Eizo
Maruyama, Tohachiro
Maruyama, Gunjiro
Masaki, Jikyo
Masaki, Shozaemon
Mashiko, Shinobu
Mashita, Junzo
Masuda, Gosaku
Masuda, Komin Ran
Masuhara, Kenichi
Masuoka, Baiichi
Matani, Matayoshi
Matano, Konin
Matsubara, Seiichi
Matsubayashi, Shushin
Matsuda, Ishichi
Matsuda, Kengo
Matsuda, Ryugen
Matsuda, Yoshio
Matsuda, Yoshio
Matsudo, Yorisuke
Matsuhara, Fusao
Matsui, Kakusuke
Matsui, Seijiro
Matsui, Totaro
Matsui, Yutetsu
Matsukawa, Kameo
Matsumoto, Hajime
Matsumoto, Katsuichi
Matsumoto, Kazumi
Matsumura, Tomatsu
Matsumura, Tomoji

Matsumura, Yasuzo
Matsuno, Kanroku
Matsuo, Kumaichi
Matsuo, Umesuke
Matsuoka, Yoki
Matsushima, Umata
Matsushita, Kintaro
Matsushita, Shichigoro
Matsushita, Shigemitsu
Matsushita, Yukichi Roy
Matsuuki, Kinichiro
Matsuura, Gyokuei
Matsuura, Issei
Matsuura, Masaji
Matsuura, Shuun
Matsuyama, Isekichi
Mayeda, Buntaro
Mayeda, Kiichi
Mayekawa, George Teijiro
Mena, Eichi
Miaki, Taneichi
Michida, Yaichi
Miho, Katsuichi
Mikami, Shuji
Miki, Yasuemon
Mikuni, Matagoro
Minami, Fukutaro
Minami, Masajiro
Minami, Nobuichi
Minami, Yaemon
Minamino, Rikichi
Minato, Kuhei
Minato, Masami
Misaka, Minoru
Mishima, Shinichi
Mitani, Masayoshi
Mitoma, Isuke
Miura, Genpei
Miura, Koshiro
Miura, Kozo
Miura, Nobuichi
Miwa, Masaharu
Miwa, Masamichi
Miwa, Nakazo
Miya, Takeshi

Miyagawa, Frank Jukichi
Miyagawa, Shintaro
Miyagi, Genei
Miyagi, Takeo
Miyagi, Yukioto
Miyagishima, Kanekichi
Miyahara, Kiroku
Miyaji, Kohei
Miyake, Tanzo
Miyake, Shigeru
Miyaki, Riyohei
Miyako, Kozo
Miyama, Shigeru
Miyama, Tadashi
Miyamoto, Buntetsu
Miyamoto, Kazu
Miyamoto, Manzo
Miyamoto, Nihei
Miyao, Shigemaru
Miyasaki, Hiseki
Miyashiro, Tokushi
Miyashita, Toshiyuki
Miyata, Kumao
Miyata, Kyoichi
Miyazaki, Kingo
Mizukami, Harry Bunkichi
Mizuki, Kashitaro
Mizumoto, Shigeki
Mochizuki, Kanryu
Momii, Kizaemon Ikken
Monzen, Kiyoto
Moriguchi, Nobuyuki
Morimoto, Takichi
Morinaga, Kaoru
Morita, Inosuke
Morita, Koetsu
Morita, Ramon
Morita, Shizuo
Morita, Takeshi
Morita, Tatsukichi
Morita, Tatsuo
Morita, Tokichi
Motoshige, Hiroshi
Motoshige, Tatsuo
Mukaeda, Katsuma

Mukai, Kenso
Mukai, Seizaburo
Murai, Koh
Murai, Masao
Murakami, Jinkichi
Murakami, Minoru
Murakami, Takuo
Murakami, Teizaburo
Muranaka, Eiichi Roy
Muraoka, Saburo
Murata, Shunichi
Mutobe, Ryujin
Mutow, Kichitaro
Nada, Yujiro
Nagaishi, Gengo
Nagakura, Eizo
Nagamatsu, Ikugoro
Nagamine, Haruyuki
Nagano, Kiro
Nagao, Masaji
Nagasaki, Toyokichi
Nagase, Yoshio Masaomi
Nagashima, Sadami Frank
Nagashima, Yohochi
Nago, Ninryo
Naito, Kyojo
Nakadate, Yojiro
Nakagama, Shintaro
Nakagawa, Kosaburo
Nakagawa, Sakuji
Nakagawa, Shintaro
Nakahara, James
  Toshimarau
Nakahata, Shiro Y.
Nakama, Ginhachi
Nakamichi, Kosaku
Nakamoto, Hidekichi
Nakamoto, Shotaro
Nakamura, Kyutaro
Nakamura, Akimatsu
Nakamura, Gongoro
Nakamura, Hiroichi
Nakamura, Juro
Nakamura, Koichiro
Nakamura, Kokichi

Nakamura, Megumu
Nakamura, Minosuke
Nakamura, Naoshi
Nakamura, Sadamu
Nakamura, Shigeichi
Nakamura, Tatsuji
Nakamura, Teiji
Nakamura, Tomoaki
Nakamura, Yoshio
Nakane, Kyoji
Nakane, Naka
Nakano, Kiyoshi
Nakano, Tamejiro
Nakashima, Kintaro
Nakashima, Teiji
Nakata, Toshio
Nakatani, Shinzo
Nakatsuka, Ichiro
Nakatsuka, Kinsaburo
Nakayama, Dengo
Nakayama, Hatsutaro
Nakayama, Hozui
Nambu, Genya
Namikawa, Shirokichi
Nanbara, Ryuichi
Nanbara, Tadao
Narumi, Jutaro
Nase, Masao
Niimi, Tokuichi
Nikki, Yoshitaro
Nimura, Yoshitsugu
Nishi, Bunpachi
Nishi, Kaneyoshi
Nishi, Kinji
Nishi, Mojuro
Nishibata, Kinbei
Nishida, Yoshifusa
Nishii, Hironori
Nishiki, Kakujiro
Nishimoto, Teijiro
Nishimura, Sueji
Nishina, Masao
Nishina, Nobu
Nishina, Siezo
Nishina, Tamizo

Nishino, Mitsunari
Nishioka, Heisuke
Nishisaka, Tadaji
Nishiyama, Matsujuro
Nishizawa, Kosan
Nishizawa, Yuko
Nishizu, Shinjiro
Niwa, Seihichi
Nobuhira, Kiroku
Nonaka, Kanezo
Nonomura, Yuko
Nonoguchi, Chiyoichi
Noritake, Motoo
Nose, Masao
Nozawa, Yoshinori
Obata, Soichi
Obayashi, Joe Uichiro
Ochiai, Ekichi
Oda, Hakuai
Odo, Shunichi
Oekawa, Tokushi
Ogata, Kazuhiko
Ogata, Sueo
Ogawa, Seichi
Ogawa, Yoshio
Ogi, Koichi
Ogura, Ukichi
Ohara, Shigeo
Ohara, Shozo
Ohata, Seiichi
Ohki, Kinzo
Ohta, Gentaro
Ohta, Kunio
Ohye, Honi
Oi, Joei
Oishi, Sakae
Oishi, Yojiro
Oka, Bunji Ben
Oka, Harry Suekichi
Okada, Masanosuke
Okaji, Toyomi
Okamiya, Yoshikazu
Okamoto, Hisajiro
Okamoto, Kazumi
Okamoto, Komo

Okamoto, Toyotaro
Okamura, Juichi
Okamura, Suyeichi
Okamura, Yasutaro
Okano, Ryoshin
Okawa, Gendo
Okazaki, Shigeo
Oku, Tohkichi
Okubo, Tometsugo
Okumoto, Yoshimi
Okuno, Bunshichi
Okura, Momota
Okura, Seido
Okuyama, Eitaro
Onaga, Buzen
Onaga, Rincho
Onishi, Junichi
Onishi, Shotaro
Onizuka, Tsuneto
Ono, Kameichi Frank
Ono, Shoroku
Ooka, Jinichiro
Ooka, Kan Yutaka Hiroshi
Orita, Isaku
Osada, Zenzaburo
Osaki, Junji
Oshima, Shigeo
Otake, Tamaichi
Otoi, Masunosuke
Otsubo, Togo
Ouchi, Moriichi
Oyama, Fukujiro
Oye, Kumejiro
Ozaki, Junji
Ozaki, Kamesaburo
Ozaki, Otokichi
Ozaki, Sawajiro J.
Ozawa, Yoshikiyo
Rikimaru, Isamu
Rikimaru, Mataji
Ryono, Densuke
Ryono, Masukichi
Ryono, Michihiko
Ryono, Otamatsu
Saiki, Takaichi

Saito, Haruto F.
Saito, Jogen
Saito, Motoi
Saito, Haruto
Saito, Shigetoshi
Sakabu, Kansaku
Sakai, Kunisuke
Sakai, Tokutaro
Sakaino, Bunro
Sakakura, Kotaro
Sakakura, Saichi
Sakamaki, Kazuo
Sakamoto, Kuichi
Sakamoto, Munetaka
Sakamoto, Sanji
Sakamoto, Seiichi K.
Sakamoto, Masao
Sakashita, Rikitaro
Sakaue, Sokuma
Sakimura, Masaichi
Sakimizuru, Atsuo
Sako, Toshio
Sakogawa, Itsuji
Sakurada, Jisaku
Sano, Moritaro
Sano, Tsunetaro
Sarashina, Shinri
Sasahara, Yoshitaro
Sasai, Myoshu
Sasaki, Giichi
Sasaki, Kosaku
Sasaki, Masami
Sasaki, Shozo
Sasaki, Shunji
Sasaki, Tadao
Sasaki, Takeichi
Sasaki, Yoshinobu
Sasame, Takashi
Sata, Hijime
Sato, Chihiro
Sato, Chosuke
Sato, Chuji John
Sato, Hiroshi
Sato, Ichio
Sato, Kikujiro

Sato, Kiyoshi
Sato, Kosaku
Sato, Matsujiro
Sato, Meijiro
Sato, Mikitaro
Sato, Rikitaro
Sato, Susumu
Sato, Taichi
Sato, Takeo
Sato, Yazo
Sato, Zentaro
Sawamura, Shigenori
Sawamura, Shohei
Sayegusa, Kinzo
Segawa, Hikoshiro
Seki, Genzo
Seki, Kyoichiro
Sekiyama, Isami
Seko, Idayu
Seko, Kaichi
Senba, Tatsumi
Serizawa, Hideyuki
Shiba, Kakuo
Shibata, Hiroshi
Shibata, Kaizo
Shibata, Shin
Shibuta, Mizuho
Shigekane, Shigezo
Shigekuni, Aisuke S.
Shigemoto, Osuke
Shigenaga, Kakuro
Shigekane, Shigezo
Shima, Hynosuke
Shimada, Kanetaro
Shimamo, Kohei
Shimazaki, Taichiro
Shimizu, Mitsuhiko
Shimizu, Takazo
Shimizu, Toraichi
Shimizu, Usuke
Shimizu, Yasajiro
Shimoda, Hanzo
Shimokawa, Hanzo
Shinoda, Masaichiro
Shinishi, Sotaro

Shinohara, Heijiro
Shinozaki, Kenjiro
Shintani, Ichimatsu
Shintani, Ritsusuke
Shinzato, Nangi
Shiode, Shoichi
Shiogi, Sadaji
Shioji, Hachijiro
Shiokawa, Tomio
Shiota, Takezo
Shiotani, Motoi
Shiraishi, Hikokuma
Shiraishi, Miyuki
Shirakana, Tokio
Shirakawa, Choichiro
Shirakawa, Tokio
Shirasu, Jukaku
Shiroyama, Kansaku
Shitanishi, Iwataro
Shoda, Seiichi
Sodetani, Yukiyasu
Sogawa, Masao
Sokabe, Miyuki
Sonoda, Santaro
Sotomaru, Harry M.
Suetomi, Koten
Sueyasu, Yonezo
Sugano, Tomikichi
Sugimara, Mankichi
Sugimoto, Seiichi
Sugimoto, Tokikichi
Sugimura, Genta
Sugimura, Sankichi
Sugino, Masami
Sugiyama, Ichitaro
Sukegawa, Denzaburo
Sukegawa, Takeo
Sukegawa, Tosuke
Sumi, Toraichi
Sumida, Daizo
Sumida, Shinzaburo
Suminaga, Konosuke
Sunago, Harukichi
Suto, Sataro
Suyama, Yasugoro
Suzue, Shigeo

Suzuki, Asakichi
Suzuki, Frank Bunichi
Suzuki, Eijiro
Suzuki, Hiroshi
Suzuki, Kakutaro
Suzuki, Kikuo
Suzuki, Noboru
Suzuki, Sadaichi
Suzuki, Tojuro
Tabata, Sam Sokichi
Tachibana, Chikamori
Tada, Kinichi
Tagawa, Shizuma
Taguwa, Asatoshi
Tahara, Hiroshi
Tahara, Kameo
Taira, Takakichi
Taira, Tomotaka Henry
Taira, Yojo
Takahashi, Giichi
Takahashi, Masao
Takahashi, Rien
Takahashi, Saburo
Takahashi, Shodo Seytsu
Takahashi, Terusone
Takahashi, Tokue
Takahashi, Wataru
Takahashi, Giichi
Takaki, Suekuma
Takaki, Umekichi
Takakuwa, Shujiro
Takanishi, Kazuichi
Takano, Itaro
Takano, Morizo
Takano, Nagaki
Takao, Fusakichi
Takao, Inosuke
Takaoka, Ryosaburo
Takase, Yutaka
Takashima, Kamekichi
Takashima, Yoshiro
Takata, Giichi
Takei, Torao
Takemoto, Hikoju
Takemoto, Yasuo
Takemura, Seiji

Takeoka, Daiichi
Takeshita, Muneyoshi
Takesue, Tsuyoshi
Taketa, Torao
Takeuchi, Masato
Takeuchi, Tsuneo
Takido, Kanekichi
Takigawa, Ikutaro
Takumi, Torihiko
Tamari, Shinnosuke
Tamashiro, Eitai
Tambara, Asakichi
Tamekuni, Shonen
Tamura, Katsuchika
Tamura, Makitaro
Tanagi, Koi
Tanaka, Giichi
Tanaka, Kakuo
Tanaka, Katsuichi
Tanaka, Kumao
Tanaka, Kyuhachi
Tanaka, Masayoshi
Tanaka, Ryohei
Tanaka, Sadamatsu
Tanaka, Tamaichi
Tanaka, Yaroku
Tanaka, Yasutaro
Taniguchi, Manabu G.
Taniguchi, Miake
Tanikawa, Atsuji
Tanioka, Kiro
Tanji, Shizuma
Taoka, Yahei
Tashiro, Manabu
Tashiro, Masanobu
Tateishi, Yoshimasa
Tateoka, Harry Hisashi
Tateyama, Mitsuyoshi
Tatsuguchi, Goki
Tatsuno, Ryuji
Tatsutani, Gengin
Tawara, Hitoshi
Terao, Ichiro
Teraoka, Hisahiko
Teraoka, Takehiko
Terasaki, Mannosuke

Terashita, Motokichi
Toakirin, Jinshichi
Tobe, Kisoe
Tobita, Kanji
Toda, Shoshin
Toda, Taiyu
Tofukuji, Koshiro O.
Togioka, Setsugo
Toguri, Makoto
Toko, Takao
Tokuda, Seichi
Tokuyama, Jitsutaro
Toma, Tsurumatsu
Tomihiro, Senichi
Tominaga, Asabei
Tominaga, Hisashi
Tomio, Harry Tomozo
Tomita, Kazuo
Tomiyama, Michio
Tomiyama, Takashi
Tomooka, Toyokichi
Tonai, Genoro
Torazawa, Heitaro
Toshima, Isao
Toyama, Takeo
Toyama, Takinosuke
Toyama, Tetsuo
Toyoda, Setsuzo
Toyofuku, Hatsutaro
Toyofuku, Ichiji
Toyofuku, Tanzo
Toyota, Fred Shizutaro
Tsubakizaki, Chiyozo
Tsuboi, Teruo
Tsuchida, Sadakazu
Tsuda, Noboru
Tsude, Mokuryu
Tsuge, Giko
Tsuha, Kenjitsu Jitsushige
Tsuji, Iwao
Tsuji, Tsuneemon
Tsuji, Tomoji
Tsujita, Bill Akira
Tsujiuchi, Shunichi
Tsumagari, Takeji
Tsunemoto, Hajime

Tsuno, Yoshitaro
Tsunoda, Chikashi
Tsunoda, Kensaku
Tsunoda, Kogyo
Tsunoda, Yoshiyuki
Tsurushima, Genjiro
Tsuboi, Teruo
Uchida, Setsuzo
Uchiyama, Keijiro
Udo, Daisaku
Udo, Tsunejiro
Ueda, Ichiro
Ueda, Nisuke
Uehara, Saburo
Uehara, Tokuya
Uemura, Mitsuo
Uenishi, Kozo
Ueno, Chujiro
Uenura, Mitsuo
Ueoka, Sokan
Umeda, Motoharu
Umehara, Shodo
Umeki, Seisuke
Uno, Hikaru
Uno, Setsujiro
Urakawa, Tomehichi
Urushibata, Kojiro
Usuda, Masaaki
Uyeda, Kyoichi
Uyeda, Mototaro
Uyeda, Tetsusaburo
Uyeda, Toraichi
Uyeji, Kame
Uyeji, Kiutaro
Uyemura, Katsuji
Uyeno, Hampei
Uyeno, Sakujiro
Uyeno, Tomoichi
Uyenoyama, Shutetsu
Uyesugi, Sekichi
Wada, Ichiro R.
Wada, Konosuke
Wada, Masaharu
Wada, Sueki
Wada, Takashi
Wada, Umeo

Wakayama, Jitsuji
Wakayama, Katsuichi Tom
Watanabe, Genzo
Watanabe, Ittetsu
Watanabe, Iwaki
Watanabe, Koichi
Watanabe, Masataro
Watanabe, Nobu
Watanabe, Shingo
Watanabe, Tadashi
Watanabe, Tamotsu
Watanabe, Tomoichi
Watanabe, Yataro
Watanabe, Yoshio
Watanabe, Yoshio
Watanabe, Yoshitaka
Watanabe, Yozo
Watanabe, Sadakichi
Watanabe, Yoshio
Watanuki, Mitsugoro
Yabe, Giichi
Yabuno, Tsukasa
Yama, Manabu
Yamada, Jutaro
Yamada, Takeshi
Yamada, Tazaburo
Yamada, Tomokichi
Yamada, Toramatsu
Yamada, Wazo
Yamahiro, Nisuke
Yamamoto, Gengo
Yamamoto, Hisataro
Yamamoto, Kimaru
Yamamoto, Kiyoshi
Yamamoto, Kizo
Yamamoto, Kyunosuke
Yamamoto, Masamichi
Yamamoto, Yotaro
Yamanaka, Heiichi
Yamane, Goichi
Yamane, Seiichi
Yamane, Tomoyuki
Yamanouchi, Teijiro
Yamasaki, Naosaburo
Yamashita, Gihachi
Yamashita, Hiroto

Yamashita, Toshimi
Yamashita, Seiji
Yamatani, Kosaku
Yamauchi, Asao
Yamawaki, Genkichi
Yamazato, Jikai
Yanagihara, Kanekichi
Yanigisawa, Honzo
Yara, Chosei
Yasui, Masuo
Yasui, Ryoichi Johnny

Yoda, Kichisuke
Yodogawa, Senzaburo
Yokota, Seiichi
Yokota, Toshikatsu
Yonahara, Ryosen
Yonezawa, Yoshiro
Yoshida, Ichita
Yoshida, Kenji Frank
Yoshida, Suehiko
Yoshii, Eisaku
Yoshikawa, Gentaro

Yoshikawa, Toyokichi
Yoshimasu, Masayuki
Yoshimura, Kichigoro
Yoshinaka, Seiichi
Yoshio, Kikumatsu
Yoshioka, Asagoro
Yoshioka, Rikimatsu
Yoshitomi, Junichi Joe
Yuasa, Fukukichi
Yui, Kamekichi
Yukita, Yoshitaro

NOTE

1. Detention Rosters: Camp Livingston, Louisiana; Subject Files, 1942–1946; Records of the Office of the Provost Marshal General, 1920–1975, Record Group 389; National Archives at College Park, College Park, Maryland. Many thanks to Duncan Ryūken Williams for his work in removing duplicate names and correcting spelling errors found on the original rosters as part of his work on the Ireichō, a component of the larger Irei: National Monument for the WWII Japanese American Incarceration project.

Appendix II

The poems below are from the "Original Writing 4th Poetry Reading and Critique Session, August 1942," which can be found in the Ozaki Collection AR1, Box 9, Folder 15, at the Japanese Cultural Center of Hawai'i.

All translations and notes on translations of poems from the 4th Poetry Reading are courtesy of the Japanese Cultural Center of Hawai'i volunteer: Yoko Waki, with volunteers Jean Toyama, Florence Sugimoto, and Sheila Chun. *Note:* Muin is the pen name of Otokichi Ozaki, a Japanese language school teacher from Hilo, Hawai'i Island. Seiha is Shoichi Asami, a Japanese language newspaper editor from Honolulu, and Suikei is Kumaji Furuya, a businessman from Honolulu. We do not know the given names of the other poets.

題詠　「船」「別」
Themes: "Ship" and "Separation"

1.　救命具つけてデッキに居並べば輝く太陽青き海原
Lined up on the deck
with life jackets on
we see the sunlight sparkle
across a stretch of
blue ocean

2.　送還ときまりたる日今布哇なる同胞のこと胸内に迫り来
The date of my return
from internment now set
I feel for
my Hawaii friends
left behind

3.　思ひ出の配所の松に日は落ちて別れ名残るか蝉しきりなく　　　かつろく
Remembering the pines
as the sun sets
in my place of exile,
the cicadas singing
as if in farewell

Katsuroku

4.　別れの日子は指に怪我をしてゐしがふと気になりぬ朝の目ざめに　　無音
Awakened in the morning
I remember my child
and worry about his finger,
injured on the day
we parted

Muin

5.　いずこまで續く苦難ぞ残る身の想ひ果てなし友を送る日　　　青波
How long will my suffering last
I wonder
as I watch
my friends depart
and I remain behind

Seiha

6.　圓かなる月も蝕しぬ囚はれの群の別るゝ日の近き宵　　　むめいし
Like the waning of a full moon
the day of parting
for our group of internees
draws near

Mumeishi

7.　君船に南洋の月仰ぐ時知れ其も大き日の本の空　　　しうんほう
As you look at the moon
from a ship on the South Seas
you realize
how vast the skies are
above Japan

Shiunhou

8.　信号に船はぴったり止まりて船壁を打つ波の音する
At the signal
the ship stops suddenly
Only the sound of the waves
hitting the sea wall
can be heard

9.　なゆきそとほゝゑみてまた君泣きぬ鐘に花散る宵なりしかな。　　ろせい
So you are going
she smiles and sobs
in the evening
flowers scatter
at the sound of the bell

Rosei

10.　送別会同胞吾等は満歳を贈とせり何なき身なれば。　　せいがく
As a parting gift
to a friend
we say "banzai"
since we have nothing
else to offer

Seigaku

11.　十日あまり空を仰がず海を見ず恨めしきかな牢獄の船　　ろせい
Over ten days
without seeing sky
nor sea
imprisoned on this ship
I am bitter

Rosei

雑詠
Miscellaneous poems

1.　なびき来る煙に脂の香して松の古株焼き居り暮々　　しうんほう
The smell of resin
in the smoke wafting
from the burning
old pine
as darkness falls

Shiunhou

2.　愛で飼へる亀と兎に囚はれの憂さを残して人の去りゆく　　しうんほう
Leaving behind
his beloved
turtle and rabbit
he is filled
with sadness

Shiunhou

3. ホノルルに心残して送らるゝ護送船團物々しかも
My heart remains
in Honolulu
as a large convoy
of ships leaves
with much fanfare

4. 親しさの草花に夏は別れゆくいとしき子等の姿にも似て　　かつろく
Summer bids farewell
to familiar flowers
How similar to
the fading sight
of my dear children

                Katsuroku

5. 兵となって下のデッキに子は乗れり父なる人は囚はれにして　　無音
The son rides below the deck,
a soldier
His father,
a prisoner,
aboard the same ship

                Muin[1]

6. いや遠く捕はれてあれば無事といふ便りさへ子は疑ひ止まず　　青波
Imprisoned
so far away
my children
doubt my letter
telling of my well-being

                Seiha

7. のどけさや見張りの塔の番兵が欠伸して居りかげろうの中に
（キャンプマコイの春）　　ろせい
(Spring in Camp McCoy)
In the tranquility
a soldier
in the watch tower
yawns
in the warm haze

                Rosei

8. さみどりのながながし葉の松直ぐにのびそろひたる森の下道
Green pine leaves
grow straight and long
along the path
in the woods

Appendix II

9. （船）我心船ゆく君に従ひてともに仰がん故郷の月
My heart wants to follow you
onto the ship
so we can view
the moon together
from our hometown

10. アメリカの南の果てに廻り来て松の林に蛍飛ぶ見る　　　　すいけい
Having gone around
the farthest tip
of the South American continent
I now see fireflies
in the pine forest

　　　　　　　　　　　　　　　　　　　　　　　　　　　　　Suikei

11. 待てど待てど家の音信（おとずれ）絶えてなき日のみ続きて今
　　 日も暮れ行く　　　　　　　　　　　　　　　　　　　　ろせい
Waiting and waiting
day after day
yet no letter comes
and the sun sets
today again

　　　　　　　　　　　　　　　　　　　　　　　　　　　　　Rosei

12. 逢ひに来し末の娘の唯だぼつねんとものも言ひ得ぬ姿目にしむ
　　　　　　　　　　　　　　　　　　　　　　　　　　　　かつろく
My youngest daughter visits,
a lonely figure
unable to say a word
My eyes begin to tear

　　　　　　　　　　　　　　　　　　　　　　　　　　　　Katsuroku

13. にはか雨に軒下によればゲラウヘアと雨の小庭に追はれ食ぶる
　　（ホノルル移民局）　　　　　　　　　　　　　　　　　むゐん
(at the Honolulu Immigration Station)
A sudden rain
"Get outta here!"
Chased from under the eaves
we eat in a small yard
in the rain

　　　　　　　　　　　　　　　　　　　　　　　　　　　　Muin[2]

14.　妻も子もひたすらわれを引止むレパトリユート決しかねつも　すいけい
To repatriate or not
How difficult to decide
with wife and children
imploring me
not to

                                                                  Suikei

15.　捕はれてここの敵地に幾度か送り迎へる今宵この月　　　　青波
Imprisoned in the enemy's land
how many times
have I seen this moon
rise and fall

                                                                   Seiha

16.　[?]のベッド針の山とも覚えつれ百日(モモカ)臥すとも心なづまず
　　　　　　　　　　　　　　　　　　　　　　　　　　　せいがく
Even if I sleep on it
one hundred times
I will never get used to
this bed,
a mountain of needles

                                                                 Seigaku

17.　ガードは親しく吾に語らへどあな腹立たし敵兵彼は
The guard talks to me
So friendly
How maddening
that he is a soldier
of the enemy

NOTES

  1. Note Courtesy of JCCH: Translations of this poem also appear in Nakano and Nakano, *Poets behind Barbed Wire*, 29 and Honda, *Family Torn Apart*, 73. Also see this latter citation for a description of the circumstances of this poem.

  2. Note courtesy of JCCH: A translation of this poem also appears in *Poets behind Barbed Wire*, 20.

Index

Page numbers followed with "n" refer to endnotes.

ABC lists, 74–76, 78–80, 84n44, 111, 133
Alexandria, Louisiana, 3, 6, 7, 87–92, 94–96, 98n43, 103, 113, 133, 135–36, 139, 194, 220, 221, 237–38, 257
alien agitators, 46, 47
Alien and Sedition Acts of 1798, 111
Alien Enemies Act of 1798, 24, 26, 111–12, 114n10
Alien Enemy Hearing Board, 23, 121–26
Alien Land Act of 1913, 91
Americanism, 39, 45, 59, 135; Americanization, 42–44, 66, 90
American Sutra (Williams), 84n44, 168
Angel Island/Fort McDowell, California (U.S. Army), 127–28
anti-Asian legislation, 1, 9, 22, 28n10, 35
anti-Asian sentiment, 35, 91, 113; anti-Japanese sentiment, 43, 91–92
Arata, Seikichi, 250
Archives, role of, 4, 10–13, 260
art exhibits (Camp Livingston), 175–76,

Asami, Shoichi (Seiha), 7, 167, 244–45; poetry by, 203, 245, 281, 282, 284, 286
Assembly Inn, Montreat, North Carolina (State Department Special Division), 187, 206–7, 213
Awa Maru ship, 7, 242–45

barbed wire disease, 129
baseball (Camp Livingston), 162, 164–65, 187
Bendetsen, Karl R., 21, 27n6
Berge, Wendell, 213
Bicknell, George, 74, 75, 79, 80n6, 119
Board of Officers and Civilians, hearings of. *See* Alien Enemy Hearing Board
Bon Odori (bon dance), 107–09, 110nn2–3, 128, 170, 219, 227n77, 259; origins of, 110n2
Buddhism, 40–42, 53–54, 78, 84n44, 148, 168, 216, 235–36; Hongwanji, 40–41, 66; Jōdo-shū, 40, 53–54, 109
Burke-Wadsworth Bill. *See* Selective Service and Training Act
Burns, John, 74–75, 79, 119

287

Index

Cable Act. *See* Married Women's Independent Nationality Act of 1922

camp arts and handicrafts (Camp Livingston), 175–81; art exhibitions, 176; handicrafts, 176, 177, 179–80, 249; painting and calligraphy, 254–56, 258–59

Camp Beauregard, Louisiana (National Guard), 89, 94, 98n43

Camp Forrest, Tennessee (U.S. Army), 148, 183, 212

Camp Livingston, Louisiana (U.S. Army), 2, 12, 23, 94–96, 104, 113, 115n17, 135–36, 139, 144–45, 212, 237–38, 241, 245, 248, 257, 258; Army translators, 147; arrival to, 143–45; art exhibits, 175–76; ban on Japanese language newspapers, 167; baptisms, 168; Buddhist practice, 148, 168–69; camp commanders Dunn and Weaver,146; camp environs, 144–45, 150–51, 157n52; celebrations of life events, 169; closure of, 241; clothing, 143, 151; communication concerns, 187; construction of, 94–95, 113–14; daily life, 149; exchange of arts to families, 179–80; faith, ritual, and religion of internees, 167–69; food and cooking, 152–53; *gaman* practice, 179–81; governance and self-advocacy, 149, 166; haiku and tanka of, 177–79; housing, 144; interactions with guards,146–47; Internee College, 165; internee demographics of, 145–46, 155n27; internee museum, 176, 181; Japanese Prisoners of War (POWs), 148, 249; Kuga, Jihei memorial service, 169; labor dispute at, 161–62; labor in, 159–63; living conditions in, 148–53; mail, 184–87; memorial services, 169–70; military personnel, 146–47; musical instruments, 199n45; music classes/concerts, 166; Panama internees, 144, 145, 147, 164, 166, 172n27; paper publication, 167; petitions, 190; pine needlecrafts of, 176–77; pine trees of, 144–45, 150; poetry readings and critique sessions, 178–79, 281–86; religious gatherings, 167–70; sports activities in, 163–65; temperature in, 150–51; transfer from camp to camp, 127–30, 139–40, 194–95; *utai* or Noh singing class, 165–66; visit from International Red Cross, 186–87; visitors to, 135–36, 186–94; visits of sons in military, 191–92; wildlife, 150, 157n52

Camp McCoy, Wisconsin (U.S. Army), 148, 156n44, 191–92, 197nn31–32; poem written about, 284

Camp Shelby, Mississippi (U.S. Army), 191, 197n29, 250

Cardinaux, Alfred, 186, 207, 217, 254–56

Chikuma, Masayuki, 145, 166–67

citizenship, 35–36; of American-born children of Japanese parents, 35–36; dual, 36, 48n6, 66; Japanese ineligibility for, 35. *See also* expatriation; repatriation to Japan

Civilian Exclusion Orders, 19–20, 26n1

Civil Liberties Act of 1988, 22, 26

Clark, Mary F., 215, 216, 229n90, 229n96, 269

clothing of internees (Camp Livingston), 143, 151

Commission on Wartime Relocation and Internment of Civilians, 10, 22, 25

consular agents (*toritsuginin*), 39–40, 48, 48n6, 59, 65, 76–79, 82nn25–26, 82n30, 84n44, 119, 122, 123, 125, 213; defined, xii

Cook, Terry, 10–11

Criminal Investigation Division of the Department of Justice, 77, 78

Crystal City Family Internment Camp
(DOJ), 211–22; art exhibitions, 220;
camp scrip, 214–15; celebration
of holidays, 219; closure of, 222;
construction of, 212–13; description of,
211–12; Farm Security Administration,
212; *gaman*, 220; gardens in, 215;
grocery store, 214; hospital in, 219;
housing, 213–14; Internal Relations
Division of, 214; Japanese Young
People Division, 216; jobs in camp,
218–19; religious faith, 216; schools
in, 216–18; swimming pool, 216,
226n48; tanka club, 219–20; tensions
within, 218, 220
Custodial Detention Lists. See ABC lists

Dance classes (Camp Livingston), 165
Delimitation Agreement, 74
DeWitt, John, 26n1
difference between internment and
incarceration, xi, 24, 26
Dillingham, Benjamin Franklin, 52–53
Dunbar, Anthony W., 10
Dunn, Colonel John, 146–47, 164, 168,
175, 188–89

eiju dochaku (settle down to the soil),
34–35
Eisenhower, Dwight D., 95
Ellis, Mabel B., 217
Enemy Alien Internment Program, 12,
22–25, 154n22
enemy aliens, 22, 24; camp for, 113;
confiscation of items of, 113;
detention of, 24, 112; internment,
22–26, 84n50, 111, 112, 114n10;
Proclamation 2525, 111–13, 114n10;
prohibition of possessions, 112
Espionage Act of 1917, 82n28
Executive Order 9012, 19
Executive Order 9066, xi, 19, 21–22,
26, 27n6, 113, 114n10
Expatriation Act of 1907, 35
expatriation petitions, 36, 40, 48n6

family incarceration camps. See War
Relocation Authority (WRA) camps
family internment camp. See Crystal
City Family Internment Camp (DOJ)
family reunification, 204–7, 213–14
Federal Bureau of Investigation (FBI),
22, 63, 65, 73–80, 84n50, 119,
133–34
Fifth Column agitators, 63, 68n31
Fischer (YMCA representative), 189–
90, 197n25
forced removal, xi, 1, 20, 24, 27n6,
114n10, 137
Fort McDowell, California (U.S. Army).
See Angel Island/Fort McDowell,
(California) (U.S. Army)
Fort Missoula, Montana (U.S. Army),
145, 195
Fort Sill, Oklahoma (U.S. Army),
11–12, 128–30, 139, 145, 242;
description of shooting of
Kanesaburo Oshima, 129–30; present
day, 11
442nd Regimental Combat Team, 191,
207n3
Fuchida, Mitsuo, 101–3
Fujihana, Reverend Kyōdō, 215, 225n38
Fujimura, Bunyu, 148, 153, 162
Fujinkai (Women's club), 59, 67n13
Fukuhara, Hisashi, 177–78
Fulton, Alexander, 88, 97n10
Funerals and memorial services (Camp
Livingston), 169–70
Furuya, Kaetsu, 128, 140n1, 160
Furuya, Kumaji (Suikei), 120, 150, 151,
161; poems by, 143, 144, 150, 162,
176, 179, 194, 281, 285, 286

G-2 operations, 64, 74, 80n6
gaman, 24, 29n18, 179–81, 220, 225n37
General Headquarters (GHQ) Louisiana
Maneuvers, 95–96
Geneva Convention of 1929, xi, 23,
115n17, 146, 161–63, 186, 199n45,
212

Gentlemen's Agreement of 1907, 34, 38n27, 38n31
golf (Camp Livingston), 163–64, 187
Gripsholm, M.S. *See* repatriation to Japan
Grove Park Inn, Asheville, North Carolina (State Department Special Division), 206

Hale'iwa, Hawai'i, 42, 51, 54, 57–61, 65, 66, 68n19, 77, 102, 103, 108, 109, 234, 243, 244, 253; history of, 51–54
Hale'iwa Hotel, 53
Hale'iwa Jodo Mission, 54, 57–59, 62, 68n20, 102, 104, 108, 109, 122, 186, 204, 205, 234, 235, 237, 242, 259
Hamada, Itsuo, 245
haole, 39, 48n3, 51, 65, 69n41, 74
Harris, Verne, 12
Hastings, Emiko, 10
Hawai'i, 31; Americanism, 39; anti-Japanese sentiment in, 43; arrival of the missionaries, 51; Buddhism, 40–42, 53–54; compulsory education, 42; consular agent in, 39–40; contract laborers, 32–34; Dillingham's railroad, 52–53; ethnic diversity of agricultural laborers, 44, 45, 47, 52; Hale'iwa Hotel, 52–54; *Issei* in, 35–36, 39, 42–43; Japanese Educational Association, 43; Japanese immigrants to, 32–34, 40–42; Japanese language schools, 39, 42, 43, 47, 48, 49n19; Japanization of, 46; Japanese planters leaving from, 47; *luna* (overseer), 33, 41, 44, 58; *Nikkei* in, 35–36, 39, 42–44, 48; plantation labor force strike, 44–48; poor treatment to laborers, 33; population, 32, 39; racial issues, 45–46; sugar plantation, 31–34, 51–52
Hechler, Ted, 102
Herzig-Yoshinaga, Aiko, 10
Hillebrand, William, 32

holehole, 38n20
holehole bushi, 33–34
Honda, Hiroshi, 258–59
Hongwanji Sect, 40–41
Honolulu Immigration Station, 119, 121; poem written about, 285
Honouliuli Internment Camp (U.S. Army), 258–59
Hoover, J. Edgar, 77–80, 137n3, 213, 247, 250n1
Hughes, John Harold, 122

Ichiba, Isao, 78
I Hear You Call, Pine Tree (Noguchi), xiii
Imamura, Bishop, 41
Immigration Act of 1924, 9, 28n10, 38n31
Immigration and Naturalization Service (INS), 23, 130n6, 154n22, 206, 212
imonbukuro (comfort kits), 40, 76
incarceration, 19, 24; defined, xi; Japanese Americans, 21, 22; *Nikkei*, 22; wartime, 22; in WRA camps, 25
INS. *See* Immigration and Naturalization Service (INS)
Intelligence Bureau Board, 126
International Committee of the Red Cross (ICRC), 185–87, 207, 212, 254, 256. *See also* Cardinaux, Alfred
Internee College (Camp Livingston), 165
Internee newspaper (Camp Livingston), 167
Internee self-governance (Camp Livingston), 149, 166
internment, 22, 24–26; defined, xi; enemy alien, 22–26, 84n50, 111, 112, 114n10
internment serial number,126, 128, 132n29, 149, 151
Ishida, Reverend Nitten, 255–56
isolationism and neutrality of United States, 93
Issei, 21–25, 76; defined, xi; discrimination against, 36; as enemy

aliens, 2, 111–14; in Hawai'i, 35–36, 39, 42, 43; internment, 22–26, 84n50, 111, 112, 114n10
Ito, Michio, 165, 167, 171n24

Japanese Consulate (Honolulu), 35–36, 39–40, 63, 64, 76–78; consul general, 41, 82nn25–26. *See also* consular agents (*toritsuginin*)
Japanese Cultural Center of Hawai'i (JCCH), 258, 281–86
Japanese Educational Association, Hawai'i, 43, 59
Japanese immigrants. *See* Issei
Japanese Imperial Navy, 63–64, 79–80, 101, 103, 148; receptions for training ships of, 63–64
Japanese language schools (Hawai'i), 42–44, 47, 48, 49n19, 58–59, 65, 78, 79
Japanese nationality, 35–36
Japanese naturalization ban, 35
Japanization of Hawai'i, 46
JCCH. *See* Japanese Cultural Center of Hawai'i (JCCH)
Jerome, Arkansas (WRA), 135, 225n37, 249
Jōdoshū sect, 40, 53–54; Honen Shonin, 54
Judo (Camp Livingston), 164
jus sanguinis (right of blood), 35, 36
jus soli (birthright citizenship), 35

kabuki play (Camp Livingston), 166–67
Kanazawa, Kanemi, 75
Kano, Reverend Hiram Hisanori, 145–46, 149–51, 155nn26–27, 161–62, 165, 167–69, 175–76, 184, 186, 190, 237–38, 253–54; Kohara family and, 238
Kashiwa, Reverend Ryuten, 66, 120–21, 130n3
Katagiri, Mineo, 61
Kelly, W.F., 218
Kendi, Ibram X., 9
Kibei Nisei, xi

Kohara, Jackie, 90, 96
Kohara, Kay, 90
Kohara, Manabu, 87, 89–93, 96, 103, 221, 238, 239; involvement in local community and business groups, 92; photography studio in Louisiana, 92; truck crop farming, 90
Kohara, Marion, 3, 7, 90–92, 103–4, 134–36, 237, 257; FBI investigation, 134; recollection of Pearl Harbor, 103–4; WRA camp visits, 135
Kohara, Saki, 89–91, 96, 104, 113, 133–36, 221, 237–39; American-ness of family, 134–35; FBI investigation of photography studio, 133, 134; hosting Nikkei, 135–36; Miyamoto visit to, 221; photography for Army camps, 135. *See also* Shima, Saki
Kohara, Sammy, 90, 96, 133
Kohara, Tommy, 90, 96, 237–38
Kooskia Internment Camp (DOJ), 195, 199n46
Krueger, Walter, 95
Kuga, Jihei, 169
Kurahara, Jane, 258–59
Kusao, Takegoro, 120, 121, 130n3

labor in Camp Livingston, 159–63; class one labor, 159–60, 162; class two labor, 160–62; disputes, 160–62; forced labor, 161–62; manual, 159, 162
Latin America, internees from, 1, 24, 130n6, 145, 154n22, 211, 222, 250n1. *See* Panama, internees from; Peru, internees from
Lazarus, Emma, 8
Lear, Ben, 95
Leary, Richard K., 147
letter writing (Camp Livingston), 183–85, censoring process, 185; regulations regarding, 184–85
Lewis, G.L., 204
life in Camp Livingston, 143–53
Lili'uokalani (Hawaiian Queen), 41, 51

Livingston, Robert, 94, 99n44
Lordsburg Internment Camp (U.S. Army), 181, 182n17, 213
Louisiana Maneuvers, 12, 93–96, 248, 249
Louisiana Maneuvers and Military Museum, 3, 249, 257
Loyalty expressed in affidavits (Camp Livingston), 186

Makiki Christian Church, 42–43
manual labor (Camp Livingston), 159, 162
Manzanar, California (WRA), 27n8, 225n37
Married Women's Independent Nationality Act of 1922, 35
Marshall, George C., 93
Masaki, Mitsuko, 205–6, 243–44. See also Sumida, Mitsuko
Masaki, Reverend Jikyo, 7, 205, 243–44
Mayfield, Irving, 74, 79, 82n26
Meisho Young Buddhist Association (Y.B.A.), 59, 65, 66
MID. See Military Intelligence Division (MID)
Midkiff, John H., 65–67, 121–26; 204; support of Japanese community, 66; testimony at Reverend Miyamoto's hearing, 124–25; visit to internees at Sand Island Detention Center (U.S. Army), 121
Miho, Katsugo, 191
Miho, Katsuichi, 191
Military Areas 1 and 2, 20, 26n1
Military Intelligence Division (MID), 63–65, 74, 75
Miyamoto, Carol, 60, 83n38, 195, 205, 207, 211, 213, 214, 233; graduation at Crystal City, 217; language broker, 77; visit to Kohara family, 221. See also Miyamoto, Taeko
Miyamoto, Clifford, 4, 60, 113, 195, 203–7, 208n4, 211, 213, 220, 226n50, 228n87, 228n89, 233–34, 241–42, 258, 267; childhood at Crystal City, 216; Dillingham Farm work, 203. See also Miyamoto, Terufumi
Miyamoto, David Kanji, 60, 203–5, 221, 233, 258. See also Miyamoto, Kanji
Miyamoto, Fumi, 7, 58–61, 113, 195, 203–5, 207, 211, 213, 214, 229n89, 238–39, 239n2, 244; instructor at language school, 58; visit to Kohara family, 220–21
Miyamoto, Kanji, 58, 60. See also Miyamoto, David Kanji
Miyamoto, Kayoko, 60–61, 68n20
Miyamoto, Kazuo, 83n31, 163–64
Miyamoto, Keiko, 60, 121, 195, 205, 207, 211, 213, 233, 238
Miyamoto, Nui, 57, 58
Miyamoto, Osamu, 58, 60–62, 204, 235–36, 239n5
Miyamoto, Reverend Buntetsu, 4, 57–67, 74, 77–80, 87, 102, 104, 107, 114, 128, 195, 203, 204, 233–34, 257–58, 264–65; Alien Enemy Hearing Board on (findings of, 125; recommendation for parole, 126); as Archbishop, 236; arrest and detention in camp, 119–21, arrival to Hawaii, 57; basic personnel record, 120; as a Bishop, 234–36; calligraphy, 236–38; children, 60–62; as consular agent, 59, 77–78, 122, 123, 213; execution of powers of attorney, 186, 204; family (at Crystal City Camp, 213–22; reunification, 204–7, 213–14); Hale'iwa Jodo temple, 108–9; hearing process, 121–24; ISN-HJ-131-CI as identification in the camp, 126; Kohara family's visit to, 238; leading the Bon celebrations, 107–9; life in Camp Livingston, 144, 145, 151–52; as minister on Oahu, 57–62, 107; non-repatriation request, 221; petitions for luggage, 6,

151–52; as religious and educational leader, 61–62; returning home, 234; safeguarding the temple and school, 186, 204; at Sand Island Detention Center, 120–21; sermons of, 234–35, 241–42; summary of information of, 122
Miyamoto, Taeko, 58, 60. *See also* Miyamoto, Carol
Miyamoto, Terufumi, 60, 242. *See also* Miyamoto, Clifford
Miyasaki, Seiichi, 204
Moran, Richard, 257
Mori, Ishiko, 219, 228n78
Mori, Motokazu, 219, 228n78
Mukaeda, Katsuma, 163, 164
Muroyama, Reverend Jitsujo, 53–54, 57
music (Camp Livingston), 166, 199n45
Myer, Dillon S., 21, 249

Nagata, Donna K., 25
The New Colossus (Lazarus), 8
Nicholson, Herbert V., 188–89, 197n21
Nikkei, 19–22, 24, 25; defined, xi; in Hawai'i, 35–36, 39, 42–44, 48; incarceration of, 19–22
Nisei, 40, 42, 43, 47; citizenship of, 35–36; defined, xi; loyalty to America, 43
Noguchi, Yone, xiii
Noh theater (Camp Livington), 165–66

Oahu Sugar Strike of 1920, 45–46, 58
Office of Naval Intelligence (ONI), 63–65, 74, 75, 78
Ohta, Reverend Kunio, 177, 208n13; handicrafts of, 265
Okumura, Reverend Takie, 42–43, 49n19
100th Infantry Battalion, 250
ONI. *See* Office of Naval Intelligence (ONI)
Organic Act of 1900, 34
O'Rourke, Joseph L., 212, 214, 216, 218, 222, 223n8, 224n22
Orphanage in camp (WRA), 21, 27n8

Oshima, Kanesaburo, 11, 129–30
Oshita, William, 147
Oyakoko (filial piety), 61
Ozaki, Otokichi (Muin), 128, 190, 281; poems by, 192, 282, 284, 285
Ozawa v. United States, 35

Palmer, Reverend Albert W., 31, 45–47
Panama, internees from, 144, 145, 147, 164, 166, 172n27, 190. *See also* Latin America, internees from; Peru, internees from
Patton, George, 64–65, 69n40
Pearl Harbor attack, 1, 19, 22, 25, 79–80, 101–4, 107, 111, 119, 133–34, 148, 211, 243
Personal Justice Denied, 22, 28n14, 114n10, 154n22
Peru, internees from, 145, 148, 166–67, 222, 229n91. *See also* Latin America, internees from; Panama, internees from
poetry: haiku and tanka, 177–79, 245, 281–86
poetry written in Camp Livingston, 143, 144, 150, 162, 176, 178–79, 194, 203, 281–86
POWs. *See* Prisoners of War (POWs)
Presidential Proclamation 2525, 6, 111–13, 114n10
Presidential Proclamation 2526, 6, 111
Presidential Proclamation 2527, 6, 111
Presidential Proclamation 4417, 26
Prisoners of War (POWs), 2, 3, 23, 148, 156n44, 164, 191, 199n45, 249; treatment of, 146
Public Proclamation No. 1, 26n1
Public Proclamation No. 4, 26n1

racial discrimination, 91–92
racism, 21, 91–92; Hawai'i, 31, 45–46. *See also* anti-Japanese sentiment
Reciprocity Agreement with the United States in 1875, 37n7
Redress Movement, 10, 21–22, 26

Red River Campaign, 88–89
Registration Act of 1939, Hawai'i, 77, 82n28
religion, 40–42, 78, 168. *See also* Buddhism
Religious gatherings (Camp Livingston), 167–70
repatriation to Japan, 130n6, 152, 195, 221, 229n89, 229n91, 244–45; of Miyamoto family, 204–7
Ritchie, Barbara, 253
Robinson, Greg, 91
Rohwer, Arkansas (WRA), 135, 192, 193
Roosevelt, Franklin Delano (FDR), 19, 63, 93, 94, 103, 104; Proclamation 2525, 111–13, 114n10
Roosevelt, Theodore, 62

saiho-maru (boat that heads to the west), 109
Saito, Hiroshi, 59–60, 146; wife of, 59–60
Sakamaki, Kazuo, 104, 148
Sand Island Detention Center (U.S. Army), 120–21, 126
Santa Fe Detention Center (DOJ), 181, 195, 182n17, 227n77
Segregation in the South, 91–92, 198n37
Selective Service and Training Act, 94
Shima, Saki, 89. *See also* Kohara, Saki
Shimizaki (Lieutenant Commander), 101, 103
Shimizu, Mitsuhiko H., 160, 163, 188
Shivers, Robert, 73–79, 81n23, 82n30, 119
Short, Walter, 77, 82n28, 112
Soga, Shigeo, 167
Soga, Yasutaro (Keiho), account of, 130n3, 155n26, 182n17, 227n77
Spanish consuls (de Garay), 190
sports (Camp Livingston), 163–65
State Department representative (Herrick), 190
Sueyasu, Yonezo, 249

Sumida, Mitsuko, 243–44. *See also* Masaki, Mitsuko
Sumo (Camp Livingston), 164
Surveillance of Japanese, 62–65, 68n39, 69n41, 69n43, 73–80, 80n6, 82nn25–26

Taisho Gakko, 42, 49n20, 54, 57–59
Takahashi, Reverend Seytsu, 168, 169
Takasago, tale of, 261–64
tengoku (heaven), 33, 37n15
Tillman, F.G., 77–78
Tomita née Ohta, Ella Miyeko, 177, 205, 208n13, 217
toritsuginin. *See* consular agents
Toyama, Sadao, 184, 191–92, 197nn31–32
Toyama, Tetsuo, 169, 170, 183–85, 191–92, 197n32
Toyota, Fred, 194, 198n39
Toyota, Toshiko, 194, 198n39
Truman, Harry, 191

"un-American," 39, 42–43, 47, 186
United States: policies of isolationism and neutrality, 93, 98n34; Japan relations, 62–63, 79
U.S. Army Camps, xi, 1, 2, 5, 12, 23–25, 84n44, 149, 211, 212
U.S. Department of Justice (DOJ) Camps, xi, 1, 2, 5, 12, 22–26, 84n44, 84n50, 115n17, 149, 154n22, 181, 183, 195, 211, 212, 250
USS *Queenfish*, 7, 243
Uyeda, Clifford, 91

Wahiawa, Hawai'i, 52, 53
Waialua, Hawai'i, 51–53, 64–66, 119–21, 125, 130n3, 186, 204; expatriation campaign, 48n6; Japanese Language School, 58–59; Sugar Company, 52, 53; Waipahu strike of 1904, 41

War Relocation Authority (WRA) camps, xi, 1–3, 19–26, 84n44, 114n10, 130n6, 135, 146, 180, 182n16, 183, 186, 192, 195, 212, 225n37, 249
Wartime Civil Control Administration (WCCA), 20, 27n6, 205
Weaver, Colonel, 146–47
Williams, Duncan Ryūken, 25, 84n44, 155n27, 168, 236, 280n1
Wilson, Woodrow, 112

yagura (tower), 108, 128
Yamashita, Angela (Yukiko), 180, 190, 192, 193
Yamashita, Gihachi, 139, 151, 152, 157n50, 160, 165, 169–70, 176, 179–80, 182n15, 183, 190, 192–94, 198n37, 227n77, 248
Yamashita, Lillian (Yetsuko), 176, 179, 180, 193, 194, 198n37
Yamashita, Tsugio, 183
YMBAs. *See* Young Buddhist Associations (YBAs)
YMCA representative (Hibbard), 189–90
Young (representative of the State Department), 186
Young, Betsy, 258
Young Buddhist Associations (YBAs), 45, 59, 66

About the Authors

Hayley Johnson is the head of the Open Scholarship and Government Publications department at LSU Libraries at Louisiana State University.

Sarah Simms is the Undergraduate & Student Success Librarian at LSU Libraries at Louisiana State University.

www.ingramcontent.com/pod-product-compliance
Lightning Source LLC
Chambersburg PA
CBHW070014010526
44117CB00011B/1569